Languages and Their Status

Languages and Their Status

Timothy Shopen
Australian National University

under the auspices of the Center for Applied Linguistics

Winthrop Publishers, Inc.   Cambridge, Massachusetts

Library of Congress Cataloging in Publication Data

Main entry under title:

Languages and their status.

    Includes bibliographies.
      1. Language and languages. 2. Language and
culture. I. Shopen, Timothy.
P106.L319   301.2'1   78-10973
ISBN 0-87626-485-2

Photo Credits

p. 2, Photo courtesy of A. Brian Deer, Caughnawaga Cultural Center;
pp. 28, 29, Photos from *The First Day*, Department of Indian and
Northern Affairs, Canada; pp. 90, 148–49, Novosti Press Agency,
London; p. 331, Hu Yu-Chih, "Phonetic Script Helps Literacy," *China
Reconstructs*, vol. 8, no. 8, p. 26

Jacket design by Ann Washer

© *1979 by Winthrop Publishers, Inc.*
  17 Dunster Street, Cambridge, Massachusetts 02138

10 9 8 7 6 5 4 3 2 1

Contents

Illustrations

Introduction

Languages and Their Status comes with a companion volume, *Languages and Their Speakers*. These books are written for a general audience with an aim to provide an introduction both to languages themselves and to their social functions. Each chapter is an essay on what it means to be a speaker of a particular language, in this volume Mohawk, Hua, Russian, Cape York Creole, Swahili, and Chinese, in the companion volume Jacaltec, Maninka, Malagasy, Guugu Yimidhirr, and Japanese. For each language we pose the question "What kind of language is it, among the languages of the world?"; at the same time we look at speakers and examine the ways languages gain their use and subsistence among them. Whereas in the companion volume we explore the grammatical and cultural principles people have learned to become members of various language communities, here we take a complementary approach: we examine the part languages play in the evolution and structure of communities and in turn the ways in which languages are shaped by the social forces impinging on their speakers.

Languages adapt themselves to cultural change, but they have structural peculiarities and inertia of their own so that cultures must adapt themselves to languages as well. Interwoven as they are with the thought and customs of their speakers, languages are an influence in the direction of social change. Cultures have intimate links to particular languages: take a language away from a culture, replace it with another, and that culture will be radically altered. To begin to understand societies one must be aware of languages, and languages in their specific details.

We live in a world where different languages, and even small contrasts between dialects, are powerful markers of identity and status. The pace of competition and change has been intense.

"Do you not feel shame at authorizing only three languages and condemning other peoples to blindness and deafness?"—so asked Saint Constantine-Cyril in the ninth century, challenging the Church in the West and defending Slavic as a language as good as any other.[1] In 1600

---

[1] Quote in English translation from Roman Jakobson, "The Beginning of National Self-Determination in Europe," *The Review of Politics*, 7, 1945, pp. 29–42, reprinted in J. A. Fishman, ed., *Readings in the Sociology of Language*, Mouton, The Hague, 1972, pp. 585–97.

English had no more than half as many speakers and not as much prestige as French, Spanish, or Italian. The status of English has moved up since then and the number of its speakers has increased nearly two hundredfold, though not through any improvement in the language itself: the English of 1600 was the English of Shakespeare. At the time of the French Revolution, it appears that less than half the twenty-six million people living in France spoke French as their first language and perhaps as many as twelve million spoke it a little or not at all.[2]

Times change. Not just prestige is at stake, but the more fundamental question of survival. Even though people are capable of being fluent speakers of both a local language and a language of wider communication, a lingua franca, there has been a tendency ever since the first empires for local languages to be *replaced* by ones with greater status. Sometimes this has been something imposed from above, but so also it can come from the local people themselves. The conflict between cultural diversity and the unity of large societies is a vital issue of our time, and nowhere is this more apparent than with languages.

The first two chapters of this volume discuss minority languages; the remaining four, lingua francas. Marianne Mithun and Wallace Chafe narrate the experience of a community struggling to keep alive its language, the Iroquoian language Mohawk. The status of Mohawk is similar to that of other native languages of North America: most face the danger of extinction by the end of this century. The authors give us an idea of the task involved in learning Mohawk, a polysynthetic language which will often render in a single word what it takes a number of words to say in English; then they go on to tell how a new generation of primary-school children has learned the language with the aid of a bilingual education program. Efforts like those of the Mohawk people are gaining momentum in various minority communities of North America and Western Europe.

John Haiman describes Hua, a Papuan language of New Guinea. Hua has an elegant system of verb morphology used to link clauses and keep track of the identity of subjects. By involving us in the discovery of some of the central principles of the language, the author gives amplitude to the crucial lesson we can learn from the Hua, an appreciation of the human capacity for language learning and multilingualism. The ordinary Hua speaker is master not only of this language but has need for and speaks fluently several other different but equally complex languages.

Bernard Comrie portrays Russian in terms of word order and functional sentence perspective, case-marking, agreement, and the tense-aspect system. He relates its development from common Slavic to a world language, the situation with standards and dialects in the USSR,

---

[2]Louis-Jean Calvet, *Linguistique et Colonialisme*, Payot, Paris, 1974.

and its use as a lingua franca over that large and linguistically diverse country. One is tempted to generalize from the Russian example about large urban societies: in spite of a government program for the use of local languages along with Russian, many languages are in the process of being replaced by Russian.

From Terry Crowley and Bruce Rigsby we have the description of a very different kind of lingua franca, a creole language, Cape York Creole. The authors relate how an ethnically diverse community has arisen on that northeastern tip of Australia bringing the need for a lingua franca, and how the people there have created a new language for themselves, one that has become the first language of many of them. They describe its structure with concern for the continuum of low to high-prestige forms typical of creole languages. The Aboriginal languages being replaced by the creole are similar to Guugu Yimidhirr, described in the companion volume.

Tom Hinnebusch describes Swahili, an example of a widely used lingua franca with relatively few first-language speakers, one that has gained a role of central importance in commerce, cultural diffusion, and political unification in East Africa. We learn about the structure of the language with its noun classes, verbal concord, and tense-aspect system. This in turn enables us to understand something about the many varieties of Swahili and the process that has gone on to standardize the language. Besides describing the varieties of the language that have native speakers, the author gives us an introduction to pidgin Swahili, spoken extensively as an auxiliary language. Like all pidgins, it is a limited means of expression, but highly useful and easy to learn.

In the final chapter Charles Li and Sandra Annear Thompson present Chinese, the language of the world with the greatest number of speakers and one with a long history as a lingua franca. The Chinese-speaking area has had as much linguistic variation as there has ever been in large areas of Europe, yet socially there has been extraordinary unity as can be seen in the traditional reference to a single Chinese language. Li and Thompson give us an idea of this unity within diversity, describing the major dialects in terms of their sound structure, word formation, and syntax, and then describing the society with the important changes that have taken place since the 1949 revolution, the reforms of the language and the writing system, the vast extension of literacy, and the use of the Mandarin dialect for unifying the country.

ACKNOWLEDGMENTS

The development of *Languages and Their Status* and *Languages and Their Speakers* would not have been possible without the generous support of the National Endowment for the Humanities, the Center for

Applied Linguistics, and the Australian National University. At the Center for Applied Linguistics, Peggy Good gave me excellent assistance from the beginning; and at various times Begay Atkinson, Peg Griffin, John Hammer, Diana Riehl, and Roger Shuy helped me surmount hurdles that lay in the way.

In the final editing of this volume the person who has been most helpful is Frances Morphy. Other people whose judgments have been of great aid include Peter and Randy Austin, David Bradley, Bill Bright, Hilary Chappell, Margaret Craig, Colette Craig, Terry Crowley, Bob Dixon, Talmy Givón, Mary Haas, Aubrey Parke, Graham Scott, Ellalene Seymour, Agnes Shopen, and Joe Williams. I am grateful to Paul O'Connell of Winthrop Publishers for his support and encouragement, as well as to John Covell, Herb Nolan, and Pat Torelli for valuable work in the production of these books. The fine maps in both volumes are the work of Val Lyon of the Department of Geography in the School of General Studies at the Australian National University. My thanks to all.

Timothy Shopen
Canberra, Australia

Languages and Their Status

I

Recapturing the Mohawk Language

Marianne Mithun

Wallace L. Chafe

1 CAUGHNAWAGA

The trip across the bridge from Montreal is short: a few moments amid roaring trucks and cars, past the Seagram's factory, and over the murky, swirling St. Lawrence. A small Quebec village comes into view on the southern bank. A church steeple flashes silver in the sun. Ancient stone and wood houses nestle close to each other along narrow, winding roads near the water. What a pleasant surprise it is to find an old-fashioned Quebec settlement so close to a bustling city.

Turning off the highway, we bump along a road lined with high

Marianne Mithun teaches linguistics at the State University of New York at Albany. Her research is primarily in the areas of syntax, semantics, diachronic linguistics, and Iroquoian languages. Over the past five years, she has been involved in the development of a number of programs designed to prepare native speakers of Iroquoian languages to teach their languages effectively to younger generations of English-speaking Iroquoians.

Wallace L. Chafe teaches linguistics at the University of California at Berkeley. One of his major concerns has been the nature and history of American Indian languages. He has written descriptive studies of Seneca and Onondaga, two languages closely related to Mohawk, and has compared these and other related languages to reconstruct the history of the Iroquois language family.

bushes. Colorful wood frame houses begin to appear, surrounded by lush gardens. Dogs are everywhere. At the intersection, foregoing the opportunity to drink Coca-Cola at what appears to be the *Teiont-ska'hónhkhwa'* restaurant, we turn right. Lafleur's market looks like a good place to pick up a snack.

Sounds of hearty laughter are coming from inside the store. The words are faint but each comment seems to be greeted with fresh bursts of glee. The group inside is a mixed one. Several middle-aged women are milling around the meat counter at the back, one accompanied by a teenaged boy. An old man is chuckling as he chooses from the selection of canned Chinese food. He is clad in jeans and a lumberjacket, but the women are stylishly dressed and look as if they might be French Canadians.

It is hard to catch what is being said, but it is clear that plenty of wisecracks are being exchanged. Replies are snappy, yet no one seems to interrupt anyone else. The butcher adresses one of the women in heavily accented English. Clearly, he is Quebecois. Perhaps the women are not French Canadians after all.

As a bell jingles over the front door of the market, one of the women calls out, "Shé:kon. Tasatáweia't. Skennen'kó:wa ken?" A husky fellow of about thirty-five strides in. He flashes a toothy smile. "Shé:kon. Skennen'kó:wa. A:ké, wakhwisenhé:ion." One of the other women asks, "Ka' nón iéhse'skwe' ne tio'karáhsen?" The fellow grins again:

Tio'karáhsen   tiontenhninòn:tha'   iekatehnhwaori'tí:ne'skwe'   tánon' entiatén:ron Teiowí:sonte' tontaiakeniá:ken'ne' tho takahnhwaori'tak-wénhtara'ne'. Ne ne tho nikari'takerí:ten' ne ne Teiowí:sonte' tsi Tioh-tià:ke iehatehnhwaori'tí:ne'skwe'.[1]

The chatter and merriment continue, but the teenaged boy is clearly bored.

The bell jangles again and several more teenagers burst into the market, along with two smaller children. They are giggling and teasing each other in clear Canadian English. The smallest child, a girl of six or seven, catches sight of the older folks and shyly steals up to one of the women. "Shé:kon. Skennen'kó:wa ken?" she squeaks in her tiny voice.

---

[1]All Mohawk examples were checked by Mary McDonald of Akwesasne, New York, whose help is gratefully acknowledged. In the Mohawk spelling system used here, *t, k, ts,* and *i* are pronounced *d, g, dz,* and *y*, respectively, when they are immediately followed by a vowel; *ti* is pronounced like English *j; th* and *sh* are not pronounced as they are in English, but as *t* and *s* followed by *h*. The symbol ' indicates a glottal stop. A vowel followed by : is a long vowel, and a vowel followed by *n* within the same syllable is nasalized. The acute accent mark ´ indicates a high pitched vowel, and the grave accent mark ` a vowel with falling pitch.

"Skennen'kó:wa," comes the reply. Who are these people, living in what appears to be a traditional Quebec village? Why are older people and the youngest children speaking one language, while teenagers speak another?

2 HISTORY

When Europeans first became acquainted with the area which is now upstate New York in the seventeenth century, it was inhabited by what has since come to be known in English as the League of the Iroquois. This confederacy of five (later six) Iroquois nations, closely related in customs and language, had been formed sometime previously as a way of preserving peace internally and of cooperating in political and military operations against their adversaries. From east to west, more or less in the order in which Europeans first encountered them, they were the Mohawks, Oneidas, Onondagas, Cayugas, and Senecas. (The Tuscaroras joined them from North Carolina in the early eighteenth century.) Although they have been subjected to strong pressures toward acculturation from the white society which has surrounded them, these people have managed, in different ways and to different degrees on about a dozen reservations in the United States and Canada, to retain a significant portion of the rich culture of their ancestors.

The Mohawks were first found living in the valley of the river in New York State which bears their name. Those who knew them best in the early years were French missionaries from Montreal who journeyed south seeking converts. Discovering quite soon that it was difficult for the new Christians to maintain their faith within the Mohawk villages, the missionaries hit upon the idea of establishing a community of "praying Indians" outside of Montreal. The first such converts were persuaded to take up residence in a place called La Prairie in 1667. The community quickly flourished and attracted other settlers from the Mohawk valley and elsewhere. Its best-known inhabitant during the early years was a young woman named Kateri Tekakwitha. Converted to Catholicism while she was still a child in the village of her birth, she moved to La Prairie at age twenty-one and died only three years later, having apparently set a remarkable example of piety and penitence.

Mohawks from this group did not lose their taste for warfare, however, and sometimes joined the French in raids on English towns, the best known of which occurred at Deerfield, Massachusetts, in 1704. English settlers captured in these raids were often brought back to the Caughnawaga community, where they were assimilated through adoption and marriage. Family names like Jacobs, Williams, Rice, McComber, Tarbell, and Stacey attest to this early English influence on the community.

FIGURE 1.1 **The Area in the North Where Iroquoian Settlements Were**
Located at the Time of Columbus, with Neighboring Algonkian and Siouan Peoples

The tribes in the shaded area spoke languages of the Iroquoian family, as did the Cherokee and Tuscarora farther south. Iroquoian was one of several dozen language families of native North America; these families embraced a total of about 300 distinct languages. The immediately surrounding languages were mostly of the Algonkian family, except for a few Siouan languages like Tutelo directly to the south.

Source: George Peter Murdock and Timothy J. O'Leary, *Ethnographic Bibliography of North America, Vol. 4: Eastern United States*, Human Relations Area Files Press, New Haven, Conn., 1975, p. 50.

The settlement was moved several times from La Prairie to other locations along the St. Lawrence River, until it reached a permanent home on what is now the Caughnawaga Reserve by 1719. Between 1755 and 1759 some of the inhabitants of Caughnawaga moved to a new settlement farther up the river called St. Regis. Known today most

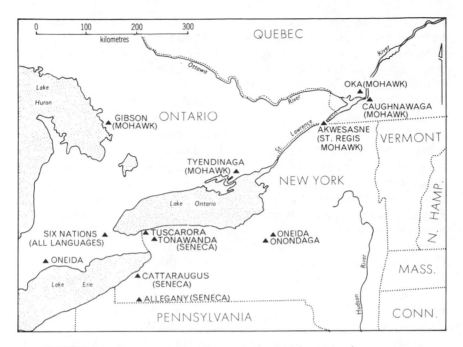

FIGURE 1.2 *Iroquois Reservations and Languages at the Present Time*

*Other speakers of Oneida live in Wisconsin, and of Cayuga in Oklahoma.
Most of these reservations have instituted native language teaching
programs.*

Source: Elisabeth Tooker, *The Iroquois Ceremonial of Midwinter*, Syracuse University
Press, Syracuse, N.Y., 1970, p. xii.

commonly as Akwesasne, this reservation straddles the U.S.-Canadian
border and is the only Mohawk reservation in the United States. For the
most part the Iroquois sided with the British during the American
Revolution. After the war those Mohawks who had remained in the
original Iroquois homeland moved to Ontario, where their descendants
still live on the Six Nations Reserve west of Hamilton.

While the Caughnawaga group retained much of its Indian heritage
during the eighteenth and nineteenth centuries, there was considerable
assimilation of white cultural patterns where they proved useful. As an
alternative to warfare, many Caughnawaga men became active in the fur
trade, which remained as an important activity until well into the
nineteenth century. This occupation was gradually supplanted by timber-
rafting on the St. Lawrence and Ottawa Rivers, and often by participation in traveling circus shows. In 1884 fifty men from Caughnawaga
spent nearly a year in Egypt demonstrating boatmanship to the British
and Egyptians on the Nile. In 1886, the erection of a bridge across the
St. Lawrence with one end on the Caughnawaga Reserve stimulated

interest in high steel work. Since that time work on structural steel has become the principal occupation of Caughnawaga men, who have contributed to the erection of bridges and skyscrapers across North America. An offshoot of the Caughnawaga community has grown up in Brooklyn, New York, closer to the scene of employment. The Mohawk language may thus be heard in a Brooklyn bar or church, as well as hundreds of feet in the air at a new building site.

Those members of the Caughnawaga community who speak Mohawk at the present time are primarily the adults over about thirty or forty years of age and many young children. Most of those who do not understand Mohawk at all are the teenagers and young adults. They constitute the first generation at Caughnawaga to grow up learning only English, and that fact contributed to a painful search for identity which many of these young people experienced during a period of extensive change in community values. As they attended high school in nearby Chateauguay, it was apparent that many of them looked different from their white classmates, and they certainly felt different in ways difficult to define. There was in fact a feeling that they possessed something their neighbors lacked, but it was impossible to identify exactly what it was. Through some inexplicable change in the world around them, it had suddenly become "in" to be Indian, but regrettably it was just at this time that the clearest symbol of their Indianness, the Mohawk language, had become lost to them. As we shall see, it has been in large part because of this situation that we heard a young child speaking Mohawk to an older woman in the market, while any teenagers present were confined to English.

The sudden decline in the use of the native language over a single generation has hardly been unique to the community at Caughnawaga. The same pattern has appeared at the same time in the majority of Indian communities across both Canada and the United States. Allowed to run its course, it will lead to the extinction of most of the ancestral languages of these communities, languages still numbering nearly two hundred, before the beginning of the next century. Is such a loss inevitable, or, given the desire, can a community do something to retard or reverse it? A familiar institution among many ethnic minorities is the extracurricular language class, meeting after school or on Saturdays with the goal of transmitting the group's language to children. Could a device such as this revive the use of Mohawk among children at Caughnawaga? Let us look at a few of the things a speaker of English must learn in order to speak Mohawk.

3 LEARNING MOHAWK

The province of Quebec fosters the learning of French by all its citizens, but an English speaking student who expects the learning of Mohawk to be similar to the learning of French is in for a surprise. English and French belong to the same language family, and in fact French vocabulary and grammar profoundly influenced the English language during the period following the Norman Conquest. Notice the similarity between the French and English sentences below:

Au zoo,   Michel   admirait   les   tigres,   mais   il
At the zoo, Michael   admired   the   tigers,   but   he

préférait   les   éléphants.
preferred   the   elephants.

Equivalents can be found for nearly every word, and the words appear in the same order in both sentences. No such resemblances can be found between English and Mohawk. Some idea of the magnitude of the differences can be gained from looking at both a literal and a free translation of the conversation we overheard in the market:

Shé:kon.   *Tasatáweia't.*   *Skennen'kó:wa   ken?*
again   toward-you-enter   peace-great   question
Hello there.   Come on in.   How are you?

    Shé:kon.   *Skennen'kó:wa.*   *A:ké,   wakhwisenhé:ion.*
    again   peace-great   oh,   my-strength-is-dead
    Hi.   I'm fine.   A bit tired, though.

Ka'   nón   iéhse'skwe'   ne   tio'karásen?
what   place there-you-go-ing   the   as-it-was-evening
Where were you last night?

    Tio'karáhsen   tiontenhninòn:tha'   iekatehnhwaori't-
    as-it-was-evening   there-one-sells   there-I-self-fool
       Last night, crazy as I am, I went off to the store,

    í:ne'skwe'   tánon'   entiatén:ron   Teiowí:sonte'
    going-was   and   we-two-friends   it-ice-makes
                             to-each-other
       and when I came out with my friend Teiowí:sonte',

    tontaiakeniá:ken'ne'   tho   takahnhwaori'takwénhtara'ne'.
    back-past-here-we-two   there   here-past-it-fool-fall-did
    returned-did
       the fool fell flat on his face, right in public.

Ne   ne   tho   nikari'takerí:ten'   ne   ne   Teiowí:sonte'
The   the   there so-it-story-kind   the   the   it-makes-ice
    That's what happens when you take a rascal like

tsi   Tiohtià:ke   iehatehnhwaori'tí:ne'skwe'.
so   there-it-crosses   there-he-self-fool-go-ing-was
    Teiowí:sonte' to Montreal.

Obvious differences can be found in the ordering of words. In English we would not be likely to say, "In the evening to the store I was going," but if we allow for differences within the words themselves, that is the way the Mohawk speaker expressed it. Although a variety of factors influence the order in which the ideas within a sentence are arranged, there is a general tendency in English to state the most important new information at the end of a sentence, whereas in Mohawk such information tends to come earlier. Assuming that the important new information in this example was the notion "to the store," we find it natural in English to say, "I was going *to the store*," while a Mohawk speaker finds it most natural to say, "*to the store* I was going."

It is also true that the order of words in Mohawk is more variable than it is in English. Suppose, for example, that an event occurred which would be appropriately communicated in English by saying, "The girl hit the boy." If we should change the order of the words in this sentence, either the meaning would be changed or we would produce a sentence that would not be grammatical English. Thus, to reverse the order of the two nouns and say "The boy hit the girl" would communicate an entirely different event. To place the verb at the beginning or end of the sentence would produce something ungrammatical: "Hit the girl the boy," or "The girl the boy hit." In Mohawk, rearranging the words neither changes the meaning nor produces an ungrammatical sentence. All of the following sentences communicate the same event:

Ieksá:'a	*wahonwá:ienhte'*	*raksá:'a.*
girl	hit	boy

Raksá:'a	*wahonwá:ienhte'*	*ieksá:'a.*
boy	hit	girl

Wahonwá:ienhte'	*ieksá:'a*	*raksá:'a*
hit	girl	boy

Ieksá:'a	*raksá:'a*	*wahonwá:ienhte'.*
girl	boy	hit

To be sure, these sentences differ in their appropriateness for different contexts. As we saw, the element conveying the most important information is usually placed at or near the beginning of a sentence. Thus, if the speaker were answering a question as to who hit the boy, it would be most appropriate to mention the girl first. If there were a question as to the person the girl hit, the boy would be mentioned first. But in all four of these Mohawk sentences it is clear that the girl did the hitting, and that the boy was the person who was hit.

How do Mohawk speakers keep track of the aggressor and the victim in sentences like these? Compare the following two sentences:

Ieksá:'a   raksá:'a   wahonwá:ienhte'.
girl   boy   hit
   The girl hit the boy.

Ieksá:'a   raksá:'a   wahshakó:ienhte'.
girl   boy   hit
   The boy hit the girl.

The only difference between the two sentences is within the last word, the verb. The gender of the person who does something and the person to whom something is done is encoded into every Mohawk verb. Thus, in the first sentence the element *-honwa-* shows that a female person did something to a male person. In the second sentence the element *-hshako-* indicates that a male person did something to a female person. A Mohawk who heard these words, regardless of their order, would have no difficulty in knowing who did what to whom. You may have noticed that in these examples the gender of the participants is also marked in the nouns themselves. In comparing the words for "boy" and "girl" we can see that they are identical except for their initial parts. The common *-ksá:'a* in fact means "child," while the initial *ie-* and *ra-* specify "female" and "male," respectively. Thus in these sentences the gender of the participants in the hitting is marked in both the nouns and in the verb.

   As you might imagine, the pronouns are not the only clues helping to untangle who did what to whom. If this were so, the system would collapse whenever all participants in an event were of the same gender. There are, in fact, two other kinds of clues.

   One of these is semantic. In a sentence like the next one, both the subject and the object are neuter, so the pronouns provide no syntactic information.

Takò:s   onòn:ta'   wa'kahnekì:ra'.
cat   milk   it-it-drank
   The cat drank milk.

Everyone knows, however, that milk does not drink cats and that cats do drink milk, so it is easy to decipher the sentence.

   Finally, if neither gender differences nor plausible semantics disambiguate a sentence, a basic subject-first word order is resorted to. The first nominal in a sentence is interpreted as the subject and the second as the object. Rearrangement of constituents is thus blocked when it results in confusion. If Kor hit Sak, for example, the event could be described as follows (Kor and Sak are names of men):

Kor   wahó:ienhte'   Sak.
Kor   he-him-hit   Sak.
   Kor hit Sak.

Reversing the names would reverse the meaning of the sentence. The expression of case relations is thus considerably more complex in Mohawk than in English, involving the interraction of several different factors, namely, gender-marking on verbs, semantic probabilities, and sometimes word order.

Probably the most striking difference between the two languages stems from the fact that Mohawk belongs to a language type linguists have labeled 'polysynthetic,' a type which has a tendency to pile as much information as possible into a single word. When Europeans first encountered this phenomenon they were apt to comment that these languages could express in a single word what it would take a whole sentence to say in English or French or Spanish. Whereas an English verb has only a few inflectional forms—so that, for example, *see, sees, saw, seeing* and *seen* exhaust the different forms for that verb—languages like Mohawk allow for hundreds of different forms. In fact, if we allow for the fact that the object of a sentence can be incorporated into a Mohawk verb, the number of different forms of such a verb is virtually unlimited.

Learning a polysynthetic language appears at first to be a monumental if not impossible task. Is it necessary to memorize a different long word for every sentence one would ever want to use? Actually, Mohawk speakers constantly understand and produce words they have never heard before. Learning Mohawk involves learning regular rules for building up words from smaller, meaningful chunks of language. Anyone who knows these elements and has mastered the rules for combining them can create new words.

One of the first words in the market conversation was:

> *tasatáweia't*   Come in!

If the speaker had been outside, she would probably have said:

> *ia'satáweia't*   Go in!

Compare these two Mohawk words. Note the similarities in their forms and meanings. Which parts appear to be linked to the difference in meaning?

A construction worker on a scaffold might yell to his partner hauling up something from below:

> *tashará:tat*   Lift it up here!

The partner might then hand it over to him with the instructions to send it on up higher:

> *ia'shará:tat*   Lift it up there!

Compare two more commands which might be heard on the site:

    taskahrátho   Tip it over this way!
    ia'skahrátho   Tip it over that way!

What conclusion can be drawn from a comparison of these commands? If you knew the word:

    ia'satkáhtho   Look over there!

what would you do upon hearing the following?[2]

    tasatkáhtho

If you knew the meaning of:

    ia'saròn:tat   Shoot in that direction!

how would you react to this?[3]

    tasaròn:tat

Yelling at the pitcher, baseball catchers often say:

    tasá:ti   Throw it here!

How would a catcher tell the pitcher to throw it somewhere else?[4] If the command for "Write to that place" is:

    ia'shiá:ton   Write there!

how would you tell someone in Mohawk to write here, to this place?[5] By knowing how to use what linguists specializing in Iroquoian languages call the 'cislocative' prefix *ta-* "here" and the 'translocative' prefix *ia'-* "there," a speaker can produce new verbs from many simple commands.

    A hunter might be heard to whisper to his companion:

    saròn:tat   Shoot!

---

[2]"Look here!"

[3]"Shoot this way!"

[4]*ia'sá:ti* "Throw it that way!"

[5]*tashiá:ton*

If the companion misses, he might hear:

> *sasaròn:tat*   Shoot again!

At the construction site, you might hear the command:

> *skahrátho*   Tip it over!

followed, soon afterward, by:

> *saskahrátho*   Tip it back over again!

Again, examine the differences in form and meaning within these pairs. What change in form seems to convey what change in meaning? Now, given the following:

> *satkáhtho*   Look!

how would you respond to:[6]

> *sasatkáhtho*

On the basis of the verbs:

> *shiá:ton*   Write (it)!
> *skòn:rek*   Hit it!

can you imagine how a Mohawk speaker would say:[7]

> Rewrite (it)!
> Hit it again!

Knowing this so-called 'iterative' prefix *sa-* further adds to the number of commands one can create.

To see how, knowing these commands, it is possible to create statements of fact, examine the following words:

> *shiá:ton*   Write!
> *shiá:tons*   You are writing./You write.
>
> *skahrátho*   Tip it over!
> *skahráthos*   You are tipping it over./You tip it over.

---

[6]"Look again!"

[7]a. *sashiá:ton* b. *saskòn:rek*

satkáhtho	Look!
satkáhthos	You are looking./You look.

With this information, what would you expect the following verb to mean?[8]

    saròn:tats

Given the following commands:

shní:non	Buy it!
skòn:rek	Hit it!

how would you say:[9]

You are buying it./You buy it.
You are hitting it./You hit it.

The *-s* suffix, it turns out, expresses either ongoing action or habitual action.

    An ongoing action can be specified as having taken place in the past through the addition of another suffix:

shní:nons	You are buying it.
shní:nonskwe'	You were buying it.
skòn:reks	You are hitting it.
skòn:rekskwe'	You were hitting it.

With this information, you can predict the meaning of:[10]

    satkáhthoskwe'

How would you say in Mohawk:[11]

You were tipping it over.
You were writing.

From these examples, you can see that Mohawk speakers do not

---

[8]"You are shooting./You shoot."

[9]a. *shní:nons* b. *skòn:reks*

[10]"You were looking."

[11]a. *skahráthoskwe'* b. *shiá:tonskwe'*

have to learn every word of their language as an isolated unit. In fact, you may already have found yourself able to form new words on the basis of the patterns described so far. Mohawk speakers have control of many other prefixes and suffixes which alter the meanings of simple verbs in various ways, expressing for example negation, surprise, simultaneity of events, the probability or desirability that something will happen, causation, reversal of actions ("untie" as opposed to "tie"), and several tenses and aspects.

Now notice that the verbs in the foregoing examples were all understood to have the subject "you." It is likely they contain some clue to the identity of their subjects. Compare the following pairs (the double *kk-* beginning the fourth example represents a single sound, like French [k], 'fortis,' but longer):

shará:tats	You are lifting it.
khará:tats	I am lifting it.
skahráthos	You are tipping it over.
kkahráthos	I am tipping it over.

The situation should be clear. From these pairs, and the verb,

shiá:tons   You are writing.

the meaning of the following verb can be inferred:[12]

khiá:tons

Given the verbs:

satkáhthos	You are looking.
saròn:tats	You are shooting.
shní:nons	You are buying it.

can you predict the Mohawk words for the following?[13]

I am looking.
I am shooting.
I am buying.

Again, by learning to change the so-called 'pronominal prefix' which expresses the subject of the verb from "you" to "I," we have succeeded

---

[12]"I am writing."

[13]a. *katkáhthos* b. *karòn:tats* c. *khní:nons*

in doubling the number of Mohawk words now available to us.
Now look back at the simple command forms:

shiá:ton	Write!
shará:tat	Lift it!
skòn:rek	Hit it!
saròn:tat	Shoot!
shní:non	Buy it!
satkáhtho	Look!
skahrátho	Turn it over!

What type of subject appears in these verbs? In English the "you" subject of commands is usually omitted. In Mohawk it is always present. Verb stems never stand alone. Not only is the subject always present, but it also provides more information than the English "you." Compare the commands in the next two pairs:

shiá:ton	Write!
senihiá:ton	Write, both of you!

shará:tat	Lift it!
senihará:tat	Both of you lift it!

If you know the command:

skòn:rek	Hit it!

when would you use the following command?[14]

senikòn:rek

How would you tell two people to:[15]

Tip it over!

Languages having separate 'dual' forms, like those in the preceding examples, usually also have separate 'plural' forms. Listening to the following Mohawk commands, you will hear a difference between orders given to two people and those issued to three or more:

senihiá:ton	You two write!
sewahiá:ton	You all (three or more) write!

senihará:tat	You two lift it!
sewahará:tat	You all lift it!

---

[14] To say "You two, hit it!"

[15] *senikahrátho*

Which part of the word signals a change in the number of people addressed? When would the following verbs be used?[16]

>   *sewatkáhtho*
>   *sewaròn:tat*

How would you say the following?[17]

>   Buy it! (speaking to two people)
>   Buy it! (speaking to three or more people)

We have seen that these pronominal prefixes differ for first and second person (according to whether they refer to the speaker or the hearer), and also for singular, dual, and plural number. There are in addition two sets of first-person dual and plural prefixes:

>   *iakenihiá:tons*   We two (not including you) are writing.
>   *iakwahiá:tons*   We all (not including you) are writing.
>
>   *tenihiá:tons*   You and I are writing.
>   *tewahiá:tons*   We all (including you) are writing.

The prefixes that begin with *iake-* or *iak-* indicate that the person being spoken to is not included in the subject of the verb, whereas the prefixes beginning with *te-* indicate that the person being spoken to *is* included. Known by linguists as the difference between 'exclusive' and 'inclusive' forms, this distinction is a very common one in Native American languages. How would a Mohawk convey the following ideas if he wanted to exclude the person he is talking to?[18]

>   We (two) are lifting it.
>   We (three or more) are lifting it.

How would he say these two things if he wanted to include the person listening?[19]

Third-person pronominal prefixes in Mohawk are differentiated not only by number but also by gender:

---

[16]a. "All of you, look!" b. "You all shoot!" Notice that when two *a* vowels come together they are simplified to a single *a*.

[17]a. *senihní:non* b. *sewahní:non*

[18]a. *iakenihará:tats* "We (dual exclusive) are lifting it," b. *yakwahará:tats* "We (plural exclusive) are lifting it"

[19]a. *tenihará:tats* "We (dual inclusive) are lifting it," b. *tewahará:tats* "We (plural inclusive) are lifting it"

rahará:tats	He is lifting it.
iehará:tats	She is lifting it./One is lifting it.
kahará:tats	It is lifting it./She is lifting it.

If we look only at the first of the meanings given in each case, we could conclude that Mohawk simply makes a distinction between 'masculine,' 'feminine,' and 'neuter,' the last including animals as well as inanimate objects. One complication, however, is that the prefix *ie-* in the second word can mean not only "she" but also "one," like French *on* or German *man*. Comparison with related languages suggests that this was the original meaning of the prefix, and that in some of the Iroquois languages its meaning was extended to the feminine category. We can note in addition that the prefix *ka-* in the third word also sometimes means "she." When a Mohawk speaker uses the word *kahará:tats* to mean "She is lifting it," he is treating the woman he is talking about in a detached, impersonal, perhaps slightly disrespectful style. If he says *iehará:tats* he is communicating a more personal, perhaps more respectful attitude towards her. The difference is a subtle one, and it presents the learner of Mohawk with the need to make an important decision whenever he wants to talk about a woman—a decision as difficult as, for example, knowing when to say *tu* or *vous* in second-person reference when speaking French.

What two different meanings might a Mohawk speaker have in mind when using each of the following words?[20]

> *iehiá:tons*
> *kahiá:tons*

How would a Mohawk say each of the following?[21]

> He is tipping it over.
> She is tipping it over (with a personal attitude toward her).
> She is tipping it over (with a detached attitude toward her).
> One is tipping it over.
> It is tipping it over.

These examples have provided only a glimpse of the complex Mohawk pronominal prefix system. We have seen that these prefixes differ for first, second, and third person, for singular, dual, and plural number, for 'inclusiveness' or 'exclusiveness' in first-person dual and plural, and for three genders (with certain alternative meanings) in the

---

[20]a. *iehiá:tons* "She is writing./One is writing." b. *kakiá:tons* "It is writing./She is writing."

[21]a. *rakahráthos* b. *iekahráthos* c. *kakahráthos* d. *iekahráthos* e. *kakahráthos*

third person. One of the ways in which this complexity is increased still further is through the use of prefixes that refer to objects rather than subjects of verbs, as well as of prefixes that refer to various combinations of subjects and objects. Look, for example, at the differences between these pairs of verbs:

khará:tats	I am lifting it.
khehará:tats	I am lifting her.
kkòn:reks	I am hitting it.
khekòn:reks	I am hitting her.

The words beginning with *khe-* show that a feminine singular object is present, as well as a first-person singular subject. In all, more than sixty different pronominal prefixes are used in Mohawk verbs.

There is another complexity exhibited by these prefixes. Most of them occur in several different forms, depending among other things on how the following verb stem begins. What are the two different forms exhibited by the second-person dual prefix in the following examples?

shará:tat	You (singular) lift it!
senihará:tat	You (dual) lift it!
satkáhtho	You (singular) look!
tsatkáhtho	You (dual) look!

The easiest way to answer this question is to begin by determining where the verb stems meaning "lift it" and "look" begin, and a simple way to do that is to separate off the second-person singular prefix, which we already know is *s-*, from the remainder of the words containing it:

s + hará:tat	You (singular) lift it!
s + atkáhtho	You (singular) look!

In this way we can identify the stems -*hará:tat*, meaning "lift it," and -*atkáhtho*, meaning "look." What, then, is the form of the second-person dual prefix that occurs with -*hará:tat*? What form occurs with -*atkáhtho*?[22] The first of these is the form of the prefix that occurs before 'consonant stems,' for example, stems beginning with *h*. The second is the form that occurs before stems beginning with *a*. Given that the second-person singular form for "shoot" is as follows:

saròn:tat	You (singular) shoot!

---

[22] *seni-* and *ts-*, respectively.

how would a Mohawk say:[23]

You (dual) shoot!

A similar kind of alternation between different forms of the same prefix can be observed with the feminine singular prefix. Compare, for example, the following words:

iehará:tats	She is lifting it.
iontkáhthos	She is looking.

What is the form of the feminine prefix that occurs before stems beginning with *a*?[24] This question is a little more difficult to answer, since apparently the prefix in this case "swallows up" the initial *a* of the stem. If you understand how this works, and if you remember the stem that means "shoot," you should now be able to construct the Mohawk word that means:[25]

She is shooting.

The entire pronominal prefix system in Mohawk exhibits a large amount of this kind of alteration of different prefix forms, so that another challenge in learning the language is to learn exactly how each prefix will appear with different types of stems.

The pronominal prefixes do not occur with verbs only; they also accompany nouns to indicate who the possessor of an object is. Note, for example, how some of the prefixes already familiar to us are used with the noun stem *-konhsà:ke* meaning "face":

kkonhsà:ke	my face
skonhsà:ke	your face
rakonhsà:ke	his face
iekonhsà:ke	her face

Note the following words indicating someone's possession of a foot:

kahsi'tà:ke	my foot
sahsi'tà:ke	your foot

---

[23] *tsaròn:tat*

[24] *ion-*

[25] *ionròn:tats*

Try now to identify the stem meaning "foot," and then predict how the following would be said in Mohawk:[26]

> her foot

If you are told that the prefix *ra-*, meaning either "he" or "his," also "swallows up" the initial *a* of an *a*-stem verb or noun, how do you suppose the following would be said?[27]

> his foot

Given that the noun stem meaning "ear" is *-ahonhtà:ke*, try to construct the Mohawk words for all of the following:[28]

> my ear
> your ear
> his ear
> her ear

Like a number of other Native American languages, Mohawk exhibits a particularly interesting grammatical phenomenon known as 'noun incorporation.' Noun stems can appear inside of verbs. The following words are often heard over Mohawk dinner tables:

ka'wahrákon	The meat is delicious./delicious meat
kahnenna'tákon	The potatoes are delicious./ delicious potatoes
kasahe'tákon	The beans are delicious./delicious beans
ka'wahrakenrì:ta'	The meat is fried./fried meat
kahnenna'takenrì:ta'	The potatoes are fried./French fries
kasahe'takenrì:ta'	The beans are fried./fried beans

In Mohawk there is no special grammatical class of adjectives, as there is in English. There is in fact no overt distinction between the assertion "(something) is delicious" and the adjectival phrase "delicious (something)"—hence the two meanings given for each of the preceding words. Each of these words begins with the neuter singular pronominal prefix *ka-*, which might be thought of as expressing grammatical 'agreement' with the neuter subject, but which has no direct translation in English.

---

[26] *ionhsi'tà:ke* (stem *-ahsi'tà:ke*)

[27] *rahsi'tà:ke*

[28] a. *kahonhtà:ke* b. *sahonhtà:ke* c. *rahonhtà:ke* d. *ionhonhtà:ke*

The remainder of each word consists of an 'incorporated' noun stem followed by a verb stem. The verb stems have the following forms:

-ákon   be delicious
-kenrì:ta'   be fried

What, then, are the forms of the noun stems in these words?[29] Note that each noun stem has an extra *a* at the end when it occurs before a verb stem beginning with a consonant. This 'stem-joiner' vowel saves the speaker from having to pronounce difficult sequences of consonants like *hrk*.

Now, if the noun stem meaning "corn" is *-nenhst(a)-*, how would a Mohawk be likely to compliment her hostess with a word meaning:[30]

The corn is delicious.

On the basis of:

kana'tarákon   The bread is delicious.

what would be a likely term for "fried bread"?[31] Another food found on a Mohawk table might be:

kanenhsterá:ken   white corn

What, then, would the following word refer to?[32]

kahnenna'terá:ken

What would a Mohawk call:[33]

white beans
white meat

The adjectival verbs exemplified here all incorporate their subject nouns. Transitive verbs on the other hand—those with both subjects and objects—usually incorporate their objects. Recall the verb:

shní:non   Buy it!

---

[29] a. *-'wahr(a)-* "meat" b. *-hnenna't(a)-* "potatoes" c. *-sahe't(a)-* "beans"

[30] *kanenhstákon*

[31] *kana'tarakenrì:ta'*

[32] "white potatoes"

[33] a. *kasahe'terá:ken* b. *ka'wahrerá:ken*

What would you do in response to the following request?[34]

  shnenna'tahní:non

How would you say:[35]

  She is buying corn.
  He is buying bread.
  I am buying beans.

As you might imagine, Mohawk speakers do not usually borrow nouns from another language (English or French) and incorporate them into such verbs. Occasionally, however, such a borrowing does take place, as in:

  kashrimpserákon

Can you guess what this word means?[36] The following may be harder to guess:[37]

  katiakare'tsherákon

Sometimes the source language may be French, as with:

  kakare'tsherákon   The cake is delicious./delicious cake

The noun stem here appears to be *-kare'tsher-*, which is based on the French word *galette*. How might a Mohawk speaker say:[38]

  She is buying cake.

What do you suppose the verb stem is in the following word?[39]

  ranóhares   He is washing it.

When an object noun is incorporated with this stem, the initial *n* is lost; in other words, the stem becomes *-óhares*. Given the following noun stems:

---

[34]"Buy potatoes!"

[35]a. *ienenhstahní:nons* b. *rana'tarahní:nons* c. *ksahe'tahní:nons*

[36]"delicious shrimp"

[37]"delicious chocolate"

[38]*iekare'tsherahní:nons*

[39]*-nóhares*

-nenhst-   corn
-tsiser-   glass, window

How would you say the next sentences in Mohawk?[40]

He is washing the corn.
He is washing the window.

There is in Mohawk an extra, so-called 'middle voice' element that indicates that an action is performed on something that belongs to or is a part of the subject. Thus, with the noun stem *-ia't-* "body" we find:

   katia'tóhares   I'm washing my body (not someone else's).

What part of this word expresses the middle voice meaning?[41] Recall now the word:

   kkonhsà:ke   my face

As you may have noticed, these words for body parts all end in *-à:ke* when they are spoken as separate words. The bare noun stem itself, however, is the portion of the word lying between the pronominal prefix (in this case *k-*) and the ending *-à:ke*. What, then, is the form of the noun stem meaning "face"?[42] Recall that "my foot" is *kahsi'tà:ke*. How would a Mohawk say:[43]

I am washing my face.
She is washing her foot.

What do you suppose it would mean to say the following, without the middle voice element?[44]

   kkonhsóhares

Many other elements may be found within Mohawk words, but the point to all this discussion is that the learner of Mohawk has to do considerably more than learn single vocabulary items which can be strung together in some simple way to form sentences. One of the most formidable tasks such a learner faces is to acquire the ability to form Mohawk words in a productive way. The present fluent speakers of the

---

[40]a. *ranenhstóhares* b. *ratsiseróhares*

[41]*-at-*

[42]*-konhs-*

[43]a. *katkonhsóhares* b. *iontahsi'tóhares*

[44]"I am washing the face/its face (not my own)."

language acquired unconsciously during their childhood all the necessary rules for putting together Mohawk stems, prefixes, and suffixes in a way that expresses what they want to say, and they are able to do it automatically without being aware of the rules themselves at all. Learning the language means learning how to do this.

But it is not enough simply to know how to put words together and how to combine them into sentences. One must also know how certain words can be extended to other uses. For it is frequently the case that a Mohawk word can have not only a literal meaning, but also one or more metaphorical or idiomatic uses. The word *iontaweià:tha'*, for example, means literally "one enters," but it can also be used as if it were a noun referring to a "doorway" or "passageway." In fact, it is used not uncommonly to mean "a place where people hang out," and even, with an interesting metaphorical extension, "a brothel."

In this light we can look back again to the conversation in the market and note that the word *tiontenhninòn:tha'* means literally "there one sells." It is, however, also the word for "store," and was so used in this conversation. At the beginning of the same sentence in which this word appears, there is also the word *tio'karáhsen*, which is also literally a verb: "as it was evening." In this sentence, however, it is most comfortably translated "last night." From one point of view the entire sentence consists of three verbs in a row:

> *tio'karáhsen*   *tiontenhninòn:tha'*   *iekatehnhwaori'tí:ne'skwe'.*
> as-it-was-evening   there-one-sells   there-I-fool-self-going-was

But taking into account the Mohawk tendency to use verbs as if they were nouns, we can be satisfied with the more comfortable translation, "Last night, crazy as I am, I was going to the store."

It is also true that in learning Mohawk, as in learning any new language, the ear must become attuned to new sounds and learn to disregard others. Sounds which go by unnoticed in English can easily change the meaning of a Mohawk word. The difference between a slightly rising tone and a slightly falling one distinguishes *oká:ra'* "story" from *okà:ra'* "eye," or *onón:ta'* "hill" from *onòn:ta'* "milk." A slight puff of breath before a consonant also changes meaning: *ohsóhkwa* "color" is different in this way from *ohsò:kwa'* "nut." The length of time a vowel is sustained (as indicated by the colon) can likewise affect meaning: *tó:ka'* "I don't know" has a longer first vowel than *tóka'* "if." A glottal stop (a catch in the throat) is as important as any other consonant. The addition of two glottal stops changes *wakhiá:ton* "I have written" to *wa'khiá:ton'* "I wrote."

Clearly, then, for a native speaker of English to learn Mohawk is a sizable task. Such a person must master the Mohawk sound system, Mohawk word construction, and Mohawk sentence structure. And he must master them not as passive facts, like the knowledge that the

Declaration of Independence was signed in 1776, but as active skills to be automatically and unconsciously applied during the course of a conversation. We have seen how radically each of these levels of language structure differs from its English counterpart. Is it only a vain hope that English speakers can be led to acquire the intricacies of such a complex system?

4 BILINGUAL EDUCATION

Obviously the language can be acquired, since one thousand Mohawks at Caughnawaga speak it perfectly. Clearly they know how to use the complex phonological, morphological, and syntactic patterns described earlier. But this linguistic knowledge was acquired without the speakers' awareness, and most speakers are still unaware on a conscious level of what they know about their language. Imagine your reply to a linguist's request for a succinct but thorough description of the rules for forming questions in your language. You can create questions with ease, but can you just as quickly state the directions for doing so? Do you remember learning to form questions as a child?

Children acquire grammatical structures and processes simply by making generalizations about the patterns they hear around them all day long. Rules are not explained. Children, and, to some extent, adults, can acquire second languages in much the same way. Exposed to sentence and word patterns in strong enough doses, they can also form generalizations quite unconsciously. Well-chosen examples can be much more effective than explanations. The problem with second-language acquisition is usually the length and quality of exposure. Learners do not normally hear specific sentence patterns in sufficient quantity and concentration to be able to acquire the rules for forming them. Fifteen minutes a day of random Mohawk utterances will never produce competent speakers. The crucial requirement is that students must be exposed to example after example of precisely the structures they are expected to learn. To produce and present language courses which will do just that, a thorough, conscious understanding of these structures is necessary. Explicit explanations to the children may never be given, but teachers must be capable of selecting specific patterns for each language lesson.

Five years ago, a group of dedicated Mohawk teachers responded to the challenge of mastering the structure of their language in order to create an effective language curriculum. Over a period of several years, the Mohawk teachers devoted their entire summers, as well as their weekends during the winter to mastering Mohawk structure. They then began to construct a curriculum which would build knowledge of structure and vocabulary in somewhat the order children would acquire them naturally if Mohawk were their first language. The result is a curriculum specifying which structures and vocabulary are introduced every day of the school year, for each grade.

The teachers themselves have developed extraordinary teaching skills. Their goal is to teach children a way of thinking, not simply a translating skill. For this reason, no English is spoken in the classroom. Children learn Mohawk in Mohawk. Teachers must not only know which structures they want to expose children to, they must also be experts at the monolingual approach, using objects, charades, and pictures to convey meaning. They are trying to establish a direct link for children between the Mohawk language and their world. The method is working well.

They are succeeding in a way never dreamed possible by many other Mohawk speakers. The language is now being taught to all children at Caughnawaga from nursery school through grade six, and to those who want it in high school. What is more, these young people are actually learning how to speak, how to put together new sentences correctly, and even how to build new words on their own. Encouraged by, and even envious of the new skills of the children, adults who did not speak the language have begun to ask for classes for themselves. At present there are four adult Mohawk classes in the community, each at a different level, and there is a demand for more.

FIGURE 1.3   A Bilingual Classroom at Caughnawaga

The accomplishment of these goals has not been easy. A tremendous amount of hard work and dedication was involved. There were many obstacles to be overcome, not the least of which sometimes originated among good speakers of the languages. One of the most important ingredients of such a language program is the attitude of the community. It can guarantee failure or be a major factor in success. If the approximately one thousand native speakers of Mohawk at Caughnawaga chose to speak Mohawk constantly to each other and were not hesitant to speak it to the children, the latter would be exposed continually to the language and would want to know it. They would have

FIGURE 1.4   *Children at Caughnawaga Learning Mohawk*

They learn the language by talking about the things around them, instead of by studying textbooks. They learn about their community and its government while watching slides of the people and places they have grown up with and by taking field trips around town. Mohawk can be learned easily when the children can actually see what the words represent.

excellent models to learn from, and the spirit—the special flavor of communication among Mohawk speakers—would be passed on to new generations quite naturally.

Many Mohawks, however, have reasons for not supporting such a program and for choosing to speak English most or all of the time. One reason has been a belief that Mohawk must be an old-fashioned language, appropriate for talk about bows and arrows or corn, but useless or inconvenient in the modern world. Such critics can point to the cumbersomeness of certain modern Mohawk words in comparison with their English equivalents. For example, the word for "telephone" is *iontewennata'ahstáhkhwa'*, literally "one uses it for inserting the voice."

Anyone who knows Mohawk, however, cannot help but be aware of its vitality, its adaptability to the changing needs of its speakers. A good example can be observed in any large eastern metropolis. If you could listen to the steelworkers erecting skyscrapers in New York City, balanced on tiny platforms high above the traffic jams, you would be likely to hear them wisecracking in the same language used only a few hundred years ago by woodland hunters and gatherers. The Mohawk language seems to suit their needs quite satisfactorily, as well as provide a constant source of entertainment and solidarity. It provides its speakers with a range of different styles, each of them appropriate for different occasions, different audiences, different speakers. The jargon of steelworkers is different indeed from the elaborate oratorical style employed at Mohawk ceremonies, a style rich in metaphor and imagery, where elaborate descriptions often take the place of simple nouns. Steelworkers' language and ceremonial language both differ conspicuously from speech used within the home, or among speakers of different ages. Even within a community of a thousand speakers there are many styles to choose from, according to one's situation and one's purposes.

But the most important objections to the language program stem from the earlier experiences of the people who are now the good speakers of the language. It is they who learned Mohawk as a first language in childhood. Like Native Americans elsewhere, they suffered considerably when they entered school. They were ridiculed and punished for not speaking English. Many were taught to cover up their heritage. Later on, those who could not speak excellent English often faced discrimination in their search for jobs. To be successful in this world, it became necessary to be a fluent speaker of English. The Mohawks were and are generally successful.

Now that English has nearly replaced Mohawk as a first language in the community, now that children no longer know the language, now that traditions risk being forgotten, there is a sudden painful awareness of the loss of roots. Mohawks can finally be especially proud of who they are, but they must search hard to rediscover just what it means to be Mohawk, just how they are different from the white population surrounding them. It was at the urging especially of young people who were feeling this loss most keenly that the teachers set about their work in the first place.

What will these people have gained if their efforts are successful? There are relatively few monolingual Mohawk speakers, so rudimentary communication between generations is not the reward. The chief reward will be in the recapturing of a personal and social identity that was on the verge of escaping forever. It will be in the intimate participation in an ancestral culture of great richness and diversity. And it will be in the ability to contribute personally to an ancient and continuing linguistic tradition where language is valued in a way that has long been lost to speakers of English.

If we say of someone that he is a good speaker of English, we generally mean that he uses correct grammar. In fact, we would be most likely to make such a comment about a foreigner who had learned the language. To say that a person's English is not good usually indicates the use of socially stigmatized forms such as "ain't" or "he didn't do nothing." If we comment on quality of style, we are usually referring to writing ability. Among Mohawks the situation is different. Skill in both formal, oratorical style and in colorful informal style are highly valued and appreciated. A skillful use of metaphor and of connotatively rich terminology are noticed by all. Many of the words now in common use in the language reflect this imaginative style: *wahia'nikonhró:kten'* "they despaired," but literally "they came to the end of their minds" or *waharihó:wanahte'* "he announced," but literally "he made the word large." Linguistic skill in Mohawk is not limited to the proper use of grammatically correct forms. There is a pride in making use of the resources the language offers in the most effective way possible.

Mohawk conversations are typically accompanied by much laughter. Funny stories are treasured and retold. They lose a great deal in translation, but the following two stories may give some idea of the nature of Mohawk humor:

> Long ago a man went to get wood in the forest. He hitched two horses side by side to a wagon. The horses' harness was made of eel skin. As he arrived at the forest, it started to rain. He finished cutting the wood, and loaded it onto the wagon and started for home. He got the horses to go, but the wagon did not move. Their harness started to stretch. The wagon remained in the forest. As he arrived at his home, he removed the harness from the horses and hung it on the fence. During the night the eel skin dried and started to shrink. He woke up in the morning and looked out of the window, and to his surprise he saw the wagon parked next to the fence, full of the wood that he had cut.[45]

> Once there were two very good, but competitive friends. One was from Akwesasne, and the other from Caughnawaga. Not a day went by that

[45]As told by Frank Jacobs, Jr.

they did not have a friendly argument about one thing or another. Each one used every little thing as an excuse to top the other. They were both the proud possessors of dogs, and each thought that his dog was much smarter and stronger than the other. One day the dogs had a fight, as dogs are prone to do. The two men thought that this was a fine time to find out which dog was really stronger. Each man was sure his dog would win, so sure in fact that they made quite a big wager. The dogs went at it so ferociously that fur was flying in every direction, and they raised such a cloud of dust that it was impossible to see which animal was winning. When all the dust had finally settled, all that was left lying on the ground were two tails. That should have ended the argument, but the two friends immediately measured to see which tail was longer.[46]

Much Mohawk humor depends on playing with words, often in the manner which we call punning. Thus a favorite joke among women which cannot really be translated goes something like, "Would you like to put milk in your tea?" "No, the tea is too hot." The humor lies in the fact that the word for milk, *onòn:ta'*, is also the word for breast. Whether the frequency of word play can be attributed to the spirit of the language or of its speakers, Mohawks create constant merriment with their linguistic manipulations. Knowing the language means being able to participate in this form of enjoyment too, a form inaccessible to those who speak English alone.

There are those who feel that projects aimed at the revitalization of a language are doomed to failure, that at best Indian children should be taught a few words of the language of their parents and grandparents to display on request—that that is the best which can be done. For Mohawk children, however, the link with the past has not been broken yet. There are still many at Caughnawaga who can share their knowledge with the children of today. Because of the energy and dedication of the Mohawk teachers, a dream is coming true. Girls and boys of elementary school age are already using Mohawk again spontaneously outside of school. With support from the community, these children just may grow up with a sense of who they are and where they have come from.

Onkwehshón:'a.	*Ietshiiatahónhsatat*	*oh*	*nahò:ten'*
people	listen-to-them	what	kind-of-thing
People.	Listen to	what	

ionkhihsothokon'kénha'	*rón:ton'.*	*Onkwehshón:'a.*
our-deceased-grandparents	they-are-saying	people
our ancestors	are saying.	People.

Shé:kon	*ionkwahronkhátie'*	*ionkhihsothokon'kénha'*
still	we-are-continually-hearing	our-deceased-grandparents
We are still	continually hearing	our ancestors'

---

[46]As told by Annette Jacobs.

raotiwén:na'.	*Onkwehshón:'a.*	*Ionkhihsothokon'kénha'*
their-voices	people	our-deceased-grandparents
voices.	People.	Our ancestors

rón:ton'	*"Sásewatst*	*ne*	*sewawén:na'.*"[47]
they-are-saying	use-them-again	those	your-words
are saying,	"Use	your language again."	

SUGGESTIONS FOR FURTHER READING

Bonvillain, Nancy. *A Grammar of Akwesasne Mohawk.* National Museum of Man, Ethnology Division, Mercury Series, Paper 8. Ottawa, 1973.

Useful for those interested in knowing more about the language.

Devine, Edward James, S. J. *Historic Caughnawaga.* Montreal: Messenger Press, 1922.

A history of Caughnawaga from a Jesuit point of view.

Hertzberg, Hazel W. *The Great Tree and the Longhouse.* New York: Macmillan, 1966.

A recent survey of Iroquois culture, written for high school students.

Hewitt, J.N.B. *Iroquoian Cosmology, First Part.* Bureau of American Ethnology, Annual Report 21, pp. 127–339. Washington, D.C., 1903.

Contains a Mohawk version, with English translation, of the Iroquois creation myth.

Michelson, Gunther. *A Thousand Words of Mohawk.* National Museum of Man, Ethnology Division, Mercury Series, Paper 5. Ottawa, 1973.

Chiefly a dictionary, but with a brief grammatical introduction. Deals with the Caughnawaga dialect.

Mithun, Marianne, ed. *Kanien'kéha' Okara'shón:'a, Mohawk Stories.* New York State Museum Bulletin 427. Albany, 1976.

A collection of stories from Caughnawaga in Mohawk and English. The source of the stories by Frank Jacobs, Jr., and Annette Jacobs quoted in this chapter.

Morgan, Lewis Henry. *League of the Ho-de'-no-sau-nee, Iroquois.* New York: Corinth Books, 1962.

Originally published in 1851. The classic nineteenth-century work on the Iroquois by one of the founders of modern anthropology.

Wilson, Edmund. *Apologies to the Iroquois.* New York: Vintage Books, 1966.

An excellent, readable introduction to the modern Iroquois and some of their traditions, with an introductory chapter by Joseph Mitchell on "The Mohawks in High Steel."

---

[47]Adapted from Frank Jacobs, Jr.

II

Hua
A Papuan Language of New Guinea

John Haiman

INTRODUCTION

Perhaps a quarter of the world's languages are spoken on the island of New Guinea, by an indigenous population of not many more than three million people. Some of these languages, particularly those spoken around the coastal areas, are Melanesian; they are closely related to Hawaiian, Indonesian, Javanese, Malagasy, and a large number of other Austronesian languages spoken by peoples throughout the Pacific. Their nature and their historical relationships have been intensively studied and are fairly well known. But most of the languages of New Guinea are not Melanesian. These other languages, known collectively as the Papuan languages of New Guinea, are still almost completely unknown to all but the populations who speak them. Their historical and structural relationships to other languages of the world, even to each other, are for the most part completely unexplored.

Hua is one of these languages, the first language of about 3,000 subsistence gardeners in the Lufa subdistrict of the Eastern Highlands. This essay will discuss what it means to be a speaker of Hua.

John Haiman teaches linguistics at the University of Manitoba in Winnipeg, Canada. He has spent a total of two years at Lufa and is finishing a full-scale grammar of Hua for publication as a book. His main theoretical interests are language change and language universals, with particular reference to the constant relationships between morphology and meaning in unrelated languages.

35

When the number of native speakers of a language is so small the speakers know at least one, more probably several, other languages as well. To a striking degree this is true of the Hua.

The Hua are typical Eastern Highlanders in that they reside patrilocally: that is, on marriage women go to live in the village of the husband. For generations, perhaps centuries, the Hua have contracted most of their marriage alliances with the Gimi, Siane, and Chimbu peoples, whose languages differ from Hua, impressionistically, as much as French, German, and Russian differ from English. Children born of such marriages grow up bilingual. When they in turn marry, they learn the first language of their spouse, which may be different from that of either their mother or their father.

Prolonged intermarriage has made the community phenomenally multilingual. In a survey of 359 adult speakers in 1974, it was found that 305 were fluent in Gimi, 287 in Siane, and 103 in Chimbu. A smaller number of people spoke at least half a dozen other languages. Only two respondents claimed to be totally monolingual, and only eleven knew only one other language besides Hua. All the others spoke at least two, and many were fluent and at ease in four or five.

Within the last twenty-five years, another language, Neo-Melanesian, also known as Pidgin English, has gained currency in the

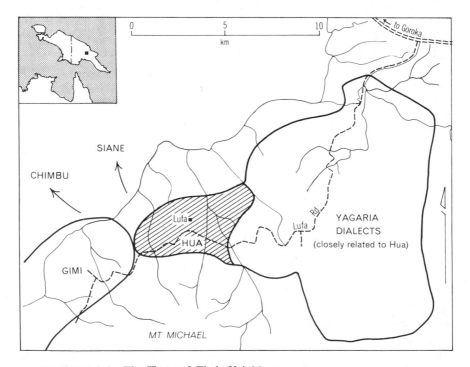

FIGURE 2.1   The Hua and Their Neighbors

FIGURE 2.2   *Kamani Kutane Transcribing a Hua Text*

A resident of Sara village, less than half a mile from Lufa station, Kamani is the author's friend and main informant. With the equivalent of a primary school education in English, he learned to write his language almost effortlessly. Here the author is showing him how to write a sound for which the alphabet he has learned in school has no symbol, the glottal stop. Kamani is one of the handful of people out of the 359 surveyed who were "only" bilingual: he is fluent in Hua and Pidgin. His wife, a native speaker of Chimbu, has a passive—and increasing—command of Hua, while he has a passive command of Chimbu. They have one daughter, aged two, who will grow up learning both Hua and Pidgin. It is not certain that she will also grow up with a speaking knowledge of Chimbu, though if she eventually marries a Chimbu man, as is likely, she will be forced to become fluent in this language as well.

Highlands, replacing all others as the most widely spoken second language among the young. Originally a much simplified English used by Europeans in their contacts with New Guineans, it has now achieved the status of a national language. It is the language of debates in the Papua New Guinea House of Assembly, of the media, and of New Guineans from different parts of the country with no common native language. Pidgin has achieved this important status, not as one might suppose as a result of colonialist intervention by Australian overlords, but at least in part in spite of intervention. Sir Hubert Murray, the most illustrious administrator of the colony in the heyday of Australian imperialism, was so disgusted with what he conceived to be the uncouth properties of Pidgin, that he attempted to abolish it as a medium of communication in favor of Police Motu, itself a simplified version of Motu, a locally spoken Austronesian language. His attempt failed, but even now, more than three decades after his death, all government schools educate their children in English, and if Pidgin is allowed at all in the classroom it is as a bridge to facilitate the acquisition of English.

Like Sir Hubert, one may condemn Pidgin English for its radically simplified structure or for its relatively small vocabulary. Yet without it the very notion of a single independent nation of Papua New Guinea would be inconceivable.

In some ways, the impact of Pidgin on the Hua is to be regretted. First learned by adult males who were recruited as manual laborers on government public works projects, it is now spoken, or at least understood, by everyone under the age of twenty. Naturally, it is the medium most Hua people use to communicate with Europeans and with government employees (policemen, truck drivers, clerks, schoolteachers, medical orderlies, and their families), almost all of whom come from other parts of the country. Moreover, it is increasingly the language used by newly betrothed couples who in past times had no recourse but to learn each other's language in order to communicate at all. Nowadays, because a young man and woman from different language communities already have one language in common, they need not bother to learn any other. Nor can it be disputed that Pidgin is a much more valuable acquisition than a language like Gimi, which, like Hua, is spoken by only a few thousand people. Culturally though, something has been lost. It is as if a native speaker of English were to substitute for French as his second language something like Esperanto. Admittedly, Pidgin is a universal language which really *is* spoken by a large number of people, not just by scattered enclaves of idealists, but like Esperanto, it has (as yet) little in the way of a cultural tradition.

More significant is the fact that Pidgin may replace Hua, even between native speakers of that language. Not surprisingly, replacement now occurs in contexts where Hua lacks terminology. For example, much of the language of card games, even that not directly related to the game, is carried on in Pidgin.

Pidgin is also the language habitually used by people when drunk. Although it is true that beer and spirits have recently been introduced by Pidgin-speaking foreigners, it is unlikely that drunken brawls are conducted in Pidgin out of deference to that fact. Nor can this explain

FIGURE 2.3   Roko Kevao and His Children

*Like most adult Hua males, Roko is almost perfectly bilingual in Hua and
Gimi. Both his mother and his wife are native speakers of Gimi, and it is
likely that the children will hear enough Gimi during their childhood to be
perfectly fluent in the language before they marry. Roko is fluent in Chimbu
and in three fairly closely related dialects of Siane, known to the Hua as
Kma, Rapagu, and Zavezufa, and knows them only slightly less well than
Gimi. His Pidgin is comparatively rudimentary. Both in his command of
native languages and his relative weakness in Pidgin, Roko is typical of
Hua males of his approximate age. He was already an initiated man when
the first European contact was made in 1950, which makes him about fifty
at the time this photograph was taken.*

the fact that a great deal of cursing, drunk or sober, is in Pidgin, particularly since Hua has a large number of pungent (but rather infrequently used) cursewords of its own. It is possible that both of these contexts in which Pidgin is used are related to a phenomenon known to New Guinea ethnographers as "wild man behavior," a tolerated way of letting off steam by going mildly berserk, damaging property, making a tremendous racket, and beating people up. Excesses committed while temporarily mad are not held against one afterwards. It is possible, though not certain, that the use of Pidgin rather than one's own language while engaged in wild man behavior makes one less accountable for one's behavior afterwards—as if the culprit were to say "Look, I wasn't even talking one of our languages, so how could you hold me to account for what I said?"

Although it seems unlikely at this point that Pidgin will soon replace Hua as the vehicle of everyday conversation, some Hua people predict that their grandchildren will grow up speaking only Pidgin. If mass emigration to Goroka and other urban centers should weaken the structure of village-based social life, their prediction may come true.

Like every other language which has evolved over thousands of years, Hua has developed into an instrument uniquely qualified to express the culture and concerns of the people who speak it. Many of its terms, those at the very heart of Hua culture, are untranslatable or meaningless in any other language.

Consider, for example, a word like *bade* "boy," which we have just translated, successfully it would seem, into English. In fact this word is composed of two words, *ba* "woman" and *de* "man"; etymologically, a boy is half woman, half man. Etymology reflects a cultural belief: people are not born male and female in Hua thinking, but achieve masculinity and femininity through a series of initiation rites. At their initiation boys are subjected to a number of trials, including nose-bleeding and induced vomiting to "purge themselves of the woman within them." The word *bade* resonates with these beliefs and is quite literally untranslatable into English, Pidgin, or any other language.

There are many other words like this in Hua, as there are in every other language, including English. Consider our homely word "bread." Surely, there should be no difficulty in translating it. And yet, this word has associations—"bread and wine," "daily bread," "thou shalt eat thy bread by the sweat of thy brow"—which it cannot have for anyone outside Christian culture. As the staff of life, bread is best translated into Hua as *bza* "sweet potato," which of course has yet other associations. And so it goes.

The loss of Hua, like that of any language, means the loss of an entire culture; the two happen together. There is no way that such a loss can occur painlessly, and it must always be reckoned a tragedy.

The loss, of course, is diminished if the new language, in this case

Pidgin, has also had a chance to evolve a richness and flexibility suitable to meet the needs of those who speak it. Pidgin English, at this time the *first* language of only about 10,000 people in all of New Guinea, has not yet had this chance. As succeeding generations grow up using it for all their work and play, it will ultimately develop into a rich and resonant language which will be adapted to the needs of the people who employ it. But this takes generations. In the meantime it simply cannot compare with the resources and associations of Hua, so it is to be hoped that it does not supplant Hua too early for this reason alone.

In any case, we have partially answered the question of what it means to be a speaker of Hua. If you are over forty, it means to be a speaker of two other Highlands languages as well, and possibly of Pidgin; if you are under forty, but over twenty, it means speaking two other Highlands languages and Pidgin as well as Hua; and if you are under twenty, it means speaking Pidgin as well as Hua, and possibly one other Highlands language also.

Primarily of course, to be a speaker of Hua means to be a speaker of Hua, a language utterly unlike any other which you, the reader, are likely to know, yet one which, for all its superficial strangeness, obeys familiar principles. In the following pages we make an attempt to learn some of these principles. We take as our point of departure the formulas of greeting and farewell.

1 THE VERB SYSTEM

1.1 Stems and Endings

Kamani has just come to your house across a level space. You greet him:

> *Ape?*   Have you come?

to which he answers:

> *Oe.*   I have come.

If he has climbed up to reach you, you greet him. (The sign /'/ represents the glottal stop, and is the sound of *t* in a phrase like "hit me" in casual speech):

> *Ai'ape?*   Have you come up?

to which he answers:

> *Ai'oe.*   I have come up.

Ape?	Have you come?	*Ai'ape?*	Have you come up?
Oe.	I have come.	*Ai'oe.*	I have come up.

If he has climbed down a hill to reach your house, the greeting is:

Ormipe?   Have you come down?

to which the response is:

Ormue.   I have come down.

If he greets you first, he will say:

Baipe?   Are you here?

to which your response is:

Baue.   I am here.

Orm-ipe?	Have you come down?	*Ba-ipe?*	Are you here?
Orm-ue.	I have come down.	*Ba-ue.*	I am here.

Note that these greetings are in the form of questions and answers, much like our greetings "How are you?" and "I'm fine." Like these greetings, they are not really requests for information at all. A foreigner may be somewhat taken aback, because the questions seem to him pointless. But like the word *bread*, these words have a communicative function which cannot be rendered by an accurate translation alone. To some extent, this function cannot be predicted and is 'formulaic'; compare English "So long," whose meaning as a formula of farewell cannot be predicted from the meanings of the words which compose it. Nevertheless, even formulaic expressions do reflect something about the culture: from the greeting "How are you?" a question about general health, a foreigner might infer that we were preoccupied with health; from the Hua greetings, with their discrimination of upward, downward, and level movement, one might infer, without glancing at a map, that the Hua were a mountain people. And these inferences are of course correct.

Consider now the farewells. Kamani is about to take his leave of you. He says, rather brusquely:

Bai!   Stay!

to which you respond, even more brusquely, with one of the following:

U!   Go!
Rmu!   Go down!
Hau!   Go up!

depending on the direction in which he is going. In English, such an interchange would be impolite in the extreme. In Hua, it is the polite standard way to take one's leave.

These questions and commands are now simply forms to be memorized; once the principles underlying their formation are understood, however, you will be able to utter any questions and make any response to a question. Hua has virtually no irregular verbs.

We have at this point, the following verb forms:

	Imperative	**I**	**You**
be	*bai*	*baue*	*baipe*
go	*u*	. . .	. . .
come	. . .	*oe*	*ape*
go up	*hau*	. .	. . .
go down	*rmu*	. . .	. . .
come up	. . .	*ai'oe*	*ai'ape*
come down	. . .	*ormue*	*ormipe*

A speaker of Hua knows a complex but regular set of rules which allows him to generate any verbal form if he knows the 'imperative' alone. That is, knowing the words in column one, he can not only produce the words in columns two and three, but also sentences with subjects "he," "we," and "they," both questions and answers. We are now going to do what any Hua child can do so effortlessly: learn these rules, and save ourselves the trouble of memorizing a very large number of verb forms.

All imperatives end in one of the three vowels /i/, /o/, or /u/. Some end in /i/: *Bai* "Stay!" *Mi* "Give it!" *Kri* "Plant it!" *Gai* "Take care of it!" Others end in /o/: *(En)O* "Come!" (the existence of the prefix *en-* in the imperative of the verb "come" is one of the two irregularities in all of Hua verb formation) *Do* "Eat!" *Bro* "Put it!" and *Iro* "Stop it!" Finally, some imperatives end in /u/: *U* "Go!" *Rmu* "Go down!" *Hau* "Go up!" *Hu* "Do it!" *Hefu* "Break it!"

Now let's take another look at the verb forms for some of these verbs:

		Imperative	**Have you...?**	**I have...**
/i/	be	*bai*	*baipe?*	*baue*
	give it	*mi*	*mipe?*	*mue*
/o/	come	*(en)o*	*ape?*	*oe*
	eat	*do*	*dape?*	*doe*
/u/	go down	*rmu*	*rmape?*	*rmue*
	do it	*hu*	*hape?*	*hue*

What regularities can be observed here? Whenever the subject of the verb is "I," the verb has an ending -*e*; whenever the subject is "you," the verb has the ending -*pe*. In addition, the 'verb stem,' that is, the part of the verb that remains, also changes, and the nature of the change seems to depend on the final vowel of the imperative.

Note that both verbs in final /i/ behave alike; so do both verbs in /o/; and so do both verbs in /u/. To see whether you have figured out *how* they behave, you might try to predict how to say:

/i/ { Have you planted it?(recall that the imperative is *Kri!* "Plant it!"),
{ I have planted it.

/o/ { Have you stopped it? (recall that the imperative is *Iro!*)
{ I have stopped it.

/u/ { Have you broken it? (recall that the imperative is *Hefu!*)
{ I have broken it.

The principles which allow you to translate these sentences are the following:

Stem Rule 1

When the subject is "I,"
final /i/ becomes /u/ (e.g., *bai* becomes *bau* in *Bau-e* "I am (here)"),
final /u/ and final /o/ remain (e.g., *do* remains in *Do-e* "I ate"; *hu* remains in *Hu-e* "I did").

When the subject is "you,"
final /i/ remains (e.g., *bai* remains in *Bai-pe?* "Are you here?"),
final /o/ and final /u/ become /a/ (*do* becomes *da* in *Dape?* "Have you eaten?" and *hu* becomes *ha* in *Ha-pe?* "Did you do (it)?").

Thus the correct forms for the sentences above are: *Kripe? Krue Irape? Iroe Hefape? Hefue.*

Suppose now that you and a companion meet and greet not one

person, but two together. Kamani and Kiomu have come across a level space to your house. You will say to them:

not *Ape?* Have you come?
but *A've?* Have you two come?

They will answer:

not *Oe.* I have come.
but *O'e.* We two have come.

If they greet you first, they will say to the two of you:

not *Baipe?* Are you here?
but *Bai-'ve?* Are the two of you here?

and you will answer:

not *Baue.* I am here.
but *Bau'e.* We two are here.

Now, if you were to greet Kamani's entire family, you would say to them:

not *Ape?* Have you come?
but *Ave?* Have you all come?

and they would answer:

not *Oe.* I have come.
but *One.* We all have come.

If they greeted you and your family, they would say:

not *Baipe?* Are you here?
but *Baive?* Are you all here?

and you would answer:

not *Baue.* I am here.
but *Baune.* We are all here.

Once again, we find a recurrent pattern, which emerges clearly if we summarize in a table the behavior of *bai* (an /i/ verb), *o* (an /o/ verb), and *rmu* "go down" (a /u/ verb). The reader is invited to fill in the gaps in the following paradigms:

		Imperative	Have you two . . .?	We two have . . .
/i/	be	*bai*	*bai've*	*bau'e*
	give	*mi*	———	———
/o/	come	*(en)o*	*a've*	*o'e*
	eat	*do*	———	———
/u/	go down	*rmu*	*rma've*	*rmu'e*
	break	*hefu*	———	———

		Imperative	Have you all . . .?	We all have . . .
/i/	be	*bai*	*baive*	*baune*
	give	*mi*	———	———
/o/	come	*(en)o*	*ave*	*one*
	eat	*do*	———	———
/u/	go down	*rmu*	*rmave*	*rmune*
	break	*hefu*	———	———

You have been able to predict the forms of the other sentences by virtue of the following generalizations:

> Whenever the subject of the verb is "you two," the ending is -*'ve*.
> Whenever the subject of the verb is "we two," the ending is -*'e*.
> Whenever the subject of the verb is "you all," the ending is -*ve*.
> Whenever the subject of the verb is "we all," the ending is -*ne*.

Moreover the *verb stem* changes in accordance with:

Stem Rule 2

When the subject is "we two" or "we all,"
final /i/ becomes /u/ (e.g., *bai* becomes *bau*),
final /o/ and final /u/ remain (e.g., *do* doesn't change).

When the subject is "you two" or "you all,"
final /i/ remains (e.g., *bai* remains *bai*),
final /o/ and final /u/ become /a/ (e.g., *do* becomes *da*).

But now if we compare Stem Rules 1 and 2, we discover that a generalization is possible. Combining Rules 1 and 2, we arrive at:

Stem Rule 3

If the subject is "I," "we two," or "we all,"
>   final /i/ becomes /u/ (thus *bau-e, bau-'e, bau-ne*),
>   final /o/ and final /u/ remain (thus *do-e, do-'e, do-ne*, and *hu-e, hu-'e, hu-ne*).

If the subject is "you," "you two," or "you all,"
>   final /i/ remains (thus *bai-pe, bai-'ve, bai-ve*),
>   final /o/ and final /u/ become /a/ (thus *da-pe, da-'ve, da-ve*, and *ha-pe, ha-'ve, ha-ve*).

What is shared by "I," "we two," and "we all" is that the *speaker* is included. What is shared by "you," "you two," and "you all," is that the *person spoken to*, but not the speaker, is included. Thus, we may restate Stem Rule 3 as follows:

If the subject includes the speaker,
>   final /i/ becomes /u/,
>   final /o/ and final /u/ remain.

If the subject includes the person spoken to, but not the speaker,
>   final /i/ remains,
>   final /u/ and final /o/ change to /a/.

What about sentences whose subject includes *neither* the speaker *nor* the person spoken to, ones whose subjects are "he," "she," "it," "the two of them," or "all of them"?

In fact, Hua makes no distinction between "you two" and "the two of them"; nor does it distinguish between "you all" and "all of them." Thus questions like *Dave? Rmave?* and *Mive?* really have two possible English translations. To put the matter in another way, you are able to provide Hua translations for unsuspected sentences like:

Have **they** come?   (recall *O!* "Come!")
Have **they** come up?   (*Ai'o!* "Come up!")
Have **the two of them** eaten it?   (*Do!* "Eat!")
Are **they** here?   (Bai! "Be here!" or "Stay!")

which will be identical with the sentences:

Have **you all** come?
Have **you all** come up?
Have **you two** eaten it?
Are **you all** here?

Namely *Ave? Ai'ave? Da've? Baive?*

A plausible but nevertheless mistaken conclusion to draw from such facts is that because the Hua language does not distinguish between "you two" and "the two of them," neither can its speakers. Rather than demonstrate the falseness of this conclusion directly, we can illustrate the status of the argument on which it is based by considering a similar case in English.

The English pronoun system consists of the pronouns "I," "you," "he," "she," "it," "we," and "they." Disregarding differences in gender, we may say that there exists a correlation of number, with one exception. Corresponding to "I" is the plural "we"; corresponding to "he," "she," and "it" is the plural "they." But there is no plural pronoun corresponding to "you." The language does not distinguish between singular and plural here. Do we infer that English speakers are unable to distinguish between a single addressee or several because of this? Obviously not.

Turning to gender, we note that a distinction is made between masculine "he," feminine "she," and neuter "it": but this distinction is made only in the third-person singular. Are we to infer from this that English speakers are unable to distinguish gender in themselves or in the people that they address? In the same way, there is no reason to believe that the Hua perception of the world is determined by the categories which happen to be recognized in their language.

In the singular, Hua does make a grammatical distinction between "you" and the third-person singular, although, unlike English, it makes no distinction in gender among third-person singular entities. By looking at questions of the form "Has he (she, it) . . . ." we can see the nature of the rules which determine the endings and the verb-stem alternations with third-person singular subjects:

		Imperative	Has he . . .?
/i/	be	*bai*	*baive*
	give	*mi*	—————
/o/	come	*(en)o*	*eve*
	eat	*do*	—————
/u/	go down	*rmu*	*rmive*
	break	*hefu*	—————

Once again there is a recurrent pattern for both the endings and the verb stem. When the subject is "he," "she," or "it," the ending on the verb is -*ve*. The verb stems are governed by the following principle:

Stem Rule 4

When the subject is "he," the verb stem is subject to the following alternations,

final /i/ remains (e.g., *bai* doesn't change),
final /o/ becomes /e/ (e.g., *do* becomes *de*),
final /u/ becomes /i/ (e.g., *rmu* becomes *rmi*).

We can integrate the stem rules into one comprehensive statement as follows:

Stem Rule 5

(a) If the subject includes the speaker (I, we two, we all),
final /i/ becomes /u/,
final /o/ and final /u/ remain unchanged.

(b) If the subject can include the person spoken to, but not the speaker,
final /i/ remains unchanged,
final /o/ and /u/ change to /a/,

(c) If the subject of the verb can include neither the hearer or the speaker (and this is true only of verbs which are third-person singular),
final /i/ remains unchanged,
final /o/ changes to /e/,
final /u/ changes to /i/.

There seems to be some important way in which /o/ and /u/ are similar and distinct from /i/: whenever /i/ remains unchanged, both /o/ and /u/ undergo some change; conversely, whenever /o/ and /u/ remain unchanged, /i/ undergoes some change.

When it undergoes a change, /i/ can change to /u/.
Both /o/ and /u/ change to /a/.
Where they differ, /o/ changes to /e/, and /u/ changes to /i/.

Let us now analyze the five vowels of Hua, to see if there is any way in which we can characterize the set of vowels /o, u/ as opposed to /i/, and the set /u, i/ as opposed to /o, e/.

The vowels /i/ (as in *beat*) and /e/ (as in *bait*) are pronounced with the tongue in the front of the mouth; /o/ (as in *goat*) and /u/ (as in *hoot*) are pronounced with the tongue in the back of the mouth. Both /i/ and /u/ are uttered with the tongue very high; /e/ and /o/ with the tongue in mid position; and /a/ (as in *aah*) with the tongue extremely low in the mouth.

	Front	**Back**
High	i	u
Mid	e	o
Low	a	

Now let us look at the parts of Stem Rule 5 rule one-by-one. According to part (a) when the subject includes the speaker, the final vowel must be back. Since /o/ and /u/ are already back vowels, they remain unchanged. Of the three vowels affected only /i/ is front; since the rule does not specify any change in tongue height, /i/ becomes the corresponding *high back* vowel /u/.

According to part (b), when the subject can be understood to include the person spoken to, but not the speaker, final *back* vowels must be lowered to /a/. Since /i/ is not a back vowel, the rule allows it to remain unchanged, and only /o/ and /u/ are affected.

Part (c) of Stem Rule 5 means that when the subject can't be understood to include either the speaker or the person spoken to, the final vowel must be *front*. Since /i/ is already a front vowel, the rule does not effect any change. Both /o/ and /u/ are back vowels and must be changed to front vowels. Since the rule does not specify any change in tongue height, /o/ (a mid back vowel) is changed to the corresponding *mid front* vowel /e/, while /u/ (a high back vowel) is changed to the corresponding *high front* vowel /i/.

Stem Rule 5 can be restated as follows:

(a) When the subject includes the speaker, final vowel must be *back*.
(b) When the subject can be understood to include the *person spoken to*, but not the speaker, final *back* vowels change to /a/. (Note particularly that verbs with subjects "they two" and "they" may be understood to have subjects "you two" and "you all" and are thus subject to part (b) of the rule.)
(c) When the subject can include *neither* the speaker *nor* the person spoken to, final vowel must be *front*.

The subject of any verb must be such that *one* of parts (a)–(c) of the rule applies to the verb stem.

It is understood that when the final vowel of the verb stem as given in the imperative already happens to satisfy the conditions specified in parts (a)–(c) of Stem Rule 5, then they will leave the verb stem unaffected. In technical jargon, the rules will apply *vacuously* in these cases.

For example, part (a) will effect a change only in verb stems ending in the front vowel /i/. It changes:

bai	to	*bau*	"be"
mi	to	*mu*	"give"

But it applies *vacuously* to *do, iro,* and *hu*:

do	remains	*do*	"eat"
iro	remains	*iro*	"stop it"
hu	remains	*hu*	"do it"

In the same way, part (b) will effect a change only among verb stems ending in one of the back vowels /o/ or /u/. It changes:

do	to	*da*	"eat"
hu	to	*ha*	"do"

But it applies *vacuously* to *bai* and *mi*:

bai	remains	*bai*	"be"
mi	remains	*mi*	"give"

Finally, part (c) of Stem Rule 5 will effect a change only in verb stems whose final vowel is not already front, namely verb stems in final /o/ or /u/. It changes:

do	to	*de*	"eat"
hu	to	*hi*	"do"

But it applies *vacuously* to *bai* and *mi*:

bai	remains	*bai*	"be"
mi	remains	*mi*	"give"

The three subrules of Stem Rule 5 lie at the heart of Hua phonology and will figure in our discussion again and again. They will allow a speaker of Hua correctly to utter and to understand (in technical jargon again, to *generate*) all the forms in Table 2.1.

TABLE 2.1 *Conjugations for -i, -o, and -u Root Verbs*

	-*i* root	-*o* root	-*u* root
Imperative	***Bai*** "Stay!"	***Do*** "Eat!"	***Hu*** "Do (it)!"
First-Person			
Singular	*bau-e*	*do-e*	*hu-e*
Dual	*bau-'e*	*do-'e*	*hu-'e*
Plural	*bau-ne*	*do-ne*	*hu-ne*
Second-Person			
Singular	*bai-pe*	*da-pe*	*ha-pe*
Dual	*bai-'ve*	*da-'ve*	*ha-'ve*
Plural	*bai-ve*	*da-ve*	*ha-ve*
Third-Person			
Singular	*bai-ve*	*de-ve*	*hi-ve*
Dual	*bai-'ve*	*da-'ve*	*ha-'ve*
Plural	*bai-ve*	*da-ve*	*ha-ve*

Before leaving these rules as something to be taken for granted in Hua grammar, we might say a few words about their status in languages generally.

Rules like Stem Rule 5, stated in their most general terms, specify that a 'grammatical' fact (for example, the fact that the subject includes the speaker) determines a 'phonological' fact (for example, that the final vowel in a verb must be *back*). Rules of this sort are called 'ablaut' rules and are extremely common. Indeed it may come as something of a surprise that you are familiar with such ablaut rules in English. Rather than having mastered rules like those in Stem Rule 5, a speaker of English has mastered rules like these:

A. When the verb refers to *past time* (a grammatical fact), the vowel changes from /ɪ/, the sound in "bid," to /ae/, the sound in "bad" (a phonological fact). Thus, it changes present tense "swim" to past tense "swam" and it changes:

> *sink*   to   *sank*
> *stink*   to   *stank*
> *ring*   to   *rang*

B. When a noun is *plural* (a grammatical fact), the vowel changes from /u/ to /i/ (a phonological fact). Thus it changes:

> *goose*   to   *geese*

Rules A and B differ in matters of detail from Stem Rule 5 and affect only a small number of words in English, whereas Stem Rule 5 applies to every verb in Hua. But the same general principle underlies them.

1.2   How to Ask Questions

We have seen that, depending on the subject, certain endings are added to the verb. Our results so far may be tabulated thus:

Subject	Ending	
I	*-e*	
you	*-pe*	(Q)
he	*-ve*	(Q)
we two	*-'e*	
you two/they two	*-'ve*	(Q)
we all	*-ne*	
you all/they all	*-ve*	(Q)

But some of these endings (all those marked with a Q) occur in yes/no questions, whereas the others occur in declarative sentences which are answers to these questions. The question now arises whether the difference between questions and answers is represented in some way in the endings themselves. Are there really two sets of endings, one for questions, and another for answers?

It turns out in fact that there are, as we can guess from hearing a simple interchange like:

Baive?   Is he here?
Baie.   (Yes), he is here.

From this, we immediately conclude that the first ending, *-ve*, occurs in questions, and that the second *-e*, occurs in answers. In principle, we must revise our table of endings:

Subject	Question	Answer
I	_____	*-e*
you	*-pe*	_____
he	*-ve*	*-e*
we two	_____	*-'e*
you two/they two	*-'ve*	_____
we all	_____	*-ne*
you all/they	*-ve*	_____

That is, we must recognize the fact that the system of endings is more complicated than it first appeared, and that certain endings remain to be discovered. Hua uses one set of endings for yes/no questions and another for different sentence types.

From a consideration of sentences like these:

Baine.   You are here.
Dane.   You have eaten.
Rmane.   You went down.
Ai'ane.   You have come up.

we conclude that the answer ending when the subject is "you" must be _____.

In the same way, examination of the sentences:

Bai'e.   You two/they two are here.
Da'e.   You two/they two have eaten.
Rma'e.   You two/they two went down.
Ai'a'e.   You two/they two have come up.

indicates that the answer ending when the subject is "you two/they two" must be _____.

Finally, we must conclude from an examination of sentences like:

Baie.   You all/they are here.
Dae.   You all/they ate.
Rmae.   You all/they went down.
Ai'ae.   You all/they have come up.

that the answer ending when the subject is "you all/they all," is _____.

Now we discover that for the seven possible subjects, we have not seven distinct endings, but only three, according to the following rules:

When the subject is "I," "he," or "you all/they," the ending is *-e.*
When the subject is "we two" or "you two/they two," the ending is *-'e.*
When the subject is "you" or "we all," the ending is *-ne.*

Now let us turn our attention to the question endings. We notice that there is a common ending when the subject is "he" or "you all/they all": the ending *-ve.* Among the assertive endings, too, there is one common to verbs with these two subjects. In addition, verbs with the subject "I" also share this ending, *-e.* This observation might lead us to believe that verbs with the subject "I" would also have the same interrogative ending as verbs with subjects "he" or "you all/they." In fact, this is the case. In questions the following rules apply:

When the subject is "I," "he," or "you all/they," the ending is *-ve.*
When the subject is "we two" or "you two/they two," the ending is *-'ve.*
When the subject is "you" or "we all," the ending is *-pe.*

These are not the only sets of verbal endings subject to such a three-way alternation. Others include the exclamatory endings (used in sentences like "There he was!") and the endings of verbs in relative clauses (as in "the pig which I killed," where the verb *killed* occurs with a special ending).

The verb stem directly before any such ending is subject to the three vowel alternation subrules (a)–(c) of Stem Rule 5. See Table 2.2.

Information questions (those with a question word like *who, what, where, when* or *why*) are already marked by the question word *kzo'* "who," *da'auana* "what," *aigatoga* "where," "whither," etc. at the beginning of the sentence. The verb ending in such questions will be the same as in statements. Thus, for "What did you eat?":

>   *Da'auana da-**ne**,*
> not *Da'auana da-**pe***

TABLE 2.2   The Full Set of Verb Endings Learned So Far

Subject	Yes/No Questions	Statements
I	*-ve*	*-e*
you	*-pe*	*-ne*
he/she/it	*-ve*	*-e*
we two	*-'ve*	*-'e*
you two/they two	*-'ve*	*-'e*
we all	*-pe*	*-ne*
you all/they	*-ve*	*-e*

Armed with this knowledge, you are in a position to construct a large number of questions and answers. All you need to know is the imperative form of the verb, subrules (a)–(c) of Stem Rule 5, and the list of endings given in Table 2.2. To illustrate, consider a new verb *Krukrufu!* "Run!" Suppose you want to say:

Are they running?

Since the subject is "they," the final /u/ of the verb changes to /a/ (by part (b) of Stem Rule 5).

Since the sentence is a yes/no question, the ending is *-ve* (by Table 2.2). Consequently, the translation is *Krukrufave?*

Given the imperative *Ebgi!* "Hit him!" predict the Hua for:[1]

a. Did you hit him?
b. You two hit him.
c. We all hit him.

(Examples with footnotes are ones which are posed as problems for the reader, and for which answers are provided in the footnotes. The reader may also wish to refer to the summary of rules and tables of examples in the Appendix.)

Given the imperative *Kipa kzo!* "Light a fire!" predict the form of the next sentences (note that the verb *kzo* "light" should not be confused with the question word *kzo'* "who?" which ends in a glottal stop).[2]

a. I lit a fire.
b. Did he light a fire?
c. They lit a fire.

---

[1]a. *Ebgipe?* b. *Ebgi'e.* c. *Ebgune.*

[2]a. *Kipa kzoe.* b. *Kipa kzeve?* c. *Kipa kzae.*

Essentially, what you are doing is very similar to solving a puzzle in mathematics, except that you are manipulating sounds rather than numbers according to fixed rules. Both kinds of problem-solving are like games. A number of linguists are convinced that a large part of a child's ability to acquire language is a capacity for play of exactly this sort. Learning a language by discovering rules and manipulating them is an aesthetic experience; it is none the less so for being almost entirely unconscious. As adults, of course, we lose the capacity to perform these manipulations unconsciously when learning a new language, but, we acquire a heightened capacity to appreciate the order and creative power of language.

2   WHO DOES WHAT TO WHOM

If you try now to translate a sentence like:

Who did he give it to?

you will get in Hua:

Kzo' mie?   Who did **he** give it to?

Similarly, you can translate sentences like:

Who gave it to him?

since the pronoun "who" is the same whether it represents the giver or the receiver:

Kzo' mie?   Who gave it **to him**?

The problem is to figure out the meaning of the questions. As we have seen, the same sentence *kzo' mie* can mean either "Who did he give it to?" or "Who gave it to him?" This section will show some of the ways in which Hua speakers solve this problem and answer the question "Who is doing what to whom?"

Consider first the English sentences:

Max kissed Hortense.
Hortense kissed Max.

In the first, the one who does the kissing is *Max*; in the second, *Hortense*. English grammar uses the syntactic device of word order to specify who is doing what to whom: the one who does it precedes the verb, the one to whom it is done follows.

This device is by no means universal, and there was a time in the history of English when it was much less frequently used than now. Sentences like the following were possible:

Her kissed he.
Him kissed she.

Although we now find such sentences unacceptable, we are able to identify the doer in each case as the one named *after* the verb: we can do this because English still has a handful of nominal expressions which occur in different forms ("he" vs. "him") depending on whether the expression identifies the doer or the recipient of the action.

Finally, English has a relatively exotic device, the passive construction, which also allows one to identify the doer and recipient of the action. Consider the two sentences:

Hortense was kissed by Max.
Max was kissed by Hortense.

These sentences are, of course, perfectly grammatical in modern English, and we are able to identify the doer in each case as the one named *after* the verb; we can do this because English has a passive construction in which the verb occurs in a special form (*be kissed by* rather than *kissed*) which marks the first named as the recipient of the action, and the second as the doer.

Among the many devices Hua uses to mark the identity of the doer is word order, but this order differs slightly from that of English, in that the verb almost always stands at the end of the sentence. The name of the doer precedes that of the name of the recipient of the action, as in:

Max Hortense kissed.
Hortense Max kissed.

Very frequently, of course, some participants are not named at all. Rather, we have sentences like:

a. I kissed her.
b. Max kissed her.
c. He kissed Hortense.

Consider first, the sentence (a) "I kissed her." How do we distinguish this from the sentence "She kissed me" in Hua? Recall that there are no pronouns like "I" and "she" whose relative order could decide the problem.

These sentences are really no problem in Hua, as we have already seen: thanks to Stem Rule 5 and the endings of Table 2.2, Hua has an elaborate system of rules whereby a verb 'agrees' with its subject. Given that the verb "kiss" is *vzaro' bro*, we can easily identify the subjects of:

Vzaro'broe.   (Subject can only be "I.")
Vzaro'bree.   (Subject can only be "he," "she.")

But how do we distinguish between "She kissed *me*" and "She kissed *you*?" The distinction is an important one, and is not made simply by identifying the subject.

As we have seen, Hua has an elaborate method of marking agreement between *subject* and verb. It also has an entirely different, and much simpler method, of marking agreement between a human *object* and a verb. Consider the following sentences below (in the first one the third-person singular object agreement marker is null or zero, "$\emptyset$"):

Mie.   He gave it to him.
Dmie.   He gave it to me.
Kmie.   He gave it to you.
Rmie.   He gave it to us.
Pmie.   He gave it to them.
Ra'mie.   He gave it to the two of us.
Pa'mie.   He gave it to the two of them.

So, too:

Dvzaro'bree.   She kissed me.
Vzaro'broe.   I kissed her.

Given the verbs *go* "look at," *gai* "take care of," and *gorai* "fool," or "trick," what is the meaning of the following sentences?[3]

a. *D-gorai-pe.*
b. *K-gau-e.*
c. *R-ge-e.*

You can also translate the following sentences into Hua (with a little checking back):[4]

a. I took care of him.
b. You looked at her.
c. We fooled them.

---

[3]a. Did you fool me? b. I took care of you. c. He looked at us.

[4]a. *Gaue.* b. *Gane.* c. *Pgoraune.*

The real problem arises with sentences (b) and (c). How does Hua distinguish between the next two sentences?

Max kissed her.
She kissed Max.

or between:

He kissed Hortense.
Hortense kissed him.

or, for that matter, between:

Who did he give it to?
Who gave it to him?

Word order will not help here, since there is no word for unstressed pronouns like "he" or "she." Rather than a three-word sentence in which the subject precedes the object, Hua presents two-word sentences like:

Max kissed.
Hortense kissed.
Who gave?

Moreover, since both subject and object are third-person singular entities, the fact that the verb agrees with the subject and object doesn't isolate the subject: since the verb is third-person singular, the subject could be either "Max" or "her," either "Hortense" or "he"; and either "who" or "he." In the same way, the third-person singular object prefix on the verb could refer to either "Max" or "her"; either "Hortense" or "him"; and either "who" or "him."

In fact, as we have seen, sentences like these are ambiguous. Recall that *Kzo' mie?* can mean either "Who gave it to him?" (*kzo'* is doer) or "Who did he give it to?" (*kzo'* is recipient). Very often, Hua tolerates this ambiguity, but Hua also has a possible means of eliminating this ambiguity. It corresponds to the second device available to languages like English, the use of different 'case forms' (like "he" vs. "him"). In the following sentences we show the distribution of a suffix -*bamu'*, which helps distinguish doer from recipient in sentences like the preceding one. You are invited to figure out the principle which regulates the distribution of this suffix. Sentences preceded by an asterisk are ungrammatical in Hua:

*Kzo'**bamu'** mie?*	Who gave it to him?
Kzo'mie?	Who did he give it to?
*Busa'**bamu'**mie.*	Busa gave it to him.

Busa' mie.	He gave it to Busa.
Busa' baie.	Busa is here.
*Busa'bamu' baie.	Busa is here.
Busa' rmie.	Busa went down.
*Busa'bamu' rmie.	Busa went down.
Busa'bamu' ebgie.	Busa hit him.
Busa' ebgie.	He hit Busa.
*Busa'bamu' ebgie.	He hit Busa.
Busa'bamu' iftehie.	Busa lost it.
Busa' iftehie.	Busa got lost.
*Busa'bamu' iftehie.	Busa got lost.
Kzo'bamu' bkaie?	Who swallowed it?
Kzo' bkaie?	Who got drowned?
*Kzo'bamu' bkaie?	Who got drowned?

To see whether you have learned the principle, you might determine which of the following sentences are possible in Hua and which are not.[5]

a.	*Kzo'bamu' krie?*	Who planted it?
b.	*Kzo'bamu' frie?*	Who died?
c.	*Busa'bamu' nie.*	Busa bit him.
d.	*Busa'bamu' nie.*	He bit Busa.
e.	*Busa'bamu' ai'eve?*	Has Busa come up?
f.	*Busa'bamu' rinai'eve?*	Has Busa brought it up?
g.	*Mni'bamu' nirinavie.*	The water carried him off.
h.	*Mni'bamu' deve?*	Did he drink the water?
i.	*Mni'bamu' hadeve?*	Did the water dry up?

If you have learned this principle correctly, you will see that it is somewhat different from the one which operates in English to distinguish forms like "he" and "him." In sentences with transitive verbs, English distinguishes between subjects (like "he") and objects (like "him"). Hua also distinguishes between subjects (which occur with the suffix *-bamu'*) and objects (which occur without this suffix).

There remains the problem of marking the subjects of intransitive verbs (those which occur without objects), like "walk," "sit down," "stand still," "sleep," "die," "stay " and so on. English like most of the other languages with which you are likely to be familiar (such as French German, Latin, Russian, and Greek) treats subjects of intransitive verbs the same as subjects of transitive verbs. Thus, we say "**He** sits down" rather than "**Him** sits down."

In the construction with *bamu'* on the other hand, Hua, like Basque, Eskimo, Mayan languages, and most of the aboriginal languages of

---

[5]Examples b, d, e, h, and i are ungrammatical.

Australia (see the chapters in the companion volume *Languages and Their Speakers* on the Mayan language Jacaltec by Colette Grinevald Craig, and the Australian language Guugu Yimidhirr by John Haviland), chooses to class these with the *objects* of transitive verbs. Thus, the subject of an intransitive verb like the object of a transitive verb, can never occur with *-bamu'*; this suffix is reserved for the subjects of transitive verbs alone.

This kind of classification may seem rather strange to speakers of English. Yet there is no logical reason why the subjects of intransitive verbs should be classified as similar to either subjects of transitive verbs or objects of transitive verbs. A third perfectly logical possibility is that they should constitute a third category distinct from the other two, and this is what happens in some other languages, like Takelma (an American Indian language). What English and Hua are doing is reducing three categories to two; neither language's solution is more "logical" than the other.

Hua

Subject of transitive verb	(occurs with *-bamu'*)
Subject of intransitive verb ⎱	
Object of transitive verb ⎰	(occurs with no suffix)

English

Subject of transitive verb ⎱	
Subject of intransitive verb ⎰	(*he, she, they*)
Object of transitive verb	(*him, her, them*)

In respect to the construction with *-bamu'*, Hua is an ergative language, and the suffix which marks the subject of transitive verbs, (that is, *-bamu'*) is called the ergative case marker. Languages like English are called nominative-accusative languages, or subject-marking languages: the subject of all verbs, irrespective of transitivity is said to be in the nominative case. (For a particularly clear example of a nominative-accusative language, see the description of Russian in the following chapter.)

3   HOW TO TELL TIME : TENSE

On the basis of the examples we have given so far, it seems that one of the distinctions Hua does *not* make is between past and present time. Thus *baie* means "he **is** here," and *ai'ane* means "You **have come** up." In fact, *baie* can also mean "He **was** here," or "He **has been** here," while *ai'ane* can mean "You **are** coming up."

The salient distinction in Hua is between past or present on the one hand, and *future*, on the other hand, which is marked on the verb in a special way. In this section, we discuss both the meaning and the formation of the future.

Once again, it will be helpful to begin with a comparison. Consider the English sentences:

I **am** breathing	I **was** breathing
You **are** breathing	You **were** breathing
He **is** breathing	He **was** breathing

and so on. In each of these, an 'auxiliary verb' which precedes the 'main verb' *breathing* marks the verb in a special way: the auxiliary verb *be* indicates that the action described by the main verb is to be understood as continuing in the present or the past; in addition, the auxiliary verb is the only one which changes depending on the nature of the subject; the main verb remains constant irrespective of the person of the subject.

Hua also has a variety of auxiliary verbs which share this property: they agree with the subject in that they are subject to Stem Rule 5 and take the endings of Table 2.2, whereas in combination with an auxiliary verb the main verb does not make this agreement. Hua auxiliary verbs differ from their English counterparts in that they do not precede, but rather follow the main verb. Where English has "will see" Hua has "see will."

The Hua future auxiliary verb is *gu*, which we may translate "will." Since it is a verb with a final /u/, we know everything we need to know about future tense forms. Remembering that the main verb remains constant (as in English), you may be able to provide translations for:[6]

a. I will be here. (*bai* "be here")
b. You will be here.
c. He will be here.
d. We two will be here.
e. You two/they two will be here.
f. We all will be here.
g. You all/they will be here.

using Table 2.2 and the parts (a)–(c) of Stem Rule 5.

In fact, the main verb remains absolutely constant only when it happens to be an /i/ verb like *bai*. Both /o/ and /u/ verbs undergo a minor change:

Dogue.	I will eat.
Dogane.	You will eat.

---

[6]a. *Baigue.* b. *Baigane.* c. *Baigie.* d. *Baigu'e.* e. *Baiga'e.* f. *Baigune.* g. *Baigae.*

Dogie.	He will eat.
Dogu'e.	We two will eat.
Dega'e.	You two will eat.
Dogune.	We all will eat.
Degae.	You all/they will eat.

That is, in /o/ verbs, the /o/ changes to /e/ in the case where the subject is either "you two/they two" or "you all/they."

Given the pervasive symmetry which characterizes the Hua verb system, you should be able to predict the future forms for a /u/ verb like *rmu* (You might take another look at the vowel chart presented in the discussion of Stem Rule 5). How would you translate the following sentences?[7]

   a. I will go down.
   b. You will go down.
   c. He will go down.
   d. We two will go down.
   e. You two/they two will go down.
   f. We all will go down.
   g. You all/they all will go down.

Elsewhere in the verb system, whenever /o/ changes to /e/, the vowel /u/ changes to /i/. The same is true in the preceding sentences. This minor change which affects both /o/ and /u/ verbs can be subsumed by the following rule:

Stem Rule 6

The final vowel of a verb is fronted when its subject is either "you two/they two" or "you all/they." Otherwise no change occurs.

The question now arises, when does Stem Rule 5 apply, and when does Stem Rule 6? The answer to this is very simple if the grammar as a whole is considered, but given the limited data presented here, it must be taken on trust.

We have seen that there are endings like *-e, -'e, -ne* for assertions and content questions, and endings like *-ve, -'ve, -pe* for yes/no questions. A large number of other endings in Hua exhibit this kind of three-way alternation, among them *-ma, -'ma, -pa* in certain subordinate clauses, and *-mane, -'mane, and -pane* in exclamations.

When a verb stem is followed directly by one of these three-way

---

[7]a. *Rmugue.* b. *Rmugane.* c. *Rmugie.* d. *Rmugu'e.* e. *Rmiga'e.* f. *Rmugune.* g. *Rmigae.*

endings, it is subject to Stem Rule 5. In all other cases but one, it is subject to Stem Rule 6.

Let us look at the future forms of *rmu* "go down" and see how they illustrate this contrast:

Rmugue.	I will go down.
Rmugane.	You will go down.
Rmugie.	He will go down.
Rmugu'e.	We two go down.
Rmiga'e.	You two/they two will go down.
Rmugune.	We will go down.
Rmigae.	You all/they all will go down.

Each single word actually consists of two verbs followed by an ending:

		Verb		**Auxiliary Verb**		**Ending**
Rmugue	=	*rmu*	+	*gu*	+	*e*
Rmugane	=	*rmu*	+	*ga*	+	*ne*

Since the auxiliary verb *gu* is directly followed by the three-way ending (*-e, -'e, -ne*) it is subject to Stem Rule 5; since the main verb *rmu* is not directly followed by such an ending, it is not subject to Stem Rule 5; since the main verb *rmu* is not directly followed by such an ending, it is subject to Stem Rule 6.

The one exception is the second future auxiliary verb *su* "may," which also follows the main verb and accordingly should cause that main verb to be subject to Stem Rule 6. For the verb *rmu*:

*Rmu-su-e.	May I go down!
*Rmu-sa-ne.	May you go down!
*Rmu-si-e.	May he go down!

But, as the asterisks indicate, these sentences are ungrammatical, and what we find instead is:

Rmi-su-e.	May I go down!
Rmi-sa-ne.	May you go down!
Rmi-si-e.	May he go down!
Rmi-su-'e.	May we two go down!
Rmi-sa-'e.	May you two go down!
Rmi-su-ne.	May we go down!
Rmi-sa-e.	May you all go down!

That is, the auxiliary verb *su* is itself subject to Stem Rule 5, but before the auxiliary verb *su*, final /u/ of *rmu* becomes /i/. There is one other context in which the /u/ becomes /i/: before the three-way ending when the subject includes neither the speaker or the addressee. In this context, /o/ becomes /e/ and /i/ remains constant. The same is true before the auxiliary verb *su*, which gives us our Stem Rule 7 (the last!):

Stem Rule 7

Before the auxiliary verb *su*, the final vowel of the verb is "fronted."

Thus, for *go* "look" or "see," we have sentences like:

Gesue	May I see it. Let me see it.
Gesie	May she see it.
Pgesae	May they see them.

On the same principle, you can construct sentences like the following:[8]

a. Let me go down.
b. Let them go down.
c. Let him go down.
d. Let them stay here.
e. Let us stay here.

from the verbs *rmu* "go down" and *bai* "stay."

The *su* "future" does not seem to correspond to a true future tense at all; rather, its meaning corresponds to a category called the "subjunctive mood," marginally represented in English by sentences like the preceding ones and wishes like "God save the Queen" and "Let that be a lesson to you."

We might argue that all wishes of this sort are really wishes for the future, but we have a more pragmatic basis for so confidently identifying *su* as a future verb like *gu*.

Very simply, the *su* future is the only one possible in questions. Moreover, it is the only future in either yes/no questions, or 'question-word questions,' which are thus multiply ambiguous. For example, the question:

Kzo' rmisie?

---

[8]a. *Rmisue.* b. *Rmisae.* c. *Rmisie.* d. *Baisae.* e. *Baisune.*

can mean any of the following:

Who will go down?	(corresponding to the statement "He will go.")
Who may go down?	(corresponding to the wish "May he go.")
Who wants to go down?	(corresponding to the reported wish "He wants to go.")

and the sentence:

Kzo' rmugie?

with a *gu* future verb is absolutely impossible and meaningless in Hua.

Knowing about future questions, you are now able to say sentences like the next ones (recall that "what" is *da'auana,* and "where" is *aigatoga*).[9]

a.   Should I go down?
b.   May I eat it?
c.   What should I do?
d.   What should I eat?
e.   What should he eat?
f.   What will he eat?
g.   Where will he go down to?
h.   Where should we go down to?

We hit a snag, however, when we come to the question "When will he come?" which we might try to translate as:

Aituvita esie,   (given that *aituvita* is "when")

However, the question word "when" in this context must have the form *aituvita-'a.* This form is used when the verb is in the future.

Nor do we find this to be an isolated fact about a single word: all adverbs of time occur in two forms like this, the one form for past time, the other form identical to the first with the added suffix *-'a* for future time. Thus (the reader is invited to fill in the blanks):[10]

---

[9]a. *Rmisuve?* b. *Desuve?* c. *Da'auana hisue?* d. *Da'auana desue?* e. *Da'auana desie?* f. *Da'auana desie?* g. *Aiagatoga rmisie?* h. *Aiagatoga rmisune?*

[10]c. *miti itga'a* tomorrow night d. *kenaga* in the distant past, *kenaga'a* in the distant future e. *dti* this morning, *dti'a* tomorrow morning f. *fzuga* earlier.

	Past		**Future**
a.	*ega* yesterday		*ega'a* tomorrow
b.	*urga* day before yesterday		*urga'a* day after tomorrow
c.	*miti itga* last night		*miti itga'a* _____
d.	*kenaga* _____		_____ in the distant future
e.	_____ this morning		*dti'a* _____
f.	_____ _____		*fzuga'a* later

For a very specific reason, certain adverbs of time do not occur in two forms:

miti	today
he	right now

What is the reason?

Notice what this tells us about past, present, and future tenses in Hua. As far as verb endings on the verb are concerned, we have seen that Hua makes no distinction between past and present times; a sentence like *baie* can mean either "He is here" or "he was here" indifferently. From evidence of this sort alone, however, it is not possible to conclude that the language, (let alone the speakers of the language), is incapable of making the distinction. As we have just seen, this distinction is made very neatly by the language in its treatment of adverbs of time: adverbs which specifically refer to past time can occur with the suffix -*'a* and then refer to a future time equally distant from the present. Adverbs which specifically refer to present time do not occur in two forms, since the distance from the present, namely zero, would be the same in both cases.

4 HOW TO JOIN SENTENCES

4.1 Medial Verbs

Whereas English, and possibly most of the other languages of the world, have a variety of conjunctions like "and," "before," "because," "after," "when," and "if" to join sentences, Hua, like many other languages of New Guinea, has none of these. Rather, it has a variety of constructions, called medial verb constructions, which express the meanings of these and other conjunctions. These constructions, more than any other, give Hua its characteristic stamp as a language of a different sort from those spoken in most other parts of the world.

The purpose of this section is to describe the forms and account for the meanings of some of these constructions whereby most logical and

temporal relations between sentences are expressed. Consider first the
following English sentences:

Max frightened Hortense **and** she ran away.
After Max frightened Hortense, she ran away.
Because Max frightened Hortense, she ran away.

These three sentences must have something in common, because they
are all translated into the same sentence in Hua. What this something is,
we can see for ourselves if we investigate more closely some of the
properties of the conjunction "and."

On the surface, "and" simply joins two sentences in the same way
that a plus sign joins two numbers. But whereas in addition, the order of
numbers is irrelevant ($3 + 1$ means the same as $1 + 3$, namely 4), in
sentences the same change in order can entail profound differences in
meaning:

Max sold the copyright and made a fortune.
Max made a fortune and sold the copyright.

In the first sentence, not only does the action of "selling the copyright"
precede the action of "making a fortune," but the latter event is
understood to be a consequence of the former. In the second sentence,
the situation is reversed, and "making a fortune" precedes and entails
"selling the copyright."

In most languages, unless the relationship is in some way specifically
denied (for example, by means of conjunctions like "before" and
"although"), the relative order of two sentences will tend to imply a)
that even as the first sentence precedes the second in the time of
speaking, so too will the action that it describes precede that of the
second sentence; and b) that the event described in the second sentence
will be interpreted as a consequence of the event described in the first.
Given the validity of these correlations, it is not surprising that in Hua
the same construction should translate "and," "because," and "after."
These are the meanings implied simply by the fact that the two
sentences occur in order.

Let us now examine the construction itself. A typical sentence with
a medial verb might look something like this:

Minaroga	*rmu-*	*gana*	*baie*
down there	go down	(Medial Ending)	he stayed

I went down there **and** he stayed.
After I went down there, he stayed.
Because I went down there, he stayed.

The medial verb consists of the verb stem *rmu* "go down," and the medial ending *gana*. Somehow, the combination of these two elements specifies that the subject of the medial verb is "I."

Since we have seen other cases where the verb ending reflects the nature of the subject, we might assume that the ending *gana* is found with all medial verbs whose subject is "I."

We may put this to the test by looking at another sentence:

Na kva' hu- gana baie
this deed do (Medial Ending) he stayed
    I did this deed and he stayed.
    After I did this deed, he stayed.
    Because I did this deed, he stayed.

Once again, the medial verb consists of the verb stem *hu* "do" and the medial ending *gana*. Note that the verb stem *hu*, like the verb stem *rmu*, is exactly as it is in the imperative. Both verbs, of course, are /u/ final.

Let us see what happens when the medial verb is one whose imperative stem ends in /o/—for example, *go* "look at," or *o* "come."

Go- gana baie
look at (Medial Ending) he stayed
    I looked at him and he stayed
    After I looked at him, he stayed.
    Because I looked at him, he stayed.

The ending, first of all, is *gana* again. The verb stem is *go*, exactly as it is in the imperative.

O- gana baie
come (Medial Ending) he stayed.
    I came and he stayed.
    After I came, he stayed.
    Because I came, he stayed.

The ending is again *gana*, and the verb stem *o* has undergone no change.

Let us turn finally to medial verbs whose stems end in /i/: verbs like *mi* "give" and *kri* "plant":

Mu- gana baie
give (Medial Ending) he stayed
    I gave it to him and he stayed.
    After I gave it to him, he stayed.
    Because I gave it to him, he stayed.

The ending *gana* is constant, but the verb stem *mi* has changed to *mu*.

Kru-   *gana*   *baie*
plant it   (Medial Ending)   he stayed
   I planted it and he stayed.
   After I planted it, he stayed.
   Because I planted it, he stayed.

Once again, the ending *gana* is unchanged. But the verb stem *kri* has changed to *kru*. Let us sum up our results so far. When the subject of the medial verb is "I," then 1) the medial ending is *gana*, and 2) the final vowel of the verb stem is subject to the following changes: final /o/ and final /u/ remain, but final /i/ changes to /u/. If we refer to our vowel chart in section 1.1, we can simplify the second part somewhat as follows: the final vowel of the verb stem is *back*. But this rule is now very familiar: it is identical with subrule (a) of Stem Rule 5, reiterated here in its entirety:

Stem Rule 5

(a) When the subject includes the speaker, final vowel must be *back*.
(b) When the subject can be understood to include the *person spoken to*, but not the speaker, final *back* vowels change to /a/. (Note particularly that verbs with subjects "they two" and "they" may be understood to have subjects "you two" and "you all" and are thus subject to subrule (b).)
(c) When the subject can include *neither* the speaker nor the person spoken to, final vowel must be *front*.

    This suggests certain lines of inquiry. If subrule (a) applies to medial verbs whose subject is "I," it should also apply to medial verbs whose subject is "we two" or "we." In that case, subrule (b) should apply to medial verbs whose subject is "you," "you two/the two of them," "you all/they." And subrule (c) should apply to medial verbs whose subject is "he," "she," "it."
    But Stem Rule 5 applies only to verb stems that immediately precede an ending which occurs in three forms, like the assertive (*-e, -'e, -ne*) and the interrogative (*-ve, -'ve, -pe*). Let us call these 'threefold endings.'
    Therefore, the medial ending *gana* must be one of these threefold endings. And therefore, we should be able to predict other medial verbs which occur with the ending *gana*:

When the subject is:	The assertive ending is:	The interrogative ending is:	The medial ending is:
I, he, you all	*-e*	*-ve*	*gana*
we two, you two	*-'e*	*-'ve*	_____
you, we	*-ne*	*-pe*	_____

That is, if *gana* is a three-way ending, then it should also occur with medial verbs whose subject is "he" or "you all."

To recapitulate the argument, the fact that medial verbs with the subject "I" are subject to subrule (a) of Stem Rule 5 before the medial ending *gana* suggests to us that all medial verbs are subject to the appropriate subrule of Stem Rule 5, depending on their subjects; it also suggests that the medial ending *gana* must be a threefold ending like the assertive and the interrogative. What the other forms of the medial ending are is of course not yet known, but we conjecture that in any case the same form will be found when the subject of the medial verb is "he" and "you all."

The verb stem of medial verbs whose subject is "he" will be subject to subrule (c) of Stem Rule 5, namely, that the final vowel is *front*.

The verb stem of medial verbs whose subject is "you all" will be subject to subrule (b) of Stem Rule 5, namely, that final *back* vowels change to /a/.

The verb ending for both of these medials should be *gana*. Let us now try to construct the sentences:

He went down there and he stayed.
You all went down there and he stayed.

We already have a model for these sentences, namely:

Minaroga	*rmu-*	*gana*	*baie*
down there	go down	(Medial Ending)	he stayed

    I went down there and he stayed.

By our hypothesis, everything in this sentence will remain constant for the two new sentences that we wish to construct, *except* the final vowel of the medial verb stem. In the model sentence, the subject of the medial verb is "I," and subrule (a) of Stem Rule 5 applies (vacuously), leaving *rmu* unchanged.

If the subject is "he," subrule (c) should apply, changing *rmu* to *rmi* (recall that /i/ is the front vowel corresponding to /u/). Thus:

Minaroga   rmi-   gana   baie
down there   go down   (Medial Ending)   he stayed
    He went down there and he stayed.

And this is correct!
    If the subject is "you all" (or "they"), subrule (b) should apply changing *rmu* (whose final vowel /u/ is back) to *rma*. Thus:

Minaroga   rma-   gana   baie
down there   go down   (Medial Ending)   he stayed
    You all went down there and he stayed.

and this too is correct!
    Given now the model sentence:

Na kva' hugana baie.
    I did this deed and he stayed.

Construct the following sentences:[11]

  a. **He** did this deed and he stayed.
  b. **You all** did this deed and he stayed.

Given the model sentence:

Go- gana baie.
    I looked at him and he stayed.

You can construct the sentences:[12]

  a. **He** looked at him and he stayed.
  b. **You all** looked at him and he stayed.

Given the model sentence:

Mugana baie.
    I gave it to him and he stayed.

You can construct the sentences:[13]

  a. **He** gave it to him and he stayed.
  b. **You all** gave it to him and he stayed.

(You will note that the last two sentences are the same in Hua.)

---

[11]a. *Na kva' higana baie.* b. *Na kva' hagana baie.*

[12]a. *Gegana baie.* b. *Gagana baie.*

[13]a. *Migana baie.* b. *Migana baie.*

All that is needed to crown our efforts with complete success is to predict the form of the *other* medial endings. Clearly, once we know these, we can specify the form of any medial verb.

And it happens that we can make a reasonably confident guess at the form of one of these missing endings, although we have never seen or heard it. This is the ending of the medial verb whose subject is "we two" or "you two."

If we take another look at our partially completed list of three-fold endings, we notice a correlation between the first and the second forms in the first two columns.

When the first form is *-e*, the second is *-'e*; when the first form is *-ve*, the second form is *-'ve*. In each case, the second form is the same as the first, preceded by /'/. If this pattern is general, the second medial will have the same form as the first, preceded by /'/, namely *'gana*.

And having guessed this ending, we can make predictions about medial verbs whose subject is "we two" or "you two." The verb stem of medial verbs whose subject is "we two" must be subject to subrule (a) of Stem Rule 5—the final vowel must be back.

The verb stem of medial verbs whose subject is "you two" must be subject to subrule (b) of Stem Rule 5—final *back* vowels change to /a/. Given the model sentence:

> *Minaroga rmugana baie.*
> I went down there and he stayed.

we can attempt to construct the following sentences:

> **We two** went down there and he stayed.
> **You two** went down there and he stayed.

By our hypothesis, the medial verb ending in both cases will be *'gana* rather than *gana*.

When the subject is "we two," subrule (a) applies vacuously to the verb stem *rmu* (whose final vowel is already back) leaving it unchanged: *rmu*. Thus:

Minaroga	*rmu-*	*'gana*	*baie*
down there	go down	(Medial Ending)	he stayed

> **We two** went down and he stayed.

which is correct.

When the subject is "you two," subrule (b) applies to the verb stem *rmu*, changing it to *rma*. Thus:

Minaroga   rma-   'gana   baie
down there   go down   (Medial Ending)   he stayed
   You two went down there and he stayed.

which again is correct.

Consequently, we have shown that our guess was right. The medial ending when the subject of the verb is "we two" or "you two" is *'gana*, and the verb stem itself is subject to the appropriate subrules of Stem Rule 5.

Given now the model sentences:

Fu mugana dee.   (*mi*   give)
   I gave him pork and he ate it.

Ai'ogana rmie.   (*ai'o*   come up)
   After I came up, he went down.

construct the following sentences:[14]

   a.   We two gave him pork and he ate it.
   b.   After you two gave her pork, she ate it.
   c.   Because we two came up, he went down.
   d.   After you two came up, she went down.

(Don't let the conjunctions and the pronoun "she" confuse you. Remember that in Hua, the medial construction is equivalent to "after" and "because" clauses and that there is no distinction between "he" and "she.")

It remains to discover the form of the medial ending when the subject of the medial verb is "you" or "we." There is no way that we can predict this from any regularities we have seen so far. In fact, it is *nana*. We may fill in our working list of three-fold endings. See Table 2.3.

To see now how thoroughly you have mastered the application of the Stem Rule 5, you might try to construct sentences with medial verbs ending in *nana*.

What subrule applies when the subject of the medial verb is "you"? When the subject of the medial verb is "we"?

Having answered these questions, try to construct the sentences:[15]

   a.   **You** went down there and he stayed.
        (*rmu*   go down;   *bai*   stay)
   b.   **We** went down there and he stayed.

_____

[14]a. *Fumo mu'gana dee.* b. *Fumo mi'gana dee.* c. *Ai'o'gana rmie.* d. *Ai'a'gana rmie.*

[15]a. *Rmanana baie.* b. *Rmunana baie.* c. *Ai'anana baie.* d. *Ai'onana baie.*

TABLE 2.3 *Some Threefold Verb Endings*

Subject	Assertive	Yes/no Question	Medial
I, he/she, it, you all/they	-*e*	-*ve*	-*gana*
we two, you two/they two	-'*e*	-'*ve*	-'*gana*
you, we	-*ne*	-*pe*	-*nana*

  c. **You** came up and he stayed.   (*ai'o* come up)
  d. **We** came up and he stayed.

We now have the impression that the medial verb ending is another three-way ending like the assertive and the interrogative. There is much more to it than this.

So far, the subject of the final verb has always been "he." In all the examples we have looked at, however, the subject of the medial verb has varied while the following subject has been kept constant. Consider now the following sentences:

Ai'egana rmie.	He came up and **she** went down.
Ai'egada rmue.	He came up and **I** went down.
Ai'egaka rmane.	He came up and **you** went down.
Ai'egata'a rmu'e.	He came up and **we two** went down.
Ai'egatina'a rma'e.	He came up and **you two** went down.
Ai'egata rmune.	He came up and **we** went down.
Ai'egatina rmae.	He came up and **you all** went down.

We find that the ending *gana* which seemed to be irreducible, actually consists of two parts; the part which is emphasized here agrees with the subject of the *following verb*.

That is, we seem to have discovered that the endings *gana, nana,* and the rest, really consist of two endings, a medial ending, which agrees with the subject of the medial verb, and a second ending, which we might call the anticipatory ending, which agrees with the subject of the following verb:

Medial Ending (a three-way ending)	**Subject**
-*ga*	I, he, you all, they all
-'*ga*	you two, we two, they two
-*na*	you, we

Anticipatory Ending (not a three-way ending)	Following Subject
-da	I
-ka	you
-na	he
-ta'a	we two
-tina'a	you two, they two
-ta	we
-tina	you all, they all

The medial verb thus *agrees* not only with its own subject, but with the subject of the following verb. To construct a medial verb, we need two pieces of information about it. Conversely, the medial verb by itself conveys two pieces of information: the nature of its subject, and the nature of the following subject.

To construct a sentence like:

We went up and they went down.

a speaker of Hua must go through the following logical steps:

1. The verb "go up" is *hau*, a /u/ final verb.
2. Since the subject of the medial verb is "we," subrule (a) of Stem Rule 5 applies, in this case vacuously, since /u/ is already a back vowel.
3. The medial ending when the subject is "we" must be *na*.
4. The anticipatory ending when the following subject is "they" is the same as when it is "you all," namely *tina*.
5. Consequently the medial verb is *haunatina*.
6. The verb "go down" is rmu, a /u/ final verb.
7. Since the subject of this verb is "they," subrule (b) of Stem Rule 5 applies, converting *rmu* to *rma*.
8. The final ending when the subject is "they" must be *e*.
9. Consequently the final verb is *rmae*.
10. Consequently, the whole sentence is:

Haunatina rmae.

Naturally a Hua speaker can perform all these operations with computer-like rapidity and in blissful unawareness of their complexity by the time he is five or six years old. Furthermore, he has no impression or recollection of a long and difficult learning process in acquiring this fantastic ability. Like all of us, he has learned his language, the most complex skill he will ever have, completely unconsciously. The magnitude of his achievement can only be properly appreciated by someone who tries to approach his language (or any other) from the outside, as an adult language learner.

As such an adult language learner, you might try to construct the following sentences, going through the same logical steps:[16]

a. After he went down, I came. (go down *rmu*; come *o*)
b. He gave me pork and I ate it. (give *mi*; eat *do*)
c. Because he kissed her,
   she hit him (kiss *vzaro'bro*; hit *ebgi*)

Time yourself!

Sentences like "He gave him pork and he ate it" are in English ambiguous: we don't know whether the person who did the giving is the same as or different from the person who did the eating. No such ambiguity arises in Hua; in all the sentences we have discussed so far the subject of the first verb is *different* from the subject of the second.

It remains to investigate the medial verb construction used when the subject of the medial verb is the *same* as the subject of the final verb, as in sentences like:

I went up and then (I) went down.
We killed it and (we) ate it.
They hit him and then (they) ran away.

All the medial verbs we have discussed so far indicate a change of subject. Those used to translate the preceding sentences indicate constancy of subject. We call them 'like-subject medials.'

Whereas a change-of-subject medial verb consists, as we have seen, of the following elements:

Verb Stem + Medial Ending + Anticipatory Ending

a like-subject medial consists simply of:

Verb Stem + Anticipatory Ending

There is no medial ending. Note the perfect logic of this absence: change-of-subject medial verbs have to carry two pieces of information, the identity of their own subjects and the identity of the subject of the following verb. To carry this information, they have two endings, the medial and the anticipatory endings. Like-subject medial verbs, on the other hand, if they had both endings, would be carrying the same information twice. This unnecessary reduplication is dispensed with by the elimination of the medial ending. Consequently, the verb stem directly precedes the anticipatory endings.

---

[16]a. *Rmigada oe.* b. *Fu dmigada doe.* c. *Vzaro'bregana ebgie.*

The importance in Hua of keeping track of whether successive subjects are the same or different (a phenomenon commonly called "switch reference" in its various manifestations around the world) is highlighted by the fact that there are alternate forms of some of the anticipatory endings for just this distinction. Corresponding to *tina* in the two change-of-subject endings *tina'a* "you two/they two," and *tina* "you all/they all," we have *reta* in like-subject endings. Thus in the first verbs of like-subject constructions—medial verbs that carry no medial endings—we have *reta'a* "you two/they two," and *reta* for "you all/they all."

For example, compare:

Egatina gae.   He came and they all looked at it.
            (change of subject)

Ereta gae.   They all came and looked at it.
            (same subject)

Like-subject is signaled not only by absence of a medial ending in this case, but by the distinct anticipatory ending. It is not surprising that this elaboration of forms should come about in cases where "third persons" can be involved, for these are just the ones where one could otherwise most often be confused about who is doing what. Consider:

The boys were on one side of the room, the girls were on the other, and they were watching while they jumped up and down on the trampoline.

Such a passage would be completely unambiguous in Hua. We have altogether the following inventory for the anticipatory ending:

Anticipatory Ending (not a three-way ending)	Following Subject
-da	"I"
-ka	"you"
-na	"he"
-ta'a	"we two"
-tina'a	"you two/they two" as unlike-subjects
-reta'a	"you two/they two" as like-subjects
-ta	"we"
-tina	"you all/they all" as unlike-subjects
-reta	"you all/they all" as like-subjects

Two questions now arise. Is the verb stem subject to any vowel changes? If so, to which ones?

Stem Rule 5 applies to verb stems which directly precede a three-way ending. The anticipatory endings, as we have seen, are not three-way endings, and therefore, we would predict that Stem Rule 5 does not apply to like-subject medial verbs.

On the other hand, we have said earlier that Stem Rule 6 applied to all other verb stems except those which preceded the auxiliary verb *su* "may." We thus predict that Stem Rule 6 applies to like-subject medial verbs as follows:

Stem Rule 6

When the subject is "you two" or "you all," the final vowel must be *front*. Otherwise, no changes are made.

Let us try now to construct a sentence like:

I have come up and I am here.

1. The verb "come up" is *ai'o*, an /o/ final verb.
2. Since the subject of the medial verb is the same as the subject of the final verb, there is no medial ending.
3. The anticipatory ending when the following subject is "I" is *da*.
4. Since the subject of the medial verb is neither "you two" nor "you all," Stem Rule 6 does nothing to the stem.
5. Consequently, the medial verb is *ai'oda*.
6. The verb "be here" is *bai*, an /i/ final verb.
7. The final ending when the subject is "I" must be *-e*.
8. Subrule (a) of Stem Rule 5 converts *bai* to *bau* when the subject is "I."
9. Therefore, the final verb is *baue*.
10. Therefore, the entire sentence must be:

Ai'oda baue.

which is the case.

You are invited to try and translate sentences like[17]

a. They killed and cooked it.   (kill *ebgi*;   cook *gi*)
b. We two ate and went up.   (eat   *do*;   go up *hau*)
c. He came and looked at it.   (come *o*;   look at it *go*)

Naturally, a construction as complex as the medial verb should not be learned in vain. It is put to many other uses besides the ones discussed

---

[17]a. *Ebgireta gie.* b. *Dota'a hau'e.* c. *Ona gee.*

up to this point. In the following paragraphs are mentioned just some of these other uses.

4.2 Prolonged or Repeated Activity

In the English sentence:

He went on and on and on and on . . . until he finally arrived.

the notion of prolonged "going" is expressed by a repetition of the word "on" and the adverb "finally." In Hua, a sentence like this would be translated by a repetition of the medial verb for "go":

U-	*na*	*u-*	*na*	*u-*	*na*	*u-*	*na*	*vzahie*
go	and he	go	and he	go	and he	go	and he	he arrived

4.3 Adverbs of Manner

In the English sentence:

He went down quickly.

the adverb "quickly" modifies the verb "went down." There are no adverbs of manner in Hua. There are *verbs* like *brgefu* "be quick," *fzehu* "be slow," *sokohu* "be good," and *sekofu* "be cautious." Thus:

Brgefie.	He is quick.
Fzehie.	He is slow.
Sokohie.	He is good.
Sekofie.	He is cautious.

To say something like "He went down quickly" (or "slowly," "well," "cautiously") Hua continues to use these verbs: they are made into like-subject medials:

Brgefu-	*na*	*rmie*
quick	and he	he went down

   He went down quickly.

Brgefu-	*ta*	*rmune*
quick	and we	we went down

   We went down quickly.

Given this information, you could understand the meaning of sentences like:[18]

---

[18]a. Did you come up cautiously? b. I did it well. c. Stay well!

   a. *Sekofuka ai'ape?*   (*ai'o* come up)
   b. *Sokohuda hue.*   (*hu* do it)
   c. *Sokohuka bai!*   (*bai* be, stay)

and construct others like:[19]

   a. Go down quickly!   (go down   *rmu*)
   b. Go down cautiously!
   c. I went down slowly.

4.4 Comparison

In a sentence like:

He is taller than I am.

English expresses the proposition that "he exceeds me with respect to height" by means of a complex construction, the comparative, involving the use of a comparative ending ("-er" on "tall") and a preposition "than." Hua has no such construction. It expresses the proposition through two verbs, the transitive verb *gaso* "exceed" and the verb *za'zafu* "be tall." The first of these is a like-subject medial:

D-   gaso-   na   za'zafie
me surpass and he he is tall
     He is taller than I am.

K-   gaso-   da   za'zafue
you surpass and I   I am tall
     I am taller than you.

Given the verbs *ogofu* "be short," *zapuahu* "be strong," you can understand sentences like:[20]

   a. *Ra'gasona zapuahie.*
   b. *Pgasota zapuahune.*
   c. *Gasona ogofie.*   (Remember that the object "he" is zero.)

and you can construct other comparatives like:[21]

   a. We are shorter than you.
   b. You are stronger than he is.
   c. You all are stronger than I am.

---

[19]a. *Brgefuka rmu!* b. *Sekofuka rmu!* c. *Fzehuda rmue.*

[20]a. He is stronger than we two. b. We all are stronger than you all/them all. c. He is shorter than him.

[21]a. *Kgasota ogofune.* b. *Gasoka zapuahane.* c. *Dgasereta zapuahae.*

4.5 Questions of Cause

One of the question types that we have not as yet discussed is the "why" question, such as "Why have you come?" which we might paraphrase "Because of what have you come?" The Hua translation for this sentence is:

Zahigaka   ane
why   you come
   Why have you come?

Unlike the other question words (for "who," "what," "where," "how many," etc.) in Hua, the question word "why" is variable: its form depends on the subject of the verb. Thus:

Zahigana   ee
why   he come
   Why has he come?

Zahigada   oe
why   I come
   Why have I come?

Thus, the question word "why" is a medial verb with variable anticipatory endings. The verb is *zahu*, which occurs only in the third person and means "What's the matter?"

Nor is this in any way surprising. Remember that one of the functions of medial verbs was to indicate a causal relationship between the first and second of two conjoined clauses. The literal meaning of a "why" question in Hua is:

Zahiga-   ka   ane
what's the matter   and you   you come
   Because what's the matter, you have come.

4.6 Speaking in Paragraphs

Once the Hua learner has mastered the medial constructions, he has learned *the* basic structure of his language. He will be able, for example, to provide the Hua equivalents for the English sentences that were translated in footnote 16, namely: *Rmigada oe, Fu dmigada doe,* and *Vzaro'bregana ebgie.* There is hardly a complete utterance that he will ever make without a medial verb, and many of his sentences—we would call them paragraphs—will consist of up to a dozen medial verbs leading up to one final verb, as in the Hua version of the following story:

He killed the pig and cooked it. They came and he gave them pig and they ate it and danced, and sang. Because they sang, the children didn't sleep and cried, so they stopped singing and went to bed.

More likely than not, a Hua speaker who was interested in telling you this story would use only one final verb, and his version might look something like the following Hua sentence. (Among other things, you may appreciate the way in which Hua keeps perfectly clear the switch reference between same and different subjects whereas in English it is a bit hard to know who is doing what in the story, the adults or the children.)

Fu	*ebgina*		*gigatina*		*agana*
pig	he killed and he		he cooked and they		they came and he

fu	*p*	*migatina*		*dereta*		*omo*
pig	them	he gave and they		ate and, and they		dance

hagereta	*okemo*	*hagatina*		*badevede*	*paumo*
they danced and they	song	they did and others		children	their bodies

a'vereta	*via*	*tagatina*		*okemo*
not they sleep	tears	they shed and others		song

ireta		*zupi'*	*havireta*		*vae.*
they stop and they		house in	they go up and they		they lie down.

There are other medial verb constructions which express relations like "if," "when," "while," and "although," as well as shades of meaning for which English has only approximate paraphrases. What we have done here is to look only at the most common constructions.

5   CONCLUSION: HUA IN TRANSITION

Like every other language, Hua is constantly changing its vocabulary, its sound system, and its syntax. Most of these changes take place slowly and can only be deduced from a detailed comparison with other related languages of New Guinea—a task which cannot be undertaken until these languages, most of them completely unknown, have been described. Nonetheless, there is one kind of change the origins and history of which can be fixed with absolute certainty. That is the change due to the influence of Pidgin English, a language which has gained currency among the Hua only in the last twenty-five years.

Most of the Pidgin innovations are borrowed words, and what is surprising about these words is not only their number but their nature.

Naturally, we would expect Hua, like any native language, to borrow the names of artifacts and technology with which its speakers were unfamiliar from their own culture. Just as the English language borrowed words like "tomato," "tobacco," and "sputnik" when the objects these terms denoted entered the culture of English-speaking peoples, so too Hua borrowed Pidgin words like *pasindia ka* "passenger car," *rendio* "radio," *makit* or *pakit* "market," *haussik* "hospital," *kiap* "patrol officer" (in Hua, generalized to mean "official") and *bia* "beer." There is nothing in the least surprising or uncommon about borrowing of this sort.

What is extremely interesting is that other words are borrowed for which Hua has not one, but several, terms of its own. The notion of *exchange*, for example, is basic to Hua politics, marriage, and social organization generally. There are several terms in Hua denoting various kinds of exchange, whether of women, food, or money. The word in almost universal use today, however, is Pidgin *bekim* "give back" which has been Huanized by the addition of the following support verb *hu*. Most young men and women are unaware of the more specialized terms, some of them not even recognizing them when they are uttered out of context.

The same mystery attends the borrowing of *bihainim(hu)* "follow" when Hua already has words meaning both to follow in line and to obey precepts; *opim(hu)* "open," when Hua has no less than a half-dozen verbs signifying various kinds of opening (as by lifting a cover, peeling skin or bark, removing slats, parting a curtain, etc.); *save(hu)* "know," when Hua has *go* "know by seeing" and *havi* "know by hearing"; *pasim(hu)* "fasten," "shut," when Hua has as many verbs for shutting as it does for opening; and there are many others of this sort.

Heavy Pidgin-borrowing of this sort, which seems both indiscriminate and unmotivated, is probably one of the reasons why some of the older Hua are able to predict the complete disappearance of their language within the lifetime of their children.

Yet a careful examination of this borrowing reveals an underlying pattern: the terms borrowed are general ones for which Hua has no real equivalents. For example, Hua does have a half-dozen verbs for various kinds of "opening," but no general term which would refer to all of them.

This is a kind of linguistic datum which used to occur very often in discussions of so-called "primitive" languages: "The Ooga Booga of the central Congo have 346 words for various kinds of sands but no single word for sand in general; therefore these people are incapable of making generalizations; therefore, they are incapable of abstract thought; therefore . . ."

This kind of reasoning, needless to say, is a base libel on the Ooga

Booga and is very easily refuted by a few counterexamples directed against English speakers. English has a word for eating, another for drinking, and another for smoking; however, it has no word which can designate all three. Many other languages do; Hua is one, with *do*; the mythical Ooga Booga language, with its 346 words for different kinds of sand, may well be another. Do we infer from this that speakers of English are incapable of generalizations or abstract thought? Let us hope not.

At any rate, the fact that the Hua seem to be borrowing precisely those general terms for which there are no equivalents in their language, and using them as cover terms for exactly that range of words which are related through such a general term, indicates that they most certainly are capable of generalizations.

The general concept of "opening" is present in their thinking, and when a language comes along which has a word for it, they borrow it. Hua does lose ground to Pidgin in that very often the original words with their specialized meanings are lost, but the borrowing is not random and indiscriminate.

If borrowing from Pidgin has been heavy in a quarter-century, it is impossible to guess how extensive and deep borrowing has been from Gimi, Siane, and Chimbu, with which Hua has been in contact for hundreds (or perhaps thousands) of years. The fact that Hua has maintained its integrity and autonomy for so long despite such prolonged and intimate contact is an augur for its continued life today.

SUGGESTIONS FOR FURTHER READING

The literature on Hua linguistics and ethnography is not perhaps as extensive as one might wish, and there is very little that would be accessible to the interested nonspecialist. Renck (1975) is a pedagogical grammar of Move, a closely related dialect which is almost mutually intelligible with Hua. Wurm (1971) provides a comprehensive and necessarily superficial overview of the linguistic situation in New Guinea as a whole, which attests eloquently to the paucity of our knowledge of languages of this area. Meigs (1976 and 1978) provides a revealing analysis of the sexual ideology of the Hua, which may be true for Eastern Highlands societies in general.

While exotic, the medial verb construction is not limited to Hua or even to the languages of New Guinea. Jacobsen (1967) is valuable for providing descriptions of analogous constructions in a number of Amerindian languages.

Jacobsen, W. H. "Switch Reference in Hokan Coahuiltecan." In *Studies in Southwestern Ethnolinguistics*, edited by Dell Hymes. The Hague: Mouton, 1967.

Meigs, A. "Male Pregnancy in a New Guinea Highlands Society." *Ethnology* 15: 393–407, 1976.

———. "A Papuan Perspective on Pollution." *Man* (N.S.) 13: 304–18, 1978.

Renck, G. *A Grammar of Yagaria*. Pacific Linguistics B 40, Linguistic Circle of Canberra, 1976.

Wurm, Stefan. "The Linguistic Situation in Papua New Guinea." In *Current Trends in Linguistics*, vol. 8, edited by Thomas A. Sebeok et al. The Hague, Mouton, 1971.

APPENDIX

A. *Summary of the Verb Affixes Presented in the Text*

1. Threefold Endings

Subject	Statements	Yes/No Questions	Medial Endings
I, he, you all/they all	*-e*	*-ve*	*-ga*
we two, you two/they two	*-'e*	*-'ve*	*-'ga*
you, we all	*-ne*	*-pe*	*-na*

2. Object-Agreement Markers

Number	Person	Marker
Singular	1st.	*d-*
	2nd.	*k-*
	3rd.	*∅-*
Dual	1st.	*ra'-*
	2nd./3rd.	*pa'-*
Plural	1st.	*r-*
	2nd./3rd.	*p-*

3. Endings for Anticipated Subjects

(Note: These are not "Threefold Endings.")

Number	Person	Anticipatory ending
Singular	1st.	*-da*
	2nd.	*-ka*
	3rd.	*-na*
Dual	1st.	*-ta'a*
	2nd./3rd.	*-tina'a* (for unlike-subjects)
		-reta'a (for like-subjects)
Plural	1st.	*-ta*
	2nd./3rd.	*-tina* (for unlike-subjects)
		-reta (for like-subjects)

B. *Summary of the Stem Rules*

(Note: The rules are given here in their final form and so are renumbered. The forms in the table that follows illustrate how each rule applies.)

Stem Rule 1 (corresponds to Stem Rule 5 in the text)

Before a threefold ending three subrules apply.

(a) If the subject includes the speaker, the final vowel must be back (all first-person forms).
(b) If the subject *can* include the person spoken to, final back vowels change to /a/ (all second-person forms, and in effect third-person dual and plural; this means that second- and third-person dual, and second- and third-person plural, are identical).
(c) If the subject includes neither the speaker nor the hearer, the final vowel must be front (third-person singular only).

Stem Rule 2 (corresponds to Stem Rule 7 in the text)

Before the auxilliary verb *su*, the final vowel must be front.

Stem Rule 3 (corresponds to Stem Rule 6 in the text)

Where neither Rule 1 nor Rule 2 applies, the final vowel must be front if the subject is neither first person nor singular.

C. *Table Illustrating the Stem Rules for the "Non Future" ("He ate"), the "Subjunctive" ("May he eat!"), and the "Future" ("He will eat").*

		-i **root**	*-o* **root**	*-u* **root**
Imperative		*Bai.* "Stay!"	*Do.* "Eat!"	*Rmu.* "Go down!"

1. Root + Subject "Non-Future"

   (Stem Rule 1 applies to root)

Number	**Person**			
Singular	1st.	*bau-e*	*do-e*	*rmu-e*
	2nd.	*bai-ne*	*da-ne*	*rma-ne*
	3rd.	*bai-e*	*de-e*	*rmi-e*
Dual	1st.	*bau-'e*	*do-'e*	*rmu-'e*
	2nd./3rd.	*bai-'e*	*da-'e*	*rma-'e*
Plural	1st.	*bau-ne*	*do-ne*	*rmu-ne*
	2nd./3rd.	*bai-e*	*da-e*	*rma-e*

2. Root + *su* + Subject "Subjunctive"

   (Stem Rule 1 on *su*, Stem Rule 2 on root)

Number	**Person**			
Singular	1st.	*bai-su-e*	*de-su-e*	*rmi-su-e*
	2nd.	*bai-sa-ne*	*de-sa-ne*	*rmi-sa-ne*
	3rd.	*bai-si-e*	*de-si-e*	*rmi-si-e*
Dual	1st.	*bai-su-'e*	*de-su-'e*	*rmi-su-'e*
	2nd./3rd.	*bai-sa-'e*	*de-sa-'e*	*rmi-sa-'e*
Plural	1st.	*bai-su-ne*	*de-su-ne*	*rmi-su-ne*
	2nd./3rd.	*bai-sa-e*	*de-sa-e*	*rmi-sa-e*

	-i **root**	*-o* **root**	*-u* **root**
Imperative	*Bai.* "Stay!"	*Do.* "Eat!"	*Rmu.* "Go down!"

3. Root + *gu* + Subject
   "Future"
   (Stem Rule 1 on *gu*,
   Stem Rule 3 on root)

Number	Person			
Singular	1st.	*bai-gu-e*	*do-gu-e*	*rmu-gu-e*
	2nd.	*bai-ga-ne*	*do-ga-ne*	*rmu-ga-ne*
	3rd.	*bai-gi-e*	*do-gi-e*	*rmu-gi-e*
Dual	1st.	*bai-gu-'e*	*do-gu-'e*	*rmu-gu-'e*
	2nd./3rd.	*bai-ga-'e*	*de-ga-'e*	*rmi-ga-'e*
Plural	1st.	*bai-gu-ne*	*do-gu-ne*	*rmu-gu-ne*
	2nd./3rd.	*bai-ga-e*	*de-ga-e*	*rmi-ga-e*

III

Russian

Bernard Comrie

INTRODUCTION

The aim of this chapter is twofold. In Part 1 the aim is to provide a typological outline of the grammatical structure of the Russian language, including similarities to and differences from other languages. In Part 2 the aim is to place the Russian language in its historical and current sociological setting. The account presupposes no previous knowledge of Russian, not even of the Russian alphabet (see footnote 1 on following page) although some suggestions are given for further reading on the various topics covered.

1 THE STRUCTURE OF RUSSIAN

The presentation in most of Part 1 will start with a number of Russian sentences and their English translations. Each set of examples is followed by a full discussion of the relevant issues raised by the structural characteristics of Russian illustrated in the sentences. Readers might like to try and work out for themselves, as far as they can, what features of Russian sentence structure and morphology are illustrated by

Bernard Comrie teaches linguistics at the University of Southern California. He is interested in describing languages, especially in relating language structure to language use, and has a particular interest in Slavic languages and in the languages of the Soviet Union. He has been an exchange student in the Russian Language Department of Moscow State University and a visiting scholar at the Academy of Sciences, Leningrad, where he worked with native speakers of several of the languages of the northern USSR.

91

the various sentences, before going on to read the account given subsequently.

1.1   Word Order

In the first set of sentences, we are introduced to two male characters, Maksim and Viktor:

(1) a. Maksím čitájet.
    b. Čitájet Maksím.   "Maksim reads."

(2) a. Víktor čitájet.
    b. Čitájet Víktor.   "Viktor reads."

(3) a. Maksím zaščiščájet Víktora.
    b. Maksím Víktora zaščiščájet.
    c. Víktora Maksím zaščiščájet.
    d. Víktora zaščiščájet Maksím.   "Maksim defends Viktor."
    e. Zaščiščájet Maksím Víktora.
    f. Zaščiščájet Víktora Maksím.

(4) a. Víktor zaščiščájet Maksíma.
    b. Víktor Maksíma zaščiščájet.
    c. Maksíma Víktor zaščiščájet.
    d. Maksíma zaščiščájet Víktor.   "Viktor defends Maksim."
    e. Zaščiščájet Víktor Maksíma.
    f. Zaščiščájet Maksíma Víktor.

One further piece of information is needed in order to work out what is going on in these sentences: each of the Russian sentences given is unambiguous. Thus (3a) *Maksím zaščiščájet Víktora* can only mean

---

[1]Russian examples are presented in a slightly modified version of the international transliteration system of Russian orthography. The following brief notes on pronunciation will enable the reader unfamiliar with Russian to approximate Russian pronunciation. The vowels *a, e, i, o, u* have their continental values (IPA [a], [ɛ], [i], [ɔ], [u]); *y* is pronounced farther back in the mouth than *i*, but with the same lip position (approximately IPA [ɨ]). Unstressed *o* and *a* are pronounced alike, similar to stressed *a* (see footnote 23). Unstressed *e* is *i*-like. Of the consonants, *c* is like *tz* of English *quartz*; *č* like *ch* of English *cheese*; *š* like *sh* of English *shoe*; *x* like *ch* of English (Scottish) *loch* (voiceless velar fricative, IPA [x]); *ž* like *s* of English *pleasure*. There is a phonemic distinction between nonpalatalized and palatalized consonants, e.g., *brát* "brother," *brát'* "to take": palatalization of a consonant is indicated by a following *j* before a vowel, by a following ' before a consonant or at the end of a word. Elsewhere, *j* is like the *y* of English *yes*; the sequence consonant + ' + *j* is thus pronounced as a palatalized consonant followed by the sound of English *y* (as in *yes*). Consonants are also palatalized before *e* and *i*. Stress is phonemic, though not usually indicated in Russian spelling; in Russian examples cited in this chapter, stress is indicated by an acute accent on the stressed vowel, e.g., *muká* "flour," *múka* "torment." For the Russian alphabet, see Table 3.3. For a more thorough treatment of Russian phonetics, see the book by Stilman listed in the "Suggestions for Further Reading."

"Maksim defends Viktor," and not, for instance, "Viktor defends Maksim." Similarly (3d) *Víktora zaščiščájet Maksím* can only mean "Maksim defends Viktor." The reader should now be able to make some headway in unraveling the other sentences (though the data provided so far give no indication of what distinguishes members within each group of sentences (1), (2), (3), or (4)).

In English, an important aspect of basic semantic differentiation of sentences is carried by word order. In general, for a given meaning in English only one word order is possible, and other word orders either carry a different meaning or have no meaning at all. Thus, if we change the order of *Viktor reads* to **reads Viktor*, we end up with a nonsentence (indicated by an asterisk). If we change the order *Viktor defends Maksim* to *Maksim defends Viktor*, then we change the meaning: in the first sentence, Viktor is defending and Maksim is being defended, whereas in the second sentence, Maksim is defending and Viktor is being defended. The two sentences clearly refer to two quite different situations. If we change the word order to **defends Maksim Viktor* or **Viktor Maksim defends*, then again we have a nonsentence of English. The first thing to note about the Russian sentences cited is that changing the word order does not change the basic meaning of the sentence: each of (3a)–(3f), for instance, describes exactly the same situation, where Maksim is defending and Viktor is being defended. We shall return in a moment to the differences between each of these descriptions of the same situation. Russian is, for this reason, often referred to as a "free word order language." What this means is that differences in word order do not affect the basic semantics of the sentence. By contrast, English is a "fixed word order language." In such a language differences in word order carry different meanings, and some word orders are not possible at all. Although it is generally true that Russian has free word order whereas English has fixed word order, it would be more accurate to say that Russian has freer word order than English, since there are some instances where Russian word order is fixed, and some instances where English word order is free. For instance, in Russian, prepositions precede their nouns, just as in English, so that both languages have fixed word order in this case (*u Víktora*, not **Víktora u*, that is *beside Viktor*, not **Viktor beside*). In both languages, adjectives usually precede their nouns (as in *stáryj dóm* "old house" from *stáryj* "old" and *dóm* "house"). Conversely, English word order is less rigid than usual when it comes to placing adverbs of time, so that both *Today Maksim is reading* and *Maksim is reading today* are possible in English, just as their literal translations are in Russian: *Segódnja Maksím čitájet*, *Maksím čitájet segódnja*.[2]

---

[2]Russian *segódnja* is pronounced as if spelled *sevódnja*.

The question that obviously arises now is how Russian speakers keep apart expressions referring, for instance, to Maksim defending Viktor and to Viktor defending Maksim. English does so by using word order, the usual word order being Subject–Verb–Object, so that in "Maksim defends Viktor," Maksim is identified as the subject and Viktor as the object. From the examples already given, it is clear that Russian does not use word order in this way, yet as already pointed out none of the Russian sentences cited is ambiguous. Careful examination shows that in these sentences, the names of Maksim and Viktor each appear in two forms: a form with no added ending (*Maksím, Víktor*) and a form with the ending *-a* (*Maksíma, Víktora*). In each sentence where Maksim is the subject, this noun appears without an ending, as *Maksím*; similarly, where Viktor is the subject, this noun appears as *Víktor*. In each sentence where Maksim is the object, we find the form in *-a*, *Maksíma*; similarly, where Viktor is the object, we find *Víktora*. This should be verified by looking again through each of the example sentences.

Thus Russian distinguishes subject from object not by means of word order, but by means of its morphology. Objects have a different ending from subjects, here the difference between *-a* and Ø (the latter being the symbol linguists use to mean 'nothing at all'). Such noun forms as *Maksím* and *Maksíma* are referred to as different "cases" of the same noun. In general, English nouns do not show a case distinction between subject and object, indeed for most nouns the only case form in English, apart from the basic form with no ending, is the genitive with the ending *'s*, as in *Maksim's book*. Some of the English pronouns do have a case opposition between subject (e.g., *I, they*) and object (e.g., *me, them*), however, as in the following sentences:

(5)   I defend them.

(6)   They defend me.

Such case-marking is marginal in English and does not in fact lead to greater freedom of word order. One cannot say *them defend I* meaning the same as *I defend them*, or indeed meaning anything at all, because the order Subject–Verb–Object is fixed in English. It is usual to call the case used for the subject of a sentence the "nominative" (e.g., English *I*, Russian *Víktor*), and the case used for the object of a sentence the "accusative" (e.g., English *me*, Russian *Víktora*). Listing the different case forms of a word that has cases is called "declining" the word; the corresponding list or paradigm is called a "declension."

Since word order is not, in general, used in Russian to convey basic semantic differences, we may ask just what differences are conveyed by members of the foregoing sets of synonymous sentences. For ease of exposition, the discussion will be limited to sentences with three constituents—subject, verb, and object, in various orders. There will be no discussion of sentences with the verb in initial position because these would require a much fuller treatment and because they are statistically rather rare.[3] Consider first the following questions and answers. In each example, the question asks for a specific piece of information by using the interrogative pronoun *któ* "who" (the nominative) or *kogó* "who(m)" (the accusative);[4] the answer uses the most natural word order for an answer to that question. Again, readers may like to work out the governing principles for themselves before reading further.

(7)　A　*Któ zaščiščájet Víktora?*
　　　　　Who defends Viktor?
　　　B　*Víktora zaščiščájet Maksím.*
　　　　　Maksim defends Viktor.

(8)　A　*Kogó zaščiščájet Maksím?*
　　　　　Who(m) does Maksim defend?
　　　B　*Maksím zaščiščájet Víktora.*
　　　　　Maksim defends Viktor.

(In both English and Russian it would, of course, be possible to give a one-word answer instead of a whole sentence. In English, one could answer "Maksim" to (7) and "Viktor" to (8). In Russian, one could answer *Maksím* to (7), using the nominative case because Maksim is understood as subject of "defend"; compare the nominative *któ*. In Russian, one could answer *Víktora* to (8) using the accusative case, as Viktor is understood as object of "defend"; compare the accusative *kogó*.)

　　In these two brief dialogues, we see that the answer to (7) has the order Object–Verb–Subject, whereas the answer to (8) has the order Subject–Verb–Object. The reason for putting the subject last in (7) and the object last in (8) is related to the informational structure of the dialogue. In asking a question with an interrogative word like "who(m),"

---

[3]The book by Bivon listed in the "Suggestions for Further Reading" reports a statistical analysis of word order in sentences with three constituents (subject, verb, and object, in various orders). If we use S for subject, V for verb, and O for object, then the relative frequencies are: SVO 79 percent; OVS 11 percent; OSV 4 percent; VOS 2 percent; SOV and VSO, each 1 percent. The remaining 2 percent is made up of sentences where one constituent is interrupted by another.

[4]Word order in questions would take us rather far afield, since certain other principles are involved. Note in particular that the interrogative pronoun usually occurs sentence-initially in both Russian and English. Readers are asked to take the word order in questions for granted and to concentrate on the word order of the answer. Note that the declension of *któ* is irregular; moreover, the accusative *kogó* is pronounced as if spelled *kovó* (compare footnote 12).

the questioner takes certain things for granted, but requires an additional piece of information. For instance, in asking (7), speaker A assumes that someone is defending Viktor, but asks for the additional piece of information as to who that someone is; the new information contained in B's answer is that Maksim is that someone (Viktor's defender). In the answer, the fact that Viktor is being defended is old information; the fact that Maksim is related to this situation, as defender, is new information. One of the basic principles of Russian word order is that new information is placed at the end of the sentence. Thus in B's answer to (7), the new information *Maksím* comes at the end. Conversely, in (8) speaker A takes for granted that Maksim is defending somebody, and asks for new information, namely the identification of this somebody. In B's answer, that Maksim is defending is old information; the new information is the identity of the person he is defending, whence *Víktora* occurs sentence-finally. The difference can be represented diagrammatically as follows:

(7')   Víktora zaščiščájet   /Maksím.
        OLD INFORMATION   /NEW INFORMATION

(8')   Maksím zaščiščájet   /Víktora.
        OLD INFORMATION   /NEW INFORMATION

A slightly more complex set of examples is provided by the following four brief conversations, which introduce two new male characters, Aleksej and Boris. The main point at issue is the word order of A's last sentence in each conversation:

(9)   A   *Maksím ubivájet Alekséja.*
            Maksim kills Aleksej.
       B   *A Víktora?*[5]
            What about Viktor?
       A   *Víktora Maksím zaščiščájet.*
            Maksim defends Viktor.

(10)   A   *Maksím ubivájet Alekséja.*
            Maksim kills Aleksej.
       B   *A Víktor?*
            What about Viktor? (i.e., What does Viktor do?)
       A   *Víktor Alekséja zaščiščájet.*
            Viktor defends Aleksej.

---

[5]Note the accusative ending here, contrasting with the nominative in (10); the meaning here is thus "What is happening to Viktor?" whereas in (10) it is "What is Viktor doing?"

(11) A *Maksím zaščiščájet Alekséja.*
           Maksím defends Aleksej.
      B *A Víktora?*
           What about Viktor? (i.e., Who defends Viktor?)
      A *Víktora zaščiščájet Borís.*
           Boris defends Viktor.

(12) A *Maksím zaščiščájet Alekséja.*
           Maksim defends Aleksej.
      B *A Borís?*
           What about Boris? (i.e., Who(m) does Boris defend?)
      A *Borís zaščiščájet Víktora.*
           Boris defends Viktor.

As far as distribution of old and new information is concerned, precisely the same principle is involved in these four exchanges as in examples (7) and (8). In the final sentence of (9), *Víktora Maksím zaščiščájet*, speaker A takes for granted that Maksim is doing something to Viktor from the previous exchanges, so this is old information, and he adds the new information that what Maksim is doing to Viktor is defending him. In (10), speaker A takes for granted that Viktor is doing something to Aleksej, and adds the new information that the relation of Viktor to Aleksej is that of defender. In both these sentences, then, the new information is carried by *zaščiščájet* "defends," which thus occupies sentence-final position. In (11), on the other hand, speaker A takes for granted in the last sentence that someone has been defending Viktor (old information), and adds the new information that the identity of this someone is Boris; thus *Borís* appears sentence-finally. Similarly, in (12), speaker A takes for granted in his last sentence that Boris has been defending someone, and adds the new information that this someone is Viktor, whence *Víktora* occurs sentence-finally.

However, the discussion so far does not explain why, in each of these four last sentences by A, there is a particular noun that occurs sentence-*initially*, and this brings us to another principle of Russian word order. In discourse, it is generally the case that a sentence expresses some comment about some entity (person or thing). In the examples given, this is particularly clear, because in each interchange speaker B explicitly asks for information about either Viktor, as in (9)–(11), or Boris, as in (12), with the question *A Borís?* "What about Boris?" etc. In other words, assuming that he is being reasonably cooperative, when speaker A replies in (9), he says something about Viktor; the same is true in (10) and (11), whereas in (12) the previous discourse constrains A to tell B something about Boris. The noun phrase referring to the entity the sentence is about is called its "topic" (or "theme"). The rest of the sentence, which tells something about the topic, is called its "comment" (or "rheme"). From the examples given, we can induce another principle of Russian word order: the topic normally occurs sentence-initially. What we know about them can be shown diagrammatically by breaking each of the third sentences in (9)–(12) into old and new information on the one hand (the division is indicated by means of a single slash), and into topic and comment on the other (this division is indicated by means of a double slash):

(9′)   TOPIC   //COMMENT . . . .
       Víktora   //Maksím   /zaščiščájet.
       OLD INFORMATION   / NEW INFORMATION

(10′) TOPIC   //COMMENT . . . .
       Víktor   //Alekséja   /zaščiščájet.
       OLD INFORMATION   / NEW INFORMATION

(11′) TOPIC   //COMMENT . . . .
       Víktora   //zaščiščájet   /Borís.
       OLD INFORMATION   / NEW INFORMATION

(12′) TOPIC   //COMMENT . . . .
       Borís   //zaščiščájet   /Víktora.
       OLD INFORMATION   / NEW INFORMATION

A number of terms found in current linguistic literature refer to the division of a sentence into topic and comment, and into old and new information. Perhaps the most common in English is "functional sentence perspective" (FSP); in Russian the usual term is *aktuál'noje členénije predložénija* "topical sentence articulation." Other terms found (apart from obvious ones like "topic-comment structure") are "communicative dynamism," "communicative structure," and "information(al) structure." In general, word order in Russian is determined by functional sentence perspective, whereas functional sentence perspective plays a less important role in determining word order in English. When we say that Russian has free word order, we mean that differences in word order do not affect the basic meaning of a sentence; we do not mean, of course, that any word order can be used with impunity in any text, since as we have seen different word orders differ in the functional sentence perspective they express. English has far fewer examples of this than Russian, but there are some. As we have already noted, in English, time adverbs can occur in several positions, as in the pair "Today Maksim is reading" and "Maksim is reading today." However, in answer to the question "When is Maksim reading?" one could reply "Maksim is reading today," but not "Today Maksim is reading." In other words, in English, new information time adverbs may not appear sentence-initially; rather, they appear sentence-finally, just as in Russian.

English does, of course, have ways of marking differences in functional sentence perspective, despite its more rigid word order. For instance, new information can be marked as in the following example simply by having the constituent expressing the new information carry the main sentence stress (marked by double accent): "Maksím defends Viktor" (in answer to "Who defends Viktor?"). The use of the passive in English often serves to bring the agent noun phrase to sentence-final position, so that in response to the same question one could answer "Viktor (or "He") is defended by Maksim." Other syntactic constructions can also be used, such as clefting ("It's Maksim who defends Viktor") and pseudoclefting ("The one who defends Viktor is Maksim"), accompanied by slight differences in FSP, but all marking "Maksim" as new information. Although Russian does have constructions corresponding formally to the English passive, clefting, and pseudoclefting, they are used much more rarely than in English, since differences in FSP are usually made in Russian simply by changing the word order. In both languages, the new information normally bears sentence stress, but Russian, especially written Russian, is much more systematic in ensuring that the new information, hence the constituent bearing main stress, occurs sentence-finally.

1.2 Morphological Typology

To start this section, we shall enlarge the range of our data by introducing two female characters Vera and Sveta. Readers are again encouraged to try and work out for themselves what is going on in these sentences, as far as possible, before reading the ensuing discussion. The principles of word order, are precisely as in previous examples; from example (17) onwards only some of the possible word orders are given:

(13) a. Véra čitájet.
     b. Čitájet Véra.

    "Vera reads."

(14) a. Svéta čitájet.
     b. Čitájet Svéta.

    "Sveta reads."

(15) a. Véra zaščiščájet Svétu.
     b. Véra Svétu zaščiščájet.
     c. Svétu Véra zaščiščájet.
     d. Svétu zaščiščájet Véra.
     e. Zaščiščájet Véra Svétu.
     f. Zaščiščájet Svétu Véra.

    "Vera defends Sveta."

(16) a. Svéta zaščiščájet Véru.
    b. Svéta Véru zaščiščájet.
    c. Véru Svéta zaščiščájet.
    d. Véru zaščiščájet Svéta.   "Sveta defends Vera."
    e. Zaščiščájet Svéta Véru.
    f. Zaščiščájet Véru Svéta.

(17) a. Véra zaščiščájet Maksíma.   "Vera defends Maksim."
    b. Maksíma zaščiščájet Véra.

(18) a. Maksím zaščiščájet Véru.   "Maksim defends Vera."
    b. Véru zaščiščájet Maksím.

Each of the sentences just given, like each of the sentences of examples (1)–(4), is unambiguous.

On the basis of the examples given, it will be seen that, just as there is a distinction between nominative *Maksím* and accusative *Maksíma*, so nominative *Véra* is distinct from accusative *Véru* and nominative *Svéta* from accusative *Svétu*. In (13), (15), and (17) Vera is subject and, so, appears in the nominative, *Véra*. In (16) and (18) Vera is object and, so, appears in the accusative, *Véru*. In (14) and (16) Sveta is subject and appears in the nominative, *Svéta*. In (15) Sveta is object and appears in the accusative, *Svétu*. The forms of *Maksím* are as predicted on the basis of the discussion of the previous section. Maksim is subject of (18), whence nominative *Maksím*; Maksim is object of (17), whence accusative *Maksíma*. For nouns like *Véra* and *Svéta*, the nominative has the ending *-a*, the accusative has the ending *-u*; contrast them with nouns like *Maksím* and *Víktor*, where the nominative has no ending, and the accusative has the ending *-a*.

It has become apparent that different nouns have different endings to express the same case: for example, the accusative ends in *-a* for *Maksím*, but in *-u* for *Véra*. Moreover, the same ending can express different cases with different nouns: for example, *-a*, which indicates accusative case in *Maksíma*, indicates nominative case in *Véra*. In fact, Russian has a number of declensional classes, and for each such class, the set of morphological endings is, at least in part, different from the endings for other classes. If we exclude a few irregularities, there are four main declensional classes in modern Russian, which are usually referred to as 1a, 1b, 2, and 3.[6] In general, one can tell from the nominative singular form of a noun which declensional class that noun belongs to. The only real exception is the small third declension, since nouns in this declension end in a consonant just like those of class 1a,

---

[6]Nouns in classes 1a and 1b have different endings in the nominative and accusative, but generally the same endings for other cases; for this reason, they are treated as subdivisions of the first declension.

although the other cases have different endings. Nouns of class 1a end in a consonant; examples are the names *Maksím* and *Víktor*, or the common nouns *rabótnik* "workman," *vóron* "raven," *avtóbus* "bus," *zavód* "factory," *stakán* "glass/tumbler." Nouns of class 1b end in -*o*, or -*e*, depending on the last consonant of the stem; for example, *bolóto* "marsh," *plát'je* "dress." Nouns of the second declension end in -*a*, like the proper names *Véra* and *Svéta* and the common nouns *žénščina* "woman," *sobáka* "dog," and *úlica* "street." The relatively small third declension again has nouns ending in a consonant; for example, *mát'* "mother," *mýš'* "mouse," *dvér'* "door."

Readers may be wondering if there is any significance to the fact that male names like *Maksím* and *Víktor*, along with the male occupation name *rabótnik* "workman" occur in class 1a, whereas the female names *Véra* and *Svéta*, along with the specifically female *žénščina* "woman" occur in a different declension, the second. The answer is that there is a significance to these facts, one which we shall explore in the next subsection.

Let us now examine some sentences illustrating the use of common nouns of classes 1a and 2 similar to the foregoing sentences with proper names. In the following examples, note that Russian does not have articles corresponding to the English definite article "the" or the indefinite article "a(n)." Other than this, these sentences illustrate no new grammatical points; only a very few of the possible word orders are shown.

(19) a. Maksím zaščiščájet rabótnika.
     b. Rabótnika zaščiščájet Maksím.
                         "Maksim defends the workman."

(20) a. Rabótnik zaščiščájet žénščinu.
     b. Žénščinu zaščiščájet rabótnik.
                         "The workman defends the woman."

(21) a. Žénščina zaščiščájet Svétu.
     b. Žénščina Svétu zaščiščájet.
                         "The woman defends Sveta."

(22) a. Véra zaščiščájet vórona.
     b. Zaščiščájet Véra vórona.
                         "Vera defends the raven."

Although we have already illustrated the nominative forms of each of the declensional classes, a few more details of accusative formation are still required for a complete illustration. It should be possible to work them out from the following examples, all of which are about Vera observing something. In each example the noun referring to that something will be in the accusative case. Only the word order Subject–Verb–

Object is given, and each example begins "Vera observes . . . ." The noun to be used as object is given in its nominative form to the left of each sentence.

	Nominative	"Vera observes . . ."
(23)	Maksím	Véra nabljudájet Maksíma.
		"Vera observes Maksim"
		(and so on).
(24)	rabótnik "workman"	Véra nabljudájet rabótnika.
(25)	vóron "raven"	Véra nabljudájet vórona.
(26)	avtóbus "bus"	Véra nabljudájet avtóbus.
(27)	zavód "factory"	Véra nabljudájet zavód.
(28)	stakán "glass/tumbler"	Véra nabljudájet stakán.
(29)	bolóto "marsh"	Véra nabljudájet bolóto.
(30)	plát'je "dress"	Véra nabljudájet plát'je.
(31)	Svéta	Véra nabljudájet Svétu.
(32)	žénščina "woman"	Véra nabljudájet žénščinu.
(33)	sobáka "dog"	Véra nabljudájet sobáku.
(34)	úlica "street"	Véra nabljudájet úlicu.
(35)	mát' "mother"	Véra nabljudájet mát'.
(36)	mýš' "mouse"	Véra nabljudájet mýš'.
(37)	dvér' "door"	Véra nabljudájet dvér'.

With most of the declensional classes, the situation is very straightforward. For instance, all nouns of class 2 (*Svéta, žénščina, úlica*) have their accusative in *-u* (*Svétu, žénščinu, úlicu*); all nouns of class 1b have their accusative in *-o* or *-e*, just like the nominative (*bolóto, plát'je*); all nouns of class 3 have their accusative in a consonant, the same as the nominative (*mát', mýš, dvér'*). The additional problem is caused by nouns of class 1a, since some have an accusative in *-a* (*Maksím, rabótnik, vóron*), while others have the accusative in a consonant, just like the nominative (*avtóbus, zavód, stakán*). The single distinguishing feature that separates these two groups from one another, is a semantic feature: nouns referring to living beings, that is, to human beings and animals,[7] have the separate accusative in *-a*, whereas nouns referring to nonliving objects (and abstract concepts) have the accusative like the nominative. In Russian grammar, it is usual to use the term "animate" to

---

[7]Plants are treated as nonliving for this purpose; for example, *Véra nabljudájet dúb* "Vera observes the oak" (*dúb* "oak").

describe nouns referring to people and animals, and "inanimate" for other nouns. Thus *Maksím*, *rabótnik*, *vóron* (and also, of course, *Svéta*, *žénščina*, *sobáka*, *mát'*, *mýš'*) are animate, whereas *avtóbus*, *zavód*, *stakán* (and, of course, *bolóto*, *plát'je*, *úlica*, *dvér'*) are inanimate. The rule for forming the accusative of nouns of declension 1a is: add the ending -*a* if the noun is animate, but if it is inanimate, add no ending. We should note, incidentally, that there are relatively few animate nouns in declension 3 (in particular, extremely few nouns referring to human beings), and hardly any at all in declension 1b. Readers might like to start thinking why it is that animate nouns of class 1a, but not inanimate nouns of this class, nor nouns of the typically inanimate classes 1b and 3, have this special accusative form.

The following list shows the common nouns that have been used so far together with their plural forms. Proper names, like *Maksím* and *Svéta*, do not have plurals. Some details of Russian pronunciation and spelling will be necessary to clarify some of the apparent anomalies in the examples listed. After *k*, *g*, and *x*, Russian writes and pronounces *i*, never *y*; the same is true after all palatalized consonants (for example, *t'* stands for a palatalized *t*, while *ti* stands for palatalized *t* followed by the vowel *i*). Thus the fact that some plurals end in -*i* while others end in -*y* is not relevant to the point at issue. With this caveat, it should now be possible to work out the rules for forming the nominative plurals of nouns:

(38)	Nominative Singular	Nominative Plural	
Declensional Class			
1a	*rabótnik*	*rabótniki*	workmen
	vóron	*vórony*	ravens
	avtóbus	*avtóbusy*	buses
	zavód	*zavódy*	factories
	stakán	*stakány*	glasses/tumblers
1b	*bolóto*	*bolóta*	marshes
	plát'je	*plát'ja*	dresses
2	*žénščina*	*žénščiny*	women
	sobáka	*sobáki*	dogs
	úlica	*úlicy*	streets
3	*mát'*	*máteri*[8]	mothers
	mýš'	*mýši*	mice
	dvér'	*dvéri*	doors

---

[8]The noun *mát'* (and also *dóč'* "daughter") is slightly irregular in that in all forms, apart from the nominative-accusative singular, the stem is *mater'*- (*dočer'*-).

These examples show that plural-formation is relatively straight-forward in Russian: nouns of class 1b form their plural in -*a*, while all other nouns (classes 1a, 2, and 3) form their plural in -*y*/-*i*. Once again, the importance of declensional classes is apparent, though here the distinction between them lies only in the difference between class 1b and all the rest. And again, we see that the same ending can have different values in different declensional classes. In what we have seen so far, -*a* can be either the accusative singular ending (class 1a, animate), or the nominative singular ending (class 2), or the nominative plural ending (class 1b).

The next set of examples shows these various nouns in the plural acting as objects of sentences, that is, in the accusative case. For simplicity, we have retained the same frame as before, "Vera observes X." This new set of data will enable the reader to work out the rules for forming the accusative plural of nouns of the various classes:

	Nominative	"Vera observes . . ."
(39)	rabótnik	Véra nabljudájet rabótnikov.
		"Vera observes the workmen"
		(and so on, object nouns always plural).
(40)	vóron	Véra nabljudájet vóronov.
(41)	avtóbus	Véra nabljudájet avtóbusy.
(42)	zavód	Véra nabljudájet zavódy.
(43)	stakán	Véra nabljudájet stakány.
(44)	bolóto	Véra nabljudájet bolóta.
(45)	plát′je	Véra nabljudájet plát′ja.
(46)	žénščina	Véra nabljudájet žénščin.
(47)	sobáka	Véra nabljudájet sobák.
(48)	úlica	Véra nabljudájet úlicy.
(49)	mát′	Véra nabljudájet materéj.[9]
(50)	mýš′	Véra nabljudájet myšéj.
(51)	dvér′	Véra nabljudájet dvéri.

In these examples, it is clear that declensional class is to some extent relevant in forming accusative plurals, but that is not the whole story. Nouns of class 1a have either the ending -*ov* or the ending -*y*/-*i*, the latter being like the nominative plural. Nouns of class 1b have the ending -*a*, like the nominative plural. Nouns of class 2 have either the ending -∅

---

[9]The stress of the accusative plural *materéj* (and similarly of *dočeréj* "daughters" and *myšéj* "mice") is irregular, and should be disregarded.

or the ending -*y*/-*i*, the latter as in the nominative plural. Nouns of class 3 have either the ending -*ej* or the ending -*y*/-*i*, the latter as in the nominative plural. Since animacy turned out to be relevant for certain singular nouns (those of class 1a), one might be tempted to check whether animacy is relevant in the formation of the accusative plural too. And this is one of those intuitions that pays off: animacy is indeed the determining factor. For each of the animate direct objects above, there is a special accusative case distinct from the nominative (in -*ov* for Class 1a, in -∅ for class 2, in -*ej* for class 3). In contrast, all the inanimate nouns have the accusative plural exactly the same as the nominative plural.[10] (A tabular summary of these forms appears in Table 3.1 at the end of the next subsection.)

One implication of the discussion so far is that the ending -*a* for animate nouns of declension 1a indicates the accusative singular form, whereas the ending -*y* indicates the nominative plural form, the ending -*ov* the accusative plural. Thus each such ending indicates (apart from indication of declension class) both the case and the number of the appropriate form. In these endings, it makes no sense to ask what part of the ending indicates case, and what part indicates number, because each of the endings is morphologically indivisible. The same is true if we examine the other cases, in the singular and plural. Russian is usually analyzed as having six cases; in addition to the nominative and accusative, these are the genitive, dative, instrumental, and prepositional. The endings of these cases in declension 1a, in singular and plural, are as follows:

(52) **Singular**

genitive -*a*, dative -*u*, instrumental -*om*, prepositional -*e*

Plural

genitive -*ov*, dative -*am*, instrumental -*ami*, prepositional -*ax*

---

[10]As noted above, there are a few animate nouns in declension 1b; they have not been introduced into the main body of the text, as all of them are nouns declined like adjectives (for which see section 1.3). One of these nouns is *živótnoje* "animal." Its accusative singular is also *živótnoje*, because for nouns of declension 1b the accusative singular is like the nominative singular irrespective of animacy. The nominative plural is *živótnyje*, and the accusative plural is *živótnyx*. In the plural, then, animate nouns of class 1b, like animate nouns of all other declensions, have a distinct accusative form. Quite generally, in Russian, the differences between declensional classes are much less in the plural than in the singular (see also section 1.3). Even the difference suggested above between the animate accusative plural of class 1a (in -*ov*) and that of class 3 (in -*ej*) can be misleading, since nouns ending in certain consonants in declension 1a, in particular nouns ending in all of those consonants which are possible at the end of words of class 3, have the animate accusative plural in -*ej*. In fairness to the reader, it must be pointed out that Russian morphology, in its details, is even more complex than is indicated by the examples chosen here. Students specializing in Russian spend a lot of their time simply learning the morphology—often failing to see the wood for the trees. The aim of this section is to provide an overview of the basic system, and although this means abstracting away from many points of detail, we do feel that an overview of this kind is justified and valuable.

These forms suffice to show that there is no regularly identifiable morphological segment or sequence of segments common to a given case in both singular and plural. Similarly, there is no regularly identifiable segment or sequence of segments common to all cases in a given number (all singular cases as opposed to all plural cases). Languages with a morphological system of this type, where various categories are fused into a single affix, are referred to as "flectional." All the Slavic languages are highly flectional, and in this they are like the older Indo-European languages (see section 2.1). English tends not to have affixes combining a number of categories, though there are some exceptions, such as the verbal ending -*s*, as in "He hits," which combines person (the third person, compare with "I hit"), number (the singular, compare with "They hit"), and tense (the present, compare with "He hit").

Some languages with several cases and a number distinction like Russian operate in a different way, always keeping distinct the affix for case and the affix for number. In Turkish, for instance, plural is indicated by the ending -*lar*, which is followed by the same set of endings as are used in the singular. In the following paradigm for the Turkish noun meaning "man," the reader is invited to parse the forms to see the consistent marking for accusative, genitive, plural, and so forth.

(53)

Turkish

	Singular	Plural
nominative	*adam*	*adamlar*
accusative	*adami*	*adamlari*
genitive	*adamin*	*adamlarin*
dative	*adama*	*adamlara*
locative	*adamda*	*adamlarda*
ablative	*adamdan*	*adamlardan*

Languages with a morphology like Turkish are called "agglutinative" (or "agglutinating"), a term formed from the Latin *gluten* "glue." It is as if the different endings, each one carrying a single piece of information, were glued on one after the other. For languages with a reasonable number of morphological categories, the difference between flection and agglutination is one of the main distinctions in morphological type.

We may now return briefly to a question that was posed above but not answered—namely, why it is that animacy should be relevant in the formation of the accusative case. In particular it is useful to determine why it is that animate nouns tend to have an accusative case distinct from the nominative, whereas inanimate nouns tend simply to use the same form as the nominative. The reason for this apparently arbitrary piece of morphology seems to lie in the relations among objects in the outside world, or at least in our conception of the real world. In general, when we are concerned with the sorts of situations that are described by means of transitive verbs—verbs that enter into the construction Subject–Verb–Object (irrespective of word order)—then we are almost invariably concerned with situations where some animate object is performing some physical or abstract action on some other object, which may be animate or inanimate. Only very rarely is it necessary to describe a situation where an inanimate object is performing an action (physical or, more usually, abstract) on some other object (animate or inanimate). Hardly any of the sentences we have examined so far would make sense with an inanimate subject; only with the verb *zaščiščájet* "defends, protects" could one conceive of an example like *Dvér' zaščiščáj-et Véru* (*ot šúma*) "The door protects Vera (from noise)."

In general, inanimate nouns do not occur as subjects of transitive verbs in Russian. With an intransitive verb—one without an object—there can be no confusion between subject and object, simply because there is no possible object, so the distinction between nominative and accusative is irrelevant. With a transitive verb, confusion is going to be more likely, in the absence of morphological discriminators, with animate nouns, since these are likely to occur as either subject or object of a transitive verb. Because inanimate nouns are unlikely to occur as subjects of a transitive verb, the same form of an inanimate noun can, with reasonable safety, be used for both nominative and accusative. With intransitive verbs it will be subject, with transitive verbs it will almost invariably be object.[11] There is thus less need for an overt opposition between nominative and accusative for inanimate nouns.

It is possible to construct sentences in Russian using nouns that do not distinguish nominative from accusative, sentences in which the case-marking does not indicate which noun is subject and which object. This does, of course, mean that both nouns must have ambiguous form, as in examples (56) and (57), though not as in (54) or (55), where the fact that one noun is unambiguously accusative (*Víktora*), or one unambiguously nominative (*Víktor*), determines by elimination the case of the other:

(54) a. Mát' zaščiščájet Víktora.
     b. Víktora zaščiščájet mát'.   "Mother defends Viktor."

(55) a. Víktor zaščiščájet mát'.
     b. Mát' zaščiščájet Víktor.   "Viktor defends mother."

(56)   Mát' zaščiščájet dóč'.

(57)   Bytijé opredeljájet soznánije.

---

[11]The fact that all nouns of the second declension have distinct accusative forms in the singular is, synchronically, an anomaly; historically, it is a relict of an earlier system in Slavic before the animacy distinction developed as a grammatical category. Animate nouns of declension 1b and 3 are also exceptional in the singular in that their nominative and accusative forms are identical; they are few in number.

(*Dóč'* in (56) means "daughter." The new lexical items in (57) are *bytijé* "being, existence," *opredelijájet* "determines," *soznánije* "consciousness.") The question now arises as to how sentences like (56) and (57) are interpreted. Are they felt to be completely ambiguous, (meaning, respectively, either "The mother defends the daughter" or "The daughter defends the mother," and either "Being determines consciousness" or "Consciousness determines being")? Or is some principle of interpretation used by means of which they are interpreted unambiguously? In fact, barring indications to the contrary, such sentences are nearly always interpreted unambiguously, with the order Subject–Verb–Object. Thus example (56) would usually be taken by native speakers of Russian to mean "The mother defends the daughter." To express the meaning of "The daughter defends the mother" native speakers would prefer the word order of (58).

(58)   *Dóč' zaščiščájet mát'.*

Similarly, example (57) would usually be taken to mean "Being determines consciousness"; so strong is this tendency that this sentence is used in Russian books on Marxism to express this, one of the basic tenets of Marxist epistemology, without any Russian-speaking ideologist fearing that the sentence will be given the inverse meaning, which would be quite contrary to Marxist ideology, and which would be expressed as follows:

(59)   *Soznánije opredeljájet bytijé.*
        Consciousness determines being.

The fact that such 'morphologically ambiguous' sentences are in fact usually given unique interpretations, on the basis of the word order Subject–Verb–Object, is one of the pieces of evidence in favor of saying that Russian, despite its 'free' word order, does have a 'basic' word order, and that this basic word order is Subject–Verb–Object. Another piece of evidence is the much greater statistical frequency of this word order (see footnote 3). Studies of how children acquire Russian as their native language also show that during the early stages of acquiring Russian, children tend to interpret sentences according to a Subject–Verb–Object word order, even where this is contradicted by the morphological indications. Thus, if faced with sentence (60), small children would tend to interpret it as meaning "The woman defends Viktor," a meaning it cannot have for older children and adults.

(60)   *Žénščinu zaščiščájet Víktor.*
        Viktor defends the woman.

1.3 Agreement

The next four examples introduce a new verbal form. As usual, all possible permutations of word order are permissible, subject to differences in functional sentence perspective. Given this information, the reader should be able to work out the difference between the verbal forms *zaščiščájet* and *zaščiščájut*:

(61) *Rabótnik zaščiščájet žénščinu.*
      The workman defends the woman.

(62) *Rabótniki zaščiščájut žénščinu.*
      The workmen defend the woman.

(63) *Rabótnik zaščiščájet žénščin.*
      The workman defends the women.

(64) *Rabótniki zaščiščájut žénščin.*
      The workmen defend the women.

Clearly, the different verbal forms are connected with the number of the participants involved in the situation. Moreover, the forms *zaščiščájet* and *zaščiščájut* both occur when the object is singular (in (61) and (62)) and when it is plural (in (63) and (64)), so that the number of the object is not a relevant factor. In both (61) and (63), where *zaščiščájet* occurs, the subject is singular; in both (62) and (64), where *zaščiščájut* occurs, the subject is plural. In other words, the verbal form in *-et* occurs with a singular subject, the verbal form in *-ut* with a plural subject. Since the choice of verbal form is determined by the number of the subject, we may say that the verb "agrees" in number with its subject (the corresponding noun is "agreement," or "concord"). The verbal form *zaščiščájet* can be called singular, the verbal form *zaščiščájut* plural.

English too has a limited amount of verb–subject agreement. (Some other languages also have verb-object agreement. One such is Hua, spoken in Papua New Guinea, described in the preceding chapter). In English we say "The workman defends" but "The workmen defend" ("defends" is singular; "defend" is plural). If we take into account the other persons of the verb, namely, first person (singular "I," plural "we") and second person ("you," both singular and plural), then we see that in the present tense English has, for regular verbs, only two forms: one in *-s* for the third-person singular, and one in *-ø* for all other combinations of person and number (only *be* has more distinctions). In the past tense of regular verbs, even this distinction is lost, since the past tense ending *-ed* shows no variation for person and number (only *be* varies in the past tense, with its alternation between *was* and *were*). In

Russian, verbs in the present tense have different forms for each of the six possible combinations of person and number:

(65) *Já čitáju.*   I read.

(66) *Tý čitáješ'.*   You read. (Singular)

(67) *Ón čitájet.*   He reads.

(68) *Mý čitájem.*   We read.

(69) *Vý čitájete.*   You read. (Plural)

(70) *Oní čitájut.*   They read.

Thus the forms *čitájet* and *zaščiščájet* are, strictly speaking, third-person singular, contrasting in number with the third-person plural *čitájut* and *zaščiščájut*, and contrasting in person with the first-person singular *čitáju*, and the second-person singular *zaščiščáješ'*.

Given the preceding discussion and the information that *zavód* is a noun of declension 1a meaning "factory" and *lípa* a noun of the second declension meaning "lime tree," the reader should be able to translate the following sentence into English:

(71) Zavód zaščiščájut lípy.

It should first be realized that neither of the noun forms is unambiguous as to case, since both *zavód* (inanimate noun of class 1a) and *lípy* (plural of inanimate noun of class 2) could be either nominative or accusative. However, the verb form *zaščiščájut* is unambiguously plural, so its subject must be plural. Thus the subject of the verb can be *lípy*, and not *zavód*, and the sentence means "The lime trees protect the factory," not "The factory protects the lime trees," which would be *Zavód zaščiščájet lípy*, or any permutation of these words. Sentence (71) has the word order Object–Verb–Subject, and is quite unambiguous, given the verb form.

In Russian, verbs are not the only part of speech to agree in number with nouns: adjectives must also agree. In the following sentences, various nouns are accompanied by the adjectives *stáryj* "old" or *xrábryj* "brave" in the appropriate form. The stems of these two adjectives are *star-* and *xrabr-*, respectively. The reader is invited to work out from these examples what principles are involved in the morphology of adjectives. The nouns and verbs should all be familiar to you from previous examples. All the examples are in the word order Subject–Verb–Object.

(72) Stáryj rabótnik zaščiščájet xrábruju žénščinu.

(73) Xrábryj rabótnik zaščiščájet stáryx žénščin.

(74) Stáryje rabótniki nabljudájut stáryj avtóbus.

(75) Xrábraja žénščina zaščiščájet stárogo rabótnika.[12]

(76) Stáryje žénščiny nabljudájut stároje plát'je.

(77) Stáraja mát' zaščiščájet xrábryx rabótnikov.

(78) Stáryje máteri nabljudájut stáryje plát'ja.

(79) Stáryj avtóbus zaščiščájet stáryx materéj.

(80) Xrábryj rabótnik zaščiščájet stáruju mát'.

(81) Stáryje rabótniki nabljudájut stáryje avtóbusy.

(82) Stáraja žénščina nabljudájet stáryje dvéri.

(83) Stáryje žénščiny nabljudájut stáruju úlicu.

(84) Stáraja mát' nabljudájet stáruju dvér'.

(85) Stáryje máteri nabljudájut stáryje úlicy.

Now you can check your understanding of these sentences against the following glosses:

(72) The old workman defends the brave woman.

(73) The brave workman defends the old women.

(74) The old workmen observe the old bus.

(75) The brave woman defends the old workman.

(76) The old women observe the old dress.

(77) The old mother defends the brave workmen.

(78) The old mothers observe the old dresses.

(79) The old bus protects the old mothers.

(80) The brave workman defends the old mother.

(81) The old workmen observe the old buses.

(82) The old woman observes the old doors.

(83) The old women observe the old street.

(84) The old mother observes the old door.

(85) The old mothers observe the old streets.

It is clear from these examples that there is a close relation between the various adjective endings and the case endings of the various declensional classes, but this relation is not absolutely straightforward. The most obvious discrepancy is in the plural. Plural nouns have, in the

---

[12]The ending -*ogo* is pronounced as if spelled -*ovo*.

nominative (and the accusative for inanimate nouns), -*y*/-*i*, except for class 1b, which has -*a*, but all adjectives agreeing with such nouns have -*yje*. Animate nouns have in the accusative the ending -*ov*, -∅ or -*ej* according to declensional class, but all adjectives have -*yx*. In other words, in the plural in Russian, adjectives in a given case take the same ending irrespective of the declensional class of the noun with which they are agreeing; the endings are -*yje* (nominative and inanimate accusative) and -*yx* (animate accusative). Note also the discussion of *životnoje* "animal" in footnote 10. As noted in that footnote, differences between declensional classes are much less in the plural than in the singular, and with adjectives the difference is lost altogether. For a tabular summary of these forms, see Table 3.1 at the end of this subsection.

In the singular, there appears at first sight to be an absolute correspondence between declensional class and adjective form. Adjectives agreeing with nouns of class 1a have -*yj* in the nominative and inanimate accusative (the nouns end in -∅), and -*ogo* in the animate accusative (the nouns end in -*a*). Adjectives agreeing with nouns of class 1b have the ending -*oje* in the nominative and accusative (the nouns end in -*o* or -*e*). Adjectives agreeing with nouns of class 2 have the ending -*aja* in the nominative (the nouns end in -*a*) and -*uju* in the accusative (the nouns end in -*u*).

Unlike the other declensions, nouns of the third declension are not accompanied by adjectives having distinct endings for agreement with that declension. Instead the adjectives accompanying the third-declension nouns *mát'* and *dvér'* have the same endings as if they were accompanying nouns of the second declension. In this connection, we may note that whereas sentence (58), reproduced here as (86) is morphologically ambiguous, morphological ambiguity does not result if the third-declension nouns are accompanied by adjectives, as in (87) and (88).

(86)   *Dóč' zaščiščájet mát'.*
        The daughter defends the mother. (Or, conceivably: "The mother defends the daughter.")

(87)   *Xrábraja dóč' zaščiščájet stáruju mát'.*
        The brave daughter defends the old mother.

(88)   *Xrábruju dóč' zaščiščájet stáraja mát'.*
        The old mother defends the brave daughter.

Earlier in this section, when nouns of declension 2 were first introduced, the following correlation was noted in passing: proper names of males tend to belong to class 1a, whereas proper names of females tend to belong to class 2. In fact the correlation is more general than this: nouns referring to male human beings and male domestic animals tend to belong to class 1a; nouns referring to female human beings and female domestic animals tend to belong to class 2 (although a small number belong to class 3). Names of other animals and inanimate objects or abstract concepts are scattered through all the declensional classes. One can usually tell which declensional class a given noun belongs to from its ending in the nominative singular (except that nouns ending in certain consonants may belong to either class 1a or class 3, as mentioned earlier).

In addition to the division into declensional classes, Russian nouns also divide up into three classes on the basis of adjective agreement. One agreement class consists of nouns referring to male human beings and domestic animals, plus some other nouns, typically of class 1a. A second class consists of nouns referring to female human beings and domestic animals, plus some other nouns, typically of declensional class 2 but also including virtually all the (few) nouns of declensional class 3. A third class contains only names of animals and inanimate objects (including abstract concepts), all in declensional class 1b. Because of the partial correlation between these adjective-agreement classes and natural (biological) sex, in speaking of Russian and other languages with this kind of system, there has arisen a tradition of using names for these agreement classes similar, though not identical, to the sex names. Nouns of the first agreement class, including males, are called "masculine"; those of the second agreement class, including females, are called "feminine"; those of the third agreement class are called "neuter." The agreement classes are called "genders." Thus of the nouns in sentences (72)–(85), the masculine nouns are *rabótnik* and *avtóbus*; the feminine nouns are *žénščinu, úlica, mát',* and *dvér'*; the neuter noun is *plát'je* (*Bolóto* "marsh" and *živótnoje* "animal" are also neuter nouns. For some thorough discussion of other phenomena relevant to the notion of gender, see section 1.2 of Chapter V in this volume on Swahili noun classes and section 2.3 of the first chapter in the companion volume on noun classifiers in Jacaltec.).

The general rule for adjectives in the singular in Russian is thus that they agree with their noun in number, case, and gender; in the plural, they agree in number and case only. In the singular, for masculine gender, the adjectival endings are *-yj* (nominative and inanimate accusative) and *-ogo* (animate accusative); for the feminine gender the singular adjectival endings are *-aja* (nominative) and *-uju* (accusative); for the neuter the singular adjectival ending is *-oje* (nominative/accusative).

One discrepancy between declensional class and gender has already been noted: feminine nouns are distributed between classes 2 and 3. Apart from a small number of anomalies, there is one further important discrepancy: a number of masculine nouns, all of them referring to male human beings, belong to the second declension, for instance *déduška*

TABLE 3.1 Summary of Russian Noun and Adjective Morphology

	Singular			Plural		
	Nominative	Accusative Inanimate	Accusative Animate	Nominative	Accusative Inanimate	Accusative Animate
Noun						
1a	-∅	-∅	-a	-y/-i	-y/-i	-ov (-ej)
1b	-o/-e	-o/-e		-a	-a	-∅
2	-a	-u		-y/-i	-y/-i	-∅
3	-∅	-∅		-i	-i	-ej
Adjective						
Masculine	-yj	-yj	-ogo ⎫	-yje	-yje	-yx
Neuter	-oje	-oje	-ogo ⎬			
Feminine	-aja	-uju	-uju ⎭			

"grandfather." These nouns are declined exactly like feminine nouns of the second declension, but where agreement depends on gender, they take masculine agreement, as in:

(89) *Stáryj déduška zaščiščájet xrábrogo rabótnika.*
      The old grandfather defends the brave workman.

(90) *Xrábryj rabótnik zaščiščájet stárogo dédušku.*
      The brave workman defends the old grandfather.

Further discrepancies between gender, sex, and declensional class will be discussed in subsection 2.5.1.

The morphology of Russian nouns and adjectives for the nominative and accusative cases is summarized in Table 3.1.

1.4 Tense and Aspect

In an introductory account like the present chapter, the example sentences are necessarily somewhat vapid, because it is necessary to keep to a relatively restricted vocabulary. The vocabulary is restricted in particular to avoid as far as possible morphological irregularities which would lead us astray from the basic points to be considered, although morphological irregularities happen to include some of the commonest words in any language. The reader may feel that some improvements could have been introduced by varying the verb forms a little more: every one of the examples cited to date is glossed by an English sentence with the verb in the simple present, despite the plethora of verbal forms that English offers. (For example, alongside "defends," English has "is defending;" alongside "defended," there is "used to have been defending," etc.) In Russian, all the verbal forms quoted have had the endings *-et* or *-ut*, or the corresponding forms for other persons. We shall now go on to look at some of the other verbal forms in Russian, a discussion which will highlight the rather different organization of verbal categories in Russian, paralleling categories of English. It is because of this different organization that the discussion to date was simplified by sticking to one and the same set of forms.

First, a morphological difference between Russian verbs in the past tense and those in other tenses will be illustrated. It has already been shown that, in the present tense, Russian verbs agree with their subject in person and number (with a single ending providing a combined marker for person and number, for example *-em* for first-person plural). Regular verbs in Russian have, in the past tense, the ending *-l*; where the present stem ends in *-j*, this is dropped before the *-l* of the past tense: thus the verb for "defend," whose present stem *zaščiščaj-* is already familiar to us, will have the past stem *zaščiščal-*; similarly *čitaj-* "read" has the past stem *čital-*, and *ubivaj-* "kill" has past stem *ubival-*. The following sentences show past-tense verbs with subjects of various declensional classes, genders, numbers, and persons. The reader is again asked to try and work out the principles involved before going on to the discussion below:

(91)   *Rabótnik zaščiščál zavód.*
        The workman defended the factory.

(92)   *Rabótniki zaščiščáli zavód.*
        The workmen defended the factory.

(93)   *Déduška zaščiščál zavód.*
        The grandfather defended the factory.

(94)   *Déduški zaščiščáli zavód.*
        The grandfathers defended the factory.

(95)   *Žénščina zaščiščála zavód.*
        The woman defended the factory.

(96)   *Žénščiny zaščiščáli zavód.*
        The women defended the factory.

(97)   *Mát' zaščiščála zavód.*
        The mother defended the factory.

(98)   *Máteri zaščiščáli zavód.*
        The mothers defended the factory.

(99)   *Bolóto zaščiščálo zavód.*
        The marsh protected the factory.

(100)   *Bolóta zaščiščáli zavód.*
        The marshes protected the factory.

(101)   *Já zaščiščál zavód.*
        I defended the factory. (e.g., Viktor is speaking.)

(102)   *Já zaščiščála zavód.*
        I defended the factory. (e.g., Vera is speaking.)

(103)   *Tý zaščiščál zavód.*
        You defended the factory. (Someone is speaking to, e.g., Viktor.)

(104)   *Tý zaščiščála zavód.*
        You defended the factory. (Someone is speaking to, e.g., Vera.)

(105)   *Mý zaščiščáli zavód.*
        We defended the factory.

(106)   *Vý zaščiščáli zavód.*

> You defended the factory. (Someone is addressing a group of people.)

One main difference between verb–subject agreement in the past and present tenses is obvious from a comparison of sentences (101)–(106) with the sentences preceding them. There is no difference in verbal form in the past tense according to the person of the subject. Thus we have the same verbal form, *zaščiščál*, in (91) the subject of which is *rabótnik*, a third-person singular; in (101) the subject of which is *já*, the first-person singular; and in (103) the subject of which is *tý*, the second-person singular. On the other hand, the past tense shows different forms according to the gender of the subject: this is the difference between the forms in -∅ (masculine singular), -*a* (feminine singular), -*o* (neuter singular), and -*i* (plural, irrespective of gender). Thus the masculine form in -∅ is used with *rabótnik* and *déduška*, showing that it is gender, rather than declensional class, that is relevant. The masculine form is also used with *já* and *tý* referring to a male. The feminine form is used with *žénščina* and *mát'* and also with *já* and *tý* referring to a female. The neuter -*o* is used with *bolóto*. And the plural -*i* is used with the plural of each of these, including the pronouns. The past-tense verbal endings parallel the adjectival endings, although in form, they are rather more similar to noun endings than to the endings of attributive adjectives.[13] Thus we can say that in Russian, verbs in the nonpast tenses agree in person and number with their subject; in the past tense they agree in gender and number with their subject.

Having eliminated the problem of morphological peculiarities of the past tense, we can now return to the problem of delimiting the full set of verbal forms in Russian in comparison with the range of forms in English. The following set of sentences provides one example for each Russian form, with an English gloss showing the range of possible translations, at least, in the most general cases. In the discussion from here on, it is not expected that readers should be able to figure out details of the meaning of the Russian forms just from the range of English glosses, as many details will not be clear until the fuller discussion ensues (*Knígu* "book" is a second-declension feminine noun, nominative form *kníga*).

(107)   *Víktor čitájet knígu.*

> Viktor reads/is reading a book.

---

[13]Adjectives in fact also have predicative forms with the endings ∅, -*a*, -*o*, -*y*, like noun and past tense endings, but the use of these forms would take us beyond the limits of the present chapter. In older Russian, the verbal forms in -*l* were verbal adjectives (participles), and their current morphology—more like that of adjectives and nouns than that of most of the verbal paradigm—is a relict of that period.

(108)   *Víktor čitál knígu.*
         Viktor read/was reading/used to read a book.

(109)   *Víktor búdet čitát' knígu.*
         Viktor will read/will be reading a book.

(110)   *Víktor pročitál knígu.*
         Viktor read/has read/had read a book.

(111)   *Víktor pročitájet knígu.*
         Viktor will read/will have read a book.

One striking difference between Russian and English is the relative paucity of distinct verbal forms in Russian. Russian has only the five given above: *čitájet, čitál, búdet čitát', pročitál, pročitájet.* The English glosses to these five Russian sentences give ten forms: "reads, read, is reading, was reading, used to read, will read, will be reading, has read, had read, will have read." In fact, English has yet more forms: "has been reading, had been reading, will have been reading, used to be reading, used to have been reading" (as in "Boris used always to have been drinking vodka when I arrived"), but the precise meanings of these more complex forms could only be expressed in Russian by means of an elaborate paraphrase, and for this reason we have chosen to omit them in the present discussion. From a formal viewpoint, the main difference between English and Russian is that in English nearly all these distinctions are made "analytically," that is, by combining together different words, whereas in Russian the distinctions are made "synthetically," that is, by using different morphological forms of the same word. Only one form is compound (analytic) in Russian, namely *búdet čitát'*, formed from the auxiliary verb *búdet* (which shows person and number, as in *Já búdu čitát'* "I will be reading") and the infinitive *čitát'* "to read." The Russian infinitive, corresponding closely in use to the English infinitive with the particle *to*, has the ending *-t'* for regular verbs; as in the past tense, a stem-final *-j* drops before this ending.

We may start this part of our discussion by examining tense in the Russian and English verbal systems. 'Tense' is the linguistic category that describes the location of situations in time. In both English and Russian, there is a tense distinction based on temporal location relative to the present moment. This gives a three-way tense opposition. 'Present' tense is for situations that hold at the present (though possibly extending back and forwards in time from the present); for example, Russian *čitájet*, English "reads," "is reading." 'Past' tense is for situations that held prior to the present (and which either do not hold at the present, or at least concerning which it is irrelevant whether or not they still hold); for example, Russian *čitál, pročitál*, English "read, was reading, used to read." 'Future' tense is for situations that will hold some time after the present moment (and which either do not hold at the present, or concerning which it is irrelevant whether or not they already hold); for example, Russian *búdet čitát'*, *pročitájet*, English "will read," "will be reading."[14] This kind of tense can be referred to as "absolute tense," since situations are located in time relative only to the present moment, and not with regard to any other situation.

'Relative tense,' in contrast, means that a situation is located relative to some other situation, either as being simultaneous with it, prior to it, or subsequent to it. In English, the forms "had read" and "will have read" indicate relative tense: "had read" (the so-called pluperfect) locates a past situation prior to some other past situation; "will have read" (future perfect) locates a situation as prior to some future situation. Thus the sentence "When I entered the room, Bill had removed his shoes" locates my entry in the past (prior to the present moment, in absolute tense), and locates Bill's removal of his shoes as prior to my entry (relative tense). Similarly, the sentence "We'll meet again next week, by which time Bill will have completed this assignment" locates our meeting in the future (subsequent to the present moment, in absolute tense), and locates Bill's completing the assignment prior to our meeting (relative tense).[15] Russian has no verbal forms especially indicating relative tense. The three-way opposition present/past/future in Russian relates exclusively to absolute tense, and that is why "Viktor had read the book" can only be glossed with an ordinary past tense in Russian, barring a more elaborate paraphrase, thus losing the distinction between English "Viktor had read the book" and "Viktor read the book." Thus Russian and English are similar in having the same set of oppositions for absolute tense, but differ in that Russian lacks forms corresponding to the English forms for relative tense.

---

[14]In most languages, tenses have uses going beyond their simplest definition in terms of location in time: thus in both English and Russian, the present tense can be used in vivid narrative to describe past events (*Yesterday I was sitting in the garden when up comes Joe and says...*). The correlation between tense and time is particularly weak with the future tense; compare English examples like *He'll be there now* (with modal, rather than temporal value), so much so that many linguists prefer not to treat the so-called future as a tense at all; for the present discussion, we prefer to keep to a more traditional analysis. In Russian there is a further complication, in that one of the future forms, *pročitájet*, belongs formally with the present (*čitájet*), which has led some linguists to consider this either as a present-tense form, or as a nonpast (rather than specifically present or future) form. In function, however, the form *pročitájet* parallels *búdet čitát'* rather than *čitájet*, and this is the basis for our treatment of it as a future-tense form.

[15]The form *has read* ((present) perfect) might therefore be taken to refer to a situation located prior relative to the present; however, since the present moment is the location pivot for absolute tense, this would fail to distinguish the present perfect from the simple past (*read*). In fact, the English present perfect indicates a situation that preceded the present moment but still has continuing relevance to the present: contrast "Sue has broken her arm" (i.e., the arm is now broken), and "Sue broke her arm" (where the arm may well have healed completely). Russian again has no formal opposition carrying this distinction, so both English sentences would be glossed as *Sú slomála rúku*, giving no indication of whether or not the arm is still broken. In the pluperfect and future perfect in English, the feature of continuing relevance is masked by that of relative tense.

We may now turn to the remaining distinctions, in particular the Russian distinction between, on the one hand, *čitájet, čitál, búdet čitát'*, and on the other, *pročitál, pročitájet*. These distinctions are not concerned with the temporal location of one situation relative to another or relative to the present moment, but rather with the internal structure of a given situation—more specifically, its internal temporal structure. Oppositions of this kind are referred to as "aspect." Russian thus has two aspects, usually referred to as "imperfective" and "perfective." The imperfective is exemplified by *čitájet, čitál, búdet čitát'*; the imperfective of a verb is usually referred to by the imperfective infinitive, which is *čitát'* in this case. The perfective is exemplified by *pročitájet, pročitál*; the perfective of a verb is usually referred to by the perfective infinitive, which is *pročitát'*, in this case. (Note that, despite the similarity between the terms "perfect" and "perfective," they have radically different meanings.)

English has the following aspectual oppositions: progressive (the "be . . .-ing" forms) versus nonprogressive (the other forms), and habitual ("used to . . .") versus nonhabitual (all other forms). Although both Russian and English have aspectual oppositions, there is no one-to-one correspondence between the particular aspectual oppositions that Russian makes and the particular aspectual oppositions that English makes. One point, however, is common to both languages: aspect is largely independent of tense, so that a given aspect can have several tenses.[16] (For information about tense and aspect in two quite different languages, see the next two chapters in this volume, Chapter IV, on Cape York Creole, sections 5.10, 5.11, and 5.12; and Chapter V, on Swahili, section 1.4.)

The basic difference between perfective and imperfective in Russian is that the perfective views a situation in its entirety, as a complete whole, including, but not distinguishing, beginning, middle, and end, if the situation can be broken up in this way. The imperfective does not view the situation as a whole, and most typically concentrates only on the internal part of the situation, on its internal structure, whereas the perfective abstracts away from internal complexity. This can be illustrated by contrasting *Víktor čitál knígu* and *Víktor pročitál knígu*. If someone says *Víktor pročitál knígu*, then we know not only that a past situation is being referred to, but also that the whole of the situation describable as Viktor's reading of the book is being referred to—he both

---

[16]In many grammars of English, all the verbal forms listed above are sometimes grouped together as different 'tenses,' but this is very misleading, since the distinction between tense and aspect (and, within tense, between absolute and relative tenses) must be maintained somehow. We thus disagree with analyses that claim that English differs from Russian in not having the category of aspect: both languages have this category, although the individual aspects are different between the two languages; just as both languages have case, but each language has a different set of cases.

began reading it and completed reading it at some time prior to the present. In *Víktor čitál knígu*, however, our attention is directed to the internal structure of Viktor's reading the book, and neither to the fact that he began reading it (one could imagine some supernatural being who has been reading an infinitely long text since the beginning of time) nor to the fact that he finished the book. Indeed, one cannot deduce from the imperfective that Viktor did finish the book, it is quite possible that he never finished it, as in *Víktor čitál knígu, no ne pročitál jejó* "Viktor was reading the book, but did not *read* (i.e., finish) it." Likewise we can form sentences like: *kogdá Napoleón vošjól v spál'nju, Žozefína čitála knígu; do rassvéta oná pročitála jejó* "When Napoleon entered the bedroom, Joséphine was reading a book; by dawn she had *read* (i.e., finished) it." The perfective form *pročitála* in the second part of this last sentence makes it clear that Joséphine did eventually complete the book; but in the situation referred to in the first part of the sentence, her reading the book was still in progress, and it is an internal part of this action of reading the book that is referred to. (The fact that the present moment is almost inevitably only an infinitesimal internal part of a situation explains why Russian lacks a perfective present.)

From a semantic viewpoint, there is the possibility of subdividing imperfectivity into two; that is, there are two different ways of viewing a situation as having internal structure. We can thus distinguish 'habitual' meaning from nonhabitual meaning. A habitual situation is viewed as holding or being repeated consistently over a sufficiently long period so that it can be considered typical of that long period. In English, explicit reference to habitual meaning can be given, in the past tense, by the use of the form "used to . . . ," as in "John used to read a book (every week)." It is not obligatory to make this distinction in English, however, since one can equally say "John read a book (every week)." Russian does not, in general, have a special form to indicate habituality; this is just one of the subcases of the imperfective, following from its general characterization as viewing a situation in terms of its internal structure: *Džón čitál knígu (kážduju nedélju)* is the way one translates "John used to read a book (every week)." It should be noted that although the English construction with "used to . . ." often indicates a repeated situation, as in the preceding sentence, it does not necessarily do so, since situations that are capable of being prolonged indefinitely can be treated as habitual without any need for repetition; for example "The marsh used to protect the factory" (Russian has *bolóto zaščiščálo zavód*, with imperfective *zaščiščát'*).

If we now turn to examples without habitual meaning, the reader may wonder what the precise relation is between the Russian perfective/imperfective opposition and the English progressive/nonprogressive opposition, particularly because in the foregoing examples with "read" there seemed to be one-to-one correspondence between the

English progressive and the Russian imperfective, between the English nonprogressive and the Russian perfective. And indeed the correspondence is very close, so long as we restrict ourselves to certain verbs, in particular, those referring to events (including actions) rather than states—verbs like *čitát'* "read" rather than *znát'* "know." In fact, if we exclude examples with habitual meaning (since the English progressive does not express habituality), the basic distinction between the Russian imperfective and the English progressive is that the latter is restricted, by and large, to dynamic (nonstative) verbs, so that whereas in English it is impossible to use the progressive of *know*, for instance in *when I arrived, John knew that I was near* (never *John was knowing that I was near*), it is possible to use the imperfective in the Russian gloss *kogdá já prišjól, Džón znál čto já blízko* (with *znát'*, imperfective, "know"). The relation among these various semantic aspectual distinctions is illustrated in Figure 3.1. The difference between aspect in English and aspect in Russian lies in the way the various semantic classes are grouped together to give formal classes. Russian opposes perfective to all the other aspects, which are collectively called the imperfective and which include the habitual, nonprogressive continuous and progressive. Note that we have two classes for the continuous: we reserve the term 'progressive' for continuous situations that are not states (as in "we were swimming for two hours") and 'nonprogressive continuous' for continuous states (as in "we were sick for two hours"). In the English past tense there is an optional contrast between habitual and nonhabitual (perfective, nonprogressive continuous and progressive); the most systematic contrast in English is between progressive and the rest (perfective, habitual, and nonprogressive continuous).

As a final observation on aspect in Russian, we may note that there is no general rule for forming the perfective of a given verb from its imperfective, or vice versa. Thus students of Russian have to learn, for

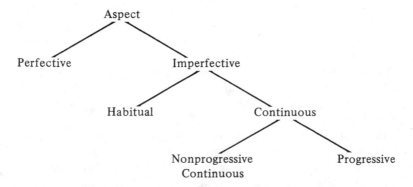

FIGURE 3.1 *Semantic Aspectual Classes*

each verb, the two aspectual infinitives of that verb; for example, *čitát'* (perfective *pročitát'*) "read," *ubivát'* (perfective *ubít'*) "kill." These two examples illustrate the commonest formal relations between perfective and imperfective. In the first, the perfective is formed by adding a prefix to the imperfective, although one cannot predict what prefix will be used for a particular verb. In the second, the imperfective is formed by adding a suffix (usually -$(y)v(a)$-) to the perfective.

2 RUSSIAN: LANGUAGE AND SOCIETY

2.1 Indo-European and Slavic

Russian, like most of the languages of Europe, belongs to the 'Indo-European' family of languages. It is thus a distant relative of English, and this relation can still be seen in the obvious similarity of some of the basic vocabulary, such as kinship terms and numerals, like Russian *brát* "brother," *mát'* "mother," *dvá* "two" (in older English the *w* was pronounced, as it still is in "twain"), *trí* "three." In some cases, related words have diverged so much in form that it takes detailed knowledge of the historical development of the two languages to establish the original relation, as with *dévjat'* "nine." Russian and English, however, are such distant relatives that for most of the vocabulary there is no such historically establishable relation. Both languages have, independently, innovated by changing the meanings of inherited forms, by borrowing words from other languages, by creating different words for new concepts, so that now English and Russian are mutually incomprehensible. To the west and southwest of the Russian-speaking area are some other languages which are much closer to Russian than is English: for instance, the Polish words corresponding to the Russian words listed above are *brat, matka, dwa, trzy, dziewięć*; the Czech equivalents are *bratr, matka, dva, tři, devět*; the Serbo-Croatian equivalents are *brat, mati, dva, tri, devet*. These languages form a subdivision of Indo-European, within which the individual languages are much closer to one another than to other Indo-European languages. The subdivision of Indo-European to which Russian, Polish, Czech, Serbo-Croatian, and some other languages noted below belong is called *Slavic*.[17] (The subdivision of Indo-European to which English belongs is the Germanic group of languages, including also German, Dutch, and the Scandinavian languages.)

At some time in the distant past, perhaps around 3000 B.C., it is assumed that the Indo-Europeans formed a reasonably homogeneous

---

[17]In Britain and some other English-speaking countries, the usual term is "Slavonic." It should be noted that of the languages spoken in this general geographical area, Hungarian and Romanian are not Slavic languages.

speech community, their language being the ancestor of the modern Indo-European languages. Because this period predates written history, there are no direct records of this language, which is often referred to as *Proto-Indo-European*. As a result of population movements and for other reasons, different sections of this original speech community broke off from one another, either losing contact completely with speakers of other Indo-European dialects or effectively isolating themselves from their neighbors so that their own dialects tended to develop along different lines. Proto-Indo-European, like nearly all attested languages, must already have had dialect differences, and with the breakup of the original speech community these dialect differences became more marked, leading ultimately to completely different languages. By the second half of the second millennium B.C., when the earliest written records of Indo-European languages started appearing, there were well-defined distinct languages, such as Hittite, (Ancient) Greek, and Sanskrit. In the course of the breakup of the Indo-European protolanguage, one of the new languages that emerged was Common Slavic, the ancestor of the modern Slavic languages; another was Common Germanic, the ancestor of the modern Germanic languages, including English.

If we compare the relations between the modern Germanic languages with the relations between the modern Slavic languages, we find that the various Slavic languages are much closer to one another than are the Germanic languages. Although speakers of the Scandinavian languages Danish, Norwegian, and Swedish can often understand one another with relatively little effort, speakers of, say, English, German, and Icelandic are in general quite unable to understand anything of a conversation in one of the other three of these languages, unless they have made a special study of that language, so great is the degree of differentiation that has been brought about by the passage of time and geographical separation. The Slavic languages are much closer to one another, and with a certain amount of effort speakers of most Slavic languages can make something of a simple conversation in almost any other Slavic language. This difference in closeness within the two language groups is a result of the fact that the breakup of Common Slavic unity occurred much later than that of Common Germanic. Almost to the end of the first millennium A.D. there seems to have been a single Common Slavic language, albeit with dialect differences that were subsequently to become the basis of different languages. By that time, Old English (Anglo-Saxon), Old High German, and Old Icelandic (Old Norse) were already distinct languages. In late Common Slavic, a series of such dialect differences provides a reasonably clear-cut division into three subgroups which are traditionally referred to as "East Slavic," "West Slavic," and "South Slavic," according to their geographic location.

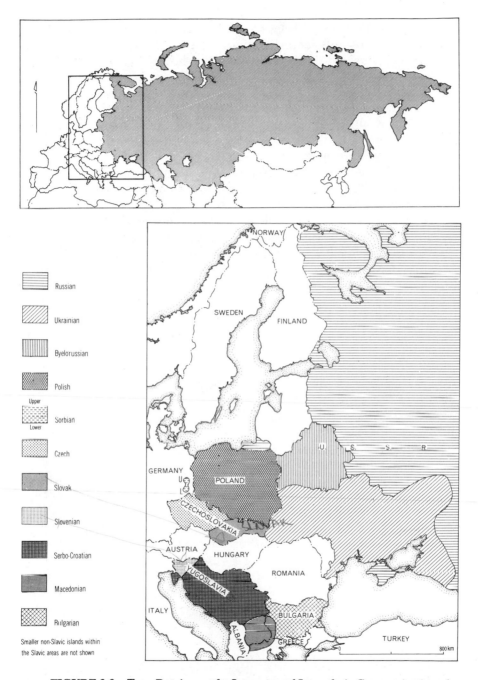

FIGURE 3.2 Top: *Russian as the Language of Interethnic Communication, the USSR.* Bottom: *Eastern Europe and the Slavic Languages Spoken as First Language.*

Source: Roman Jakobson, *Slavic Languages: A Condensed Survey*, 2nd ed., King's Crown Press, Columbia University, New York, 1955, map opposite p. 1.

From the East Slavic subgroup derive ultimately the modern East Slavic languages, Russian, Ukrainian, and Byelorussian; the last is sometimes referred to as White Russian, though this should not be confused with the political signification of the same term. From the West Slavic subgroup derive ultimately the modern West Slavic languages, Polish, Czech, Slovak, Upper Sorbian, and Lower Sorbian.[18] From the South Slavic subgroup ultimately derive the modern South Slavic languages, Bulgarian, Macedonian, Serbo-Croatian, and Slovenian. These languages are spoken in areas more or less coterminous with the corresponding political units. Russian is spoken in the European part of the Russian Soviet Federative Socialist Republic north of the Caucasus, though now also in much of Siberia and other parts of the Soviet Union. Ukrainian is spoken in the Ukrainian Soviet Socialist Republic; Byelorussian in the Byelorussian Soviet Socialist Republic (these are among the constituent republics of the Soviet Union); Polish in Poland; Czech and Slovak in Czechoslovakia (Slovakia is the eastern part); Bulgarian in Bulgaria; Macedonia in the Macedonian republic in southern Yugoslavia; Slovenian in the Slovenian republic in northwestern Yugoslavia; Serbo-Croatian in most of the rest of Yugoslavia (including the Serbian and Croatian republics). Upper and Lower Sorbian, which are distinct written languages, have no corresponding political units and are spoken in two enclaves surrounded by German-speakers near Bautzen and Cottbus in the German Democratic Republic. In addition to these modern languages, two now extinct Slavic languages have left written records; they are Old Church Slavic, a South Slavic language discussed in greater detail in section 2.2.1, and Polabian, a West Slavic language spoken until around 1700 in the neighborhood of Lüneburg in northern Germany.

Within the modern Slavic group as a whole, the languages within each of the three subgroups are in general closer to one another than they are to languages from either of the other two subgroups. This is illustrated in Table 3.2, which gives the words for "gold" and "candle" in the various modern languages. (Space does not allow a full account of the phonetics here, but it should be noted that *c* represents a sound similar to the one represented by *ts* in English *nuts*; *j* is like *y* of English *yes*; *ł* is like *w* of English *win*.) In these examples, two main distinguishing features of the three subgroups are involved. The first is the treatment of Common Slavic forms where the sequences *-or-* or *-ol-*[19]

---

[18]Kashubian is sometimes considered a separate language, in view of the considerable differences from other dialects of Polish, though its official status within Poland is as a dialect of Polish. Sorbian is sometimes referred to as Lusatian or Wendish.

[19]Common Slavic, like Proto-Indo-European, is not an attested language, and it is customary in historical linguistics to prefix hypothesized forms of nonattested languages with an asterisk (not to be confused with the use of the asterisk in syntax to indicate ungrammatical sentences).

TABLE 3.2 *"Gold" and "Candle" in the Slavic Languages*

Language	gold	candle
Common Slavic	*zolto	*světja
South Slavic		
Old Church Slavic	zlato	svěšta
Bulgarian	zlato	svjašt
Macedonian	zlato	svek'a
Serbo-Croatian	zlato	sveća/svijeća
Slovenian	zlato	sveča
East Slavic		
Russian	zóloto	svečá
Byelorussian	zolata	svjača
Ukrainian	zoloto	sviča
West Slavic		
Czech	zlato	svíce
Slovak	zlato	svieca
Polish	złoto	świeca
Upper Sorbian	złoto	swěca

occur between consonants (as in Common Slavic *zolto "gold"): in East Slavic, these sequences give -oro- and -olo-, respectively;[20] in South Slavic, they give -ra- and -la-; West Slavic is not homogeneous with respect to this feature, since Czech and Slovak give -ra-, -la-, while Polish and the Sorbian languages give -ro-, -ło-. The second is the treatment of Common Slavic *tj (as in *světja "candle"): East Slavic gives č; West Slavic gives c; while South Slavic is not homogeneous, giving št, ć (Macedonian k' regularly corresponds to Serbo-Croatian ć), and č. If we take both features together (and there are numerous other features that back up this differentiation into three subgroups), then we can isolate each of East, West, and South Slavic, although the last two are (with respect to these features, and more generally) less homogeneous than East Slavic.

It is important to bear in mind that the kinds of correspondence illustrated by, say, Russian zóloto versus Serbo-Croatian zlato are not restricted to isolated words, but are regular phonetic correspondences; compare, for instance, the Russian words voróna "crow," solóma "straw," górod "town," with their equivalents in Serbo-Croatian, vrana, slama (usually slamka, etymologically a diminutive), grad; in Polish, wrona, słoma, gród; in Czech, vrána, sláma, hrad (in Modern Polish and Czech, gród and hrad usually mean "castle"). It is the systematic

---

[20]Byelorussian has *zolata* because Byelorussian, unlike Russian, reflects the pronunciation of unstressed *o* as *a* in spelling.

nature of these correspondences that enables us to justify the tripartite division of Slavic, and in general such systematic correspondences are at the basis of work in historical and comparative linguistics.

At the beginning of the present millennium, the division between the three main subgroups of Slavic was firmly established, although the subgroups were still very close linguistically. South Slavic was cut off geographically from the other Slavic languages as a result of movements of Romance-speaking population (the modern Romanians) and the incursion of the Magyars (Hungarians). Although East Slavic had a long common frontier with Polish and a smaller common frontier with Slovak, at this period this was probably a fairly clear-cut dialect boundary, (later to be a language boundary), accentuated by the political unification of Poland at the beginning of our millennium. In fact, political developments play an important role in the later development of relations among the Slavic languages, including Russian. Let us examine East Slavic first.

2.2 Old Russian

East Slavic at the beginning of the present millennium was very homogeneous, with scarcely a trace of the later divisions that were to differentiate Russian, Ukrainian, and Byelorussian. As we are now entering the period of recorded history for the East Slavs (from the end of the first millennium A.D.), there exist actual texts from which we can draw evidence for the period concerned. It is usual to refer to texts from this early period as *Old Russian*, though Old East Slavic would be more accurate, given that the division into three East Slavic languages had not yet taken place. In fact, the main dialect division in Old Russian is between northern and southern East Slavic, divided roughly by a line running somewhat south of the latitude of present-day Moscow. At the time in question, there was no single unified East Slavic political state but, rather, a number of small political units, of which the two most important were Kiev, most of southern East Slavic, and Novgorod, the most important state in the north. This division between north and south is still the basic dialect division within modern Russian, a point to which we return in section 2.4, with examples of some of the most important distinguishing features. The main changes that were to affect this north/south division within East Slavic were 1) the separation of Ukrainian, then of Byelorussian, from the rest of East Slavic, which can then properly be referred to as Russian, and 2) the development of a band of central dialects incorporating features of both northern and southern dialects and finally providing the basis for the development of a unified Russian language. Both of these developments were fostered by political events, as will be discussed in sections 2.3 and 2.4.

2.2.1 *Old Church Slavic*   One further strand remains to be woven into the scenario. This is the effect of Christianization on the further development of the relations between the Slavic languages. A key role is played here by Old Church Slavic, a South Slavic language and the oldest documented Slavic language. In the ninth century, dialects of Slavic were spoken rather farther southwards than at present. In particular, the town of Salonika was bilingual (Greek and Slavic); Salonika is in the north of present-day Greece, and at this time was part of the Byzantine Empire, where the official language was Greek and the official religion Orthodoxy. The Slavs had not yet (with isolated exceptions) been converted to Christianity, and one of the first groups to be converted was the Moravians, in what is now Central Czechoslovakia. Upon their conversion, their prince sent an envoy to Byzantium asking to be sent someone who could teach the Slavs about Christianity in their own language. The Byzantine emperor readily agreed to this because Byzantium, unlike Rome of the same time, believed in teaching the faith to each nation in its own language. The Byzantine emperor sent two natives of Salonika, Constantine (better known under the name of Cyril, which he took when he became a monk) and his brother Methodius; both were Greek but fluent in both Greek and Slavic. Prior to leaving for Moravia, Constantine devised an alphabet for writing Slavic (more especially the Slavic dialect of Salonika) and started translating various religious works into what later came to be termed Old Church Slavic (or Old Slavic, or Old Bulgarian). Two alphabets were used, the Glagolitic and the Cyrillic, and while the precise relation between them is unclear, it is probable that the Glagolitic is the earlier; it soon fell into disuse, replaced by the Cyrillic alphabet. The Cyrillic alphabet is closely modeled on the Greek alphabet, with additional letters for sounds not found in (Byzantine) Greek—in fact, the alphabet provides a near perfect fit to the sounds of this Slavic dialect. This alphabet, in slightly modified form, still serves as the alphabet for Russian (see Table 3.3), Ukrainian, Byelorussian, Bulgarian, Macedonian, and Serbo-Croatian (especially in Serbia).

In terms of the criteria for distinguishing the three main groups of Slavic, Old Church Slavic is clearly a South Slavic language (compare the forms of *svěšta* "candle" and the forms of *zlato* "gold" in Table 3.2), indeed it must be regarded as a very peripheral South Slavic dialect, spoken at the southernmost extremity of the Slavic-speaking world (the present-day Slavic/Greek linguistic boundary runs to the north of Salonika). However, the various Slavic dialects were so close at this time, the period of the dissolution of Common Slavic, that texts composed in the Salonika dialect by Constantine were readily comprehensible to other Slavs, in particular, the West Slavs of Moravia. Although Old Church Slavic manuscripts do contain forms that clearly betray the different geographical origins of the various scribes who

TABLE 3.3   The Russian Alphabet

Russian	Transliteration	Russian	Transliteration
а	a	п	p
б	b	р	r
в	v	с	s
г	g	т	t
д	d	у	u
е	je (but e after	ф	f
	a consonant)	х	x
ё	jo	ц	c
ж	ž	ч	č
з	z	ш	š
и	i	щ	šč
й	j	ъ	″
к	k	ы	y
л	l	ь	´
м	m	э	è
н	n	ю	ju
о	o	я	ja

wrote and copied them, introducing forms from their own dialects, such differences as existed were no impediment to communication.

Unfortunately, political rivalry between Byzantium and Rome (more specifically, the pro-German party in Moravia) led to a conflict between the advocates of the Old Church Slavic Orthodox liturgy and the Latin Roman Catholic liturgy. The end result of this conflict was a division of the Slavic world into two cultural zones. There was a western zone of Roman Catholic religion, where the official language was Latin and the vernaculars developed only very slowly as written languages; these included all of West Slavic, Slovenian, and the Croatian half of Serbo-Croatian. The eastern cultural zone had Orthodox religion, with Old Church Slavic (of which later, local versions are usually referred to as "Church Slavic") serving as the liturgical language and having a profound effect on the secular language too. In this zone were most of the East Slavs, from their Christianization officially in 988, plus the remainder of the South Slavs. This cultural division still survives in the alphabets used by the different Slavic languages. West Slavic languages all use the Latin alphabet; East Slavic languages all use the Cyrillic alphabet. Of the South Slavic languages, Slovenian uses the Latin alphabet, Bulgarian and Macedonian the Cyrillic alphabet, and Serbo-Croatian may be written in either the Cyrillic alphabet (by the Orthodox Serbs) or in the Latin alphabet (by the Catholic Croats). The cultural difference survives even where religious adherence per se has disappeared.

Church Slavic has had a profound influence on the later development of the Russian language, especially on vocabulary. The earliest Russian texts are either religious texts written primarily in the local version of Church Slavic, with only occasional scribal errors or insertions revealing specifically East Slavic features; or secular texts (legal documents, treaties) written in Slavonicized, that is, influenced by Church Slavic, East Slavic. Often doublets of the type *zoloto/zlato* "gold" both occur in the same text, with no apparent reason for the choice now of the one, now the other. It is doubtful whether the Old Russian scribes consciously thought of their native East Slavic and Church Slavic as distinct languages, or even as distinct (geographical) dialects. The difference between native and Church Slavic forms was primarily stylistic: the higher the style, the more Church Slavic forms. Only in occasional private letters and commercial documents do we find pure East Slavic being written. The situation, both at this stage and in later development, is in many ways analogous to that of English (Anglo-Saxon) and Norman French in post-Conquest England, with Norman French providing most of the learned vocabulary and even some quite common words (modern English *very* is of Norman French origin), even in texts written in English. There is, of course, an important difference: Russian and (Old) Church Slavic were extremely close; many forms were exactly the same in both languages, whereas Old English and Norman French were radically different languages, the one Germanic, the other Romance. The kind of situation found in Old Russian is often referred to as 'diglossia': two varieties of the same language serve different stylistic and social functions.

Church Slavic influence can still be seen throughout modern Russian. Very often, one finds that both East Slavic and Church Slavic roots survive, the latter primarily in more learned parts of the vocabulary. Using examples with East Slavic *-oro-*, *-olo-*, and South Slavic *-ra-*, *-la-*, compare *gólos* "voice" with *soglásije* "agreement" (literally, "with-voiceness"), *pórox* "powder" with *práx* "ashes" (the remains from cremation), *korótkij* "short" with *krátkij* "brief," and *voróta* "gate" with *cárskije vratá*, literally "royal gate," referring to part of the iconostasis in an Orthodox Church. The usual modern Russian word for "town, city" is *górod*, but many city names have the stylistically elevated *-grad*, as does *Leningrád*. In some cases, there seems to be no reason for the triumph of the Church Slavic form; for example, *sládkij* "sweet" has survived where Old Russian also had *solodkij*. In modern Russian, it is usually the case that in a given meaning one can use only either the East Slavic or the Church Slavic form (apart from rhetorical verse, where more Church Slavic forms are possible), but this semantic differentiation has only gradually emerged over the course of the development of standard Russian, as we shall see in section 2.4.

2.3 Breakup of East Slavic

Returning now to internal divisions of East Slavic, we shall examine the factors leading to the separation of Ukrainian and Byelorussian from Russian, and to the unification of Russian across the old north/south dialect division within East Slavic. The main factor to be considered here is the political separation of the western part of East Slavic territory (roughly modern Ukraine and Byelorussia) from the rest of East Slavic territory. The Kievan state did not prove stable enough to withstand combined onslaughts from the west, from Poland, and from the east, from the Tatars (Turkic peoples); outside of the Kievan state, there was no unifying force during the earlier part of our millennium to withstand these incursions. The result is that the western parts of East Slavic territory became, politically, part of the Polish-Lithuanian sphere of influence, while the main body of the East Slavs were, from the thirteenth to the fifteenth centuries, under Tatar suzerainty, "the Tatar yoke."

The separation of Ukrainian from the main body of East Slavic is the more apparent, with most of the characteristic features of Ukrainian developing in the thirteenth and fourteenth centuries, in particular the shift of the originally long vowel *ě* and of lengthened *e* and *o* to give *i*: Ukrainian has *vil* "ox" and *lito* "summer," where Russian has *vól* and *léto* (Old Russian *lěto*). The most notable area of Polish influence is in vocabulary, where many Ukrainian words, especially those relating to abstract terminology and technical terms developed subsequently to the split from the rest of East Slavic, are closer to Polish than to Russian; compare Ukrainian *panstvo* "state, kingdom," Polish *państwo*, and Russian *gosudárstvo*; also compare Ukrainian *drukuvaty* "to print," Polish *drukować* (ultimately from German *drucken*), and Russian *pečát-at'*. This pattern even appears with some nontechnical terms; compare Ukrainian *čekaty* "to wait," Polish *czekać*, and Russian *ždát'*. Vocabulary differences are, in fact, the main feature making it difficult for the monolingual Russian-speaker to read a text in Ukrainian that contains any abstract or technical terminology.[21] The extent of Polish influence on Ukrainian and of isolation from Russian is more marked in the western Ukraine, which was under Polish cultural domination even during the partition of Poland, when eastern Poland was politically part of the Russian Empire, and did not revert to the East Slavic cultural area

---

[21]In this connection, we might note that it is relatively easy for a monolingual Russian-speaker to make something of a similar text written in Bulgarian, although Bulgarian is, from a historical viewpoint, much more distant from Russian than is Ukrainian. Much of Bulgarian technical and abstract vocabulary was borrowed directly from Russian, with only minor phonetic modifications, in the course of the development of literary Bulgarian during the late nineteenth century. The importance of cultural factors in language development is again apparent.

132

until the redrawing of frontiers after the Second World War. The rest of the Ukraine effectively rejoined Russia with the first partition of Poland in 1772. Some other effects of the long period of separation may be noted. First, Ukrainian was much less subject to Church Slavic influence than was Russian, so that the Ukrainian for "sweet," for instance, is *solodkyj* (compare Russian *sládkij*, noted previously); conversely, Ukrainian was more influenced by western European loanwords at this time (see the comparison of *drukuvaty* just given). Second, Ukrainian was excluded from the spread of '*akanie,*' nondistinction of unstressed *o* and *a* (see section 2.4), one of the main features shoring up the division between northern and southern dialects of Russian; with regard to *akanie*, Ukrainian is thus similar to northern Russian dialects, despite its origin as part of southern East Slavic.

Byelorussian occupies, linguistically, a position midway between Russian and Ukrainian, though it is closer to the latter. Its separation from Russian occurred with the annexation of Byelorussia by Lithuania, and the development of Byelorussian was strongly influenced by Polish after the Union of Lublin between Lithuania and Poland (1569). That Byelorussian was less isolated from Russian than was Ukrainian is illustrated by the spread of *akanie* to Byelorussian.

Whether Russian, Ukrainian, and Byelorussian should be regarded as three distinct languages or as dialects of one language has been a vexed question for much of recent East Slavic history. The Tsarist government effectively treated Ukrainian and Byelorussian as dialects of Russian. Apart from a period before the Union of Lublin when a form of Byelorussian was used as the written language of the Lithuanian state, neither Byelorussian nor Ukrainian had any official status before the Russian Revolution, although Ukrainian, at least, was developed unofficially as the medium of a clearly distinct ethnic group. Since the October Revolution of 1917,[22] all three East Slavic languages have had official status as distinct languages. Inevitably, the influence of Russian on the other two languages is strong, given political unification within the Soviet Union. Thus many modern dictionaries of Ukrainian, for instance, give the word for "ninety" as *dev'janosto* (Russian has *devjanósto*), although the traditional Ukrainian form is *dev'jatdesjat*. A standard Ukrainian written language existed, effectively, before the Revolution; this was not true of Byelorussian, and the dialect base of the standard language has been changed in the course of the development of a written language in the twentieth century, thus creating difficulties in

---

[22]The Russian calendar used before the Revolution differed by thirteen days from that used in the rest of Europe and adopted in Russia after the Revolution. The Revolution took place on October 25 according to the old calendar (whence the name 'October Revolution'), but on November 7 according to the new calendar (which is why the anniversary of the October Revolution is celebrated on November 7 in the Soviet Union).

this development, which means that standard Byleorussian is much less well established than standard Ukrainian and, especially, standard Russian.

2.4   Unification of Russian

Meanwhile, in the main body of East Slavic territory, a process of political and concomitant linguistic unification was taking place. In the struggle against the Tatars, a dominant role came to be played by the princes of Muscovy, the area around Moscow. Towards the end of the fifteenth century, Muscovy was already in control of most of European Russian proper, including Novgorod (captured in 1478), effectively the last internal resistance to Muscovite expansion. In the middle of the sixteenth century, the conflict with the Tatars was finally resolved by the capture of their strongholds of Kazan (1552) and Astrakhan (1556). The conquest of Kazan is particularly important in that it opened the way to Russian colonization of Siberia. This period thus marks the beginning of a unified Russian state.

Moscow is situated towards the southern extremity of what was originally the northern dialect area of East Slavic. Because of population movements northwards as a result of Tatar incursions, and because Moscow was a population magnet in the course of the consolidation of the Russian state, however, this southern part of the northern dialect area was strongly influenced by features of the southern dialects, adopting some (but not all) of them, giving rise ultimately to a new dialect area, the so-called central dialects, including that of Moscow. This process can be illustrated by looking at two of the most salient features that distinguish the northern and southern dialects. The first is *akanie*, or the pronunciation of unstressed *o* and *a* alike, similar to stressed *a*,[23] in the southern dialects, so that for instance *vodá* "water" is pronounced as if it were *vadá*; its plural, which has a different stress, is *vódy*, where the *o* is pronounced as such because it is stressed; contrast *travá* "grass," with original *a*, and plural *trávy*. In the northern dialects, unstressed *o* remains (*okanie*). This southern dialect feature of *akanie* was adopted by the central dialects (and also, as noted above, by Byelorussian). The second southern dialect feature is the pronunciation of *g* as a voiced velar fricative (International Phonetic Alphabet symbol [ɣ]), whereas the northern dialects have a voiced velar plosive (much as English *g* of *go*), as in *górod* "city." This southern dialect feature was not adopted by the central dialects, which thus combine some southern features with some northern features. The emergent standard language

---

[23]More accurately, when immediately preceding the stressed syllable or in word-initial position as a low-mid back unrounded vowel (IPA [ʌ]), elsewhere as a mid-central (neutral) vowel (IPA [ə]) like the *a* of English *sofa*.

was based primarily on the dialect of Moscow, i.e., on a central dialect, so that the standard language too combines features of northern and southern dialects (in particular, it requires *akanie* and plosive *g* in pronunciation; although the more conservative spelling system still writes unstressed *o*, as in *vodá*).

In this way, the dialect base of standard Russian was established, essentially, as a result of political developments. By the eighteenth century, there were still, however, two outstanding general problems in the establishment of the standard language: the relation between Church Slavic and native Russian forms and the role of loanwords. As indicated in section 2.2, at earlier stages in the development of Russian the difference between Church Slavic and native Russian was primarily stylistic, Church Slavic forms being used in the higher styles, for example, for liturgical and rhetorical writings. In the eighteenth century, the brilliant Russian polymath Lomonosov attempted to codify this stylistic difference in his theory of the three styles: Church Slavic without native Russian was to be used for the high style, as in liturgy and rhetoric; native Russian without Church Slavic (except, of course, for such forms as *sládkij* "sweet," which had ousted their native Russian equivalents completely) was to be used for the low style, as in comedy; while a mixture was to be used for the middle style, as in most drama. The subsequent development of the relation between Church Slavic and native Russian did not, in fact, follow this path. In the work of the early nineteenth-century writer Puškin, usually considered the founder of modern Russian literature, we find overall the same use of Church Slavic and native Russian forms as in the language of today: in general, for a given word either the Church Slavic or the native Russian form is used in all styles. The only real exception to this is that an artificially high-flown style can be created, for instance in rhetorical verse, by using Church Slavic forms where other styles would use native Russian.

The influx of foreign (mainly Western European) loanwords into Russian is particularly marked from the time of Tsar Peter the Great (1672–1725). Peter the Great was primarily responsible for the opening up of Russia—or rather of the Russian upper class—to the influence of Western European culture and technology. There had been loanwords entering Russian before this period, for instance from Turkic languages and, to a limited extent, from Western European languages often via Polish and Ukrainian, but it is only from this period that there is any marked influx of loanwords. The loanwords are primarily concerned with specific features of technology and technical terms in the arts, although in a few fields Russian devised its own terminology using native resources (native East Slavic and Church Slavic): for instance, Russian grammatical terminology is largely homegrown, often calquing (translating literally the component parts of) Latin or Greek terms; for example, *imenítel'nyj* "nominative" from *ímja* the Russian gloss of Latin *nomen* "name," and *vinítel'nyj* "accusative" is from *vinít'* the Russian gloss of Latin *accusare* "to accuse." As in many European languages, the problem of whether loanwords should be replaced by native neologisms has reared its head at several times in the development of Russian since the early eighteenth century. In the period immediately after the Second World War, for instance, soccer terms borrowed from English were replaced by native formations, so that *golkíper* was replaced by *vratár'* "goalkeeper" (literally, "gate-man," from Church Slavic *vratá* "gate"). Overall, the process has been one of natural acceptance or rejection of foreign words, rather than of the application of an explicitly puristic policy. It is interesting in this respect to compare Western European loanwords in Russian with those in other Slavic languages. Polish has more common everyday words of Latin origin, reflecting the greater influence of Latin on everyday life via the Catholic Church and the fact that Poland was never cut off from Western European culture in the way that Russia was. Czech and Serbo-Croatian developed later than Russian or Polish as national standard languages, and in their development were therefore more subject to nationalistic, puristic pressures against loanwords, despite the strong influence of Western culture in Czechoslovakia in particular. Thus while Russians are quite happy with the international word *teátr* "theater," as are the Poles (*teatr*), the Czechs devised their own word *divadlo* (from a root meaning "look at"), the Serbs *pozorište* (from a root meaning "see"), and the Croats *kazalište* (from a root meaning "show").[24]

By the end of the first quarter of the nineteenth century, the basic outlines of standard Russian as it is today had evolved. In particular, there had been established the dialect base of the standard language, the relation between native Russian and Church Slavic elements, and (apart from vocabulary changes due to subsequent technological and cultural developments) the limits for foreign (especially Western European) loans. For this reason, modern Russian is often defined as the Russian language from the time of Puškin (1799–1837) to the present. During the early nineteenth century, this form of Russian became the accepted mode of written and oral communication among educated Russians, many of whom had previously preferred French, in which most educated Russians of the time were bilingual. By the end of the century, Russian was the vehicle of one of Europe's major literatures.

---

[24]The different cultural history of the Serbs (traditionally of Orthodox religion and having undergone a long period of Ottoman occupation) and Croats (traditionally of Roman Catholic religion, and having undergone a long period of Austrian occupation) still shows itself in the existence of two varieties of Serbo-Croatian, which differ in vocabulary, pronunciation, and alphabet. Thus Serbs would normally say *pozorište* "theater," pronounce *sveća* "candle," and write both in the Cyrillic alphabet; Croats would normally say *kazalište* "theater," pronounce *svijeća* "candle," and write both in the Latin alphabet.

2.5 Russian in Soviet Russia

The use of the term "educated Russians" in the preceding paragraph is an important qualification on the universality of standard Russian among the Russian population throughout the nineteenth and into the twentieth century. Despite the vast geographical area across which Russian is spoken (even excluding zones of recent expansion like Siberia), Russian varies relatively little dialectally, much less so than British English or German, for instance. Nonetheless, geographical and social dialects did and do exist within Russian. Even at the beginning of the twentieth century, the majority of Russians—excluding educated town-dwellers, a smaller number of rural educated people, and an even smaller number of urban workers with a little education—spoke their local dialects, and although standard Russian was normally comprehensible to them, they did not speak it or an approximation to it. Moreover, the overwhelming majority of the population was illiterate. According to the census of 1897, only 21 percent of the population of the Russian Empire (excluding children under nine) was able to read; for European Russia, the figure was 30 percent, above the average for the Empire but still very low by Western European standards. According to the census of 1970, by contrast, 99.7 percent of the population of the Soviet Union between the ages of nine and forty-nine was able to read (the corresponding figure in 1897 for the Russian Empire was 28.4 percent). In dealing with the social development of standard Russian in the twentieth century, one of the main factors to be borne in mind is the 'democratization' of the standard language. The standard dialect of the Russian language is now the property not just of a small educated elite, but of the population as a whole. This applies in particular to the written standard language, although standardization in pronunciation and other aspects of the spoken language is also well advanced in Soviet Russia. On the other hand, various social groups that did not previously have access to the standard dialect have, in the process of their assimilation to the standard, affected the further development of that standard. Thus there is a two-way interplay between the traditional standard dialect and the dialects of the previously underprivileged classes. A process of this kind has been in action in most European countries during the nineteenth and twentieth centuries, but perhaps nowhere has the change been so marked or so sudden as in Soviet Russia.

In Russian, the influence of the traditional standard has been much more powerful overall, so that there is no real break between pre-Soviet and Soviet Russian (recall the definition noted above of modern Russian as the Russian language from Puškin to the present day). Nonetheless, certain changes that have taken place and are taking place in the development of the standard can be attributed to the influence of sections of the population that previously spoke nonstandard Russian, and have introduced these previously nonstandard features into the standard.

Detailed information on the correlation of variants within and around the standard language has become available in recent years as a result of a project "Russian language and Soviet society" carried out by the Russian Language Institute of the Soviet Academy of Sciences since the late fifties. In general, the results are very much as might have been expected where there is a choice between an older, traditional form or construction in the standard language and a newer form which is only now gaining acceptance in the standard. The newer forms tend to be used by younger speakers, by less well educated speakers, and by speakers whose work means that they have less contact with the traditional standard (like industrial workers, as opposed to writers). The results of this project are discussed in more detail in the book by Comrie and Stone referred to in the "Suggestions for Further Reading."

One of the main kinds of change in the pronunciation of Russian since the beginning of the twentieth century has been the spread of a number of spelling pronunciations. Such pronunciations owe their existence to the influence of the orthographic system; for example, many English-speakers now pronounce the *t* of *often* because it is there in the spelling. Just to give one example from Russian, educated Muscovites at the beginning of the century pronounced the verbal form *strójat* "(they) build" as if it were spelled *strójut*; nowadays, by far the more usual pronunciation is the one following the spelling *strójat*. Although in general the fit between Russian spelling and Russian pronunciation is very close, and was very close at the beginning of the century, there are several discrepancies like this, and their number has been reduced over the course of the twentieth century. The social factors leading to spelling pronunciations are interesting to consider: probably most of the speakers of nonstandard Russian who have acquired standard Russian during the twentieth century have done so with strong influence from the written language. In going over to a spoken standard, they were naturally influenced by the fact that the standard language was for them essentially the written form of the standard; they followed the standard as closely in speech as was possible and consistent with what knowledge they had about the pronunciation of educated people, but this knowledge did not always extend to small details of pronunciation.

2.5.1 *Sex and Gender Conflicts*   In section 1.3, we noted that in Russian, there is in general correspondence between the declensional class of a noun, the grammatical gender of that noun, and, if the noun refers to a human being, the natural sex of the referent of that noun, as there is in *žená* "wife" (second declension, feminine, female) and *múž* "husband" (declension 1a, masculine, male). There are a few exceptions to this rule, because several masculine nouns referring to males, especially pet names used instead of given names, belong to the second declension (*Volódja* is the diminutive of *Vladímir*; *Kólja*, the diminutive of *Nikoláj*), but in general the rule holds firmly. There are several occupations and professions which, before the October Revolution, were exclusively or predominantly carried out by men, for instance *vráč* "(medical) doctor." One of the main changes that has taken place in Soviet society during the twentieth century, especially since the Revolution of 1917, has been the opening up of the vast majority of occupations and professions to women as well as men. At present, there are in fact far more women doctors than men doctors in the Soviet Union, especially among general practitioners. This leads to a conflict between biological sex and grammatical gender, where the noun *vráč* is used in reference to a woman. The noun is of morphological class 1a, and this is quite rigid in Russian: there is no possibility of using inflections from declensions 2 or 3, to which most feminine nouns belong. However, there is variation in current usage in whether the grammatical gender of such nouns, used in reference to women, is masculine or feminine, as becomes apparent in the forms of verbs and adjectives used in agreement with them. If we want to say "The doctor has arrived," do we say *vráč prišjól* (masculine) or do we say *vráč prišlá* (feminine)? In referring to a "young doctor," do we say *molodój vráč* (masculine) or *molodája vráč* (feminine)? The general question in such instances is thus: do we follow grammatical gender or do we follow natural (biological) sex? In traditional usage the conflict arose relatively rarely, since so few occasions arose for talking about women doctors— there were almost none. But where such occasions did arise, traditional usage was quite clear: grammatical gender prevailed (hence *vráč prišjól*, *molodój vráč*), despite the slight awkwardness in having masculine grammatical forms used in reference to a woman. However, over the course of the twentieth century this usage has changed, with adjectives of feminine gender coming to be used to match the sex of the referent rather than the declensional class and traditional gender of the noun.

In a survey carried out as part of the "Russian language and Soviet society" project, native speakers of Russian were asked which of the two alternatives they preferred, taking the particular case of women doctors, among others. Their responses were classified according to the age and social group of the speaker. Of the alternants *vráč prišjól/vráč prišlá*, the oldest of the five age groups (born before 1909) showed a slight preference for grammatical agreement with the predicate form, choosing *vráč prišjól*; the ratio was 49.8 percent to 42.2 percent. (In these statistics, the difference between the total and 100 percent is composed of the "don't knows".) Each of the other four age groups, born in 1910–1919, 1920–1929, 1930–1939, or 1940–1949 preferred the form with semantic agreement (*vráč prišlá*), the greatest change having taken place among the youngest speakers (53.1 percent to 37.3 percent for those born in 1940–49). The social classification used the following categories: intellectuals (subdivided into language and literature specialists and others), white-collar workers, industrial workers, writers and journalists, students (subdivided into language and literature majors and others). Of these social groups, only writers and journalists showed preference for *vráč prišjól*, the form displaying grammatical agreement (50.7 percent to 41.3 percent). All the others preferred *vráč prišlá*, the preference being particularly marked with industrial workers (56.5 to 33.4 percent) and white-collar workers (56.4 to 34.6 percent). This accords with the view that writers and other educated speakers are particularly conservative with respect to innovations in the standard language, whereas, such innovations are introduced and spread in the first instance by social groups who did not traditionally speak the standard language (in particular, workers).

A similar test was carried out for attributive adjectives, using the expression *xoróšij buxgálter* (masculine adjective, grammatical agreement) versus *xoróšaja buxgálter* (feminine adjective, semantic agreement) "good bookkeeper," referring to a woman, The trend is exactly the same as for predicate agreement: the younger age groups gave the feminine form more often than the older age groups did; workers gave the feminine form more often than did writers and journalists. Despite the statistical trend, in absolute numbers all social groups and age groups showed preference for grammatical agreement for the attributive adjectives. (For those born before 1901, the ratio was 83.5 percent to 12.5 percent; for those born after 1940, 66.9 to 28.4 percent; for writers and journalists, 87 to 13 percent; for industrial workers, 55 to 38.7 percent).

Thus we can say that although the conflict between sex and grammatical gender is working itself out in favor of sex overall, the extent to which sex prevails is different in different parts of the grammar. Thus one finds sentences of the type *xoróšij* (masculine) *vráč prišlá* (feminine) "the good doctor arrived" used quite naturally in contemporary Russian, reflecting the near victory of semantic agreement for predicates and the much greater tenacity of grammatical agreement with attributes.

The example of natural sex versus grammatical gender agreement in contemporary Russian is of sociolinguistic interest from two viewpoints. First, the traditional assignment of sex roles is reflected in the fact that certain names of occupations have forms for only one sex and gender (usually masculine). Because of social changes language and social reality have been out of step, and the spread of semantic agreement (albeit inconsistently) can be seen as a reflection of this conflict. Second, reactions of native speakers to the traditional and to the newer usage in this matter demonstrate the correlation between different linguistic variants and different social groups. The traditional form is more likely to be preferred by older speakers and by those closest to the traditional group of educated people. The newer forms are more likely to be preferred by younger speakers and by those who have most recently been absorbed into the set of speakers of the standard language.

2.6 Russian in the Soviet Union

There is one aspect of the sociolinguistic situation of contemporary Russian that we have not mentioned at all so far. Russian-speakers form part of a much larger political entity, the Union of Soviet Socialist Republics, which comprises a number of other ethnic groups, speaking a variety of other languages in addition to Russian and the closely related Ukrainian and Byelorussian. Russian is the native language of just over half the population of the Soviet Union. Russian is spoken by 58.7 percent of the population, according to the census of 1970, from which the other statistics below are also quoted; the total population of the Soviet Union in 1970, according to this census, was about 241,720,000. It is difficult to give an exact number to the languages spoken in the Soviet Union, mainly because in many cases it is unclear whether different speech forms are to be regarded as distinct languages or as dialects of the same language, but most Soviet sources give a number around 120 to 130. Some of these languages are Indo-European, belonging to branches other than Slavic. One of these groups is Baltic, comprising the Lithuanian and Latvian languages; within Indo-European, these are the languages closest to Slavic, although the two groups are not mutually intelligible. Other Indo-European branches represented are Iranian and Armenian; the Iranian language with the largest number of speakers is Tadjik, a form of Farsi or Persian. Many languages spoken in the USSR, however, are genetically quite unrelated to Indo-European. The Soviet Union contains, for instance, many Uralic (Finno-Ugric and Samoyedic) languages, the best known being Estonian, a fairly close relative of Finnish. Turkic languages, closely related to the Turkish of Turkey, are spoken in Central Asia and some other parts of the Soviet Union. The Tungusic languages of Siberia and the Mongolian languages Buryat and Kalmuck (closely related to Mongolian proper, of Mongolia) are possibly distant relatives of Turkic, the three groups together forming the Altaic family. In the Caucasus, three language groups are represented, apart from members of other families (like Armenian). They are South Caucasian, the main language being Georgian with some three million speakers; North-West Caucasian; and North-East Caucasian. Whether any or all of these three groups are genetically related is still a matter of controversy. In Siberia, a number of languages are spoken which have few or no known related languages. Three languages, Chukchee, Koryak, and Itelmen (otherwise known as Kamchadal) form a genetically related family spoken in the far east of Siberia (in the Chukotka and Kamchatka peninsulas). Three other languages there, Yukaghir, Nivkh (otherwise known as Gilyak), and Ket (otherwise

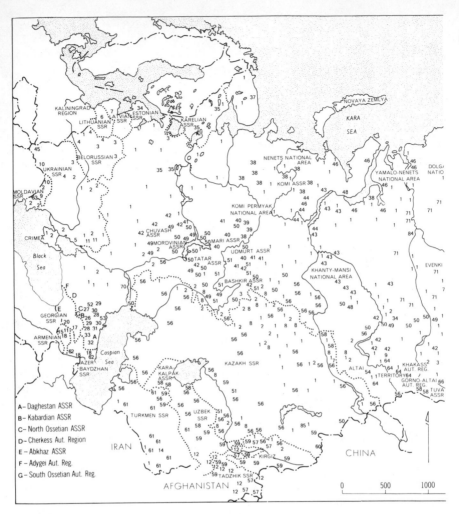

FIGURE 3.3 *Distribution of Ethnic Groups and Languages in the U.S.S.R.*

Key to map

INDO-EUROPEAN	Romance	CAUCASIAN	URALIC
Slavic	9 Moldavian	20 Georgian	**Balto-Fennic**
1 Russian	10 Romanian	21 Abkhaz	34 Estonian
2 Ukrainian	**Iranian**	22 Abaza	35 Karelian
3 Byelorussian	12 Tadzhik	23 Kabardian	36 Veps
4 Polish	14 Beludzhi (Balochi)	24 Cherkess (Circassian)	**Lappish**
5 Bulgarian	15 Kurdish	25 Adygei	37 Saame (Lappish)
Baltic	16 Tat	26 Chechen	**Permic**
6 Lithuanian	17 Ossetian	27 Ingush	38 Komi (-Zyryan)
7 Latvian	**Other Indo-European**	28 Avar	39 Komi-Permyak
Germanic	11 Greek	29 Lak	40 Udmurt (Votyak)
8 German	18 Armenian	30 Dargin	**Volgaic**
19 Yiddish		31 Tabasaran	41 Mari (Cheremis)
		32 Lezgin	42 Mordvin
		33 Agul	

Not included on the map are some languages spoken in very restricted geographical areas, such as languages of single villages in the Caucasus and Pamirs, and some languages whose speakers are everywhere a minority scattered among other ethnic groups, such as Romany, the language of the gypsies.

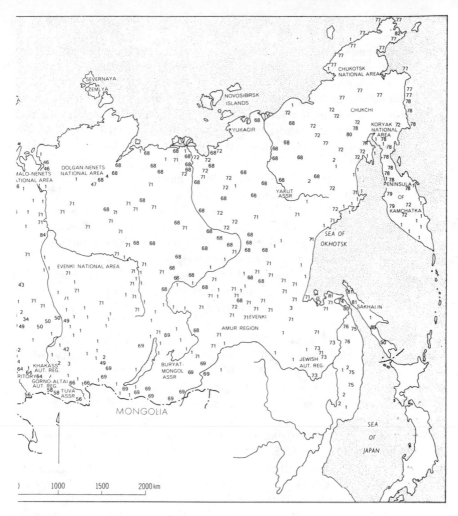

Source: E. Glyn Lewis, *Multilingualism in the Soviet Union: Aspects of Language Policy and Its Implementation*, Mouton, The Hague, 1972, map opposite p. 1.

Ugric
- 43 Khanty (Ostyak)
- 44 Mansi (Vogul)
- 45 Hungarian

Samoyedic
- 46 Nenets
- 47 Nganasan
- 48 Selkup

ALTAIC

Turkic
- 49 Chuvash
- 50 Tatar
- 51 Bashkir
- 52 Nogai
- 53 Kumyk
- 54 Karachay
- 55 Balkar
- 56 Kazakh
- 57 Kirgiz
- 58 Karakalpak
- 59 Uzbek
- 60 Uighur
- 61 Turkmen
- 62 Azerbaidzhan
- 63 Gagauz
- 64 Altai
- 65 Khakass
- 66 Tuvan
- 67 Shor
- 68 Yakut

Mongolian
- 69 Buryat
- 70 Kalmyk

Tungusic
- 71 Evenki
- 72 Even
- 73 Nanay
- 74 Ulch
- 75 Oroch
- 76 Udegey

PALEO-ASIATIO
- 77 Chukchi
- 78 Koryak
- 79 Itelmen (Kamchadal)
- 80 Yukagir
- 81 Nivkh (Gilyak)
- 84 Ket (Yenisei Ostyak)

ESKIMO-ALEUT
- 82 Eskimo
- 83 Aleut

KOREAN
- 85 Korean

known as Yenisei Ostyak), seem to be unrelated, at least closely, to any other languages at present spoken. The Soviet Union is thus a country of remarkable linguistic diversity.

In addition to languages spoken by ethnic groups that can be regarded as native to the territory of the Soviet Union, there are also languages spoken by ethnic groups who live primarily beyond the boundaries of the Soviet Union, but who for various historical reasons find themselves in part within these boundaries; for instance, in the Soviet Union there are over one million native speakers of German, nearly 400,000 of Polish, and some 245,000 of Korean.

The languages of the Soviet Union are also very diverse in terms of the number of their speakers. There are languages like Russian (142 million), Ukrainian (35 million), Uzbek, a Turkic language (9 million), that are spoken by vast populations. Conversely, in the Caucasus mountains one often finds that neighboring villages have different languages that are mutually incomprehensible, and the conditions of life in preindustrial Siberia meant that none of the native peoples ever had a population much above 20,000.

Moreover, the languages of the USSR differ considerably in the cultural and technological character of the speech community which they were, traditionally, called upon to serve. For instance, the languages of the three Baltic republics,[25] Lithuanian, Latvian, and, especially, Estonian, served communities that were if anything even more technologically oriented than Russia itself, and the independent development of these languages was fostered by a period of political independence between the Revolution and the Second World War; thus these languages are as adapted as Russian or any Western European language to express twentieth-century technological and cultural concepts. The same is true to a perhaps slightly lesser extent of Armenian and Georgian; both are languages with a long literary tradition (from around the fifth century A.D.), though long periods of Persian and Turkish domination meant that the languages failed to maintain this development uninterrupted into the modern period. At the other extreme, in the far east of Siberia one finds peoples who had had virtually no contact with western culture or technology before well into the twentieth century (with the frequent exception of their use of alcohol, to which they were introduced by unscrupulous traders in the nineteenth century). A similar distribution existed at the beginning of the century for literacy: literacy was highest in the European parts of the Russian Empire north of the Caucasus, though, as already noted, in Russia proper the literacy rate was very low by general European standards. In

---

[25]Note that "Baltic" as a geographical-political term includes all three of these territories (Lithuania, Latvia, Estonia); in referring to genetic linguistic relations, however, 'Baltic' includes only Lithuanian and Latvian, since Estonian is a Finno-Ugric language.

parts of the Caucasus and Central Asia, Arabic writing systems existed for the various languages, but these were poorly adapted to the structure of the languages concerned, and in any case literacy in these writing systems was extremely low. The majority of languages spoken within the Russian Empire simply had no written form, so the question of literacy in these languages did not arise; moreover, speakers of these languages were rarely literate in any other language.

In the Russian Empire, the policy towards languages other than Russian was very negative. Only in Poland and Finland, essentially autonomous with regard to internal affairs, were languages other than Russian used for official purposes.[26] Elsewhere Russian was the only official language of the Empire. Some local languages were actively discouraged; Ukrainian, for example, was deemed to be a dialect of Russian, and the printing of books in Ukrainian was forbidden. In general, however, the policy towards minority languages was one of neglect. Only the Russian Orthodox Church occasionally devised writing systems in these languages and wrote texts in them, and then only for the practical purpose of religious indoctrination. For the most part, the alternatives faced by speakers of minority languages were either to continue using their own languages and remain powerless and without access to modern technology, or to adopt Russian to have a chance for mobility in their own and the surrounding Russian population, a share in the government of their community, and the possibility of a better standard of living. In other words, the only alternative to assimilation was stagnation and powerlessness.

The Revolution of October 1917 changed this attitude towards the non-Russian languages. During the twenties and thirties many of the other ethnic groups—in particular, those with sizable and compact populations—were given various degrees of regional autonomy. This autonomy has been primarily administrative and cultural, rather than political, but it has provided an administrative (including educational-cultural) structure which has fostered the development of many of these languages. Writing systems have been devised for some sixty languages previously lacking one, and in general only very small ethnic groups (with populations of a few hundred, mainly bilingual in one of the larger languages) have not received writing systems for their languages. Apart from Russian, the languages spoken by the largest and/or most compact ethnic groups in the Union Republics are Ukrainian, Byelorussian, Estonian, Latvian, Lithuanian, Moldavian, Georgian, Armenian, Azerbaidjani, Kazakh, Turkmenian, Kirghiz, Uzbek and Tadjik. These languages are now used for nearly all purposes (often alongside Russian, especially where the republic contains a large Russian population). Such

---

[26]In Poland, Polish was thus used; in Finland, Swedish. The emergence of Finnish as an official language really only starts in the period after Finnish independence was obtained.

usage, in the case of the Asian languages in particular, represents a vast widening of the range of function for these languages. Most of the other written languages are used in at least the elementary grades in school, as well as in books and newspapers, and some of them have even wider use as cultural media.

Although there have been black spots in the history of nationalities policy in the Soviet Union, the general tolerance and even fostering of non-Russian languages is in marked contrast to the policies prior to 1917.

One of the tasks facing the new Soviet administration was to forge the disparate ethnic groups of the Soviet Union together into a united society modern in culture and technology. As we have seen, only very few of the languages of the Soviet Union had developed vocabularies capable of handling the kind of communication needed in such a society. Moreover, the languages of the Soviet Union are so diverse linguistically that with very few exceptions (among them Ukrainian and Russian, and many of the Turkic languages), they are mutually incomprehensible. Faced with this practical problem, and given the fact that Russian was and remains the native language of the majority of the population of the Soviet Union, the Soviet government decided, at the same time as fostering the further development of other languages, to foster the development of Russian as the basic means of communication among ethnic groups speaking different languages, and moreover to use Russian as the basis for enriching the vocabulary of those languages so far lacking the necessary cultural and technological terms. Thus to the extent that speakers of other languages do not pick up Russian from Russians living in the same area, they are taught Russian as a second language in school and have at least the option of having part or all of their subsequent education in Russian. When speakers of different languages have to communicate, it is almost invariably by means of Russian that they do so. With the exception of the few languages (such as Armenian, Georgian, and the languages of the Baltic republics) that had already come to terms with the general problem of creating new vocabulary apace with technological innovation, the other languages of the Soviet Union simply take over the Russian word. Although speakers of these languages who know Russian less well may adapt the word phonetically, they retain the Russian spelling. The aim is that such words should occur in the same Russian form in all the languages of the Soviet Union, with Russian pronunciation, as an aid to interethnic communication.

At first sight perhaps the most obvious evidence of the influence of Russian on the other languages concerns the alphabet. Apart from a few languages that have retained alphabets with long cultural traditions (in particular, the Latin alphabet for Estonian, Latvian, and Lithuanian, and their own alphabets for Armenian and Georgian), nearly all languages of the Soviet Union are written in the Cyrillic alphabet. In the early post-Revolution period, when it was felt necessary to allay fears of Russification, most of these other languages were given Latin alphabets; but since both the native language and Russian were taught in schools, it was found disadvantageous to have pupils (often including adults) having to learn two alphabets simultaneously, and so since the thirties the writing systems of these languages have used Cyrillic. Incidentally, loanwords from Russian into languages using the Cyrillic alphabet are spelled exactly as in Russian, even where this contradicts the spelling rules of the language concerned. Outside the Soviet Union, the Cyrillic alphabet is used only in Bulgaria and in Yugoslavia (for Macedonian and by the Serbs for Serbo-Croatian), and in Mongolia for Mongolian. (In Mongolia Russian serves as the prime means of contact with contemporary culture and technology).

One is naturally led to compare the linguistic policy of the Soviet Union with that pursued, at least until very recently in most other countries of Europe and North America. In these other countries, minority languages are, or were, actively discouraged, in a few cases even openly persecuted: only rarely was education in minority languages tolerated; even more rarely was such education encouraged (in material terms) by the appropriate government. Typically the most enlightened policy was one of complete neglect: if a group wanted to preserve its own language, its members would be free to do so at their own expense, but should not expect to receive any assistance or recognition from official sources. In the Soviet Union, the opportunity was provided for all languages to develop as written media of communication wherever this seemed to be viable, indeed even in a few cases where this turned out not to be viable. (For instance, some of the writing systems developed in the thirties were subsequently abandoned, since some of the small bilingual speech communities chose rather to operate primarily in their second language for writing purposes.) Literacy programs were provided, at government expense, in these languages, and books were and are being published in them, at low prices, even where the small circulation would deter the most philanthropic commercial publisher.

Despite the efforts to encourage language retention by minority groups in the Soviet Union, there are several factors operating against it, especially against the retention of languages of groups small in size or traditionally technologically unadvanced. The first of these factors is the need to come to terms with contemporary culture and technology. As already indicated, the policy that has been adopted for all languages is for them to borrow the necessary vocabulary directly from Russian, rather than create new vocabulary using native word-formation possibilities. In technical discussions requiring lots of such borrowed terms, it is often easier for speakers with a good knowledge of Russian to conduct the whole conversation in Russian than, in effect, to keep switching from their native language to Russian. For some languages,

this means that almost any conversation carried out in or about an urban environment is easier in Russian than in the native language, and with increasing urbanization and industrialization the switch from native language to Russian is accelerated. Similarly, many non-Russian parents choose to send their children to schools where Russian is the basic or sole medium of education so that their children will be better equipped to prosper in more technical careers. The second factor is the increasing consolidation of members of different ethnic groups in single farms, factories, schools, and so forth. Where a number of different ethnic groups come together to work or study, Russian is normally the only language they have in common, even if their number contains no Russians. Therefore, even if some members of the group at first speak Russian haltingly, Russian becomes the lingua franca of the group as a whole. On a larger scale, Russian is almost invariably the lingua franca of any cooperative endeavor at other than a purely local level. It is the language in which local leaders communicate with higher levels of the administrative hierarchy, thus a premium is placed on knowledge of Russian as a means of advancement to such positions. The same adoption of Russian takes place in the microsituation of a mixed family. If the parents are from different ethnic groups, then Russian will almost certainly be the only language they have in common. Because it will be the normal medium of communication within such a family, the children will normally grow up speaking only Russian, or at least speaking Russian best, a situation that will be reinforced when they are sent (as

FIGURE 3.4 *Multilingual Education in the Soviet Union*

Many of the languages of the USSR are used in the schools, either as the basic language of instruction, with Russian as a second language, or as one of the school subjects where the main medium of instruction is Russian or one of the other widely spoken languages. (The chapter-opening photograph shows a class in a Moscow Russian-language school.)
Left: *a photograph showing a Moldavian lesson. The pupil, Nadya Kokarcha, is a gypsy in the second grade, and the sentence she has just written, phonetically [vine primǝvara], means "Spring is coming." Moldavian, a Romance language close to Romanian, is the language of the Moldavian S.S.R., where it is used alongside Russian for all official purposes. Above: a photograph taken in a Kurdish school in Alagez, in the Armenian S.S.R.: under the supervision of teacher Shukroye Avdal, the pupil is writing the Kurdish version of a popular Soviet song. The first three lines of the song, in phonetic transcription [bɪra tʰɪme hæbæ tæ ʕv, bɪra tʰɪme hæbæ æ ʕzman, bɪra tʰɪme hæbæ de], mean "May there always be sunshine. May there always be the sky. May there always be Mother." The last line is "May there always be me." Most Kurds, several million of them, live outside the Soviet Union, in Iraq, Iran, and Turkey, but there are some 90,000 Kurds in the Soviet Union, mainly in the Armenian, Azerbaidjan, and Turkmen republics. During the 1930s there were Soviet schools with Kurdish as the primary medium, but since 1937 the primary medium in Kurdish schools is either Armenian, Azerbaidjani, or Turkmen, with Kurdish often still taught, however, as a school subject and used in publishing.*

they almost certainly would be in such a case) to a school where Russian is the sole medium of education.

In recent years in Western Europe and North America, there has arisen much interest in language revival and 'rescue linguistics,' where ethnic groups who have largely abandoned their respective native languages take a renewed interest in those languages, teaching them to their children, who would in the normal course of events have grown up speaking only outside languages. Such movements are often, though not always, linked to movements in favor of greater political autonomy, even separatism. No such movements (with or without political connections) seem to have gotten off the ground in the Soviet Union, and in present circumstances it is unlikely that any would, so that in future the comparison between Soviet and western attitudes towards minority languages may well indicate a more positive attitude in at least certain western societies. At present, one can say with regard to the Soviet Union that communities wishing to retain their native languages are given every moral and material encouragement to do so. Communities and individuals are equally entitled to abandon their native language in favor of Russian if they wish. Given this freedom of choice and the practical advantages following from good knowledge of Russian, assimilation to Russian is likely to become an ever more potent factor in the sociolinguistic development of the Soviet Union.

SUGGESTIONS FOR FURTHER READING

The following paragraphs list, with commentary, a small number of titles which the linguistics student not specializing in Russian may find useful for further amplification of topics that could be covered only briefly in this chapter. Only works available in English have been included; research monographs on specific points of Russian linguistic structure have not been included, except for treatments of word order and verbal aspect.

Since nearly all works dealing with Russian quote Russian examples in the Cyrillic alphabet, with English translation but no Latin-alphabet transliteration, some familiarity with Russian Cyrillic orthography is an essential prerequisite. The necessary information can be gleaned, for instance, from the manual by Leon Stilman, *Russian Alphabet and Phonetics (Columbia Slavic Studies)*, Columbia University Press, New York, 1941.

Dennis Ward, *The Russian Language Today*, Hutchinson University Library, London, 1955, is very useful for acquiring an impression of the basic phonological, morphological, and syntactic structures of Russian, plus some information on the historical and sociological setting. This work is particularly useful in the absence of any comprehensive typological study of Russian.

A general introduction to the Slavic languages is provided by Roman

Jakobson, *Slavic Languages: A Condensed Survey*, 2nd. ed., King's Crown Press, New York, 1955. G. O. Vinokur, *The Russian Language: A Brief History*, Cambridge University Press, London and New York, 1971 (translated by M. A. Forsyth from the second Russian edition, Moscow, 1959) provides a concise survey of the historical development of the language within a historical-sociological setting. Some account of developments in the Soviet period is given by Ward (1965), cited above, but for a fuller treatment reference should be made to Bernard Comrie and Gerald Stone, *The Russian Language Since the Revolution*, Clarendon Press, Oxford, 1978; this work describes changes that have occurred in the pronunciation, morphology, syntax, vocabulary, and orthography of Russian since the late nineteenth century, where possible correlating these changes with social changes, and is intended not only for specialists in Russian, but also for linguists with more general interests, especially in sociolinguistics.

E. Glyn Lewis, *Multilingualism in the Soviet Union*, Mouton, The Hague and Paris, 1972, examines sociolinguistic aspects of language pluralism in the Soviet Union, particularly in education. The only general account of the languages of the Soviet Union available in English, W. K. Matthews, *Languages of the U.S.S.R.*, Cambridge University Press, Cambridge, 1951, is unfortunately very out of date in general orientation, data, and of course in the language statistics presented. A more up-to-date replacement, providing recent statistical data and giving more emphasis to syntactic typology, is currently in preparation by Bernard Comrie under the title *The Languages of the Soviet Union*, Cambridge University Press.

Two works will be of interest to those wanting further information on Russian word order, especially in its relation to functional sentence perspective. R. Bivon, *Element Order*, Studies in the Modern Russian Language, vol. 7, Cambridge University Press, London and New York, 1971, includes statistical data based on the author's own research. O. Krylova and S. Khavronina, *Word Order in Russian Sentences*, Russian Language Publishers, Moscow, 1976 (translated from the simultaneously published Russian edition) is a very detailed presentation with exercises, intended primarily for advanced students of Russian; a big disadvantage, for present purposes, is that Russian sentences cited are not provided with English translations.

By far the most comprehensive account of Russian aspect available in English is J. Forsyth, *A Grammar of Aspect: Usage and Meaning in the Russian Verb*, Studies in the Modern Russian Language, extra vol., Cambridge University Press, London and New York, 1970. Some facets of Russian aspect are treated against a more general linguistic background in Bernard Comrie, *Aspect: An Introduction to Verbal Aspect and Related Problems*, Cambridge Textbooks in Linguistics, Cambridge University Press, London and New York, 1976.

IV

Cape York Creole

Terry Crowley

Bruce Rigsby

1 CAPE YORK PENINSULA AND THE TORRES STRAITS ISLANDS

In this chapter we present an introduction to the English-based Creole language that is spoken by many Aboriginal people and Torres Straits Islanders of the northern Cape York Peninsula region of North Queensland, Australia. Part of our intended audience is Australian, and we hope that European ("white") residents of the region who come into contact with the Cape York Creole will wish to learn more about it and study it further on their own. In particular, teachers and educators may want to develop both a hearing and a speaking command of Creole that they can use when talking with Aboriginal and Islander students and their parents who do not command Standard Australian English (SAE) well.

Terry Crowley is a Ph.D. student at the Australian National University in Canberra who is currently researching an Oceanic language in the New Hebrides. He has previously worked on Australian languages in northern New South Wales and far northern Queensland and is also interested in New Hebrides pidgin English.

Bruce Rigsby is a linguistic anthropologist who is interested in the past and present evolution of languages and cultures. An American, he shifted to the University of Queensland, Brisbane, in 1975 to continue work on Cape York Creole and several indigenous languages of Cape York Peninsula. Earlier he studied Sahaptin and Nass-Gitksan, two Native American languages of the Pacific Northwest.

Cape York Peninsula is the northeasternmost part of the Australian mainland, whilst the numerous small islands of the Torres Straits are situated between the northern peninsular area and Papua New Guinea. The general region is largely inaccessible by land and most food and other supplies are brought in by ship or plane. The population totals less than 20,000 and most people live in Reserve communities that are administered by the Queensland Department of Aboriginal and Islanders Advancement (D.A.I.A.) and by several church mission boards.

The main ethnic groups of the area are:

1. The *Aborigines*, who live in the mainland Reserve communities. Their original thirty or more indigenous languages are rapidly losing speakers as children no longer learn and use them; some are already extinct. The chapter-opening photograph shows a wedding ceremony where Aboriginal people at Bamaga Community are performing a Torres Straits Island–style dance.

2. The *Torres Straits Islanders*, who live on various of the islands and at Bamaga near the tip of the peninsula. The people of the eastern islands speak Miriam, which is related to the Kiwai language of the Fly River delta area of Papua New Guinea. The people of the western islands speak Yagar-Yagar, which is related to the Aboriginal languages of the Australian mainland.

   There are also 9,000 or so Torres Straits Islanders who reside permanently further south on the mainland in such North Queensland towns as Cairns, Townsville, and Mackay.

3. The *Europeans*, who live in mining towns and camps, on stations, and in the Reserve communities as administrators and employees of the D.A.I.A. and as missionaries. They generally speak SAE, which differs markedly in pronunciation from British and North American English.

4. The *Chinese, Japanese*, and *Malays*, who live on Thursday Island as shopkeepers and pearlers. They are generally bilingual in their native language and in SAE.

2   'PIDGINS' AND 'CREOLES' IN GENERAL

When most Australians speak of "Pidgin English" or "Pidgin," they generally think of something they also call "broken English," which is a language variety that no one takes seriously. Pidgin is a sort of simplified English, and its simplicity is believed to reflect the lesser mental abilities of its darker skinned speakers. Such misconceptions are dangerous because they serve to rationalize European ethnocentrism and they perpetuate racist stereotypes.

When a linguist or anthropologist uses the term "pidgin language," he has a technical usage in mind. A pidgin language is a *type* of language that has specific social and linguistic characteristics. Socially, a pidgin is a contact language that is used among people who have no common native language and who use the pidgin for purposes that often relate to commerce and trade. Indeed, the word "pidgin" is thought to derive from the Chinese Pidgin English pronunciation of the English word "business." Pidgin languages often develop in colonial social situations in which there are marked economic and political power differences between a small superordinate high-status group (often Europeans) and a large subordinate low-status group whose members speak no common native language. The pidgin provides a stable medium of communication among members of the subordinate group. Its use to bridge the gap between the high- and low-status groups is definitely less frequent, but it is in such cases that the superordinate speaker "simplifies" his language and speaks in an unsystematic "baby-talk" fashion.

Linguistically, a pidgin language has a limited vocabulary and its grammatical structure is considerably reduced from that of the natural language on which it is based.

Under the right circumstances, a pidgin language can acquire its own native speakers, as children come to learn it as a first language from their parents, who come to rely on it more and more. When people come to use the pidgin as their first and primary means of communication, it must undergo expansion of its vocabulary and grammar so that it can serve the full range of communicative needs of the speech community in its environment. When a pidgin language has gained native speakers and its communicative functions have thus expanded to equal those of a natural language, it becomes a 'creole' language. The term "creole" derives from a Portuguese word that referred to a Portuguese person born in the colonies; it has since taken on the additional meaning of a language "born" in the colonies as well.

When a pidgin undergoes creolization, it must increase its vocabulary many times over. This is mainly done by borrowing words from the superordinate language, but words from the several subordinate former native languages may be adopted too. The grammar—the rules of sentence structure and word-formation—becomes richer and more complex. Some examples can illustrate the point. The original pidgin may not have marked tenses in the verb, so that a sentence such as,

Him run.

could mean "He ran," "He is running," or "He will run." But when the pidgin develops into a creole, it typically comes to mark different tenses. So, in the Cape York Creole, you will now hear:

Im bin ran.	He ran.
Im ran.	He is running.
Im go ran.	He will run.

A second example is provided by sentences that contain relative clauses. Pidgin languages can do without these. So instead of saying:

The man who is fat is running.

the pidgin could well be satisfied with two simple sentences:

Man run.   Man fat.

But a full natural language usually has relative clauses. In the Cape York Creole, you will hear:

Maan wee i fet i ran go.

And a creole language *is* a full natural language in its own right that meets the full range of communicative needs of its native speakers, even though it derives from an earlier, simplified version of another natural language.

Now that you have some understanding of the technical terms 'pidgin' and 'creole,' you should be aware that popular usage of the terms is often different, partly from tradition and partly from ignorance and negative feelings toward such stigmatized languages. Very often, genuine creole languages are called pidgins. For example, Cameroon Pidgin in West Africa for many of its speakers is a creole despite its name, whereas New Guinea Pidgin is rapidly undergoing creolization in many urban and town areas of Papua New Guinea. Many Aboriginal people and Torres Straits Islanders refer to the Cape York Creole as *Pidgin* (or even *Broken English* when talking to Europeans), but it has in fact been a creole for over a generation, perhaps two.

English is not the only major European colonial language that developed pidgin and creole varieties. There was a Dutch creole spoken in the United States Virgin Islands called Negerhollands. French creoles are spoken in Haiti, Louisiana, and Mauritius. Portuguese creoles were once spoken in many coastal cities and towns of India, Ceylon, and Southeast Asia; Spanish creoles were fewer, some being spoken in a small part of the Philippines and in parts of South America.

Some creole languages have their own names: Djuka, Papiamentu, Sranan, Tok Pisin. Others do not have a particular name; the Cape York Creole is such a language. We considered calling it *langgus bla Kepyok*, but the phrase refers generically to any language of the area, and so we call it simply Creole in this chapter. This usage is technically correct, and it permits us to avoid the popularly stigmatized term Pidgin.

There is yet another possible stage in the development of a creole language. Where there is little or no contact between the superordinate language and the creole derived from it, the creole will continue to develop on its own as a separate language. This has been the case with the English-based Taki-Taki and Djuka creoles in Surinam, which was a Dutch colony from 1667, and it may well continue to be the case in New Guinea, where most Tok Pisin speakers have limited access to Standard English. However, where there is continual exposure to the superordinate language and social mobility is possible, creole speakers are likely to modify their speech towards what they perceive to be a more prestigious norm. This is especially true where the superordinate language is the primary medium of instruction in the schools and where it is used for governmental and other public purposes. In such a case, a 'postcreole continuum' is likely to develop. Among the several parts of the modern world where English postcreole situations are found are Guyana, Hawaii, and Jamaica, to name a few, and the Cape York region is another.

In the postcreole situation, speakers of the lower-status group come to learn a variety of speech forms that range from the straight creole to the standard language. They also learn a set of social norms for language use, so that the creole is considered to be appropriate for some purposes, but not for others. Individuals differ, of course, in their knowledge and ability to move between the creole and the standard, but it is the standard language that is indeed superordinate and furnishes the socially acceptable public norm. When speaking to higher-status persons, the lower-status person will adjust his speech forms upward to approximate the standard norm as closely as he can. On the other hand, among his relatives and friends, the lower-status person will use the creole—to use standard forms is to be formal and to indicate social distance. In labeling the forms that are found in a postcreole continuum, linguists use the terms 'basilect' and 'acrolect.' Basilect refers to the form of the creole that is furthest removed from the standard. It is usually the speaker's most informal variety. We will also refer to it as 'base Creole'. Acrolect refers to the form of the publicly valued superordinate standard language. Between the basilect and acrolect, there are various intermediate 'mesolectal' forms.

3   CAPE YORK CREOLE

The Cape York Creole is spoken mainly in the northern and northeastern portions of Cape York Peninsula and in the Torres Straits Islands. The data for this outline comes only from the Bamaga area, but our observations of the speech of visitors and immigrants to Bamaga from other places in this area suggest that variations or differences from the Bamaga Creole are minimal.

The historical origins of the Cape York Creole are obscure, but we will outline its history so far as we know it or can make reasonable speculations on it.

By about 1860, an English-based pidgin language called Beach-la-mar had developed and was spoken in the islands of the South Seas. It is possible that Beach-la-mar was itself derived from, or at least influenced by, the well-known Chinese Pidgin English that was brought into the region by sandalwood and trepang traders who used it in contact situations with the native peoples. The name Beach-la-mar derives from the French bêche-de-mer, which means "trepang, sea-slug." The same word is preserved today in the Cape York Creole as *bislama*, its generic word for trepang. As well, there is a descendant language of Beach-la-mar still widely spoken in the New Hebrides that is called in French "Bichelamar" and in English and the pidgin itself usually "Bislama." (See Figure 4.1.)

In the second half of the nineteenth century, sea captains (so-called blackbirders) were going to the various island groups of Melanesia, including the New Hebrides, the Solomons, New Ireland, and New Britain, to sign up or kidnap laborers (Kanakas) who were taken to work on the sugar plantations of coastal Queensland for periods of indenture lasting several years. As there is great linguistic diversity in the New Hebrides alone—over 100 languages today divided among 100,000 people—there was a strong need for a 'lingua franca' (a contact language) among the Kanakas so they could communicate among themselves. The Beach-la-mar English-based pidgin language filled this need on the plantations. Many Kanakas were repatriated to their home areas about the turn of the century, but some stayed behind, and their descendants remain in Queensland today.[1] There is disagreement among knowledgeable researchers as to whether the Kanaka pidgin was passed along to the Aboriginal people of the Queensland sugar area.

During the same period, many South Sea Islanders, especially from the Loyalty Islands, Rotuma, and Samoa, who spoke the Beach-la-mar pidgin, were brought into the Torres Straits region. Some of them came as missionaries for the London Missionary Society, but many more came as laborers in the rich shell and trepang industries. Later, some unrepatriated Kanakas from the Queensland cane plantations came to live on Mabuiag Island. The immigrants often married Torres Straits Islander women and settled. By 1898, the pidgin was well established there. We know this from the brief report on the "Jargon English" of the Torres Straits that was written by Sidney Ray, who was a member of the famous Cambridge Anthropological Expedition to the region at that time.

---

[1] We intend no disrespect by using the term "Kanaka," but restrict its reference to the period of indentured labor. Modern descendants of the indentured laborers in such cities as Mackay proudly identify themselves as "Pacific Islanders" or "South Sea Islanders."

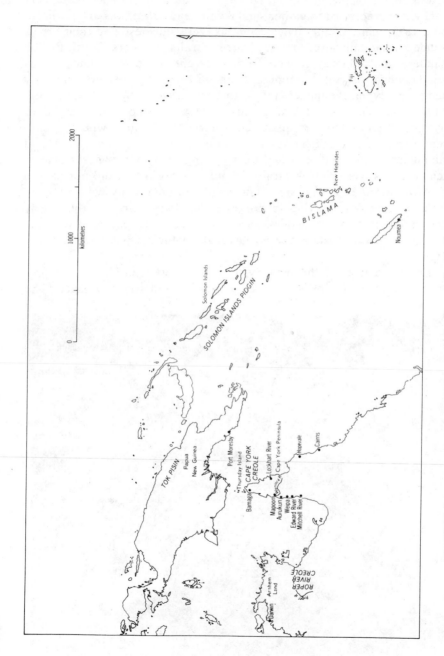

FIGURE 4.1 **English-based Pidgins and Creoles of the Southwestern Pacific Area**

159

The pidgin also spread to the Aboriginal people of the northern and eastern coasts of the Peninsula with the sandalwooders and the luggers as they were recruited to gather sandalwood and to work as divers. From about 1890, many of the lugger captains were Japanese and their crews included other Japanese, Malays, Torres Straits Islanders, South Pacific Islanders, and Aboriginal men from different places. The pidgin was their language of daily communication on board the luggers and they used it also when the luggers put in to visit native camps, missions, and centers like Thursday Island. And at Mapoon and Lockhart River missions, the missionaries instituted a dormitory system whereby children were separated from their parents, given some education and training in English and punished for speaking native languages. Some of their teachers were Torres Straits Islanders who in fact did not have a command of SAE, and young Aboriginal men commonly went to work on the luggers upon leaving school, often for long years. All this surely had an effect upon transmission of the native languages from one generation to the next and must have aided their replacement by the pidgin.

From the turn of the century, the creolization of the pidgin proceeded variously in the several communities and island villages. The

FIGURE 4.2   *Aboriginal Men at New Mapoon, Bamaga, as They Prepare to Butcher a Dugong*

FIGURE 4.3 *Mr. and Mrs. Frank Don, Whose Traditional Home is at Mapoon on the West Coast of Cape York Peninsula*

They were educated under the dormitory system that forbid Aboriginal children to speak their native languages. They can understand some of their native language, and they are fluent in Standard Australian English and Cape York Creole.

replacement of native languages by the Cape York Creole has accelerated in the past few decades, notably so at Weipa, Mapoon, Cowal Creek, and on Banks and Darnley Islands. The same is now well under way at Lockhart Community, now situated at Iron Range. At Weipa and Mapoon, the original Wenlock River languages are all but extinct, save for a handful of old men and women. At Cowal Creek, only a few people, all older than fifty-five, still use their native languages regularly. And at Lockhart, only adults over thirty or so have active command of the native language, while all members of the community speak Creole. It is the first and primary language for many young people and children there.

Further illustration of native language replacement by Creole can be seen in the following estimated numbers of speakers of languages at Bamaga Community, which includes the five smaller village communities of Cowal Creek, Umagico, Bamaga, New Mapoon, and Red Island Point. Bear in mind that most native people there are bilingual, e.g.,

most people who have come to Bamaga Community from the western
Torres Straits Islands speak both Creole and Yagar-Yagar.

Cape York Creole	1,400
Yagar-Yagar	900
Standard Australian English	100
Miriam	25
Umpila/Kuuku-Ya'u	25
Umbuygamu	5
Atambaya	4
Yadhaykenu	2
Mpakwithi	1
Lamalama	1
Barimangudinma	1
Umbindhamu	1

Although there has always been some contact in the Cape York
region between speakers of the Creole and speakers of SAE, it has been
especially over the past decade that such contact has intensified. Education by European teachers, contact with D.A.I.A. personnel, going to
films, and listening to the radio have had the net effect of attaching a
negative value to basilectal Creole, so that Aborigines and Islanders now
adjust their speech "upwards" towards SAE in many social situations.

There is something very important about such a linguistically
complex postcreole speech community that most SAE-speakers do not
ordinarily appreciate, coming as they do from fairly homogeneous
monolingual speech communities. This is that the choice of language or
language variety is 'conditioned' or 'determined' by features of the social
situation in which it is used. Yet we can all understand the importance of
such conditioned variation when it is pointed out. The choice of 'formal'
versus 'informal' styles of conversation is exactly the same kind of
thing. A thirsty workman could, for example, call out to his mate on a
hot day and say:

Ya got 'ny water, John? Shit, she's 'ot!

But a well-dressed stranger asking John for the same thing would use
a more formal style:

Excuse me, could I trouble you for a glass of water, please? It's hot
today.

To break these cultural rules, and for the stranger to use the first sentence would be inappropriate or wrong in much the same way as it is to eat peas off a knife in a restaurant. The general rule that we operate with is to match the value of our social activity (in terms of whom we are speaking to, where, what about, how important it is) with an appropriately valued speech form.

This is the same principle a speaker in a postcreole continuum situation operates with, only his range of choices is far wider than any you are used to making. In Cape York Creole, a speaker's most informal style is to all intents and purposes a different language from his most formal acrolectal style, as the basilectal varieties cannot be understood at all (or only with great difficulty) by someone who speaks only SAE. The Creole speaker has to match up a great many different speech varieties with various social situations. Let us look specifically at some aspects of grammar that a speaker has to deal with in this way.

We will look at how a Creole speaker can express possession. In the variety most removed from SAE, he would say,

Dog bla maan *i bin dai.*

for "**The man's dog** died." The same speaker could express the phrase in boldface type in quite a number of different ways:

Dog blo maan
Dog blong maan
Maan dog
Maanz dog

These alternative forms are set out such that each form more closely approaches the phrase that we use. Of course, a speaker of Creole does not simply choose one of these five alternate forms at random when he is speaking. The choice is determined by the social situation in the same way as our choice between formal and informal styles is conditioned. Our Creole speaker will match:

dog bla maan

with informal situations, such as speaking to his children or his close friends. On the other hand, he will use:

maanz dog

in more formal situations, such as speaking to the manager of the Reserve or the person selling stamps in the post office. The intermediate forms are used in intermediate social situations.

Another good example of a variable feature is the pronoun that expresses the second-person plural, like "you all." In base Creole this is sometimes heard as:

yubla

There is a whole set of alternative forms, however, gradually approaching a form that we might use. Thus:

yupla
yupela
yufla
yufela
yufelaz

In the speaker's "best" speech, he might say *yufelaz* ("you fellows"), while in his least formal speech, he will say something close to *yubla*.

Actually, in a linguistically complex situation such as that of the Cape York area, there is more to the rules of language use than this, because we have taken into account only how a speaker chooses his variety of Creole. Many speakers include in their repertoire an indigenous language as well. The following list illustrates in a general way the rules followed by an indigenous person for the choice of language or language variety at Bamaga:

Person Spoken to:	**Language Variety Used:**
European	Closest possible approach to SAE
Another native person who speaks the same indigenous language	The common indigenous language or a form of Creole close to the basilect
Another native person who does not speak an indigenous language or whose indigenous language is not the same	A form of Creole close to the basilect

This list suggests that for a European to speak to an indigenous person in anything but SAE is "breaking the rules." Indeed, for a European to do this can cause embarrassment as it can be interpreted as mockery or condescension. But it *is* possible for a European to speak to an indigenous person in Creole if their relationship is close, as base Creole is the language of familiarity. Then the Aborigine or Islander may feel pride in the fact that the European has bothered to learn his "lingo."

Anyone in the Creole-speaking area will also be able to observe how the range between the basilect and the acrolect comes into play. You will notice that some people can easily adjust along the continuum as the needs arise, whereas others experience difficulty and can manage little more than base Creole. Such are usually preschool children and very old people who have had little exposure to the "corrective" pressures of school and reading.

4   SOUNDS AND SPELLINGS

The sounds of Creole are very different from those of SAE. This is obvious even at the very first contact with Creole. It would of course be possible to use the traditional English orthography to write Creole, but it is better to avoid this, for the reason that standard orthography makes Creole look like English. You have already learned in the preceding section that Creole is *not* English; it is only similar to it. So, if you were to come across a sentence such as:

Me been come long sandbeach for catch him fish.

you would be tempted to read it as English. But if you read instead:

Mi bin kam lo sanbich fa kechim pis.

you are less likely to fall into the same trap.

Creole is not usually written, so we have had to devise our own spelling system that will accurately and unambiguously represent the sounds of the language. (Incidentally, if you are a reader living in the Cape York area and you are interested in writing down examples of Creole for yourself from speech you hear around you, it is advisable to stick as closely as possible to this spelling system.) Most of the system will be quite clear, and need no special comment, though a few points need to be mentioned.

4.1   Sound Variation with Consonants

You will find that Creole speakers do not consistently distinguish between members of the following pairs of consonant sounds:

p	*f*
s	*sh*
t	*th* (as in "*th*in")
d	*th* (as in "*th*ough")
b	*v*

So, you should not be surprised to hear of people going to the "airfort in a behicle to ply in a flane to bisit the pamily in Vrisbane." In deciding on a consistent spelling system, it is difficult to know just what to do with this sort of variation. It does seem to be that in some words, certain preferences exist. Thus, "finish" is generally heard as *pinis,* and we have decided to write it as such, whereas "finger" is generally heard as *fingga,* and is written as such rather than as *pingga.*

There is a second kind of variation in the consonants of Creole: *p* is sometimes heard as *b, t* as *d,* and *k* as *g.* These sounds only alternate when they occur between two short vowels. Thus, "paper" could be heard in Creole as either *pepa* or *peba.* Note that "baby" could only be heard as *bebi,* never as *bepi.* Note also that when the suffix *-im* is added to transitive verbs (discussed in the next section), a consonant that was originally at the end of a word now appears between two vowels. Thus, a consonant such as *p, t,* or *k* at the end of a word cannot vary, but when there is a following *-im,* the variation can be heard:

> *mek* ⟶ *mekim, megim*   make
> *gat* ⟶ *gatim, gadim*   have

4.2   Simplification of Consonant Clusters

A striking characteristic of the Creole sound system is that it tends to avoid more than one consonant at the end of a word or together in the middle of a word. This is something that also probably happens to a lesser extent in your own speech as well. Say the following words to yourself quickly:

> goodbye
> grandfather
> MacDonald River

You will probably find that you drop the *d*'s that appear before the other consonants. So, you will say: *goo'bye, gran'father, MacDonal' River* and so on. It is only in your most formal, and hence most careful, speech, that you actually pronounce these *d*'s. It is interesting to note that in words such as "Christmas," "chestnut," "fasten," "listen," "castle," and "whistle," the *t* sound was pronounced by English-speaking people at one time, giving consonant sequences such as *stm, stn, stl.* Now, the *t* is silent and is retained only in the spelling.

If you listen to Creole speakers pronouncing the following words, you will find that there is a considerable difference from SAE:

old
last
jump
hand
department
Commonwealth
Queensland
island
sergeant

What Creole speakers do is to extend the process of consonant cluster simplification just described for your own speech; they "drop" the last consonants in all the words just listed and one in the middle of "Queensland" as well. Pronunciations are actually:

ol'	=	*oul*
las'	=	*laas*
jum'	=	*jam*
han'	=	*aan*
departmen'	=	*dapaatman*
Commonweal'	=	*komanwel*
Queen'lan'	=	*kwiinlan*
islan'	=	*ailan*
sergean'	=	*saajan*

(These spellings are examples of the special spelling system that has yet to be explained; see the discussion further below.)

As an exercise, look at the words in the following list and try to guess how a Creole speaker would pronounce the consonant clusters. Be careful to cover up the answers on the righthand side:

grandfather	*gran'father*
sandbeach	*san'beach*
Townsville	*Town'ville*
landrover	*lan'rover*
ghost	*ghos'*
ask	*as'*
wasp	*was'*
nest	*nes'*
twenty	*twen'y*

4.3 Consonant Symbols

Most of the symbols used for the consonants of Creole need no special discussion, though the following have slightly different values to those of English:

th   as in "thin," never as in "the" or "lathe"

dh   like the sound of "th" in "the" or "lathe"

zh   like the sound corresponding to "s" in the words "leisure," "usually"

ng   always as in "ring" and "singer," never as in "finger," where one hears a distinct *g* sound as well as the nasal sound preceding it (recall the spelling for Creole "finger" is in fact *fingga*)

r   between two vowels in Creole, usually pronounced as a flap of the tip of the tongue against the top of the mouth behind the teeth

If you listen, you will find the *r* generally quite different from the corresponding sound in the speech of most standard English speakers, certainly different from the ordinary Australian *r*; it is more like the Scottish *r*. Listen in words such as:

hariap	hurry up
beri-im	bury (something)
orait	alright

In these words you will invariably hear the flapped *r* sound. This is always the case when the sound comes between vowels.

At the beginning of a word, *r* is sometimes pronounced as in SAE, and sometimes as a flap like the Scottish *r*. When it follows another consonant it is often pronounced like an Australian *r*; so in words such as:

difran	different
bring-im	bring
thri	three

you will not always hear the flapped *r* sound.

4.4 Vowels

It is in the vowel sounds that Creole differs most notably from SAE. The general tendency in Creole is to reduce the number of distinctive vowel sounds and to eliminate the typical drawl or glide of vowel sounds in Australian English. In thinking of English vowels you must remember that we are speaking of pronunciation and not of writing, and that we have far more vowels than the five (i.e., *a, e, i, o, u*) that you might suppose from the spelling. If you listen to the vowels as you pronounce each of the following words, you will find quite a few more than five:

big	beg	bag	bug	laugh	cook
trip	met	mat	tough	half	put
dip	leg	hang	dump	part	hood
pot	suit	cow	throw	there	here
dog	root	bough	no	bare	beer
long	troop	hound	home	air	hear

There are a few more distinct vowel sounds in SAE and other standard dialects. It would be possible to find almost a half-dozen more in the speech of most standard English speakers. (Can you think of some of these?)

What happens in Creole is that in some cases, one or more of these vowels "merge" into one sound, usually with some new phonetic value. In fact, even many of the vowels that do not merge with another vowel still change their phonetic value, and yet other vowels in SAE "split" into more than one vowel. We now describe for you the pronunciation of Creole vowels.

i. The Creole *i* sound is pronounced always as in "sit," "hit," the short, clear sound of English, from which it is derived. There is no merger of more than one vowel in the origin of this vowel.

ii. This is a longer version of *i*. We use double letters for all vowels to indicate length. In SAE, in words such as "*fee*l" and "*rea*lly," the italicized vowel sound is distinctly longer than the vowel sound in "s*i*t" and "h*i*t," but if you listen carefully to the way you say the two different vowels, you will find that there is more than just a question of length involved. If you are a standard English speaker, the longer vowels in your speech are likely to be more like "gliding" vowels, beginning with *i* and ending with a distinct *y* sound. This "glide" element is not pronounced in Creole. The vowels are pure, and so are written with the double symbol. Thus, we spell the preceding words as:

sit   *fiil*
hit   *riili*

e. This is pronounced as in SAE "bed" and "leg," and never as in "me" or "the." This Creole vowel has two sources from Australian English:

1. The vowel in "bed," "leg," "get," and so on
2. The vowel in "hat," "back," "hang," and so on

The vowels in these two sets of words in SAE are quite distinct, but in Creole they are all pronounced as *e*. So, the words given above as examples are spelled:

bed	*het*
leg	*bek*
get	*heng*

ee. This is a longer variety of *e*; pronounce this much as most Australians pronounce the vowel of "there," "Cairns," "dare," and so on. Australians should be careful not to pronounce any kind of following glide as they will find in "educated" speech; they should stick to the pure vowel of "broad" Australian here. The source of this vowel in Creole is the vowels of the standard language which we spell "-ere," "-air," "-are," etc. For example,

there	$\longrightarrow$	*dhee*
Cairns	$\longrightarrow$	*Keenz*
dare	$\longrightarrow$	*dee*
tear	$\longrightarrow$	*tee*

Note that when you see a double *ee* like this in Creole, you must be careful to avoid reading it as you would in the English word "meet" or "feet." Such words would have the vowel *ii* which has already been discussed.

a. This letter is used to represent the sound in "cup," "rub," "truck," and so on (and never the vowel sounds of "hang," "bag," "take," etc.). The Creole vowel *a* comes from the following English vowel sounds:

1. The vowel in "cup," "rub," "truck"
2. The vowel in "stop," "hot," "lot," "rock"
3. The vowel in "alive," "China," "sergeant," "department"
4. The vowel of "sandbeach"

So, the words just given in Creole become:

kap	*stap*	*alaiv*	*sanbich*
rab	*hat*	*Chaina*	
trak	*lat*	*saajan*	
	rak	*dapaatman*	

aa. Here we have the longer version of *a*; this sounds like the vowel in the SAE words "father," "half," "card," "laugh," and so on. This long vowel in Creole comes from the following sounds in ordinary speech:

1. The vowel of "card," "far," "heart"
2. The vowel of "hand," "fan," "mad," "bag," "man"
3. The vowel of "burn," "turn"

Thus, these words are spelled:

kaad	*haan*	*baan*
faa	*faan*	*taan*
haat	*maad*	
	baag	
	maan	

Notice that we have in English words such as "hat," "back," "hang," "hand," "fan," "mad," "bag," "man," a sound which we all regard as being the same. However, this particular *a* sound in English has two different correspondences in Creole; this is therefore an example of what is known as a "split." Some words have an *e*, whereas others have an *aa*: thus "hat" becomes *het* whereas "bag" becomes *baag*. How can we know whether an English *a* will become *e* or *aa* in Creole? It is possible to work out a rule. If you are a standard English speaker and in your speech, the *a* sound is followed by one of the following sounds: *b*, *p*, *f*, *v*, *t*, *th*, *l*, *s*, *z*, *j*, *ch*, *k*, or *ng*—that is, by most of the consonants— then it becomes *e* in Creole; but if your *a* is followed by *m*, *n*, *d* or *g*, then it becomes *aa* in Creole. The reason for this will be obvious if you listen carefully to yourself pronouncing the following pairs of words in English:

bat	bad	ban	bag
mat	mad	man	mag

The first column has a final *t*, and so the vowel in Creole will be *e* (e.g., *bet*, *met*). This is because the *a* sound in English is very short when it is compared with the vowels where there is a following *d*, *n*, or *g*. Where there is a following *d*, *n*, or *g* the *a* is much longer in English, and so in Creole the corresponding vowel must also be long, as in *baad*, *baan*, *baag*, *maad*, *maan*, *maag*.

Just to check to see if you have understood this rule, see if you can predict what vowel Creole will have for the boldface part of the following words:

drag	sandy	ham
badge	canter	adding
batch	barracuda	bash
sand	bang	

o. The vowel that is written as *o* in Creole is pronounced the same way as most Australians pronounce the vowel of "hot," "dog," or "long," and never as in "load" or "home." This vowel has as its origin the SAE vowels in:

1. talk, walk, tall, airport
2. dog, fog, long, rod

In Creole, these words are spelled:

tok	*dog*
wok	*fog*
tol	*long*
eepot	*rod*

You will have noticed that there are some words that have *o* in SAE (like "dog," "rod") which in Creole becomes *o*, whilst others ("stop," "lot") become *a*. The rule is the same as for deciding which *a* sounds of SAE become *e* and which become *aa* in Creole. This is a further example in Creole of a "split" taking place. So, if an *o* in your speech is followed by an *m, n, d,* or *g,* then English *o* will become Creole *o*, but if your *o* is followed by any other sound, then it will become *a*. You should also be able to predict which *o* sounds become Creole *o* and which become *a* in the following words:

log	stop
lodge	dog
botch	rod
bond	hot
bong	lot
song	rocks
oddity	foggy

oo. This is the long variety of *o* and sounds the same as the broad Australian vowel in "four," "score," or "door." Do not pronounce this as the vowel of "room," "doom," or "soup," nor as the vowel of "home," "rope," or "road." In Creole, this vowel comes from the SAE vowels in:

1. four, raw, sure, more
2. road, boat, showed, glowed, roam, home

In Creole, these words can be written:

foo	*rood*
roo	*boot*
shoo	*shood*
moo	*glood*
	room
	hoom

u. This vowel is the vowel pronounced in SAE and most dialects of English as in "foot," "hood," and so on. This vowel in Creole has only one source in SAE, and that is the vowel of words such as "foot and "hood," which in Creole will be spelled:

fut
hud

You should be careful if you see such a word written not to make it rhyme with "cut" or with "cute." This vowel is always pronounced as in "put."

uu. This is the long *u*. You must avoid the gliding *w* sound following the vowel in English words such as "moon" and "room," though this vowel is the origin for *uu*. Thus, the words just given become:

muun
ruum

4.5 Diphthongs

Although for the most part it has been stressed that the Creole vowels are "pure" (i.e., with no so-called drawl), there are some sequences of vowels that are pronounced as vowels with a glide. In the next examples, we present all of the diphthongs you will encounter. This time their pronunciation is more similar to that of "educated" varieties of Australian English than to the "broad" varieties.

ai	*saiz*	size
	trai	try
ei	*teik*	take
	dei	day
ou	*bout*	boat
	houm	home
oi	*boi*	boy
	Roi	Roy
au	*nau*	now
	haus	house

4.6 Exceptions

You have been shown in the preceding paragraphs how to predict what pronunciation a word will have in Creole. However, it is only fair to list the exceptions. These are few in number but common in use. Some of the most frequently encountered irregular forms are:

	Actual Form	When We Would Expect
goanna	*gwana*	*goena*
language	*langgus*	*lenggwij*
close up ("nearly")	*klosap*	*klousap*
match(es)	*machis*	*mechas*
Mackay	*makei*	*makai*
stingray	*tingari*	*stingrei*
tobacco	*tabeka*	*tabekou*

4.7 Sound Variation with Vowels

So far, there has been no mention of variation with vowels. But as you might expect, there is variation there as well, as with consonants. This can be in two directions—either closer towards the SAE system, or in the opposite direction, closer towards the basilect (that is, the form most removed from your own speech). The sound system presented here is *meso*lectal (that is, about midway between the basilect and the variety of English you speak). The reason we have presented this mesolectal system here is that it is the variety you are most likely to hear: with you, Creole speakers will generally adjust their speech in the direction of your standard, and it will therefore emerge in the mesolect variety. However, if you want to be able to understand Creole speakers when they are talking with each other, you ought to be acquainted with the basilectal forms as well.

We have pointed to the difference between long and short vowels, but in forms closer to the basilect, you will find that there is no such distinction. *All* vowels can simply become short. So, you will sometimes hear the following forms:

seat	*sit* (same as "sit" in your speech; "seat" and "sit" sound the same in the basilect)
feel	*fil* (same as "fill")
really	*rili*
sergeant	*sajan*
department	*dapatman*
card	*kad* ("cud" is pronounced the same)

heart	*hat*	("hot" is pronounced the same)
man	*man*	
airport	*epot*	
show	*sho*	("sure" is pronounced the same)
home	*hom*	
moon	*mun*	
room	*rum*	

and you will hear that the diphthongs *ei* and *ou* lose their second element:

take	*tek*	(same as "tech," the abbreviation of "technical")
day	*de*	(same as "dare")
say	*se*	
boat	*bot*	(same as "bought")
home	*hom*	

In the next paragraphs are five other kinds of variation you will notice.

1. At the ends of words that we have spelled with *ee* there is an alternative pronunciation *ea*, which is much more like British English than Australian (compare British and Australian pronunciations of words like "there" and "prayer"). This kind of variation is exemplified by:

there	*dhee ~ dhea*
dare	*dee ~ dea*
where	*wee ~ wea*
tear	*tee ~ tea*

2. At the end of a word, *oo* is sometimes pronounced as *oa*, like the British English pronunciation of "poor" or "Moore." Some examples of this kind of variation:

four	*foo ~ foa*
sure	*shoo ~ shoa*
more	*moo ~ moa*

3. There are Creole words we have spelled with *a* where SAE has the neutral (schwa) vowel, which is symbolized as *ə*. This vowel occurs in words such as "*a*live," "Chin*a*," and "serg*ea*nt." Actually, Creole speakers will vary here between *a* and the neutral vowel. For example,

sergeant	*sajən ~ sajan*
department	*dəparmən ~ dapatman*
Queensland	*Kwinlən ~ Kwinlan*
Commonwealth	*Komənwel ~ Komanwel*

4. Sometimes, the diphthong *ai* can become the long vowel *aa*. Recall that we have said that any long vowel, including *aa*, can be shortened in some Creole varieties. This does not apply however, when the *aa* is derived from *ai*. Examples of this kind of variation are:

I	*ai ~ aa*
size	*saiz ~ saaz*
time	*taim ~ taam*

5. The diphthong *au* is sometimes pronounced simply as *a*, i.e., the same vowel as in "cup," "such," "truck," etc. Some examples of this alternation are:

come out	*kamaut ~ kamat*
sit down	*sidaun ~ sidan*
then	*nau ~ na*

5 GRAMMAR

The grammar of any natural human language is an extremely complex set of rules and regulations about the accepted ways of combining words to form sentences and discourses. Although Cape York Creole is a language derived historically from a simplified version of English, (a version that is simplified phonetically, grammatically, and lexically), it would be wrong to assume that present-day Creole has anything less than a full grammar. Probably what it gains in simplicity in some parts, it makes up for with complexity in others.

5.1 Nouns

A noun, you will know from English, can be the name of any thing, animal, person, or place. A noun can also be described by the fact that it occurs as what we call the "subject" or the "object" of a verb. Nouns in Creole can be described in much the same way. A few Creole nouns are given as examples:

Bamaga	Bamaga
Alau	Umagico
dokta	doctor
haus	house
viikl	vehicle, car
faiasmouk	smoke
walabi	wallaby
gavaman	government

Nouns in English are either definite ("**the** dog") or indefinite ("**a** dog," "**some** dogs") and singular ("dog") or plural ("dogs"). In Creole, nouns are unmarked for all of these four features. Thus, all of these examples will be simply *dog* in Creole. You might hear a sentence such as:

Dog i sidaun.

which could be translated as:

$\begin{Bmatrix}\text{The}\\\text{A}\end{Bmatrix}$ dog is sitting down.

$\begin{Bmatrix}\text{The}\\\text{Some}\end{Bmatrix}$ dogs are sitting down.

depending on what the speaker actually saw happen. You should be careful not to add the plural *-s* to a noun when speaking Creole. This is not a characteristic of Creole, but of SAE. However, while it is true to say that Creole does not generally mark definiteness and number, it is wrong to say that it *cannot* do so. In fact, there are times when you will need to specify such things. What you do in these instances is to use the following words before the noun:

	Singular	**Plural**
Definite	dhet, det	dhem, dem, ol
Indefinite	wan	plenti

So, you will hear sentences such as:

Det nadawan bin wokabaut go.
   The other (man) went away on walkabout.
Dem imyu en plein taaki bin fait.
   The emu and the plains turkey had a fight.
Wan dog i bin singaut.
   A dog was barking.
Plenti dog i bin singaut.
   Some dogs were barking.

You will have to be careful to avoid replacing these Creole forms with the SAE ones; the SAE forms have slightly different meanings. For example, *plenti* does not necessarily mean "plenty," but "some." To express "plenty," you usually say *bigmab*, as in:

I gat bigmab walabi.
> There are plenty of wallabies.

Nor does *wan* necessarily mean "one;" it generally means "a."

5.2 Pronouns

The Creole pronoun system is quite different from that of Standard English varieties. SAE has the following forms when used as the subject of a verb:

	Singular	Plural
First person	I	we
Second person	you	you
		(But you will sometimes hear "youse" for the plural of "you")
Third-person masculine	he	
feminine	she	they
neuter	it	

In the singular, the Creole pronouns are:

First person	ai, mi
Second person	yu
Third person	i, im

The main differences from the SAE singular pronouns are that *mi* is often used as well as *ai* for "I" and that there is no distinction between "he," "she," and "it." These are all just *i* or *im* in Creole. So, you will often hear sentences such as:

Waif bla mi i insaid lo aus.
> My wife is inside the house.

***Im** bin go insaid pinis.*
> **She** has already gone in.

where *im* is used for "she," even though it sounds like (and is certainly derived from) the masculine form in standard English.

Creole does not have a simple set of plural pronouns like SAE. Instead, it has two plural sets; one is a 'dual' set, which means "two people or things" and the other is a 'plural,' which in Creole means more than two (*not* just more than one as in English). The second- and third-person forms are:

	Dual	**Plural**
Second person	yutu(pela)	yu(pela)
Third person	tupela	ol, dempela

So, *yutu* or *yutupela* means "you two," *tupela* means "they two," while *yu* or *yupela* means "you all (=youse)" and "they all" is translated by *ol* or *dempela*. For example,

> *Ol kolim seimwei laik Mpakwithi.*
> > They say it the same as the Mpakwithi.

> *Yutupela ran kam.*
> > You (two) run here.

In the first person, a distinction has to be made in Creole, depending on whether the person you are speaking to is included in the "we" or not. The forms are:

	Dual	**Plural**
Inclusive	yumi, yumtu	mipela, wi
Exclusive	mitu	mitupela, wi

This distinction in Creole is extremely important. Let's imagine a situation where there are three people in a group, A, B, and C, and A says to B:

> *Yumi go nau.*

he is saying that A and B will go, but not C, but if he says:

> *Mitu go nau.*

he means that he and C will go, but not B (who is being spoken to). If he wants all three to go, he will need to say:

> *Mipela go nau.*

(Where the pronouns are followed by the plural suffix *-pela*, you will encounter quite a range of variation in the form. The suffix sometimes reduces to *-bla* or *-pla* or *-fla*, and sometimes may be heard as *-fela*. The choice of the particular variation is decided by the formality of the situation, *-fela* being the most formal.)

There is a second set of pronouns in Creole, which have the following forms:

	Singular		**Dual**	**Plural**
First				
person	mi	**Inclusive**	yumi, yumtu	mipela, wi
		Exclusive	mitu	mitupela, wi
Second				
person	yu		yutu(pela)	yu(pela)
Third				
person	im		tupela	dem(pela)

This set of pronouns differs from the set just given in the following ways only:

1. The first-person singular has only the form *mi*. There is no *ai*.
2. The third-person singular has only *im*. There is no *i*.
3. The third-person plural has only *dem*(*pela*). There is no *ol*.

This set of pronouns is used as the object of a verb, whereas the first set is used as the subject of a verb; for example,

> *Im bin luk mi.*
> He saw me.

NEVER: *Im bin luk ai.*

5.3   Prepositions

A preposition in English is a word such as "with," "on," "to," "from," and so on, which in some way specifies the location or function in a sentence of a noun or pronoun. Creole has prepositions too, and these are for the most part similar to the prepositions of English. However, there are two prepositions that are particular to Creole (though they originate from other items in English). These are *lo* and *blo*.

The usual form of the first of these prepositions is *lo*, but before a word beginning with a vowel, it can optionally become *long* rather than simply *lo*. (There is a rule like this in English: the indefinite article *a* becomes *an* if the following word has an initial vowel.) Examples of the *lo*/*long* alternation are:

lo Bamaga	at Bamaga	*long Alau*	at Umagico
lo riva	at the river	*long Injiinu*	at Cowal Creek
lo sanbich	on the beach	*long ailan*	on the island

When the following word begins with a consonant, instead of *lo* you can sometimes hear *la*.

This preposition has a very wide range of meanings. It can mean:

1. "to"

   Ai tok lo yu.
   I am talking to you.

   Mitu bin wokabaut lo Mapun.
   We two (not you) walked to Mapoon.

2. "in, on, at"

   Im aid lo skrab.
   He is hiding in the rainforest.

   Ol sidaun lo sanbich.
   They are sitting on the beach.

   Im stap lo Bamaga.
   She lives at Bamaga.

3. "with" (instrumental)

   Im bin hitim mi long aan.
   He hit me with his hands.

4. "with" (accompaniment)

   Im wok lo yumi.
   He is walking with us.

The second preposition, *blo*, behaves like *lo* in that we optionally have the variant *blong* when the following word begins with a vowel, as in:

blo dokta	the doctor's
blong im	his

When the following word begins with a consonant, *blo* often also has the form *bla* (though when the following word begins with a vowel, *blong* does not become *blang*); for example,

blo dokta ~ bla dokta

This preposition precedes a noun or pronoun that is the possessor of something. For example,

azban blo dokta	the doctor's husband
aus blo menija	the manager's house
stik blong olmaan	the old man's stick

Creole has another construction involving prepositions that is not used in SAE. In SAE we have a series of words such as "on top," "underneath," "inside," "behind," and "in front," which express some kind of relative location (location relative to something else). Such words in Creole are followed by *lo*, in much the same way as in English these prepositions are sometimes followed by *of*. For example, we can say, "on top **of** the house," "in front **of** the house," and so on. Sometimes we do not find this "of," as in "underneath the house" or "behind the house." In Creole, however, you almost always find this *lo*; for example,

insaid long aus	inside the house
andanis lo viikl	under the car
antap lo ruuf	on top of the roof

In the preceding section on pronouns, two slightly differing sets of pronouns were presented. The first set is used in subject position and the second in object position in respect to verbs. It is the second set which serves as objects of prepositions as well; for example,

mine	*blo mi*	NEVER	*blong ai* or *blo ai*
with him	*long im* or *lo im*	NEVER	*long i* or *lo i*

You should be able to make up some Creole constructions for yourself now. Look at the phrases in boldface type in the sentences below and try to work out how you would say them in Creole. Cover the answers on the righthand side before checking to see if you were right or not.

They were **inside the sergeant's house.**	*insaid long aus blo saajan*
The fish was **right up on the beach.**	*raidap antap lo sanbich*
They are sitting **on the jetty.**	*lo jeti*
He lives **at Umagico.**	*long Alau*
He is going **to Umagico.**	*long Alau*
He hit me **with his stick.**	*lo stik blong im*
I swam **with the children.**	*lo pikanini*
They hid **behind the tree.**	*biain lo tri*

5.4 Equational Sentences

We have now looked at nouns, pronouns, and prepositions in Creole. We have learned enough now to begin looking at the way we make up sentences in the language from these smaller units. The simplest sentences in Creole are those we call 'equational' sentences. The name suggests that we are equating two things, and this is indeed what is meant by the term:

> That man is my boss.
> He is a big boy.

These sentences you will observe, both contain parts of the verb "to be." (Besides "is," other parts are "am," "are," "was," "were," and so on.) In Creole, there is no verb "to be." Instead, there are two patterns, and both are very simple.

The first pattern is that used when the first element (the subject) in the equational sentence is a pronoun. When you use this pattern, you simply place the pronoun at the beginning of the sentence and then have the second element follow it immediately, with nothing in between;

> *Im big baga.*
> He is a big fellow.

> *Mitu bos blong im.*
> We two (not you) are his boss.

The second pattern is that used when the subject is not a pronoun, but a noun. This pattern makes use of a small word called a 'concord particle.' Since you have not yet learned about how Creole uses concord particles, these will be explained first, before going on to discuss the second type of equational sentence.

5.5 Concord Particles

Here is an important rule that holds for many (but not all) Creole speakers: whenever the subject of a sentence is a noun (but not a pronoun), the rest of the sentence (the 'predicate') is typically preceded by a small particle that agrees with the noun in person. There are two concord particles:

> **Second person**   *yu*
> **Third person**   *i*

The third-person concord particle *i* is the one you will hear most frequently. Whenever a noun is used in a sentence such as:

> The dog is barking.

the concord particle must follow the Creole equivalent of "the dog" and precede the Creole equivalent of "is barking." Thus, this sentence will become:

Dog i singaut.

Whether the noun is singular or plural, the concord marker is always *i*; for example,

Plenti maan i kech-im fish daun lo riva.
    Some men are catching fish down at the river.

The other concord particle that is used in the second person is *yu*. If you are using a subject noun in the second person, in order to address somebody, then instead of introducing the rest of the sentence by *i*, you use *yu*. This kind of sentence in English would be:

You men come here!
Willie and Larry listen to me!

In sentences like these in Creole you should use the concord particle *yu*, as follows;

Olmaan yu kam ia!
    Come here old man!
Wili an Lari yu lisan mi!
    Willie and Larry listen to me!

Of course, if you are talking *about* the old man or Willie and Larry and not *to* them, then the concord particle will be *i*.

Olmaan i kam ia.
    The old man is coming here.
Wili an Lari i lisan mi.
    Willie and Larry are listening to me.

5.6 Returning to Equational Sentences

Now that you have learned about the behavior of the concord particles in Creole, we can find out more about the behavior of equational sentences. If the subject is a pronoun, you have seen that there is no concord particle. However, the structure of any sentence with a noun subject is:

Subject + Concord particle + Predicate

Hence, for equational sentences:

Det maan i bos blo mi.
> The man is my boss.

Tumach maan i stakman.
> Many men are stockmen.

This same pattern is used for other sentences which are only slightly different from equational sentences. By 'equational' sentences, we mean those of the form:

noun/pronoun = noun

We can also have 'descriptive' sentences, in which the second element is some kind of descriptive element such as an adjective or an expression describing a place, for example:

Im prapa kruk.
> He is very ill.

Ol ded.
> They are dead.

Det maan i tumach spaak.
> That man is very drunk.

Dog i andanis long aus.
> The dog is under the house.

Give yourself another test. Look at the sentences in the left-hand column below and work out how to say them in Creole (without cheating!)

Listen to me Roy!	*Roi yu lisan mi.*
The kangaroo is dead.	*Kanggaru i ded.*
This man is a sergeant.	*Dis maan i saajan.*
These men are sergeants.	*Dis maan i saajan.*
I am running.	*Mi ran.*
They are running.	*Ol ran.* or *Dempela ran.*
The sky is blue.	*Skai i blu.*
The rain is coming.	*Rein i kam.*

5.7 Existential Sentences

There are sentences in English which you use to say whether or not something exists. The technique for expressing these sentences (which we will call 'existential' sentences) is to use "there" + a form of the verb "to be" + noun. So, we say:

There are mangoes on the ground.
There are no people on the wharf.
There's a lot of rain in The Wet.

When Creole expresses such existential sentences, you will hear constructions quite different from those you use in English, since Creole has no word which can translate "there," and we have already seen that there is no verb "to be." What one does in Creole is to imagine that there is a noun at the beginning of the sentence (in much the same way that in English one imagines there is a noun in "It's raining." That there is no noun in the English sentence is shown by the fact that it is quite ridiculous to ask "What is raining?") You saw in the previous section that where a sentence has a noun at the beginning, the rest of the sentence must be preceded by the concord particle *i*. Also, to express the existential sentence, we must insert following the concord particle *i* the word *gat*. When you wish to express the negative existential ("there isn't," "there aren't"), the word *gat* is replaced by *nogat* (which often appears without the preceding particle *i*); for example,

> *I gat manggo lo det tri.*
>> There are mangoes on the tree.

> *I gat tumach rein.*
>> There is a lot of rain.

> *I nogat maan lo jeti.*
>> There are no men on the wharf.

> *Nogat grog lo kantiin tanait.*
>> There is no grog in the canteen tonight.

> *I gat piksa lo Mapun.*
>> There is a film at Mapoon.

5.8   Impersonal Sentences

In the sentence "It's raining," it was pointed out that the "it" here does not really refer to anything in particular. The sentence only expresses the idea "There is raining." The use of "it" is purely conventional. Such constructions are called 'impersonal' sentences.

Because Creole has no verb "to be" and because the pronoun *im* can only refer to real things, it is predictable that a construction quite different from that of SAE is used in Creole for impersonal sentences. Once again, you have to pretend that there is a noun at the beginning of the sentence. Since we are imagining that there is a noun, the rest of the sentence must be preceded by the concord particle *i*:

I rein.
> It is raining.

I prapa hat.
> It is very hot.

I orait.
> It is OK.

There is a second kind of impersonal sentence in English. It is used when we are talking about time; for example,

> It is afternoon.
> It is three o'clock.

In Creole however, you do not express these sentences in the same way as you express sentences such as "It is raining." Instead, the time sentences just given are expressed as:

I kam fa aftanun.
I kam fa tri aklak.

There is once again no subject, but the concord particle still makes its appearance before the verb. After the verb you will hear the preposition *fa.*

5.9   Verbal Sentences

We are now in a position to look at the behavior of genuine verbal sentences. All of the sentences discussed so far are unusual in that they either do not contain verbs or they do not contain subjects (or both). However, most of the sentences you will hear in Creole (and in English) are sentences which have subjects and verbs.

The behavior of sentences which have a subject and a verb is fairly simple. If the subject is a pronoun, we simply place the pronoun first and the verb second, as in:

Mi ran.
> I am running.

Ol waak lo Bamaga.
> They work at Bamaga.

Tupela stap long Alau.
> They (two) live at Umagico.

Where the subject is a noun, you have to place before the verb the concord particle *i* that has already been described and exemplified in some detail. For the reader's better understanding, some examples of the use of *i* before verbs are given:

> *Baad i flai.*
>> The bird is flying.
>
> *Olmaan i singaut.*
>> The old man is shouting.
>
> *Walabi i kamaut fram skrab.*
>> The wallaby is coming out of the rainforest.

Actually, the verbal sentences just discussed are the simplest type of verbal sentence in Creole. When the verb has an object (all examples above have only a subject, but no object), then the construction becomes a little more complicated, though it is still quite regular. The kinds of sentences we are about to look at are like the following English examples:

> I bought **some food** from the store.
> He dug **the ground.**
> They squashed **the mangoes.**
> They caught **a dugong.**

When expressing such sentences in Creole, we use the same word order as we have in English; first you have the subject, then the verb, and then the object. As with all other verbal sentences, if the subject is a noun, the verb must be preceded by the concord particle *i*, and if the subject is a pronoun, this concord particle is absent. There is one additional fact, however, which you will notice when a verb has an object. This is that the verb itself is usually followed by the suffix *-im*. There are only a few verbs that do not take this suffix. These are *luk* "see," *savi* "know," *kaikai* "eat," and *lisan* "listen to," as exemplified by:

> *Im bin luk mi.*   (NEVER   ... *luk-im* ...)
>> He saw me.
>
> *Ol bin kaikai dugong.*   (NEVER   ... *kaikai-im* ...)
>> They ate dugong.
>
> *Roi bin lisan mi.*   (NEVER   ... *lisan-im* ...)
>> Roy listened to me.

All other transitive verbs (verbs with objects) have this suffix *-im*, e.g.:

> *Mi bin bai-im kaikai.*
>> I bought some food.

Dog i bin bait-im mi.
   The dog bit me.

Im bin dig-im graun.
   He dug the ground.

Olmaan i kas-im chek.
   The old man is cashing a check.

It is possible for this *-im* suffix to be lost if there is a following object, though this is uncommon, or it is sometimes simply reduced to *-i* or *-a* without being completely dropped. So although the usual form is:

Im bin chak-im spia.
   He threw the spear.

you will occasionally have the alternate forms:

Im bin chak-i spia.
Im bin chak-a spia.
Im bin chak spia.

There are instances where a verb which carries this transitive suffix *-im* has no following object. This construction is used when the object is a third-person pronoun, either singular or plural. So we hear:

Sili baga i bin dringk-im.
   The silly fellow drank it.

Dog i bin bait-im.
   The dog bit him/them.

Yupela pul-im.
   You (all) pull it.

If the verb is one of the four transitive verbs that never take the suffix *-im* (*savi, kaikai, lisan,* and *luk*), then the third-person pronoun objects follow the verb as separate words; for example,

Mi no luk im.
   I didn't see him.

Mi no savi dempela.
   I don't know them.

The *-im* suffix is added to a transitive verb (except for the verbs just mentioned) if the object is a pronoun. So:

Im bin kik-im yu lasnait.
> He kicked you last night.

Olmaan i go bai-im dempela kaikai.
> The old man will buy them some food.

There are some complications in the use of this suffix *-im* with verbs such as:

pikap	pick up
kataut	cut out
digap	dig up
pudaun	put down

When these verbs are pronounced without the *-im*, as they are written here, they are quite definitely pronounced as though they are one word. However, when they take an object, the *-im* suffix goes at the end of the verb as we would regard it as in English, rather than at the end of the whole word. Thus:

> *Ol bin pikimap manggo.*
> > They picked up the mangoes.
>
> NEVER: *Ol bin pikapim manggo.*

Even the new element *pikimap* is pronounced as a single word, however, and the *ap* element cannot be separated as it is in English and placed at the end of the sentence. So, while in English we can say:

> They picked the mangoes up.

you will *never* hear in Creole the sentence:

> *Ol bin pikim manggo ap.*

It can only be:

> *Ol bin pikimap manggo.*

See if you can pick out which sentences below have *-im* on the verb. (Remember to cover up the answers on the righthand side.)

The crocodile took the goanna's teeth.	*Krok i bin tekim tiit blo gwana.*
The crocodile ran away with his teeth.	*Krok i bin ran lo tiit blong im.*

The crocodile put the teeth in.	*Krok i bin pudimin tiit.*
The brolga dug the ground up.	*Brolga i bin digimap graun.*
I ate some dugong.	*Mi bin kaikai dugong.*
I know that man.	*Ai savi det maan.*
The mosquitoes bit him.	*Moskito i bin baitim.*

5.10 Verbal Modifiers

Immediately preceding a verb in Creole, you will sometimes find one of the following two modifiers:

go   (Future Tense)
bin   (Past Tense)

Very often, a verb will be preceded by nothing, in which case the verb can be present tense, future tense, or past tense. So, when trying to interpret a sentence such as:

Maan i ran.

do not be misled by its appearance. Although it looks like "The man ran," it can actually have three meanings:

The man ran.
The man is running.
The man will run.

It is only if you especially need to indicate that the action takes place in the past or the future that you use the verbal modifiers *go* and *bin*. The use of these forms is illustrated by the following sentences:

Im bin kambek.
    He has returned./He returned.
Im go kambek.
    He will return.

The past-tense verbal modifier also has an alternate form *bi* that often occurs before verbs beginning with a consonant. The reader should also note that if the subject of a verb is a noun, then the concord particle *i* must still be placed before the verb. If the verbal modifiers are present, the particle *i* precedes these; for example,

Dog i bin kambek.
   The dog has returned.

Pikanini i go krai.
   The baby will cry.

5.11 Presentence Modifiers

Creole has a small number of words that can occur at the beginning of a sentence. Those you will hear are:

klosap	(Immediate Future)
baimbai	(Distant Future)
stil	(Continuative)
oredi	(Completive)
mait	(Dubitive)

Most of these presentence modifiers express the category that grammarians call 'aspect,' but *go* and *bin* express the 'tense' of the verb. The aspect words express the way in which the action takes place. So, *stil* indicates that the action is continuing on from an earlier state:

Stil i no bin kam.
   He hasn't come yet.

Oredi indicates that the action is now completed.

Oredi ai bin lisan Roi.
   I have heard Roy.

and *mait* expresses uncertainty:

Mait i kam fa luk mi.
   He might come to see me.

You will notice that *klosap* and *baimbai* both express tense rather than aspect, but they still occur in presentence position. They never occur in preverbal position as do *go* and *bin*. When a sentence is modified by *klosap*, the meaning is that the action will take place in the near future, but if the sentence is modified by *baimbai*, the action will take place at sometime in the long distant future; for example,

Klosap mi go luk yu.
   I'll see you soon.

Baimbai olmaan i go dai.
   The old man will die sometime.

5.12 Postsentence Modifiers

There is a second set of aspect markers that appear not at the beginning, but at the end of a sentence. These aspect words are:

pinis	(Completive)
gen	(Repetitive)
trai	(Attemptive)
nau	(Inceptive)
wanwan	(Sequentive)
yet	(Continuative)

You will observe that some aspects, namely, the completive and the continuative forms, can be expressed equally by presentence modifiers as well as by postsentence modifiers. So, for example,

Oredi i bin go.
I bin go pinis.

are synonymous, both meaning "He has gone." Similarly,

Stil i stap long Araipi.
I stap long Araipi yet.

are synonymous, meaning "He is still living at Red Island Point."
The postsentence modifier *gen* indicates that an action is being repeated, as in:

Migolo bin sut-im gen.
  The white man shot it again.

The word *trai* means to try and do something, as in:

I bin chak-im trai.
  He tried to throw it.

You must be careful to avoid using this particle as a verb as we do in English. You will not hear:

I bin trai chak-im.

in base Creole. The particle *nau* means that the action is, was, or will be just starting to take place at a particular time; for example,

Im bin go nau.
  He went then.

This particle also is likely to cause problems if it is too closely associated in meaning with English "now." You should not be surprised to hear "now" in past-tense sentences as the one just given, as *nau* in Creole does not have a present-tense meaning as it does in English. The particle *wanwan* indicates that the action was performed in sequence by a number of actors, as in:

> *Ol kaikai wanwan.*
>> They ate one after the other.

The reader should also realize that any sentence can contain more than one of these presentence and postsentence modifiers. Thus, you could hear a sentence such as:

> *Mait i go chak-im spia trai pinis.*
>> He might have tried to throw the spear.

Of course, this is a fairly complicated sentence, not one people would use every day, but they might use a sentence like this on a particular occasion, and in an appropriate context, there would be no trouble understanding what it meant.

5.13 Directional Modifiers

Verbs in Creole can be divided into verbs of motion and verbs of nonmotion (as they can also for English). Examples of motion and nonmotion verbs are:

Motion Verbs		Nonmotion Verbs	
wokabaut	walk	*sing*	sing
ran	run	*stap*	live, stay
bring-im	bring	*beri-im*	bury
keri-im	carry	*dig-im*	dig
giv-im	give	*kuk-im*	cook
swim	swim	*kaikai*	eat

In Creole, there is a major difference between these two classes of verbs. Verbs of motion can be followed by a modifier that expresses the direction of the action. If the action takes place in the direction of the speaker, then the verb is followed by the modifier *kam*, and if the action takes place in the direction away from the speaker, then the verb is followed by *go*. Thus, you will hear:

> *Ol bin ran go.*
>> They ran away.

Ol bin ran kam.
They ran here.

Note that if the verb has an object, then the directional modifiers must follow the object, for example:

Ol bin bring-im kaikai kam.
They brought the food.

Win bin teik-im peipa go.
The wind blew the paper away.

This fact suggests that we should properly regard a verb and its object as a single phrase, and that the directional modifiers follow this phrase rather than just the verb.

Note that since the postsentence modifiers, which were discussed previously, are placed at the end of a sentence, these also follow the directional modifiers; for example,

Ol bin bring-im kaikai kam pinis.
They have already brought the food.

5.14 Adjectives

There has been very little discussion of the behavior of adjectives in Creole, because the differences from their behavior in SAE are for the most part not great. When the adjective is in what we call a 'predicative' construction (as the second element of a descriptive sentence), it is preceded by the particle *i* rather than by the verb "to be" as in English. This was one of the first sentence structures you learned in Creole. In 'attributive' constructions, where the adjective qualifies a noun, it is simply placed before the noun, as in SAE; for example,

roo miit   raw meat
strong san   hot sun

and so on.

However, when an adjective is made 'inchoative' (i.e., to become something), then the Creole construction differs quite markedly from SAE. In SAE, the inchoative construction is expressed by using the verb "to become," (or more colloquially "to get"), as in:

The sun became/got hot.
He is becoming/getting old.

In Creole, however, the inchoative verb can only be *kam*. It behaves in all respects as a verb, and if the subject is a noun, it requires the particle *i* to precede it; for example,

San i kam strong nau.
>The sun is getting hot.

Im kam ool nau.
>He is getting old.

Dog i kam wail.
>The dog is getting angry.

5.15 Reduplication

By "reduplication," we mean the repetition of a word to form a new, "double-barreled" word. In SAE we seldom reduplicate words, though we do have a process similar to this when we form words such as *helter-skelter, Humpty-Dumpty, higgledy-piggledy* and so on. In Creole, it is not at all uncommon to repeat a word. When we do this, however, we change its meaning. If a noun is reduplicated, we make an adjective. So in Creole, reduplication fulfills a role similar to our suffixes *-y* or *-ish*, as in:

Noun		**Adjective**	
spat	spot	*spat-spat*	spotty
neil	nail	*neil-neil*	spiky
jam	jump	*jam-jam*	jumpy

These reduplicated adjectives are used as regular adjectives, like:

spat-spat tingari	spotted stingray
jam-jam daans	a corroboree with lots of jumping

Not only adjectives can be derived by reduplication. New verbs can be formed from other verbs by repetition. If the verb is repeated, it means to do something continuously, all over the place, or too much; for example,

Verb		**Reduplicated Verb**	
ran	run	*ran-ran*	ran about all over the place
tok	talk	*tok-tok*	growl
flout	float	*flout-flout*	float about all over the place
swim	swim	*swim-swim*	swim around
sing	sing	*sing-sing*	sing for a long time

5.16 Negative Sentences

All of the sentences that have been discussed so far are affirmative or positive, that is, simple statements of fact. If we want to express the negative, that is, denying statements of fact, in SAE, we notice the changes below:

I saw him. ⟶ I didn't see him.

You will observe that the verb "do" is inserted in the appropriate tense and the word "not" (often reduced to "-n't") follows this. The verb then follows in the infinitive form. In Creole, the formation of a negative sentence is considerably simpler. You only need to place the negative particle *no* before the verb. If the verb has the tense markers *bin* or *go*, then the negative particle precedes, but it *must* follow the particle *i* if present. For example,

Mi no bin kil-im dog blong im.
   I didn't kill his dog.

Maan i no go kambek lo haus.
   The man will not return home.

There is in Creole a second negative particle *nomo*. We should probably regard this as another of the set of postsentence aspect modifiers; it expresses a kind of negative form of the continuative marker *yet*, as in:

I stap long Araipi yet.
   He is still living at Red Island Point.

I stap long Araipi nomo.
   He is no longer living at Red Island Point.

5.17 Questions

In SAE when we want to turn a statement into a question, we have to apply a fairly complex series of rules. If we examine the sentence pair:

He saw the man. ⟶ Did he see the man?

We can see that we have placed at the beginning of the sentence the verb "do" (in the appropriate tense), followed by the subject, and then by the verb which is in the infinitive form. Creole does not have this construction at all. Instead, all you need to do is change the tone of your voice (the intonation). We do this quite often in English in fact. Thus, with:

You went fishing from the wharf?

we can distinguish the question from a statement by intonation alone. If you take the Creole statement:

Yu bin chak-im lain fram jeti?

you can make it into a question by using the same intonation as for the English sentence just given:

Yu bin chak-im lain fram jeti?

Questions are also frequently formed in Creole by placing the question tag particle *e* following the normal statement form, as in:

Yu bin chak-im lain fram jeti, e?

There is a second kind of question that can be made in English by using one of the interrogative pronouns such as "how," "where," "when," or "why." In Creole, you use the following interrogative forms:

hau	how
haumach	how much, how many
wee	where
wen	when
hu bla	whose
wanim	what

and so on. The only real difficulty here is that *haumach* is the general interrogative of quantity, where in English we use both "how many" and "how much." In English we say "how many" if we are asking about a number, but "how much" if we are asking about an amount; for example,

How many dogs?
How much flour?

In Creole, however, this distinction is not made. So you should say:

Haumach dog?
Haumach flaua?

The interrogative of possession is *hu bla*, as in:

Hu bla dis aus?
 Whose is this house?

and the interrogative for things as a whole is *wanim* rather than a form derived directly from English "what"; for example,

Wanim yu bin luk dhee?
 What did you see there?

In the section on verbal sentences, you were introduced to the suffix *-im* which marks transitive verbs in Creole. So, you may hear the sentence:

Im bin chak-im spia.
 He threw the spear.

However, if the object of the verb is an interrogative, this *-im* is not found because all interrogative pronouns are placed at the beginning of the sentence. So, if you want to ask a question about the object of the preceding sentence, you should say:

Haumach spia im bin chak?
 How many spears did he throw?

Wanim im bin chak?
 What did he throw?

But if there is an interrogative that is not asking about the object, and the object therefore still follows the verb, you will still keep the *-im* suffix; for example,

Wen yu bin bai-im kaikai?
 When did you buy the food?

Hau ol go kil-im tingari?
 How will they kill the stingray?

There is something else that should be pointed out about the word *wanim*. In the preceding sentences, it always has an interrogative meaning. However, it can occur in sentences without asking a question. You will always be able to tell the difference between *wanim* used in these two ways, because of the difference in word order. When it is used noninterrogatively, *wanim* simply means "a thing." So, you will hear:

Yu bin bring dhet wanim kam.
> You brought that thing.
> (NOT: You brought that "what.")

Yu bin kech-im mach wanim?
> Did you catch many things?
> (NOT: Did you catch many "whats"?)

It is also used as an indefinite pronoun in the form *wanimting*, as in:

Ol go dig-im wanimting.
> They will dig something.

Pikanini bin fain-im wanimting.
> The baby has found something.

5.18   Interjections

Interjections are usually very short expressions, commonly of only one word, that express a very strong and often sudden feeling. In English, some of the interjections we use are: "oh!" "boy!" "eh?" "wow!" "shit!" "bugger!" "ouch!" and so on. The interjections used by Creole speakers probably depend largely on what is their native language. Thus, an Islander speaking Creole may say *eso* for "thank you" and *waa* for "yes," whereas an Aborigine would not, and some Cowal Creek Aborigines will use *akai* as an expression of surprise whereas other Creole speakers would not. However, Creole speakers all use the following interjections very frequently, regardless of what their native language is:

1. *orait*. In narration, this interjection seems to end what we might loosely call a paragraph, and indicates that something fresh is coming up in the story. This interjection is also used very frequently in the expression *i orait*, which is the Creole equivalent of "It's OK." or "She'll be right," a common Australian expression.

2. *yawo*. This is what you say when you are taking your leave of somebody. It is equivalent to "Cheerio" or "Hooroo" in SAE. It is likely that *yawo* is more than just this however; it seems to act as a final sign of departure. You will seldom hear anybody break back into conversation after having said *yawo*. In English, you can say "Cheerio ... oh, by the way, I just forgot..." In Creole, you should reserve *yawo* for use when you know for certain there is nothing more to be said. It is a signal of no return.

3. *wanim*. You can use this as an interjection to get a speaker to repeat something you have not heard or understood, in the same way as you can say "What?" in SAE. There is no equivalent to "I beg your pardon?"; Creole does not see the need to have a special polite form here as *wanim* is quite acceptable.

4. *tru*. This interjection follows a sentence and indicates that the speaker is firmly committed to the truth of what he says, in the same way as Australians occasionally say "fair dinkum" or "true dinks"; for example,

Baimbai yu gat spia-fait tru.
You will have a spear fight for sure.

5.19   Complex Sentences

This discussion of Cape York Creole has so far centered only on simple sentences, that is, sentences with one verb (and occasionally sentences with no verbs). However, it is possible to have sentences with more than one main verb just as in SAE there are sentences such as:

He **came** to **buy** some bread.
I **have eaten** the bread I **bought**.
He **told** me not to **eat** it.
He **started shouting.**

and so on. These are what we call "complex" sentences because we can regard them as being formed from two simple sentences. For example, "He came to buy some bread" would be derived from the simple sentences:

He **came**.
He **bought** some bread.

In SAE, there are many different ways of putting the two sentences together to make a complex sentence. The two sentences just presented are joined by placing "to" at the beginning of the sentence and using the infinitive form of the verb. Another way is to place "-ing" on the verb of the second sentence as we have done in "He started shouting."
As with SAE, Creole also has a number of ways of making two simple sentences into one complex sentence. So, although many of the complex sentence constructions are very similar to those of SAE, Creole expresses such complex sentences without much of the grammar of subordination that we have in English. Therefore, there is not as much detail discussed in this section as the complications of English would suggest there is a need for. For instance in:

Roy said Larry would come.

we have a special use of "would" to indicate 'future in past time'

(Compare this with "Roy said 'Larry will come' "). In Creole this would be simply:

> *Roi sei baimbai Lari i kam.*

where the second sentence (the 'subordinate clause') simply follows the first with no marking for the future any different than in direct speech.

Despite the apparent similarity to English, however, there are some constructions that are quite different which you should be familiar with, for example:

1. Verbs such as *staat* "start," *wan* "want," *let-im* "allow," *mek-im* "cause," can be followed by another verb with nothing separating them, as in:

> *Yu mek-im singaut.*
>> You made him shout.
>
> *Im mek-im mi singaut.*
>> He made me shout.
>
> *Yu let-im maan kam.*
>> You allow the man to come.
>
> *Ol let-im mipela go.*
>> They let us go.
>
> *Im wan go.*
>> He wants to go.
>
> *Im bin staat fis.*
>> He started fishing./He started to fish.

You will be able to notice that sometimes these sentences in English differ from the Creole forms. You will have to become familiar with the difference in construction here.

2. If we want to express the purpose of an action in a complex sentence in SAE, we put the verb of the second sentence into the infinitive form, as in:

> They came **to see** us.   (i.e., in order to see us)

Creole does not use "to" in this kind of sentence. Rather it uses *fa*. So this sentence will be:

> *Ol bin kam fa luk yumi.*

Other examples of this kind of complex sentence are:

Dog i dig-im graun fa kaikai boun.
> The dog is digging the ground to eat the bone.

Olmaan i kat-im kokonat fa fiid-im pig.
> The old man is cutting coconuts to feed the pigs.

5.20 Relative Clauses

A relative clause is a type of sentence used to modify a noun in another sentence. So in SAE:

> This is the meat that I bought.

we have the relative clause "that I bought" qualifying the noun "meat." Relative clauses in SAE can be introduced by "that," "which," or "who," as in:

> That is the man **who** I was talking to before.
> This is the dog **which** bit you.

or simply by nothing:

> That is the man I was talking to before.
> This is the meat I bought.

In the speech of many Creole speakers, a relative clause is always preceded by *wee*, and it can never be left out as the relative clause markers sometimes can in SAE. So, you can have the sentences:

Dhet trokas wee ai bin fain-im ai kaikai pinis.
> The trochus which I found, I have eaten it up.

Dhet viikl wee you bin boro-im lastaim i brokdaun.
> The car which you borrowed last time has broken down.

Dhet maan wee i go wokabaut i bin dai.
> The man who went walkabout died.

It is possible in SAE to have a relative clause to a noun which is the object of a preposition; for example,

> I saw the chair you sat on.

In SAE, this kind of sentence has a preposition at the end. In Creole, you should never leave a preposition at the end of a sentence. This kind of sentence in Creole simply drops the preposition, as in:

Mi bin luk dhet teibl wee yu bin put-im buk.
   I saw the table which you put the book **on**.
Ol bin hit-im maan wee yu bin go wokabaut.
   They hit the man you went walkabout **with**.

Try translating the English sentences below into Creole (without looking at the answers on the right).

I came to tell you something.	*Mi bin kam fa telim yu wanimting.*
He shouted to the man sitting down.	*Im bin singaut lo maan wee i sidaun.*
He will eat the meat I bought.	*I go kaikai miit wee ai bin bai-im.*
They want to talk to me.	*Ol wan tok lo mi.*
This is the axe you cut the wood with.	*Diswan i tamiok wee yu bin katim wud.*

5.21 Or Else ...

In English we often say things like:

Go away **or else** I'll hit you.
Don't eat that **or else** you'll get sick.

The way to say this kind of thing in Creole is not like the pattern you are used to in English. The first part of the sentence is an order, what we call an "imperative" construction. To express the imperative, in SAE, you can see from the examples just given, that usually you use only the basic form of the verb, and nothing else. So:

Go away!
Don't eat that!

The second example is a negative imperative, which places "don't" before the basic form of the verb. In Creole, if you want to express the imperative, you use the verb as you ordinarily would, and place before it the second-person pronoun. Now, you must remember that there are three different second-person pronouns, depending on the number of people you are speaking to. So, the first sentence above could be any of the following:

$$\left.\begin{array}{l} Yu \\ Yutu(pela) \\ Yupela \end{array}\right\} \; gowei$$

The negative imperative is not formed by using "don't" as in English; rather, you place the negative particle *no* after the pronoun. So, the second sentence would be:

$$\left.\begin{array}{l} Yu \\ Yutu(pela) \\ Yupela \end{array}\right\} \; no \; kaikai \; det!$$

To express the "... or else ..." part of the sentence, you simply place the word *bifo* (or *bipo*) after the imperative sentence, and add the rest of the sentence; for example,

> *Yupela no kaikai det bipo yu fool sik.*
> Don't eat that or you'll all get sick.

> *Yupla sat-im maut bipo ai cheis yupla.*
> Shut your mouths or I'll chase you away.

6 VOCABULARY

Cape York Creole has become a fully viable language, and as such it possesses a word stock containing all sorts of terms required by specialized circumstances. Thus, for example, carpentry with its various technical procedures can be handled in Creole. And a newly introduced item of technology, such as the television (which is known only from hearsay by many Creole speakers), can be called a *piksa-baks*, by compounding two already existing Creole words.

Some of the lexical items used in Creole differ from anything you will ever hear in SAE. Such words are sometimes borrowed from the original Beach-la-mar pidgin that was introduced into the area last century. Others come from Malay (as Malay traders and laborers entered the area both before and after white contact), or (in surprisingly few cases) from the original Aboriginal and Islander languages. Some examples of these Creole words of non-English origin are:

food, eat	*kaikai*	(Beach-la-mar, originally from Polynesian)
ear	*talinga*	(Malay)
know	*savi*	(Beach-la-mar, originally from Portuguese)
child, baby	*pikanini*	(Beach-la-mar, originally from Portuguese)

whiteman	*migolo*	(?)
blossom	*kansa*	(?)
cook under ashes	*kapamari*	(?)
sarong	*lava-lava*	(Pacific?)
sweet	*susu*	(Malay)

The vast majority of words used in Creole are taken from SAE, however. The phonetic changes which take place between the words in the standard language and in Creole have been discussed in some detail. For the most part, this change in phonetic form is all that you need to know about. However, there are many cases where a word in Creole has changed slightly in meaning from the word that is used in SAE, or where two words in SAE have become one word in Creole. An example of the latter kind is:

see, look   *luk*

This convergence is typical of the basilect. Mesolect or acrolect speakers sometimes say "see" as well as "look." Other examples of this kind are:

bad	*nogud*	(from "no good")
diarrhea	*beliran*	(from "belly run")
cold (the illness)	*koolsik*	(from "cold sick")
on your back	*beliap*	(from "belly up")
live, stay	*stap*	
a lot	*tumach*	(from "too much")
beach	*sanbich*	(from "sand beach")
return	*kambek*	(from "come back")
other	*nadha(wan)*	(from "another one")
the best	*nambawan*	(from "number one")
the same	*seimwei*	(from "same way")
shout	*singaut*	(from "sing out")
	saudaut	(from "shout out")
stand	*staanap*	(from "stand up")
sit	*sidaun*	(from "sit down")
run away in anger	*stoomwei*	(from "storm away")
grab, take, get	*kech-im*	
stingray	*tingari*	
stop a vehicle for a lift	*beil-im ap*	(from "bail it up")
throw	*chak-im*	

deaf	*talinga nogud*
blind	*ai nogud*
smoke	*faiasmouk* (from "fire smoke")
be drunk	*spaak* (from "spark")
urine, urinate	*pipi* (from "pee-pee")
lie (i.e., tell a lie), pretend	*geman* (from "gammon")
cheat	*blaf* (from "bluff")
hide	*stoowei* (from "stow away")
father's elder brother	*big ankl*
father's younger brother	*litl ankl*
maternal grandmother	*greni blo madha*
Thursday Island	*tiai* (from "T.I.")
bow of canoe	*foored* (from "forehead")
Red Island Point	*araipi* (from "R.I.P.")

SUGGESTIONS FOR FURTHER READING

A good short introduction to the study of pidgin and Creole languages is the paperback by Loreto Todd, *Pidgins and Creoles*, Routledge and Kegan Paul, London and Boston, 1974. A modern classic work on the general topic, also available in paperback, is Dell Hymes, ed., *Pidginization and Creolization of Languages*, Cambridge University Press, London, 1971.

Background material and description of the Cape York Creole as spoken by Torres Straits Islanders is provided by the article by T. E. Dutton, "Informal English in the Torres Straits," which appears in W. S. Ramson, ed., *English Transported. Essays on Australasian English*, Australian National University Press, Canberra, 1970. The use of the Cape York Creole by Aboriginal people at Bamaga is treated by Bruce Rigsby, "Pidgin Talk lo Bamaga: Aboriginal English on Northern Cape York Penninsula," *Kivung*, to appear.

For a description of an Aboriginal language of Cape York peninsula (at Hopevale, refer to map, Figure 4.1), see the chapter by J. B. Haviland "How to Talk to Your Brother-in-Law in Guugu Yimidhirr" in the companion volume, *Languages and Their Speakers*, T. Shopen, ed., Winthrop Publishers, 1979.

T.C. thanks Sid Mounsey and Joan MacIlwraith of Bamaga for being interested. B.R. thanks Ross Wilson for friendship and support. Both of us, T.C. and B.R., express our deep gratitude and feelings to our many Aboriginal and Islander friends at Bamaga who shared their language and culture with us.

V

Swahili

Thomas J. Hinnebusch

INTRODUCTION

Swahili is a lingua franca, a means of communication for about 25 million ethnically diverse peoples living in Eastern Africa who speak Bantu, Nilotic, and Cushitic languages as their first languages. For these people Swahili is a second language, but on the East African coast and on the offshore islands, particularly Zanzibar, it is also the native language of some 2 million people. It began as a language spoken by only a few hundred thousand people living on the coast and spread throughout East Africa. Some of the details are clouded in prehistory, but enough is known to reconstruct an outline of Swahili's early development.

Along some thousand miles of coastline—between Mogadishu in Somalia, in the north, and the Tanzania–Mozambique border, in the south (see map)—lies the traditional Swahili-speaking area. As one might expect in such a large area, linguistic uniformity does not exist. Scattered all along this strip are hundreds of Swahili-speaking communities speaking a continuum of dialects, all more or less mutually intelligible from north to south. One of these dialects, that of the island of Zanzibar,

Thomas J. Hinnebusch is a linguist and language teacher whose main research interests include Swahili and comparative Bantu studies. After living, teaching, and doing research in Tanzania and Kenya for some four years he is presently Assistant Professor of Linguistics and African Languages at the University of California at Los Angeles where he teaches Swahili and linguistics and is Co-editor of Studies in African Linguistics. *Currently he is working on material to develop a linguistic classification of East African Bantu languages.*

is essentially the model for the kind of Swahili that is spoken in mainland Tanzania (formerly Tanganyika), most of Kenya, and parts of Uganda, and beyond into Zaire (formerly the Congo), Mozambique, Zambia, Burundi, and Ruanda.

The Swahili variants that one finds spoken away from the coast, in so-called up-country areas, range from a form commonly called standard Swahili to highly pidginized versions spoken mainly, but not exclusively, by Asian and European immigrant communities: they are known respectively as Kihindi and Kisetla. Somewhere between these extremes are variants which are spoken by the various indigenous ethnic groups, such as the Maasai, Luo, Luhya, Galla, Kikuyu, Kamba, Sukuma,

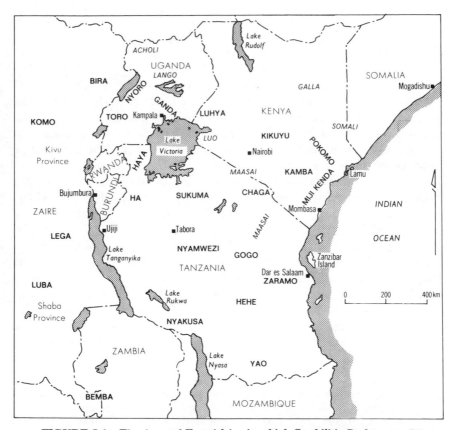

FIGURE 5.1   *The Area of East Africa in which Swahili is Spoken as a Lingua Franca*

Bantu languages are named in capitals (KIKUYU, NYAMWEZI, LUBA, etc.) and non-Bantu languages in italic capitals (MAASAI, LUO, SOMALI, etc.). This is only a small sample of the total number of distinct languages.

Chaga, Haya, and many others, variants sometimes markedly different from the Swahili spoken by first-language speakers.

The influences that create these differences are both linguistic and sociological. The first languages of these speakers is, by far, the major factor. Whether an up-country person speaks a version of Swahili which approaches the coastal norm is also a question of schooling, residence in a rural or urban setting, and exposure to mass media (radio, television, newspapers, and magazines). Diversity makes it difficult to describe Swahili; furthermore, it has not been easy for either first or second-language speakers to reach a consensus on a definition of standard Swahili, and the same kind of problem has faced educators and government officials wishing to impose standards on the language over large areas.

The basic problem was settled some time ago, and today people have a norm against which they can model their linguistic performance at the national level, even though there are differences of detail over which arguments will arise. The fact of Swahili as a lingua franca predates the rise of modern education and the establishment of national governments in East Africa. The Swahili of Zanzibar Town and very similar dialects were already widely spoken along commercially important parts of the coast and along the trade routes that wended their way into the interior. Educators, linguists, and civil servants took what they found and attempted to adapt it to their needs. This has resulted in a form of Swahili which no single group in East Africa feels completely comfortable with, but which is nevertheless the standard by which, at least, all nonnative forms of Swahili are judged today.

Most speakers of Swahili do not acquire the language as very young children; they are at least school age before they begin learning it; many acquire it as adults outside of their home villages—in market centers and towns where they travel to find employment. So it is for immigrants who came to East Africa as adults. Their success at learning Swahili often varies. People whose first language is already a Bantu language find the morphology and syntax of Swahili familiar; those whose native language is non-Bantu do not, for example native speakers of Maasai, Luo, Gujerati, and English (Maasai and Luo are Nilotic languages spoken in Kenya; Gujerati is spoken by immigrants from India and is the major Asian language in East Africa; English is the predominant language of European settlers). The responses of these various communities to learning Swahili, both linguistically and sociologically, are different. In some cases, they learn standard Swahili, but in others a form of pidgin Swahili, a language which has a highly simplified morphology and syntax.

This chapter will have two main sections. In the first we will consider the major characteristics of Swahili; in the second we will consider its place in the social fabric of East Africa.

1 THE SWAHILI LANGUAGE

1.1 The Verb and the Clause

Swahili has two prominent syntactic characteristics. One is the language's morphological classification of nouns into discrete sets. For example, nouns which have an initial *m* sound in their singular form, and *wa* in their plural form, such as *mtu* "person" and *watu* "people", belong to one class; nouns with *ki* and *vi* in their singular and plural shapes, for example *kiti* "chair" and *viti* "chairs," belong to another, and so on. The other characteristic is the role played by the verb in the organization of clauses; we'll begin with the verb.

Clauses are used to communicate minimal pieces of information, things like *Ali ran* and *Ali greeted Fatuma*. Verbs like *ran* and *greeted* are key words around which clauses are organized, and they tell us rather specific things about events or states. The verbs define a plot, and the people or things playing roles are typically designated by nouns, like *Ali, Fatuma, the man, the woman,* or by pronouns, *he, him, she, her,* all nominal expressions. We want to look at how nominal expressions are grouped around verbs to form clauses in Swahili, and how someone goes about learning this.

In both English and Swahili the word order is subject, verb and then, if there is one, object; in both languages, verbal expressions tell us about the time and other aspects of events and states, but beyond this the reader will begin to find Swahili quite different from English.

1.1.1 *Subject-Marking* Usually the first things people learn about another language are the greetings. For instance, Swahili shopkeepers on the Kenya coast make it a point to greet all their non-Swahili-speaking customers in their own languages. In turn these people quickly learn the proper Swahili greetings. Imagine yourself in this situation and consider:[1]

(1) *Hujambo.*   Hello, how are you (Sg)?
     Habari gani?   How are things?
     Habari za asubuhi?   How are things (this) morning?

Any man or woman involved in the community will also learn numbers and other practical vocabulary useful in short utterances. But then if you are to make any progress in learning standard Swahili you will have to come to grips with the structure and morphology of the

---

[1]You can attempt a fairly accurate pronunciation of these Swahili words by pronouncing vowels with Spanish or Italian values, and consonants with English values; to achieve more accurate, near-native pronunciation you would need native-speaking models to mimic.

clause. You quickly learn the Swahili equivalents of the pronouns "I" and "you" in your own language:

(2)   *mimi*   I
       wewe   you

You may hear these pronouns foregrounded in short utterances as, for instance, in answer to the greeting of *hujambo*, when the person responds by saying:

(3) **Mimi** *sijambo,* *na*   *wewe* *je?*
    I   I'm fine and **you** how/what?
    As for me, I'm fine, how about you?

Or, you may hear them used in a context such as the following where you and a Swahili-speaking friend are at the market and you hear someone say:

(4) **Mimi** *ninataka*   *maembe.*
    I   want   mangoes
    I would like some mangoes.

in answer to the fruit seller's question:[2]

(5) *Je,*   **wewe**   *unataka*   *ndizi?*
    Say **you**   want   bananas
    Say, would **you** like some bananas?

When you learn the other personal pronouns (which we list along with *mimi* and *wewe*),

(6) *mimi*   I
      wewe   you
      yeye   he, she (s/he)
      sisi   we
      ninyi   you (Pl)
      wao   they

you will be ready to understand a number of additional questions and answers, and will nearly be prepared to begin saying things such as "Do

---

[2]Questions in Swahili are pronounced differently from statements, with a distinctive rising intonation; they are not indicated by a change in word order as in English. Swahili speakers, however, often introduce a question with the particle *je*, which merely indicates that a question is about to be asked; we have translated it as "say."

they want some mangoes?" or "They want bananas." You will quickly
find out, however, that it is not enough to simply know the pronouns in
(6); you will have to learn something about the nature of the verb that
you may have missed in (4) and (5). In one, "want" is *ninataka*; in the
other it is *unataka*:[3]

(7)   **ni**-*nataka*   (used with *mimi* "I")
      u-*nataka*   (used with *wewe* "you")

As your exposure continues, you become aware that for each pronoun
(*yeye, wao, sisi,* etc.) there is a different element which is always
attached to the verb form:

(8)   *mimi*   *ni-*
      wewe   *u-*
      yeye   *a-*
      sisi   *tu-*
      ninyi   *m-*
      wao   *wa-*

Upon knowing these you have an easy time making the correct choices
to complete the following:

(9)   *Sisi* _____ *nataka ndizi.*   We want bananas.
      Wao _____ *nataka maembe.*   They want mangoes.

Swahili is like many other languages of the world in modifying the
shape of the verb to match particular subjects. Consider the intricacies
of Spanish or French in this respect, and of Russian, Hua, and Mohawk
as described in this volume. Modern English is relatively uncomplicated:
except for *to be* the most any verb has is agreement with subjects in the
present tense, and here with a distinctive form for only third-person
singular (*he/she/it*); we have *walks* versus *walk*, *has* versus *have*, and so
on. The most elaborate pattern is with *be*:

(10)   I   **am**   I/he/she/it   **was**
      we/they/you   **are**   we/they/you   **were**
      he/she/it   **is**

The match between subject and verb has to be learned by anyone
wanting to attain a standard form of spoken and written Swahili. That
this is not an easy task is attested to by the simplified forms used by

---

[3]The formal orthography writes words without any breaks or dashes in words; we do so
here to identify and focus attention on morphological units of larger structures.

speakers of pidgin Swahili, where verbs have the same form for any subject.

Let us return to the *soko* (the market) where you and your friend are making a purchase from a seller:

(11) a. *Ninyi   m-nataka   matunda   gani?*
     you   Subj-want   fruit   what
     (Pl)   Prefix   kind?
         What kind of fruit would you like?

   b. *Tu-nataka   ndizi   na   maembe   tu.*
      1st.-Pl-want bananas   and   mangoes only
      Subj
      Prefix
          We only want bananas and mangoes.

You notice immediately that your friend says *Tu-nataka* "We want" without the independent pronoun *sisi* preceding it. In fact, either of the following sets is possible as complete sentences:

(12) a. *Mimi ni-nataka.*   b. *Ni-nataka.*   I want.
       Wewe u-nataka.   *U-nataka.*   You want.
       Yeye a-nataka.   *A-nataka.*   S/he wants.
       Sisi tu-nataka.   *Tu-nataka.*   We want.
       Ninyi m-nataka.   *M-nataka.*   You (Pl) want.
       Wao wa-nataka.   *Wa-nataka.*   They want.

At first you might consider the expressions in (12a) and (12b) to be interchangeable, but it would soon become clear that they are somehow different. In the question "What kind of fruit would **you** like?" the pronoun **ninyi** gives a new focus of attention; until now the fruit seller was addressing other people, but now he shifts his attention to you and your friend and identifies you as potential buyers. In his response your friend said simply *Tu-nataka . . .* and not *Sisi tu-nataka . . . .* The identity of the subject is old information and in no need of special emphasis; the information that is important now is the fruit that you want. *Sisi tu-nataka* would be used in other contexts to convey senses such as the following:

(13) **Sisi   tu***-nataka   ndizi.*
     We   we-want   bananas

       a. **As far as we are concerned, we** would like some
          bananas.
       b. **We** (and no one else) want some bananas.
       c. **We** (not them) want some bananas.
       d. **We** (emphatic) want some bananas.
       e. **We** (new topic), **we** want some bananas.

1.1.2   *Tense-Markers*   While you are learning about pronouns, you are also learning more verbs, ones such as *buy, cook, sell, eat, go.* You hear verbs used as commands; at times you pick them out in other contexts, and a pattern begins to emerge:

(14)   a.   *Pika!*   Cook!
            Nunua!   Buy!
            Uza!   _ Sell!

        b.   *A-napika.*   S/he's cooking, S/he cooks.
            A-nanunua.   S/he's buying, S/he buys.
            A-nauza.   S/he's selling, S/he sells.

What can you make of this data? First of all, you note that when *cook, buy,* and *sell* are used in the (b) column, there is an extra element *na* associated with each verb, one not present when the same verbs are used as commands, as in (a). You might conclude that if a verb is used with a subject prefix then *na* has to be used as well; this is almost an adequate observation, but not until you hear the same verbs used in the following forms do you realize what *na* is:

(15)   *A-napika.*   *A-lipika.*   *A-tapika.*
        A-nanunua.   *A-linunua.*   *A-tanunua.*
        A-nauza.   *A-liuza.*   *A-tauza.*
        S/he is cooking.   S/he cooked.   S/he will cook.
            buying.   bought.   buy.
            selling.   sold.   sell.

The verb element *na* turns out to be a present-tense marker, *li* past, and *ta* future.

1.1.3   *Object-Markers*   We now want to shift our attention to the verb in its relationship to objects. Objects normally identify a person or thing which is affected by the action of the verb. Nouns such as *ndizi* "bananas" might be the object which the subject is buying, eating, or cooking. This much is common to all languages, but there are several other things you will have to learn about objects before you can speak or understand standard Swahili effectively.

Let us return to the market; as the transaction over bananas continues, you hear a new kind of clause. The fruit seller points to a particular type of banana (one for cooking and not eating) and asks:

(16)   *Je,   m-na-taka   ndizi   hizi?*
        Say   you-Pres-want   bananas   these
            Would you like these bananas?

Hizi is a demonstrative used by speakers to point to things close to the speaker (other forms are used when the thing is close to the listener, or at a distance from both speaker and listener). Notice the response:

(17)   *Ndiyo,   tu-na-zi-taka.*
     Yes   we-Pres-**them**-want
         Yes, we would like them.

Instead of repeating the words *these bananas* in his response, the buyer uses an object pronoun *-zi-*, which is marked on the verb, unlike the corresponding English pronoun *them*, which occurs in object position following the verb.

Here is something else to learn: if the buyer and seller were talking about mangoes instead of bananas, a different form of the object pronoun would be used; to say "We would like them," referring to mangoes, one would say *Tu-na-ya-taka* with *-ya-* instead of *-zi-*. This has to do with the division of all nouns into classes; the words for bananas and mangoes belong to different classes and require different pronouns. One must learn a different set of object pronouns for persons. For instance, compare subject-marking and object-marking in the following with the verb *-penda* "like, love":

(18) | **Independent Pronouns** | **Subject Prefixes** | **Object Prefixes** |
|---|---|---|
| a. *mimi* | *Ni-na-penda.*
I love. | *A-na-**ni**-penda.*
S/he loves **me**. |
| b. *wewe* | *U-na-penda.*
You love. | *A-na-**ku**-penda.*
S/he loves **you**. |
| c. *yeye* | *A-na-penda.*
S/he loves. | *A-na-**m**-penda.*
S/he loves **him/her**. |
| d. *sisi* | *Tu-na-penda*
We love. | *A-na-**tu**-penda.*
S/he loves **us**. |
| e. *ninyi* | *M-na-penda.*
You (Pl) love. | *A-na-**wa**-penda.*
S/he loves **you** (Pl). |
| f. *wao* | *Wa-na-penda.*
They love. | *Wa-na-**wa**-penda.*
They love **them**. |

In some cases the subject and object pronouns are identical; in others they are different. Note further that the object pronouns in (18e) and (18f) are identical; thus, out of context, *a-na-wa-penda* is ambiguous. Also note that the subject prefix in (18e) and the object prefix in (18c) are identical, but this is ordinarily not a problem for the learner because of their different positions.

There are then three sets of pronouns whose forms and usages have to be learned by the language learner. Gradually we begin to see the morphology of Swahili becoming more complex, while, so far, the meaning of these pronouns has probably not seemed too much different from languages you are familiar with.

Object pronouns, however, also function in Swahili in rather unusual ways. Remember in the market when a buyer said that he wanted mangoes? It is important now to recall that he wasn't talking about any particular mangoes, but was merely identifying the kind of thing he wanted. Such nouns are nonspecific and fit into the larger category called 'indefinite' in English: English indefinite nouns are either unmarked or marked with the articles *a* or *some*. In Swahili nonspecific nouns are left unmarked; for example:

(19)   *Ni-na-taka maembe.*
         I want (**some**) mangoes.

       Ni-na-taka nazi.
         I want **a** coconut.

Definite nouns in English are marked with the article *the*, e.g. *the mangoes, the coconut.* Definite nouns are ones that refer to things the speaker assumes will be uniquely identifiable to the listener. If someone says "Hand me *the* bananas," or "Give me *the* coconut," it is with the assumption that the listener will know which bananas or which coconut are being referred to. Swahili doesn't have definite articles, but it can indicate when a noun object is definite. It does so through a device the essential value of which is to emphasize the specific identity of objects. Compare the following pairs of sentences:

(20)   a.   *Ni-na-taka nazi.*
              I want a coconut.

            Ni-na-taka maembe.
              I want (some) mangoes.

       b.   *Ni-na-i-taka nazi.*
              I-Pres-**it**-want coconut
              I want **the** coconut.

            Ni-na-ya-taka maembe.
              I-Pres-**them**-want mangoes.
              I want **the** mangoes.

By using *both* the object noun and an object pronoun marked on the verb, a Swahili speaker emphasizes that he has a particular object in mind, and therefore (in a situation like this one) one which he assumes the hearer can uniquely identify.

When nouns or pronouns naming humans are used as objects the verb is nearly always object-marked. Observe:

(21) *Ali a-na-m-penda Hadija.*
         he-Pres-**her**-love
      Ali loves Hadija.

      Ali a-na-m-penda   mwanamke mrembo.
         he-Pres-**her**-love woman   beautiful
      Ali loves a beautiful woman.

This follows from the fact that when people talk about other people they are nearly always talking about particular or specific human beings.

1.1.4 *Standard Swahili* Let us now look at what a language learner will have found out by now about Swahili. Analyze the following clause as it might be spoken by a native speaker or by someone who speaks standard Swahili as a second language:

(22) *Mimi   ni-na-ku-penda   wewe.*
      I   I-Pres-you-love   you
      I love you.   (As for me, it is you that I love.)

The role and function of each element of this clause are summarized below:

(23) a. *mimi*   An independent pronoun identifying the subject; its use focuses special attention on the subject as a special, unique entity; translation: "as for me" or "*I*" (emphatic).

     b. *ni-*   A dependent subject pronoun agreeing with *mimi*; it is required here because verbs must be matched with their subjects; translation: "I."

     c. *-na-*   A prefix marking the time of the verbal process as 'present.'

     d. *-ku-*   A dependent object pronoun agreeing with *wewe*; it is required here because verbs have to be object marked when the object is definite and human.

     e. *-penda* The verb stem: "love."

     f. *wewe*   An independent pronoun specifying the object of the clause; its use focuses on the object as a special, unique entity; translation: "as for you," "*you*" (emphatic).

This clause, because of the double specification of both subject and object, is a very strong statement; the speaker is saying that there is no one else in the world that *he* loves, that he and his beloved are unique. Notice the difference in meaning when one or the other, or both pronouns are missing:

(24)   *Ni-na-ku-penda wewe.*
          I love **you**.   (It is you that I love.)

       Mimi ni-na-ku-penda.
          I love you.   (I'm the one who loves you.)

       Ni-na-ku-penda.
          I love you.   (no special emphasis on either subject or
                          object)

These subtle differences in meaning would be impossible without having the two ways for marking subject and object.

1.1.5   *Pidgin*   Let us shift our attention again and look at a different learning environment. If you find yourself working on a rural water project in the Kenya Rift Valley where Maasai, a non-Bantu language, and several other languages, are spoken natively, the chance is good that you will not learn standard Swahili. Only a highly pidginized version of Swahili is known there. A pidgin is by definition a language without native speakers, an auxiliary language used for communication between speakers of different native languages for a limited range of topics. You will learn some shortened forms of the greetings, and most of the vocabulary that we discussed above: the independent pronouns such as *mimi, wewe, yeye,* and most of the verb stems; but you will not learn the subject and object pronominal prefixes (*ni-, u-, a-,* etc.). As a consequence you are reduced to learning clauses which merely identify a state or event and its participants. Subject and object agreement are nonexistent, as the following examples of pidgin Swahili illustrate:[4]

(25) a.   *Yeye   nataka   ndizi.*
          he   want   bananas
          He wants bananas.

    b.   *Mimi   napenda   wewe.*
          I   love   you
          I love you.

---

[4]The major published work on Swahili pidgin is Bernd Heine, *Pidgin-Sprachen im Bantu-Bereich*, Dietrich Reimer Verlag, Berlin, 1973.

To illustrate the impoverished nature of the pidgin forms, compare what is possible in standard against both of these:

(26)	**Standard Swahili**	**Pidgin Swahili**

a. *Yeye a-na-zi-taka ndizi.*
   As for him, he wants the
   bananas.

A-na-zi-taka ndizi.
   He wants the bananas.

Yeye a-na-taka ndizi.   *Yeye nataka ndizi.*
   As for him, he wants   He wants bananas.
   (some) bananas.

A-na-taka ndizi.
   He wants (some) bananas.

b. *Mimi ni-na-ku-penda wewe.*
   I love **you**.

Ni-na-ku-penda wewe.
   I love **you**.

Mimi ni-na-ku-penda.   *Mimi napenda wewe.*
   I love you.   I love you.

Ni-na-ku-penda.
   I love you.

In each case, we see that standard Swahili has four options, each conveying a distinct nuance, while pidgin has a single invariant form. The obvious difference between the two is that pidgin has no subject or object prefixes; it does have the prefix *na-*, but this does not function as a present-tense morpheme. *Na-* serves only to identify a sentence as affirmative; the same form with *na-* would be used for future or past time reference.

In terms of identifying subjects and objects, or in terms of making simple statements that can be said to be true or false, the pidgin is equal to the standard language. Pidgin Swahili is used in a restricted set of social settings. The systematic and stylistic richness of the standard is ignored because the pidgin speaker is seldom in a situation where more than simple messages is needed; he uses his native language to express subtleties and complex thoughts, and the pidgin for simple communicative tasks. If he wants bananas and the fruit seller doesn't speak his native language, the pidgin speaker will say *Mimi nataka ndizi*; he will be perfectly well understood and will be sold some bananas (although he may be made fun of once he walks away). *Mimi nataka ndizi*

identifies him as the subject, bananas as the object, and the notion of
"want" as the connecting predicate; the standard *Mimi ni-na-(zi)-taka*
ndizi has more in it than he needs. Simple communicative tasks are
accomplished with the pidgin, without the expressive power of the
standard, or its social mobility.

The primary virtue of pidgins is that they are easy to learn, far easier
than any language with native speakers. Pidgin Swahili is no exception,
and this is easy to see. You remember that *sisi* is "we" or "us," *wao* is
"they" or "them," and *-penda* is "love"; by merely putting *sisi, wao,*
and *penda* in the correct Subject–Verb–Object order and remembering
to attach *na-* to *penda,* you say *Wao napenda sisi.* But if you want to say
the same thing in the standard language and you have forgotten the
verbal prefixes corresponding to *wao* and *sisi* and the rules for their use,
you are in trouble, and you will have to go back to the earlier discussion
of these and look them up.

1.1.6   *Verbal Extensions*   In the way they bear subject, object, and
tense prefixes, we have seen verbs as the hub of basic clause types. But
there are additional kinds of clauses where the verb plays an even larger
role signaling special relationships between subjects and objects. Take
the case where a verb has its object promoted to subject position. In the
basic clause type, said to be in the 'active voice,' a verb expressing an
action would have a 'patient' as its object, the thing undergoing the
effect of the action, and an 'actor' as its subject. In this special clause
type we have the 'passive voice' with the patient as the subject and the
actor demoted to a prepositional phrase after the verb. The passive verb
is in effect 'intransitive': it has no object. Here English has characteristics strikingly similar to Swahili:

(27) a.   Mother is cooking some food.   (Active)

   b.   Some food is being cooked by mother.   (Passive)

Food gains special prominence by being moved into subject position.
Notice the comparable Swahili sentences and what changes the verb
itself undergoes:

(28)   *Mama*   **a-na-pika**   *chakula.*
       mother   she-Pres-cook   food
          Mother is cooking some food.

       Chakula   **ki-na-pikwa**   *na   mama.*
       food   it-Pres-be cooked   by   mother
          Some food is being cooked by mother.

The new role played by *chakula* "food" is signaled by the subject marker on the verb (note the prefix shape: it reflects a further aspect of the noun class system); the verb stem *-pika* has become *-pikwa*.

Verbs contain a root + suffix which form a stem. In the case of *-pika* "cook," *-uza* "sell," *-taka* "want," and *-penda* "love," the roots are *-pik-*, *-uz-*, *-tak-*, and *-pend-*, plus the extension suffix *-a*, which is used in the simplest kinds of indicative clauses. The passive verb stem is formed in most cases (there are exceptions) by inserting *-w-* between the root and the *-a* extension:

(29)
-pik-a	cook	*-pik-w-a*	be cooked
-uz-a	sell	*-uz-w-a*	be sold
-tak-a	want	*-tak-w-a*	be wanted
-pend-a	love	*-pend-w-a*	be loved

Another clause type involves an actor-subject performing an action for the benefit of another. This role is signaled by the 'benefactive' suffix:

(30) a. *Mama a-na-pika chakula.*
　　　Mother is cooking some food.

　 b. *Mama　a-na-wa-pik-i-a　watoto　chakula.*
　　　mother　she-Pres-them-　children　food
　　　　　　　cook-for
　　　Mother is cooking some food for the children.

(31) a. *Mama a-na-leta maembe.*
　　　Mother is bringing some mangoes.

　 b. *Mama　a-na-wa-let-e-a watoto　　maembe*
　　　mother　she-Pres-them- children　mangoes
　　　　　　　bring-to/for
　　　Mother is bringing some mangoes for the children.

The *-i-* and *-e-* suffixes in the (b) clauses signal the benefactive relationship; they differ according to the sounds present in the verb root. Note the effect in the following object-marked verb forms:

(32) a. *A-na-wa-leta.*
　　　She is bringing **them**.

　 b. *A-na-wa-let-e-a.*
　　　She is bringing (something) **for them**.

The verb suffix signals a difference in roles for the object pronoun *-wa-*. There is another clause type in which patients are asserted to be getting into certain states or conditions, or to have undergone certain actions, without any cause being implied. Notice how this is signaled by the *-ik-* 'stative' suffix in (33d):

(33) a.   *Yeye a-na-u-vunja mlango.*
           He is breaking the door.

    b.   *Mlango   u-na-vunj-w-a   na-ye.*
           door   it-Pres-be broken   by-him
           The door is being broken by him.

    c.   *Mlango u-na-vunj-w-a.*
           The door is being broken.

    d.   *Mlango   u-na-vunj-ik-a.*
           door   it-Pres-become broken
           The door is becoming broken.

In (33a–c) we understand that someone or something is causing the action to happen; this is true even in (33c) where no agent is named (and notice that the English translation functions just like Swahili in this respect). In (33d) with the suffix *-ik-*, on the other hand, the presence of a cause is not asserted; the verb asserts only that its patient is entering a new state or condition. This way of describing an action is compatible with the view that events can happen spontaneously without an external cause; it is also an appropriate way of describing an event when no one is being held responsible for it. A door or a chair can become broken because they are used a great deal, because of termites, because of weather, because of wood rotting, or because of a combination of these plus other unknown causes; and any way, it would appear that people do not always think of events as having causes. If the notion of a cause *is* important, if someone is to blame, then Swahili speakers will use the verb transitively in the active voice, as in (33a), or in the passive voice, as in (33b) or (33c).

In most of the clauses that we have looked at thus far, individual actor-subjects are performing the action of the verb on a simple patient-object, but plural actor-subjects can perform actions which mutually affect one another. In Swahili this role is marked by *-an-*, the 'reciprocal' suffix. A large class of transitive verbs can be used this way; in their reciprocal forms these are, in effect, intransitive:

(34) a.   *Ni-na-m-penda Mariamu.*
           I love Mariamu.

    b.   *Mimi   na   Mariamu tu-na-pend-an-a.*
           I   and   Mariamu   we-Pres-love-
                                        each other
           Mariamu and I love each other.

In another type, actor-subjects can cause other agents to carry out some action, or undergo some activity, or cause objects to undergo a change of state; such roles are indicated by the 'causative' stem (which varies phonologically for reasons that we don't have to consider here):

(35) a. *Mimi   ni-li-chok-a.*
  I   I-Past-be/become tired.
    I got tired.

  b. *Yeye   a-li-ni-chosh-a.*
    He   he-Past-me-make tired
    He made me tired.

(36) a. *Bei   zi-na-pungua.*
    Prices they-Pres-go down
    Prices are going down.

  b. *Wauzaji   wa-na-punguz-a   bei.*
    Sellers   they-Pres-make   prices
            go down
    Sellers are reducing prices.

By using the 'reversive' suffix, the subject can be used to undo the effect of the action of the verb upon a patient-object; note the function of the *-u-* and *-o-* suffixes in the following:

(37)
-kunja	fold	*-kunj-**u**-a*	unfold
-funga	close	*-fung-**u**-a*	open
-ziba	stop up	*-zib-**u**-a*	remove a stopper
-choma	pierce	*-chom-o-a*	draw out (e.g., a knife)

These suffixes do not exhaust the possibilities, but are the most frequent and important ones. Of further interest is the fact that they can be combined to denote complex and sometimes idiomatic relationships between nouns and verbs; as an example, note the various possibilities of the verb root *-chom-*:

(38)
-chom-a	pierce, stab, thrust into
-chom-ek-a	be/become pierced (STATIVE)
-chom-ek-e-a	stick new pieces of thatch in an old roof (STATIVE + BENEFACTIVE)
-chom-ek-e-z-a	stick in by using force (STATIVE + BENEFACTIVE + CAUSATIVE)
-chom-e-a	stuff things in (e.g., a box, a bag) (BENEFACTIVE)
-chom-o-a	draw out (e.g., a thorn) (REVERSIVE)
-chom-o-le-a	draw out from (REVERSIVE + BENEFACTIVE)

Needless to say, this system of verbal morphology is not part of pidgin Swahili in any productive way. Some of the distinctions cannot be expressed at all; on the other hand, the pidgin speaker does have some resources. When he wants to say that he will cook something *for* the children, he will use *-pika* "cook" plus the preposition *kwa*, which in standard Swahili has a number of adverbial uses and is glossed by English prepositions including "to," "for," "by," "in respect to."

(39) *Ni-na-wa-pik-i-a*   *watoto*   *chakula.*   **(Standard)**
     I-Pres-them-cook-for   children   food

     Mimi   *napika*   *chakula*   *kwa*   *watoto.*   **(Pidgin)**
     I   cook   food   for   children

1.2 Noun Classes and Agreement

In the previous pages we saw examples of subject–verb agreement, and in some well-defined instances, object–verb agreement:

(40) **Subject–Verb Agreement**

*Mimi **ni**-na-nunua nazi.*	**I** am buying coconuts.
*Wewe **u**-na-nunua nazi.*	**You** are buying coconuts.
*Yeye **a**-na-nunua nazi.*	**S/he** is buying coconuts.
*Sisi **tu**-na-nunua nazi.*	**We** are buying coconuts.
*Ninyi **m**-na-nunua nazi.*	**You** (Pl) are buying coconuts.
*Wao **wa**-na-nunua nazi.*	**They** are buying coconuts.

Object–Verb Agreement

*A-na-**ni**-penda mimi.*	S/he loves **me**.
*A-na-**ku**-penda wewe.*	S/he loves **you**.
*A-na-**m**-penda yeye.*	S/he loves **him/her**.
*A-na-**tu**-penda sisi.*	S/he loves **us**.
*A-na-**wa**-penda ninyi.*	S/he loves **you** (Pl).
*A-na-**wa**-penda wao.*	S/he loves **them**.

All the agreement here is in reference to human subjects and objects, and already indicates that Swahili has an extensive system of agreement. And like other Bantu languages, Swahili has a remarkable noun class system. This becomes apparent when we see the subject and object prefixes associated with inanimate nouns: they are different from the ones used for human nouns, and they are often different from each other. Compare:

(41)   **Subject–Verb Agreement**

Chakula   ki-na-pik-w-a   na mama.
food   it-Pres-be cooked   by mother
   Some food is being cooked by mother.

Mlango   u-na-vunj-w-a   na-ye.
door   it-Pres-be broken   by-him
   The door is being broken by him.

Object–Verb Agreement

Ni-na-i-taka   nazi.
I-Pres-it-want   coconut
   I want the coconut.

A-na-u-vunja   mlango.
S/he-Pres-it-break   door
   S/he is breaking the door.

Ni-na-ya-taka   maembe.
I-Pres-them-want   mangoes
   I want the mangoes.

A-na-zi-taka   ndizi.
S/he-Pres-them-want   bananas
   S/he wants the bananas.

All Swahili nouns belong to classes which can be defined at least approximately in terms of meaning. Most of the classes go together in pairs with one for singular and one for plural. The singular/plural pairs of the same nouns are also called classes, so that we get Class 1/2, Class 3/4, etc., odd numbers referring to singulars and even numbers to plurals. Normally nouns carry singular and plural prefixes characteristic of their class, so that in Class 1/2 we get *m-tu/wa-tu* "person/people," in Class 3/4 *m-ti/mi-ti* "tree/trees," and so on. Looking at singular/plural pairs this way we can say Swahili has six classes, plus several others which do not fall within the singular/plural pattern. Noun classes are matched by verb prefixes, and they govern agreement in adjectives, possessives, and demonstratives as well.

The noun class systems of Bantu languages have all the characteristics of what we call 'gender' in European languages except that the number of classes is so high. French has a two-way division between 'masculine' and 'feminine' nouns, while Latin and German have a three-way division between 'masculine,' 'feminine,' and 'neuter' nouns; but next to a Bantu language, a language with just three noun classes seems exotically simple.

A thoroughgoing gender language has two characteristics: its nouns are divided into classes, and the classes are distinctively marked on the nouns themselves, elsewhere in the sentence, or both. Spanish is a gender language with all its nouns belonging to either the 'masculine' or 'feminine' class. The unexceptional marking of these classes takes place not on the nouns themselves, but in agreement with other parts of speech, determiners, adjectives, and pronouns: the definite article in Spanish is *el, la, los,* or *las,* depending on gender and number of the noun; for example, *el lápiz* (masculine singular) "the pencil," *la casa* (feminine singular) "the house," *los árboles* (masculine plural) "the trees", and *las flores* (feminine plural) "the flowers."

In English, we see vestiges of an earlier gender system in just the opposition that has to do with *it* versus *he* or *she*: one says "There was a **rock** there and **it** was big" versus "There was a **student** there and **she/he** was big." This is roughly the distinction between human and nonhuman nouns, with a good deal of variation in between in conversations about boats, babies and pets. The opposition between *he* and *she* has to do with sex (mostly among humans) and not gender. One says "He is a student" when talking about a male and "She is a student" when talking about a female, but the noun "student" is the same in each case. There are nouns, it is true, that select just *he* or *she*: we have *boy* and *man* versus *girl* and *woman,* and one would say "**He** is a **waiter**" and "**She** is a **waitress**." But there are many like *student* which do not; moreover, the male/female distinction exemplified in *waiter/waitress* is not consistently associated with *he* and *she*: *stallion/mare, bull/cow, ram/ewe, rooster/hen* are more frequently referred to with *it* than with *he* or *she*. If it is useful at all in English, the label 'gender' is useful only in respect to the human/nonhuman distinction.

Bantu languages outdo any of the well-known gender languages of Europe in the complexity of the agreement rules; and they have more noun classes. Whereas the familiar 'masculine/feminine' grammatical gender distinction of European languages tends to correlate at least partially with sex, sex doesn't enter into the picture in Bantu languages: corresponding to English "he," "she," and "it," Swahili has the one pronoun *yeye* used only for animate beings, and there are no other formal markings correlating with sex. A number of other distinctions prevail: most Bantu languages have a singular/plural noun class pair which includes the names of animals; another pair contains the names of elongated and narrow objects such as river, sword, and tongue; one contains the names of abstract qualities such as beauty and freedom; one consists of nouns naming people; another the names of botanical objects such as trees, plants, and bushes; there are classes in which mass nouns and the names of liquids (like water, oil, milk) are found, others with the names of useful objects and artifacts made or used by people, and so on. In all essential respects these noun classes are genders.

In this section we want to explore what learners have to know to be able to recognize class membership and the further knowledge necessary to master the agreement system.

1.2.1   *The Semantics of the Noun Classes*   Nouns typically consist of a singular or plural prefix, followed by a noun stem used for both the singular and plural. The word "person" has a *m-* prefix affixed to the stem *-tu* (*m-tu*); the plural has *wa-* (*wa-tu*). The word "pipe" has *ki-* singular and *vi-* plural with the stem *-ko* (*ki-ko/vi-ko* "pipe/pipes").

With only two exceptions, Class 1/2 names just human beings; the two exceptions are the nouns "insect" and "animal." Most nouns in this class have *m-* singular and *wa-* plural; before vowel-initial stems the prefix shapes are somewhat modified: *mw-* and *w-*.

(42)   **Class 1**   **Class 2**

m-ke	wife	*wa-ke*	wives
m-toto	child	*wa-toto*	children
m-sichana	girl	*wa-sichana*	girls
mw-alimu	teacher	*w-alimu*	teachers

While the generic nouns for "animal" (*m-nyama/wa-nyama*) and "insect" (*m-dudu/wa-dudu*) are found in the M-/WA- Class (Class 1/2) the names of individual animals and insects are found in other classes; and *not all* names denoting humans are found in Class 1/2. Many kinship terms (*mama* "mother," *baba* "father," *ndugu* "sibling" or "relative," *kaka* "elder brother," *dada* "elder sister," etc.) *formally*, according to their morphological shape, belong to Class 9/10, and this class includes the names of most animals and insects, kinship terms, and the names of many objects of foreign origin which have been borrowed into Swahili culture.

Although each noun class has certain semantic characteristics, there are many exceptions. Noun classification in the ancestral Bantu language followed consistent semantic parameters, but as the individual Bantu languages have gone their own way and developed separately, the semantic basis of the classification system has been deteriorating, more or less, in each one. This complicates the learning of the classification system in any of the present-day languages. Swahili is a case in point. The formal shape of noun prefixes takes on added importance as something consistent to hang on to, but even the formal system of noun marking is complicated. The person born into a Swahili-speaking community learns the concordial system in due course; others outside the community learn the system in varying degrees; some who are exposed to varieties of pidgin Swahili never master the system and virtually ignore it. Bear this in mind as we look at the salient semantic and formal characteristics of the remaining noun classes.

Class 3/4 (M-/MI-) nouns maintain a semantic commonality only within certain bounds. Formally, they are marked with either *m-* or *mw-* in the singular; this is identical to Class 1 (M-) nouns, but the plurals are marked with *mi-*. A lot of nouns in this class are names of things which are living, but which are non-human and nonanimate, such as plants and trees; for example, *m-mea* "plant," *mi-mea* "plants," and *m-ti* "tree," *mi-ti* "trees." This class also names things which, within a certain world view, could conceivably be living: *m-oto* "fire" and *m-oshi* "smoke," as well as *m-lima* "mountain," *m-to* "river," *m-situ* "forest," and others. Some nouns in this class are closely associated with living things, such as body parts, or are derivative of them, such as objects made from plant material or tree products:

(43) **Class 3**

		Class 4	
m-kono	arm, hand	*mi-kono*	arms, hands
m-guu	leg, foot	*mi-guu*	legs, feet
m-kia	tail	*mi-kia*	tails
m-domo	mouth, beak	*mi-domo*	mouths, lips
m-keka	mat (plant fiber)	*mi-keka*	mats
m-shale	arrow (wood)	*mi-shale*	arrows
m-fuko	bag (leather)	*mi-fuko*	bags
mw-iko	ladle (wood)	*mi-iko*	ladles

Not all body parts, however, are found in this class. Some are in Class 7/8 (*ki-chwa/vi-chwa* "head/heads," *ki-fua/vi-fua* "chest/chests"); some others are in Class 9/10 (*pʰua* "nose" (Sg and Pl)), and a lot are in Class 5/6 (*shavu/ma-shavu* "cheek/s," *sikio/ma-sikio* "ear/s"). In addition, Class 3/4 contains a rather large number of nouns derived from verbs, and others, borrowed for the most part from Arabic, that have other meanings:

(44) *m-pango/mi-pango*   plan   (< *-panga* "arrange")
      m-chezo/mi-chezo   game   (< *-cheza* "play")
      m-sumari/mi-sumari   nail   (Arabic)
      m-shahara/mi-shahara salary (Arabic)
      m-fereji/mi-fereji   ditch   (Arabic)

Despite this lack of homogeneity, there is some semantic coherence. One can predict, for instance, that the name of a new plant or tree which is introduced into East Africa will be put in this class. This happened when mango trees were introduced into East Africa from India. Along with the tree came the word; it was given Class 3/4 prefixes and added to the language: *mw-embe/mi-embe*. There are many other examples of the same sort.

We pointed out previously that both Class 1 and Class 3 nouns have identical prefix shapes. One may ask how native speakers sort these out and predict the correct plural forms. Study the following list and try to supply the correct plural forms:

(45)

Singular	Meaning	Plural
m-falme	_____	_____*-falme*
m-gomba	_____	_____*-gomba*
m-vulana	_____	_____*-vulana*
m-nazi	_____	_____*-nazi*
m-pishi	_____	_____*-pishi*

You can't supply the plural prefixes until you know the meanings of these nouns; and it is surely by meaning that speakers have formed generalizations; you could fill *wa-* and *mi-* in the blanks at random, and you probably would make some correct guesses, but you would have to be lucky to get them all correct; however, once you know that the first, middle, and last examples name human beings, you can predict their plural forms (respectively, *-falme* "king," *-vulana* "boy," *-pishi* "cook"; their plurals are formed with *wa-*); by elimination, of course, the others must be M-/MI- nouns, and you can predict the plural for these; their meanings are *-gomba* "banana plant", and *-nazi* "coconut palm" (the second you might have recalled from earlier examples), and they have *mi-* for the plural.

The next class, Class 5/6, or the so-called JI-/MA- Class, does not contain nouns that are as easily categorized semantically as those in Class 1/2 or Class 3/4. For the most part, the singular nouns in this gender or class have no prefix, because it was lost through historical sound change, but a few nouns do have a *ji-* or *j-* prefix in the singular. The plural nouns, for the most part, have *ma-*. Upon close examination, some salient features of this class's membership emerge. First there are nouns indicating parts of the body which occur in pairs:

(46) **Class 5/6**

j-ino/meno	tooth/teeth
ji-cho/ma-cho	eye/s
sikio/ma-sikio	ear/s
bega/ma-bega	shoulder/s
goti/ma-goti	knee/s
shavu/ma-shavu	cheek/s
kwapa/ma-kwapa	armpit/s
paja/ma-paja	thigh/s
ziwa/ma-ziwa	breast/s
tako/ma-tako	buttock/s

Most words denoting constituent parts of trees and plants, including their fruits, occur in this class:

(47) *tawi/ma-tawi*   branch/es
      jani/ma-jani   leaf/ves
      shina/ma-shina   trunk/s
      tunda/ma-tunda   fruit/s
      embe/ma-embe   mango/es
      ua/ma-ua   flower/s
      kuti/ma-kuti   palm frond/s
      ganda/ma-ganda   piece of bark/bark

Again, exceptions abound. While the word for "banana plant" and "coconut palm" are in Class 3/4 as we would expect, the names of their fruits are not in Class 5/6; instead *ndizi* "bananas" and *nazi* "coconut/s" are members of Class 9/10.

Finally, Class 5/6 has nouns indicating constituents of groups, as well as mass nouns and collectives, which normally have no singulars:

(48) a. *ji-we/ma-we*   stone/s
          jabali/ma-jabali   rock/s
          yai/ma-yai   egg/s
          chozi/ma-chozi   tear/s
          tumbo/ma-tumbo   stomach/intestines

      b. *ma-te*   saliva
          ma-ziwa   milk
          ma-ji   water
          ma-futa   oil
          ma-pesa   quantity of money

Notice the situation with the words for liquids, "saliva," "milk," "water," "oil," singular in English, but here plural.

Class 7/8, or the KI-/VI- Class, originally containing only inanimate objects, includes a wide range of artifacts or objects which are useful to human beings:

(49) **Class 7/8**

      a. *ki-tu/vi-*   thing/s
          ki-su/vi-   knife/ves
          ki-kapu/vi-   basket/s
          ki-ti/vi-   chair/s
          ki-kombe/vi-   cup/s

b. *ch-akula/vy-*   food/s
    ch-ambo/vy-   bait/s
    ch-uma/vy-   iron/pieces of iron
    ch-ombo/vy-   utensil/s

(Notice this way of citing singular and plural nouns: just the plural prefix is given after the slash line. Thus *ki-tu/vi-* is an abbreviation for *ki-tu/vi-tu.*)

The shapes of the prefixes in this class show variation of form following the same lines as other classes: *ki-* and *vi-* before stems beginning with consonants (49a) and *ch-* and *vy-* before vowel stems (49b).

This class also contains words for the names of things having to do with processes expressed by verbs: they sometimes name instruments, sometimes results.

(50) *ki-zibo/vi-*   stopper/s   (< *-ziba*   "stop up")
      ki-leo/vi-   intoxicant/s   (< *-lewa*   "be drunk")
      ki-lio/vi-   cry/s   (< *-lia*   "cry")
      ki-umbe/vi-   creature/s   (< *-umba*   "create")

Other nouns indicate humans with physical defects:

(51) *ki-lema/vi-*   cripple/s
      ki-ziwi/vi-   deaf person/s
      ki-bogoyo/vi-   toothless person/s

Another set indicates physical afflictions themselves:

(52) *ki-sonono*   gonorrhea
      ki-chomi   pleurisy
      ki-pindupindu   cholera

Class 9/10 has two striking characteristics: it has the most diverse semantic membership of all the classes, and it has little in the way of prefixes. We can see remnants of a prefix system from earlier stages of Swahili, but learners of the present day language have little reason to perceive any prefix–stem division in the nouns at all. The clincher is that the nouns of this class are invariant for singular and plural: *mbogo* means "buffalo" or "buffalos" depending on the context. Class 9/10 nouns had distinct singular and plural forms at earlier stages, and still do in many other Bantu languages.

Most names of animals and most kinship terms are in Class 9/10, but beyond this its semantic definition has been blurred by borrowings. One can put the nouns in three groups:

(53)   **Class 9/10**

a.   Animals

m-bogo	buffalo(s)
m-buni	ostrich(es)
n-dege	bird(s)
n-dovu	elephant(s)
ŋ-guruwe	pig(s)
pʰaa	gazelle(s)
tʰwiga	giraffe(s)
kʰobe	tortoise(s)
ny-oka	snake(s)
ny-uki	bee(s)

b.   Kinship

m-bari	clan(s)
n-dugu	brother(s), sister(s), relative(s)
mama	mother(s)
baba	father(s)
binamu	cousin(s)
shangazi	paternal aunt(s)

c.   Borrowed (Miscellaneous Meanings)

afya	health	(Arabic)
hesabu	math	(Arabic)
bakshishi	tip(s)	(Arabic)
gereza	jail(s)	(Portuguese)
meza	table(s)	(Portuguese)
motokaa	car(s)	(English)
baisikeli	bike(s)	(English)
pʰicha	picture(s)	(English)
pʰesa	money	(Hindi)

Class 9/10 is interesting phonologically. It is called the N- Class because many nouns begin with a nasal sound *m*, *n*, *ny* or *ŋ*; however, some nouns of the class begin with aspirated voiceless stops (*pʰ*, *tʰ*, *kʰ*), and others have no particular identifying mark at all. Nouns fall into two groups: those that retain a reflex of an earlier prefix form, and those that do not. A homorganic nasal is retained before roots which begin with a voiced consonant, and before vowel stems *ny-* occurs. (The combination of letters *ny* represents the palatal nasal sound, the same sound that occurs with the *n* in the middle of English "onion." Before another palatal consonant, Swahili spelling represents this sound simply as *n*, as in the sequence *nj*; here we add a distinguishing mark to give *ñ*.):

(54) *m-bari*   clan(s)
      m-begu   seed(s)
      n-devu   beard(s)
      n-dama   calf(ves)
      ñ-jaa   hunger
      ŋ-guo   clothing
      ŋ-guzo   post
      ny-ama   meat
      ny-ota   star

Notice that the nasals have the same point of articulation as the obstruents that follow them: we get *m* before *b* (labial), *n* before *d* (alveolar), *ñ* before *j* (palatal) and *ŋ* before *g* (velar). Notice further that in the case of the first two examples we have items that look in print like Class 1 or Class 3 nouns. In actuality, the pronunciation is different and there can be no such confusion. None of the initial nasals are syllabic; thus *m-bari* is heard as [ᵐbari] with just a prenasalized *b*, whereas the nouns in Class 1 and Class 3 begin with nasals pronounced as full syllables, like *m-buyu* [m̩buyu] "baobab tree." This kind of detail helps to keep the noun class system intact.

Nouns beginning with voiceless stops retain a remnant of earlier nasal prefixes by having those stops aspirated:

(55) *pʰaa*   gazelle(s)
      tʰaa   lamp(s)
      kʰaa   crab(s)

The aspiration helps to distinguish them from Class 5 nouns, singulars which also have no overt prefix, but which have their plurals with a prefix in Class 6:

(56)

Class 9/10		Class 5/6			
pʰaa	gazelle(s)	*paa*	roof	(Pl	*ma-paa*)
kʰaa	crab(s)	*kaa*	piece of charcoal	(Pl	*ma-kaa*)

There are several other noun genders. One is termed the U- Class with the prefix *u*- before consonants, and *w*- before vowels. Some of the nouns in this set have no plurals; they are typically abstract nouns, indicating such qualities as goodness, beauty, freedom, and childhood. Others have plurals and denote long, thin objects, like tongue, wick, wall, and sword, or entities which can be thought of as linear, such as time or songs. These two sets are actually derived from two distinct noun classes that still exist in other Bantu languages: a Class 11/10, where the Class 11 nouns had a prefix *lu-* at earlier stages, and a Class 14 which at earlier stages had a *bu-* prefix. Class 14 nouns are the ones without plurals. Class 10 provides plurals corresponding to singulars in both Class 9 and Class 11.

(57)   **Class 11/10**   **Class 14**

u-tambi/t^{h}ambi	wick/s	*u-zuri*	beauty
u-kuta/k^{h}uta	wall/s	*u-baya*	evil, badness
u-panga/p^{h}anga	sword/s	*w-ema*	goodness

Class 12/13, a category for diminutives in other Bantu languages, is not found in Swahili; this explains the gap in the numbering. Another noun class is Class 15; this includes all verbal nouns, infinitives, or so-called gerunds; its nouns are marked by the prefix *ku-*:

(58)   **Class 15**

ku-anguka	to fall, the act of falling
ku-penda	to love, the act of loving
ku-saidia	to help, the act of helping
ku-winda	to hunt, the act of hunting

The remaining classes are unlike the others; they are the 'locatives.' Classes 16, 17, and 18 all consist of stems from other noun classes with a locative suffix *-ni*. The resulting nouns convey notions normally express- ed by prepositions in English, such as "in," "on," "at":

(59)   *ki-chwa*   *kichwa-ni*
            head (Class 7)   on, in the head

         ny-umba   *nyumba-ni*
            house/s (Class 9/10)   at, in, to the house/s

         m-ti   *mti-ni*
            tree (Class 3)   at, in, up the tree

While there is only one form for these expressions (noun + *-ni* suffix), there are three locative classes. If a locative noun defines a 'specific' location it belongs to Class 16; if it defines a 'general' location it belongs to Class 17; and if it denotes an 'internal' location it is a Class 18 locative noun. Thus the noun *nyumba-ni* "house-Loc" can indicate either a specific, general, or internal location. These distinctions are seen in the form of modifiers of locative nouns:

(60)   **Class 16**

         nyumba-ni   *ha-pa*
         house-Loc   this-**specific place**
                  right here at this house

Class 17

nyumba-ni   hu-ku
house-Loc   this-**general place**
  this **general area around** the house

Class 18

nyumba-ni   hu-mu
house-Loc   this-**place inside**
  inside this house

1.2.2   *Subject and Object Agreement*   It is the complex agreement
system above all that makes Swahili a supergender language. Anyone
who has learned the language as an adult can tell you what a challenge it
is. If the learner is exposed often enough, either in the classroom or in
living contexts, he can soon learn to associate *m-* class words that have
wa- plurals (and not the *m-* words that have *mi-* plurals) with verbs that
are marked with *a-* and *wa-*, respectively, as in the following statements:

(61)   **M**-*toto   a-na-cheza   mpira.*
  child   he-Pres-play   ball
    The child is playing ball.

  Wa-*toto   wa-na-cheza   mpira.*
  children   they-Pres-play   ball
    The children are playing ball.

He recognizes that *a-* and *wa-* on the verb are what he learned to
associate with *yeye* "s/he" and *wao* "they." He also discovers, if he
hasn't earlier, that *wao* itself has a shape that facilitates remembering
the *wa* on the verb. With these associations made, he has no trouble
saying the following sentences and supplying the correct prefix on the
verb:

(62) a. *Yeye _____-na-taka ndizi.*
      He wants bananas.

  b. *Wao _____-na-taka ndizi.*
      They want bananas.

  c. *Wa-toto _____-na-nunua ndizi.*
      The children are buying bananas.

  d. *Wa-sichana _____-na-pika chakula.*
      The girls are cooking food.

  e. *Wa-vulana _____-na-cheza mpira.*
      The boys are playing ball.

    f. *M-vulana* _____ *-na-pika uji.*
        The boy is cooking porridge.

    g. *M-sichana* _____ *-na-cheza mpira.*
        The girl is playing ball.

    h. *M-toto* _____ *-na-uza ndizi.*
        The child is selling bananas.

Another class that the learner becomes quickly aware of is the
KI-/VI Class, because of the easy association involved. *Ki-* and *vi-* on
nouns are quickly associated with *ki-* and *vi-* on the verb:

(63) **Ki-ti**   **ki-na-vunjwa.**
     chair   it-Pres-be broken
        The chair is being broken.

     Vi-ti   *vi-na-vunjwa.*
     chairs they-Pres-be broken
        The chairs are being broken.

But, if you remember, not all *ki-/vi-* nouns have *ki-/vi-* prefixes; some
are marked with *ch-* in the singular and *vy-* in the plural, for example,
ch-akula/vy-akula "food/foods." Here the learner can get into some
trouble. He has already learned to associate *wa-*, *ki-*, and *vi-* initial nouns
with the *same* shapes on verbs. What then should he do with the
following?

(64) *Ch-akula* _____ *-na-tosha.*
     food   it-Pres-be sufficient
        There is enough food.

     Vy-akula _____ *-na-tosha.*
     foods   they-Pres-be enough
        There are enough kinds of food.

If the learner prefixes identical copies of the noun prefixes onto the
verb, he will have made an error; the proper prefixes remain *ki-* and *vi-*.

It is nevertheless the case that some verbal prefixes are easy to learn
because they are the same as the more commonly occurring shape of the
noun prefixes, to wit:

(65)

Class	Noun Class	Prefixes	Subject Concord	Object Concord
2	*wa-tu*	people	*wa-*	*-wa-*
7	*ki-tu*	thing	*ki-*	*-ki-*
8	*vi-tu*	things	*vi-*	*-vi-*
11, 14	*u-huru*	freedom	*u-*	*-u-*
15	*ku-imba*	singing	*ku-*	*-ku-*

   Object prefixes are identical to subject prefixes and are thus easy to learn, once the rule for when to mark objects is learned. The one exception is Class 1. Note the following:

(66)   *M-toto*   *a-na-kimbia.*
       child   he-Pres-run
          The child is running.

       M-kulima   *a-na-m-fukuza*   (*m-toto*).
       farmer   he-Pres-him-chase   (child)
          The farmer is chasing him (the child).

Unfortunately from the point of view of the learner, the concords for the rest of the classes are more complicated.

   Let us begin with Class 3/4 (vegetative living objects; for example, *m-ti/mi-ti* "tree/s"). The singulars with *m-* prefix govern *u-* subject concord and *-u-* object concord, while the plurals with *mi-* govern *i*, subject and object:

(67)   *M-ti*   *u-na-anguka*;   *ni-na-u-ona.*
       tree   it-Pres-fall   I-Pres-it-see
          The tree is falling; I see it.

       Mi-ti   *i-na-anguka*;   *ni-na-i-ona.*
       trees   they-Pres-fall   I-Pres-them-see
          The trees are falling; I see them.

The learner can get some help from the fact that the *i-* concordial prefix is identical to the vowel of *mi-*, but sounds are of little help in the connection between the singular *m-* noun and its *u-* concord. In the ancestral Bantu language, *m-* initial nouns (both Class 1 and Class 3) were *mu-*; the *u-* was lost due to sound change, but it is this very *u-* which is used as the Class 3 concord. Language learners have no way of knowing this, however, so it does not help them learn the correct match.

   The shapes of Class 5/6 nouns are not much help either. Remember that Class 5 nouns are for the most part unmarked, with just a few of them having a *ji-* or *j-* prefix, and that the Class 6 plurals are marked with *ma-*:

(68)   *Ji-we*   *li-na-anguka.*
       stone   it-Pres-fall
          The stone is falling.

       Tunda   *li-na-anguka.*
       fruit   it-Pres-fall
          The fruit is falling.

> **Ma**-*we*   *ya-na-anguka.*
> stones   they-Pres-fall
> > The stones are falling.

> **Ma**-*tunda*   *ya-na-anguka.*
> fruits   they-Pres-fall
> > The fruit (Pl) is falling.

We can see easily enough that the *ji-* prefix, in the few nouns where it occurs, shares its vowel with the *li-* prefix on the verb, and the same goes for the plurals with *ma-* and *ya-*. But what of *tunda* and the majority of nouns like it in Class 5 that have no overt prefix? This is a real problem, because there are many nouns in Class 9/10 which have no prefixes either (like *siagi* "butter"). Can it be the meaning of the nouns that helps? Not likely, for we have seen that the memberships of Class 5/6 and Class 9/10 are very diverse, and in fact overlap. There are, for example, liquid mass nouns in both classes: most of these are in 5/6, but 9/10 has *kahawa* "coffee," *chai* "tea," and *soda* "soda." Again it is purely formal considerations which help the learner sort things out. The language learner comes to know more than individual lexical items, and more than their meanings; he is learning a system. He learns that prefixless singular nouns which have *ma-* plurals (*tunda/ma-tunda* "fruit/fruits") have *li-* marked on the verb for the singular and *ya-* for the plural, while prefixless singular nouns with identical plurals (*pʰua/pʰua* "nose/noses," the Class 9/10 nouns) have a different set of concords. Incidentally, the Class 5 verbal concord is identical to the noun prefix of Class 5 nouns in other Bantu languages, as in *li-taxo* "buttock" (Bukusu, a language spoken in Western Kenya). Had sound change not caused the loss of the noun prefix of Class 5 (*li-tunda* > *tunda*), there would have been a perfect match between noun prefix and verbal concord.

Class 9/10 nouns have identical singular and plural forms, but there are distinct singular and plural verbal prefixes associated with them:

(69)   *Chupa*   *i-na-anguka.*
　　　　bottle   it-Pres-fall
　　　　> The bottle is falling.

　　　　Chupa   *zi-na-anguka.*
　　　　bottles   they-Pres-fall
　　　　> The bottles are falling.

　　　　Ni-na-i-ona   *chupa.*
　　　　I-Pres-it-see   bottle
　　　　> I see the bottle.

　　　　Ni-na-zi-ona   *chupa.*
　　　　I-Pres-them-see   bottles
　　　　> I see the bottles.

With other classes, singular and plural verb forms are matched with singular and plural noun forms, but here we have a situation similar to English "The fish **is** evading the shark" and "The fish **are** evading the shark"; the only "matching" is a direct one between the verb forms and the concept the speaker has in mind: if he has a group of bottles in mind he says *chupa zi-*, if only one, *chupa i-*.

The alert reader will have noticed that the noun *chupa* "bottle/s" in (69) has a shape which makes it quite similar to some nouns of the KI-/VI- Class, such as *ch-akula* "food," *ch-eo* "rank," *ch-uo* "school." Another word, *chai* "tea," is a borrowed word like *chupa* and is normally treated as a Class 9/10 noun in Swahili spoken as a first language; however, among some nonnative speakers of standard Swahili, both *chai* and *chupa* govern *ki-* concords on the verb. They hear the initial *ch* sound of these nouns and decide that they belong to Class 7/8.

We will now take another look at locative nouns, nouns such as:

(70) *meza*　　　　　+ *-ni* > *mezani*
　　　table (Class 9)　　　　　　on, in, etc. the table

　　ki-chwa　　　+ *-ni* > *kichwani*
　　head (Class 7)　　　　　　on, in, etc. the head

These nouns belong to any one of three classes—16, 17, or 18—but it is only the concord that distinguishes them; *pa-* is Class 16, *ku-* Class 17, and *m(u)-* is Class 18. As in the singular and plural of Class 9/10 nouns, the choice of concord has nothing to do with the shape of the noun itself, but just with the concept being expressed; for example:

(71) **Class 16 Concord**

　　a.　*Meza-ni*　*pa-na*　*ndizi.*
　　　　table-Loc　it-with　bananas

　　Class 17 Concord

　　b.　*Meza-ni*　*ku-na*　*ndizi.*
　　　　table-Loc　it-with　bananas

　　Class 18 Concord

　　c.　*Meza-ni*　*m-na*　*ndizi.*
　　　　table-Loc　it-with　bananas

Example (71a) conveys a *definite* meaning: the bananas are in a specific location which the speaker assumes to be uniquely identifiable to the hearer; (71b) asserts only that the bananas are located someplace with respect to the table; (71c) implies the bananas are inside the table, as in a drawer. Locative concord is one of the hardest things for a learner of Swahili to master if his first language is not already Bantu.

Let us look at another rather important case where agreement and concord are not a matching with the physical shape of nouns. There are a lot of nouns naming human beings which are formally members of classes other than 1/2:

(72)   **Class 5/6**

   jirani/ma-   neighbor/s
   jitu/ma-   giant/s

   Class 7/8

   ki-jana/vi-   youth/s
   ki-ongozi/vi-   leader/s
   ki-nyozi/vi-   barber/s

   Class 9/10

   mama   mother/s
   baba   father/s
   ndugu   sibling/s
   kʰaka   elder brother/s

They all govern Class 1/2 concord:

(73)   *Jirani a-na-kuja.*   The neighbor is coming.
       NOT   **Jirani li-na-kuja.*

       Ma-jirani wa-na-kuja.   The neighbors are coming.
       NOT   **Ma-jirani ya-na-kuja.*

       Ki-ongozi a-na-kuja.   The leader is coming.
       NOT   **Ki-ongozi ki-na-kuja.*

       Vi-ongozi wa-na-kuja.   The leaders are coming.
       NOT   **Vi-ongozi vi-na-kuja.*

       Mama a-na-kuja.   Mother is coming.
       NOT   **Mama i-na-kuja.*

       Mama wa-na-kuja.   The mothers are coming.
       NOT   **Mama zi-na-kuja.*

Any noun that denotes a human being works in this way, and so it is with animals:

(74)   *Simba a-na-kuja.*   The lion is coming.
       Simba wa-na-kuja.   The lions are coming.

Simba is formally a Class 9/10 noun, but it governs Class 1/2 concord.

The names of animals in other Bantu languages are Class 9/10 nouns, and they govern Class 9/10 concord. We can surmise that noun classification used to be a matter of semantic category and was based on a "natural" taxonomic division of the noun universe, with names of animals opposed to names of plants, artifacts, and so forth. Given the breakdown of the semantic system, agreement became mostly grammatical and based on the formal shape of nouns. But now in Swahili concord we find another natural sort of semantic classification imposing itself across the noun class system: animate versus inanimate nouns. All animate nouns govern animate concord, that is, Class 1/2 concord; all inamimate ones govern formal class concord. In practical terms the speaker first has to determine whether the noun he is talking about is animate or not, and then he can assign appropriate concord.

The animate/inanimate dichotomy reveals itself in a further interesting distinction. There is a set of words like *ji-tu/ma-ji-tu* "giant, huge person" (Class 5/6) which normally governs animate concord:

(75)   *Ji-tu a-na-wa-tisha wa-toto.*
       The giant is scaring the children.

But the same noun can govern Class 5/6 concord as well, catching a shift in meaning from "giant, huge person" to "ogre," "ogres" being out of the sphere of normal animate beings:

(76)   *Ji-tu li-na-wa-tisha wa-toto.*
       The ogre is scaring the children.

1.2.3   *Classes and Agreement in Pidgin Swahili*   There is no system of agreement in pidgin Swahili; in fact, the noun class system itself is virtually nonexistent. We must say "virtually" because there are wide differences in usage among pidgin speakers, a lot of it depending on how much exposure there has been to the standard. In Kenya-Pidgin Swahili only Class 1/2, a class of human beings, significantly enough, retains singular and plural marking: thus *m-tu/wa-tu* "person/people," *m-levi/wa-levi* "drunkard/s," *m-vulana/wa-vulana* "boy/s," etc. The other classes have merged singular and plural nouns, sometimes choosing the singular form, sometimes the plural, and making that the invariant form for singular and plural (like English "fish"):

(77)

	Standard Swahili		**Pidgin** (Sg and Pl)
Class 3/4	*m-kate/mi-*	bread/s	*mkate*
	m-ti/mi-	tree/s	*miti*
	m-to/mi-	river/s	*mto*
Class 5/6	*sanduku/ma-*	box/es	*sanduku*
	yai/ma-	egg/s	*mayai*
	goti/ma-	knee/s	*magoti*

	Standard Swahili		**Pidgin** (Sg and Pl)
Class 7/8	*ki-ko/vi-*	pipe/s	*kiko*
	ki-azi/vi-	potato/es	*kiazi*
			(or *viazi*)
	ch-akula/vy-	food/s	*chakula*
Class 11/10	*u-shanga/shanga*	necklace/s	*shanga*
	u-nywele/nywele	hair	*nywele*

Apart from Class 1/2, plurals can be marked by adding quantifiers such as "much, many" or by numerals, as in *kiko moja* "one pipe," *kiko tatu* "three pipes," *kiko ingi* "many pipes."

1.2.4 *The Noun Phrase and Agreement*   Agreement goes well beyond verb-marking in standard Swahili. In fact, any constituent which modifies a noun, adjective, demonstrative, or possessive, must agree with the class of that noun; for example:

(78) *Wa-tu   ha-wa   wa-zuri   wa-na-vi-nunua   vi-ti*
      2   2   2   2   8   8
      people   these   nice   they-Pres-them-buy   chairs

vi-le   vi-kubwa   duka-ni   hu-mu.
8   8   18   18
those   big   store-Loc   this
    These nice people are buying those big chairs in this
    store.

Mi-ti   i-le   mi-refu   i-na-ya-angukia   ma-shamba
4   4   4   4   6   6
trees   those tall   they-Pres-them-fall on   farms

ma-dogo   ya-le   ya   wa-tu   wa-le.
6   6   6   2   2
small   those   of   people those
    Those tall trees are falling on the small farms of those
    people.

The numbers in these examples indicate the class of each prefix. The agreement concords fall into two sets, nominal prefixes and verbal prefixes. Nouns and adjectives are marked with the nominal series; everything else (verbs, demonstratives, possessives, and so on) governs the verbal series:

TABLE 5.1 Swahili Concords

245

	Class	Pronouns	Nominal Prefixes: Nouns	Nominal Prefixes: Adjectives "good"	Verbal Prefixes: Subject	Verbal Prefixes: Object	Demonstratives "this"	Demonstratives "that"1	Demonstratives "that"2	Possessives "my/mine"	Relatives "who/which"
		mimi			ni-	-ni-					
		wewe			u-	-ku-					
		yeye			a-	-m-					
		sisi			tu-	-tu-					
		ninyi			m-	-wa-					
		wao			wa-	-wa-					
"person"	1		m-tu	m-zuri	a-	-m-	hu-yu	hu-yo	yu-le	w-angu	-ye-
"people"	2		wa-tu	wa-zuri	wa-	-wa-	ha-wa	ha-o	wa-le	w-angu	-o-
"tree"	3		m-ti	m-zuri	u-	-u-	hu-u	hu-o	u-le	w-angu	-o-
"trees"	4		mi-ti	mi-zuri	i-	-i-	hi-i	hi-yo	i-le	y-angu	-yo-
"fruit"	5		tunda	zuri	li-	-li-	hi-li	hi-lo	li-le	l-angu	-lo-
"fruits"	6		ma-tunda	ma-zuri	ya-	-ya-	ha-ya	ha-yo	ya-le	y-angu	-yo-
"thing"	7		ki-tu	ki-zuri	ki-	-ki-	hi-ki	hi-cho	ki-le	ch-angu	-cho-
"things"	8		vi-tu	vi-zuri	vi-	-vi-	hi-vi	hi-vyo	vi-le	vy-angu	-vyo-
"banana"	9		n-dizi	n-zuri	i-	-i-	hi-i	hi-yo	i-le	y-angu	-yo-
"bananas"	10		n-dizi	n-zuri	zi-	-zi-	hi-zi	hi-zo	zi-le	z-angu	-zo-
"string"	11		u-zi	m-zuri	u-	-u-	hu-u	hu-o	u-le	w-angu	-o-
"freedom"	14		u-huru	m-zuri	u-	-u-	hu-u	hu-o	u-le	w-angu	-o-
"to want"	15		ku-taka	ku-zuri	ku-	-ku-	hu-ku	hu-ko	ku-le	kw-angu	-ko-
"location" ("specific")	16			pa-zuri	pa-	-pa-	ha-pa	ha-po	pa-le	p-angu	-po-
"location" ("general")	17			ku-zuri	ku-	-ku-	hu-ku	hu-ko	ku-le	kw-angu	-ko-
"location" ("internal")	18			m-zuri	m-	-m-	hu-mu	hu-mo	m-le	mw-angu	-mo-

"That"1 specifies an object close to the listener, "that"2 specifies an object at a distance from both speaker and listener; possessive roots vary depending on the person of the possessor: *-angu* "my/mine," *-ako* "your/yours," *-ake* "his/her/hers," *-etu* "our/ours," *-enu* "your/yours (Pl)," *-ao* "their/theirs"; (Class 11 and Class 14 prefixes are identical to those of Class 3, including the adjectival prefix).

(79)   **Nominal**

Nouns and Adjectives

Class

wa-tu wa-zuri	2	nice people
vi-ti vi-kubwa	8	large chairs
mi-ti mi-refu	4	tall trees
ma-shamba ma-dogo	6	small farms

Verbal

Possessives, Demonstratives, etc.

Class

wa-tu ha-wa	2	these people
vi-ti vi-le	8	those chairs
mi-ti i-le	4	those trees
ma-shamba ya-le	6	those farms
wa-tu wa-le	2	those people
duka-ni hu-mu	18	in this store
ma-shamba ya	6	farms of

Adjectives are easy to learn, because generally, they take the same prefix as the noun they modify. The demonstratives, likewise, pose no real problem for the language learner, because once he knows the verbal series he can easily form the demonstrative. Possessives are troublesome since they undergo some phonological alternation. Table 5.1 gives a summary of concord markers.

By now the language learner should be able to do the following exercise:

(80)   *Ki-ti hi_____ ni _____zuri.*   This chair is nice.
       Vi-tu hi_____ ni _____baya.   These things are bad.
       Wa-tu ha_____ ni _____dogo.   These people are small.
       Tunda hi_____ ni _____bichi.   This piece of fruit is raw.
       Ma-tunda _____le ni _____bovu.   Those fruits are rotten.
       M-ti _____le ni _____refu.   That tree is tall.
       Mi-ti _____le ni _____zuri.   Those trees are nice.

It should be no surprise to find out that little of this happens in pidgin Swahili; adjectives and demonstratives are not inflected and thus do not agree. For demonstratives, usually the Class 9 forms are used and we get just *hii* for "this" and *ile* for "that"; adjectives are usually Class 9 in shape; *-zuri* "good/nice" is normally *mzuri*, a Class 1 or Class 3 form:

(81) *mtu mzuri*   good person
    watu mzuri   good people
    kiko mzuri   good pipe/s
    mayai mzuri   good egg/s

    mtu hii   this person
    watu hii   these people
    kiko hii   this pipe/these pipes
    mayai hii   this egg/these eggs

It is interesting that students in a classroom situation and children in a native-Swahili speaking situation learn the noun class system and its accompanying system of agreement, and that other speakers and learners—those not influenced by strong standard models—manage to discard it. The concern of the pidgin speaker is to get across basic messages with the least amount of effort; however, it now appears that as they are coming into more intimate contact with standard speakers through mass media and education, extreme forms of pidgin are giving way to more standard dialects.

1.3 Complex Sentences and the Role of the Verb

Up till now we have been talking about the basic clause in Swahili, essentially a string of words consisting of subject, verb, and object. We have seen how important the verb is within the clause; we now want to show how the verb signals links between clauses.

Many languages of the world can construct complex sentences such as the following:

(82) The woman who is pounding maize is old.

This combines two propositions:

(83) A woman is pounding maize. That woman is old.

Relative clause formation with the relative pronouns *who*, *which*, and *that* allows us to combine two clauses into one sentence. Swahili has a similar capability:

(84) *Mwanamke a-na-ye-twanga mahindi ni mzee.*
    woman   she-Pres-**who**-pound maize   is   old
        The woman who is pounding maize is old.

What combines and links the two clauses is the relative pronoun *-ye-*, the Swahili equivalent of English "who." It is uniquely third-person singular animate. If the antecedent—the noun or pronoun to which the relative clause refers—is third-person plural animate, or an inanimate noun of, say, Class 8, then the relative pronoun will reflect this. In other words, like other pronouns we have seen, relative pronouns in Swahili agree as in the following examples:

(85) a. *wa-nawake wa-na-o-twanga*
                      who
            the women who are pounding

    b. *vi-tabu vi-na-vyo-somwa*
                      which
            the books which are being read

If the antecedent is also an object then the verb can be object-marked as well as relativized:[5]

(86) a. **Wa-nawake** *a-na-o-wa-ona ni wazee.*
                  he-Pres-**who**-them-see
            The women he sees are old.

    b. **Vi-tabu** *a-na-vyo-vi-ona ni vy-angu.*
                  he-Pres-**which**-them see
            The books which he sees are mine.

With these examples we reach the limit of clause functions that can be marked as prefixes on verbs. The various possibilities and their allowed orders are diagrammed below:

(87)   SUBJECT + TENSE + RELATIVE + OBJECT + VERB
       PREFIX   PREFIX   STEM

This agglutination allows a great deal of meaning to be packed into one word:

(88)   *anayeyatwanga*   she who is pounding it
       a-na-ye-ya-twanga   (-*ya*- refers to *mahindi* "maize,"
       she-Pres-who-it-pound   the -*ye*- is the relative pronoun)

This can serve as an answer to the question "Who is going to get the maize?"

    In addition to relative sentences, there are several other ways in which the verb links clauses together. This can be done in what we are

---

[5]The relative pronoun consists basically of the morpheme -*o*-, which is usually marked with the appropriate agreement concord, depending on the noun class of its antecedent. The relative pronoun, however, for Class 1 nouns, and for first-, second-, and third-person singular, is -*ye*-, an exception to the general pattern. See the table of concords (Table 5.1).

calling the 'tense' slot. Languages can typically connect clauses with conjunctions, such as *and*:

(89) a.   Juma is cultivating. ⎫
                         ⎬ Juma is cultivating **and** Fatuma is
    b.   Fatuma is cooking. ⎭ cooking.

Swahili uses *na* in the same context:

(90) a.   *Juma analima.* ⎫
                       ⎬ *Juma analima **na** Fatuma anapika.*
    b.   *Fatuma anapika.* ⎭

However, there is a special case in which the conjunction is established by a prefix marked on the verb. If a Swahili speaker wishes to say that after getting home, he cultivated his garden, and after that, ate something, he would say:

(91) *Ni-li-fika*   *nyumbani,* *ni-**ka**-lima*   *shamba kidogo,*
      I-Past-arrive   I-Consec-cultivate
      *ni-**ka**-la.*
      I-Consec-eat
         I arrived home, cultivated the shamba a little, and then ate.

The prefix *-ka-* is called the 'Consecutive' marker. The first verb marked by *-li-* conveys the notion of past time; the two verbs with *-ka-* indicate only sequence after other events. Although not as frequent, sentences like the following are also possible with the future tense:

(92) *Ni-ta-enda* *kesho*   *ni-**ka**-wa*   *sawasawa.*
      I-Fut-go   tomorrow I-Consec-be alright
         I will go tomorrow, and then I'll be O.K.

One further use of the verb will serve as our final illustration of the importance of morphology in Swahili. Consider a situation where Juma did two things: one he sang and two he drummed. If he did these things separately one would most likely conjoin full clauses with *na*, but if he did them simultaneously, one can emphasize the unity of the two actions by reducing the second clause to an infinitive.

(93) *Juma* *a-li-imba.*
      Juma he-Past-sing
        Juma sang.

      Juma *a-li-piga*   *ngoma.*
      Juma he-Past-hit   drum
        Juma drummed.

Conjunction of Full Verb Forms

Juma a-li-imba na a-li-piga ngoma.　　(Separate acts)
Juma sang and he drummed.

Conjunction with the Infinitive

Juma a-li-imba na ku-piga ngoma.　　(Two acts performed
Juma sang and drummed.　　　　　　　as one)

The infinitive *ku-piga* is reduced: there is no subject marker and no tense marker, and this is why there is the strong implication that the drumming goes together with the singing, as a single act.

For the most part, the complex constructions that depend on the verb—the relative construction, conjunctions of clauses with -*ka*-, and with the infinitive—are not possible in pidgin, and, it would seem, this is primarily because pidgin has simplified the verbal morphology so drastically.

1.4   Tense and Aspect

When an English-speaker talks about some event or state of affairs, he may or may not name the time with an expression such as "last year" or "next Thursday," but he will almost always signal time reference in the verbs he uses. English has two tenses, the present and the past. "Jimmy cooks" and "Jimmy is cooking" are both in the present tense, and they contrast with "Jimmy cooked" and "Jimmy was cooking" in the past tense. To make reference to future time, one uses various constructions in the present tense "Jimmy will cook," "Jimmy is going to cook," and even "Jimmy cooks tomorrow."

Tense has time reference as its primary function, although there are special constructions where it takes on other roles: for example, as in many languages, English has special constructions that employ the past tense to signal, not past time, but "unreality," "If we *had* the money, we would take a plane," "I wish I *lived* in the country."

Swahili has three tenses:

(94)　**Present**　*Ni-na-taka*　I want
　　　Past　　*Ni-li-taka*　I wanted
　　　Future　*Ni-ta-taka*　I will want

The position for prefixes signaling tense or aspect is following the subject but before the relative or object markers, if there are any:

(95)　*a-na-ye-wa-penda*
　　　s/he-Pres-who-them-love
　　　　the one who loves them

Now consider the notion of 'aspect.' Whereas tense is concerned with the location of events and states in time, aspect is part of a verbal system that signals how events and states are *thought of* in terms of their orientation in time. The consecutive marker -ka-, which, as we may recall, is used to say things such as "I got here, cultivated the shamba a little, and then ate," is an example of aspect: it can be used with any specific time reference; what is important is the orientation of events relative to each other. In aspect systems it is typically the case that there are events which can be described from more than one point of view: "Sue read *War and Peace*" and "Sue was reading *War and Peace*" could be about the same event, but they have different aspects; the first is in the 'nonprogressive' and so implies that Sue finished the book; we see the action with a beginning, a middle, and an end; the second is in the 'progressive' and so focuses on just the process, leaving out the beginning and the end. Of course, some situations can be described in only some aspects and not others: had Sue only gotten into the process of reading the book, without finishing it, we could say the progressive ("was reading"), but not the nonprogressive ("read").

When Swahili uses the -na- present tense with a main verb, without further syntactic or contextual elaboration, it is neutral between a progressive or a nonprogressive reading:

(96) *Ni-na-pika.*   I cook.
                          I am cooking.

The contrasting notions of "action in progress" versus "action completed" come to the fore in the description of actions but not states. Just so, the progressive is not ordinarily used in English stative expressions: One ordinarily says "I am sick" but not "I am being sick." The past tense -li- and the future tense -ta- merely locate actions without implying their completion. When it becomes relevant to distinguish between "action in progress" and "action completed," Swahili makes two constructions available, the progressive and a construction with the verb "finish"; for example, in the past tense:

(97) *Ni-li-kuwa   ni-ki-pika.*
       I-Past-be   I-Prog-cook
             I was cooking.

      Ni-li-kwisha   ku-pika.
       I-Past-finish   to-cook
             I finished cooking.

In both these expressions tense is expressed on the first verb. Compare the English progressive "I *am/was* cooking." The Swahili progressive has a progressive morpheme -ki- comparable to English -ing in the second or 'main' verb, but unlike English, Swahili has subject-marking on both verbs. The same constructions are found in the future tense:

(98) *Ni-ta-kuwa   ni-ki-pika.*
      I-Fut-be   I-Prog-cook
          I will be cooking.

      Ni-ta-kwisha   ku-pika.
      I-Fut-finish
          I will finish cooking.

The progressive marker *-ki-* is used in complex sentences to signal an ongoing process that coincides with another event, as in complements for verbs of perception:

(99) *Tu-li-wa-ona   watoto   wa-ki-anguka.*
      We-Past-them-see   children   they-Prog-fall
          We saw the children falling.

      Tu-ta-wa-ona   watoto   wa-ki-soma.
      We-Fut-them-see   children   they-Prog-study
          We will see the children studying.

Note also the following:

(100) *A-ki-soma   ni-ta-furahi.*
       s/he-Prog-study   I-Fut-be happy
           If he studies I'll be happy.

This is the usual 'conditional' construction, not unlike English "With him studying, I will be happy." There is an intriguing similarity between situations where Swahili uses *-ki-* progressive prefix, and where English can use a verb with *-ing*, but while there are overlaps, the two languages have different systems. The language learner has to prepare himself for the unexpected. Compare the following:

(101) I **knew** right then that he   **was coming** (i.e., on the way).
       Past   Past Progressive

       Ni-li-jua   papo hapo   kwamba   a-na-kuja.
       I-Past-know   right then   that   he-Pres-come

Just where one might expect Swahili to use a past progressive construction, it uses what we are calling the 'present' prefix *-na-*; this is to show that the act of coming was *present to* the knowing of it. The presentness of the *-na-* is relative to the tense of the verb in the main clause. Because -*na*- is neutral as between a progressive and non-progressive reading, it is quite compatible with the idea of the "coming" being in progress.

Swahili has an aspect prefix which focuses attention on states resulting from completed processes. This is the perfect prefix -*me*-. Note the variation possible in the translation for the following sentences:

(102)	*Wa-me-pika chakula.*	They have cooked some food.
		They have got some food cooked.
	Wa-me-tengeneza gari.	They have fixed a vehicle.
		They have got a vehicle fixed.
	Wa-me-lala.	They have fallen asleep.
		They are asleep.
		They are sleeping.
	Wa-me-enda.	They have gone.
		They are gone.
	Wa-me-simama.	They have stood up.
		They are standing.
	Kiti ki-me-vunjika.	The chair has become broken.
		The chair is broken.

For an English-speaker learning Swahili, the best translations to focus on here are the ones farthest away from past time reference, and this to avoid the common error of viewing -*me*- as some kind of past-tense marker. Indeed, the situations reported on with -*me*- typically involve events in past time, but they are always completed events and the focus is on present results. English-speakers have special difficulties in Swahili saying things like "They are sleeping" and "They are standing," both about situations which in Swahili are viewed as static states rather than processes. They are likely to reason that since one uses -*na*- to say something like "They are cooking" and "They are studying" (*Wa-na-pika, Wa-na-soma*), the way to say "They are sleeping" and "They are standing" ought to be *Wa-na-lala* and *Wa-na-simama*. But these are most decidedly errors; one says instead *Wa-me-lala* and *Wa-me-simama*. It is equally wrong to say "It is broken" with -*na*-, since what matters is not so much time reference but the state that something is in at the moment of speaking: one says only *Ki-me-vunjika*.

Translations are often deceiving because there are some contexts where they are appropriate and others where they are not. Consider "He has gone" as a translation for *A-me-enda*. When a Swahili-speaker says this he means that the person is *not around*; an English-speaker saying "he has gone" could be conveying the same message, but he could equally well say it in the context where at the moment of speaking the person *is* around ("He has gone already and come back, and now he is cooking dinner"). This is why the better translation for the learner to concentrate on is "He is gone," which can only allow the inference that the person is not around.

Since a Swahili speaker uses *-me-* to assert a state that holds at the time of speaking, it is impossible for him to say:

(103)   **Ni-me-enda.*
       I-Perf-go

This is because of the difficulty of someone's being gone and at the same time being present to say it. It makes as much sense as the English "I am gone." The only way to say "I have gone" is with the verb "finish" plus the infinitive for "go":

(104)   *Ni-me-kwisha   kw-enda.*
       I-Perf-finish   to go
           I have already gone.

Here the finishing is perfect, not the going, i.e., the resulting state of having finished holds at the time of speaking.

Compare the following pairs of sentences with the present *-na-* and the perfect *-me-*:

(105)   *Wa-**na**-simama.*   They are standing up.
           Pres

       *Wa-**me**-simama.*   They are standing.
           Perf

       *Kiti ki-**na**-vunjika.*   The chair is getting broken.
           Pres

       *Kiti ki-**me**-vunjika.*   The chair is broken.
           Perf

The present is used to allow for the notion of ongoing process, the perfect for fixed states that result from completed processes. With this information the following exercise should not be difficult. The tense or aspect prefixes remain to be filled in:

(106) a. *Juma a-_____-choka.*   Juma is becoming tired.
     Juma a-_____-choka.   Juma got tired.
     Juma a-_____-choka.   Juma is tired.

    b. *Juma a-_____-kaa kitini.*   Juma is sitting down in the chair. (in the process of getting into it)

     Juma a-_____-kaa kitini.   Juma sat down in the chair.
     Juma a-_____-kaa kitini.   Juma is sitting in the chair. (in the state of being in it)

The last example of each set takes *-me-*, the middle examples should have the prefix *-li-* for location in the past, while the first ones require *-na-* for location in the present and to allow for a notion of ongoing process.

Given our present understanding, it should be no surprise to learn that negation is signaled by a prefix on the verb. Note the function of *ha-* in the following interchange:

(107) *Je, wanawake watapika?*   Will the women cook?
     Hapana, ha-watapika.   No, they will *not* cook.

To express the negative with a future tense form with *-ta-*, one prefixes *ha-* directly to the corresponding positive form: the negative of *watapika* is *ha-watapika*; *hapana* means "no," and it is the complement to *ndio* "yes." There is some variation to the shape of the negative prefix—for the first-person singular it is *si-*, so the negative of *nitapika* "I will cook" is *sitapika* "I won't cook," but this is a relatively small complication, and the future negatives are not hard to learn:

(108)	Positive	Negative
	Ndizi zitapikwa.	*Ha-zitapikwa.*
	The coconuts will be cooked.	
	Uji utapikwa.	*Ha-utapikwa.*
	The porridge will be cooked.	
	Chakula kitapikwa.	_____-*kitapikwa.*
	The food will be cooked.	
	Vyakula vitapikwa.	_____-*vitapikwa.*
	The foods will be cooked.	
	Maharagwe yatapikwa.	_____-*yatapikwa.*
	The beans will be cooked.	

The last three go like the first two: one simply supplies the negative prefix to the positive form. This pattern applies to future constructions of all sorts:

(109) *Wa-ta-kuwa   wa-ki-soma.*
       they-Fut-be   they-Prog-study
          They will be studying.

       ***Ha**-wa-ta-kuwa   wa-ki-soma.*
       Neg-they-Fut-be   they-Prog-study
          They won't be studying.

Difficulties begin when we move away from the future. Special tense/aspect markers are often required. Compare the following positive and negative statements:

(110)   **Positive**   **Negative**

       *Wa-**na**-soma.*   *Ha-wa-somi.*
          They're studying.   They aren't studying.

       *Wa-**li**-soma.*   *Ha-wa-**ku**-soma.*
          They studied.   They didn't study.

       *Wa-**me**-soma.*   *Ha-wa-**ja**-soma.*
          They've studied.   They haven't studied yet.

Contrasting with the richness of forms and expressive options in the standard tense/aspect system is the situation found in the pidginized versions of Swahili where tense/aspect prefixes are practically nonexistent. The *na-* prefix is virtually the only one to survive, but it does not function as a tense/aspect marker. Our example *Mimi napenda wewe* could mean not only "I love you," but "I loved you" or "I will love you." What the *na-* means has nothing to do with time reference: it marks a sentence as affirmative. Compare the affirmative with the negative formed with *hapana* "no": *napenda* contrasts with *penda* as the affirmative and negative forms for "love":

(111) *Mimi **napenda** wewe.*
          I love you. (I loved you, I will love you)

       *Mimi hapana **penda** wewe.*
          I don't love you. (I didn't love you, I won't love you)

One may ask then how time reference is expressed in pidgin. The answer is by adverbial expressions such as *jana* "yesterday," *kesho* "tomorrow," and *sasa* "now":

(112)   **Standard Swahili**   **Pidgin Swahili**
       Present

    Mpishi a-na-pika (sasa). ⟶ *Mpishi napika **sasa**.*
      The cook is cooking (now).

    Past

    Mpishi a-li-pika (jana). ⟶ *Mpishi napika **jana**.*
      The cook cooked (yesterday).

    Future

    Mpishi a-ta-pika (kesho). ⟶ *Mpishi napika **kesho**.*
      The cook will cook (tomorrow).

In the more radical forms of pidgin, *sasa*, *jana*, and *kesho* have become the generalized markers for present, past, and future. As for aspect, there is nothing left of the system that depends on verbal prefixes, but some nuances are communicated by combinations of words; for example, the verb *kwisha* "to finish" is used where the standard language uses the perfect prefix *-me-*:

(113)   *Kiti ki-me-anguka.*   ⟶ *Kiti kwisha anguka.*
      The chair has fallen.

Similarly, in the situations where the standard language uses the negative perfect, where as we have seen the *-me-* prefix is replaced by *-ja-*, the pidgins have achieved the same effect by taking the standard expression *bado* "still/yet" and making it into a negative adverb "not yet":

(114)   *Wa-me-pika.*   ⟶ *Wao kwisha pika.*
      They have cooked.

    Ha-wa-ja-pika (bado). ⟶ *Wao bado pika.*
      They haven't cooked (yet).

The generalization throughout is that pidgin says what it can say with a small vocabulary and without morphological complexity. This narrows the repertoire of expressions for pidgin speakers but makes the language easier to learn. Pidgin speakers are not fully accepted in areas where the language is spoken natively, or in up-country areas where standard Swahili is the norm as a national language, as in Tanzania. Throughout East Africa one can describe a continuum ranging from the most elementary pidgins through varieties that begin looking more and more like standard and native Swahili. Change is taking place in the direction of standard varieties. In the face of mass media, education, and the need to communicate in a wide range of social and cultural contexts that exceed the usual bounds of pidgins, the pidgins are giving way to the complexity and expressive flexibility of standard Swahili.

2   SWAHILI LANGUAGE AND SOCIETY

Each of the features of Swahili that we have been examining—the basic clause pattern, noun classification, agreement, and marking for tense and aspect—could be described for any number of Bantu languages. Swahili is a linguistic descendent of the same ancient language that gave rise to all the present-day Bantu languages, and more immediately, to the closely related Bantu languages spoken along the Kenya and Tanzania coasts today. But unlike these languages, Swahili has become a language

FIGURE 5.2   *Zanzibar Town (left) and the Market in Musoma, Tanzania (right)*

In Zanzibar, Swahili is the native language of all but a few of its inhabitants. In the inland town of Musoma (near Lake Victoria), there are few first-language speakers of Swahili. The Musoma town market serves a linguistically diverse area. While Swahili is the main language for commerce there, one can also hear spoken Kuria, Kwaya, and Jita (all Bantu languages), and the Nilotic language, Luo. Everywhere it is used one sees the imprint of the contact Swahili has had with multilingual communities. For example, in the photograph at the front of the chapter, we see a view of Musoma with a sign in Swahili advertising Soda Baridi. Soda *is from English;* baridi *is from Arabic and means "cold," hence "cold soda."*

of national and international importance. It is the official language of Tanzania, a national language, along with English, in Kenya, and it is widely used in Uganda, in the Shaba and Kivu regions of Zaire, and in parts of Burundi, Ruanda, and Zambia, as well as in Somalia and Mozambique. It is known and used by people of diverse ethnic backgrounds—Africans, Asians, and Europeans—and it is used in all types of communicative situations, from bargaining in marketplaces to debates in parliament.

Most people speak Swahili as a second or third language, but the number of native speakers is growing through each generation. Interethnic marriage is increasing, especially in urban areas, and many of the children of these marriages grow up speaking Swahili, often the only language their parents share. The language continues to spread and grow in numbers of speakers each year; some Pan-Africanists have even suggested, somewhat unrealistically perhaps, that Swahili could become the lingua franca of the whole of Africa. This is unlikely to happen since Swahili has no hold in other areas of Africa, especially in the large expanse of West Africa where there are a number of deeply rooted lingua francas, such as Hausa and Maninka (see Chapter II, *Maninka*, in the companion volume).

Most international languages (for example, English) have had humble origins and have come to prominence largely through the operation of nonlinguistic forces. The success of Swahili is largely an accident as far as the language itself is concerned, but is due rather to practical choices made by the people who came to use it. The language bears the imprint of this experience.

2.1 Chronological Overview

Swahili has existed as a distinct language for about nine hundred years. Before that, migrating waves of Bantu-speaking agriculturalists and fishermen emigrated from an area north of the Congo forest in the Camerouns into East and Southern Africa. In some cases they displaced previous hunting-gathering peoples and pastoralists, but in other cases they assimilated them culturally and linguisitically. Bantu is a linguistic term used to describe peoples who now live over much of the southern portion of Africa from the Camerouns in the northwest to southeastern South Africa, and from the Atlantic shores of Zaire to East Africa. Bantu languages in turn are related more distantly to most of the languages of West Africa in the Niger-Congo family.

By around 1100 A.D. these migrating peoples, ever in search of better farming country, had emerged as distinct groups. We can identify at least three of these groups of language communities from which the present day Kenyan and Tanzanian coastal languages developed. From these same ancestral languages arose the Mijikenda languages (which are spoken in an area centering on Mombasa, Kenya), Pokomo (which is spoken from the upper Tana River in Kenya to the coast), and Swahili. Given the present-day distribution of these languages, we can say that the Swahili lived originally only in the northern part of the area where they are found today. Some Swahili point to certain myths and legends which would place the point of origin somewhere along the Somali coast in an area known as Shungwaya.

To understand something of what happened to this small group of Bantu farmers and fishermen, we have to understand the global importance of the East African coast. East Africa faces the Indian Ocean. To the northeast is Arabia, a little further south of Arabia there is India, and to the east is Malaysia, China, and Indonesia. Trade between these areas is quite ancient. Early Greek and Roman records talk about settlements of seafaring peoples along the African coast, with trade controlled by Arabs. Ivory, turtle shell, rhino horn, and some coconut oil are mentioned as exports, while iron was imported. This trade was made possible by the variable winds known as the monsoons. Traders from southwest Arabia sailed to East Africa on the northeast monsoon from November to April and returned with the winds that blow in the reverse direction from June through October.

From the writings of al-Mas'udi (died *c.* 945 A.D.), an early visitor from Persia, we know that by the tenth century there were towns already established along the East African coast with a mixed population of Africans and Moslem Arabs who spoke the indigenous language.

Between the tenth and fifteenth centuries, important trading and commercial centers developed along two thousand miles of coast, from the northern city of Mogadishu in Somalia to the southern Tanzanian town of Kilwa. Mogadishu was close to the trading centers of Arabia and Persia. Kilwa prospered from the long-distance gold trade carried on with people from the interior and because it was a stopping place on the way to trading areas on Madagascar. We know of at least thirty trading centers along the coast during this period. By the fifteenth century, most of the ruling class in these towns appears to have been of mixed Arab and African ancestry whose religion was Islam. The landowners, skilled artisans, merchants, and most of the religious functionaries belonged to this class, but most of the agricultural labor and menial tasks were done by Africans, who in many cases were in a state of slavery. Many people from the interior were attracted to the amenities of coastal town life and so also to Swahili culture. Swahili language and culture spread as the trade and towns spread and by the fifteenth century was well established even on the remote Comoro Islands which lie just north of Madagascar. A new civilization evolved, one that was ethnically diverse, maritime, and looked outward toward the Indian Ocean; it was Moslem, urban, mercantile, literate in Arabic, and at least late in this period, a writing tradition developed for Swahili with Arabic script.

2.2 Colonies then Nation States: The Pressure for Standardization

By the midnineteenth century, Zanzibar came to dominate the long-distance trade that had been developing between the interior and the coast. By use of routes that had been established by inland peoples, such as the Nyamwezi and Yao, large trading caravans (Swahili *safari*) were launched inland seeking both ivory and slaves. A major stimulus for this penetration came from an increasing European interest (after the American Revolution) in trade possibilities with East Africa. Arab/Swahili settlements were established along the inland routes. Some traders and slavers penetrated deep into the Congo (present-day Zaire) and into Zambia. The Swahili of Zanzibar was the language used by the traders in their transactions with the local people, and the use of the language spread among local people.

2.2.1 *European Penetration*   It was via these trade routes that European explorers and missionaries, and following them, European administrators, penetrated the inland area of present-day Tanzania, Kenya, and Uganda. Stanley, for example, depended on Swahili traders from Zanzibar to lead him to Ujiji, where he had his well-known meeting with Livingstone, and then, somewhat later, when he crossed the continent from the east coast to the Atlantic. During the 1860s and 1870s, missionaries and the representatives of the European powers set themselves up in the inland trading centers, including Tabora, Ujiji, and Bujumbura. They saw the need of a language with which they might communicate with Africans. The obvious and immediate choice was Swahili. Edward Steere, an English missionary, was able to write this about Swahili as early as 1870:

> There is probably no African language so widely known as the Swahili. It is understood along the coasts of Madagascar and Arabia, it is spoken by the Seedees in India, and is the trade language of a very large part of Central or Intertropical Africa. Zanzibar traders penetrate sometimes even to the western side of the continent, and they are in the constant habit of traversing more than half of it with their supplies of Indian and European goods. Throughout this immense district any one really familiar with the Swahili language will generally be able to find someone who can understand him, and serve as an interpreter.[6]

By the 1890s the Germans had gained administrative control of

---

[6] E. Steere, *A Handbook of the Swahili Language* (4th ed., rev. by A. B. Hellier), The Sheldon Press, London, 1870, p. vii.

Tanganyika.[7] By that time a number of German administrators, settlers, and missionaries were learning Swahili. Swahili newspapers were founded, and reports to the German administration from village headmen were made in Swahili or German. Schools were established, and in nearly all cases Swahili was the language of instruction. The colonial administrations, both German and British, used Swahili as a means of reaching the people; in some cases Swahili was the means through which some of the people were able to reach up to the administration. Under German administration the acquisition of Swahili was enough for membership in the junior civil service, but beyond that level a knowledge of German was required. The British, who succeeded the Germans in Tanganyika after World War I, required both English and Swahili for the junior civil service. The attitude developed among at least some Africans that Swahili was useful but second best. Swahili was used in the primary schools and was a subject in secondary schools, but the rest of higher education was in English.

The need for Swahili was quickly recognized by the Europeans, even though the countervailing pressure to develop English was always present. Pragmatic considerations won out: Swahili was an established fact, a vital communicative tool in all but the highest level of society, but if that level was to rule successfully, it had to build on a preexisting foundation. Swahili was that foundation, and like it or not, the colonial governments began to deal with it through their various agencies, primarily through education. It also became obvious, very early on, that Swahili was not a homogeneous entity, that the Swahili spoken on Zanzibar and the Swahili spoken in Mombasa, for example, were different. They are mutually intelligible, but they are nevertheless different. Some of the differences are grammatical (like the tense/aspect markers), but the most obvious differences, that impressed the early educators and administrators, were differences in pronunciation and vocabulary.

2.2.2   *Dialects*   It seems fairly certain that by 1500, Swahili was spoken all along the coast, in the same areas where it is spoken today. What is not clear is how it spread and whether it spread in hopscotch fashion from one central area, or whether it spread south in slowly

---

[7]In 1895 British and German representatives, along with the Sultan of Zanzibar, who at that time controlled the offshore islands and a long strip of territory on the mainland, partitioned East Africa: Britain gained final control over Uganda and Kenya and the dominions of the Sultan; Germany consolidated its hold on the Tanganyika mainland as well as part of the coastal strip which had been governed by the sultan. After the First World War Tanganyika became a mandate of the League of Nations with Britain the mandatory power. Tangayika gained independence in 1961, Uganda in 1962, and Kenya and Zanzibar in 1963. In 1964 Zanzibar and Tanganyika formed the United Republic of Tanzania.

advancing waves. It is also not clear if one uniform Swahili dialect existed for some time and then diverged later, or whether the dialect situation was diverse from the beginning of the period of expansion. In any case, by the beginning of this century, when educators and administrators began to worry about what kind of Swahili they would use in schools throughout the East African territories, how they would write it, and so forth, there was a fairly diverse dialect situation in existence. There were two prominent dialects to choose from, those spoken in Mombasa and in Zanzibar, the largest commercial centers at that time.

Swahili dialects form a chain of mutually intelligible linguistic units linking north and south, from the Lamu archipelago (northern Kenya coast) to the Comoro Islands north of Madagascar. They form three clusters: northern, central, and southern. The northern cluster includes a number of dialects spoken on Lamu island and environs; the central cluster numbers mainly the dialects of Pemba plus several others spoken on the mainland; the southern group, perhaps more uniform than the other two groups, includes the dialects south of Bagamoyo (which is located on the northern Tanzanian coast). This group also includes KiUnguja, the dialect of Zanzibar Town, on which standard Swahili is based. Within the southern group is a cluster which has been termed the "bridge dialects" so-called because they share certain features with northern and central dialects: these are the dialects spoken in and around Mombasa, where the major dialect is known as KiMvita, after the traditional name of the island of Mombasa.

How different dialects are from each other affects how easy it is for people to understand each other. For example, KiVumba, a dialect of the central cluster spoken south of Mombasa near the Kenya-Tanzania border, has a future-tense marker -*cha*-, which corresponds to the -*ta*- of standard Swahili:

		Standard	
(115)	**KiVumba**	**(KiUnguja)**	
	ni-cha-funga	*ni-ta-funga*	I will fasten

The difference here is just in pronunciation and not meaning, however, and once this is recognized, intelligibility is not affected. But there are cases where the dialect difference is critical: whereas -*na*- is the present-tense marker in standard Swahili, in KiVumba it functions as the present perfect (the -*me*- aspect in standard):

(116)	**KiVumba**	**Standard**	
	ru-na-funga	*tu-me-funga*	we have fastened
	ku-na-funga	*u-me-funga*	you have fastened

Not only does -*na*- have a different meaning in KiVumba, but the subject prefixes are different. These are not insurmountable barriers, but such differences create larger problems when there is a greater audience, such as in the various mass media.

Past tense (-*li*- in standard) in KiVumba is marked by modifying the stem-final vowel which is normally -*a*; in past tense this final vowel is assimilated to the vowel preceeding it. This is illustrated in Table 5.2, along with the full set of subject prefixes for personal animates.

TABLE 5.2   *KiVumba Future and Past-Tense Forms Compared to Standard*

	KiVumba	Standard	
Future	*ni-cha-βara*	*ni-ta-pata*	I will get
	u-cha-rera	*u-ta-leta*	you will bring
	a-cha-βira	*a-ta-pita*	he will pass by
	ru-cha-ondoka	*tu-ta-ondoka*	we will leave
	mu-cha-chukua	*m-ta-chukua*	you will carry
	wa-cha-m-chukulia	*wa-ta-m-chukulia*	they will carry for him
Past	*si-βara*	*ni-li-pata*	I got
	ku-rere	*u-li-leta*	you brought
	ka-βiri	*a-li-pita*	he passed by
	ru-ondoko	*tu-li-ondoka*	we left
	mu-chukuu	*m-li-chukua*	you carried
	wa-m-chukulii	*wa-li-m-chukulia*	they carried for him

The tense-marker -*li*- is found in KiVumba but it marks the past negative:

(117)   **KiVumba**   **Standard**

        si-li-funga   *si-ku-funga*   I did not fasten
        kʰu-li-funga   *hu-ku-funga*   you did not fasten
        kʰa-li-fika   *ha-ku-fika*   he did not arrive
        kʰa-ru-li-fika   *ha-tu-ku-fika*   we did not arrive

Not only is the tense system different, but the subject prefix series is different, depending on the tense of the verb. The KiVumba subject prefixes correspond more closely to the Standard in the future than in the past (compare the forms in Table 5.2). In the past tense, *si*-, *ku*-, and *ka*- correspond to standard Swahili *ni*-, *u*-, and *a*-; *si*- in standard is only first-person singular in 'negative' tenses, but has both a positive and negative value in the KiVumba past. The *r*/*t* correspondence seen in the first-person plural marker (*ru*- versus *tu*-) is found in much of the lexicon where KiVumba *r* corresponds to standard *t*:

(118) **KiVumba**   **Standard**

    m-roro   *m-toto*   child
    ku-ruma   *ku-tuma*   to send
    m-ri   *m-ti*   tree
    vira   *vita*   war

Another phonological difference is seen in the correspondence of KiVumba β with standard *p* (β is a voiced bilabial fricative, the sound you get when you turn *b* into a fricative):

(119) **KiVumba**   **Standard**

    ku-βara   *ku-pata*   to get
    ku-βira   *ku-pita*   to pass
    u-βeβo   *u-pepo*   wind
    βahali   *pahali*   place
    haβa   *hapa*   here

Similar differences can be stated for other dialects, compared each with each or with standard Swahili. One of the most important contrasts socially is that between the Standard and the Swahili of the city of Mombasa, KiMvita, both in the southern cluster of dialects. Mombasa Swahili has a set of dental and postdental consonants: ţ and ḍ versus *t* and *d*, while KiUnguja has only the postdental series;[8] the *t* and *d* of KiMvita corresponds fairly regularly to the *t* and *d* of standard, but the dental series corresponds to *t*, *ch*, *d*, or *j* in standard:

	Mombasa (KiMvita)	**Standard (KiUnguja)**	
(120)			
a.	*takataka*	*takataka*	rubbish, trash
	tatu	*tatu*	three
	m-to	*m-to*	river
	ndoo	*ndoo*	bucket
	ndiyo	*ndiyo*	yes

---

[8]The dental series /ţ/ and /ḍ/ is pronounced with the tongue tip touching the back of the front incisors, while in /t/ and /d/ the tip of the tongue is raised a bit higher and in articulation touches the alveolar ridge, that is, the gum ridge above the teeth. In the conventional orthography used to write KiMvita, this distinction is not indicated, but for our purposes here the cedilla is used to mark the dental series.

	Mombasa (KiMvita)	Standard (KiUnguja)	
b.	*ku-ṭaka*	*ku-taka*	to want
	ṭano	*tano*	five
	m-ṭo	*m-to*	pillow
	ki-ṭwa	*ki-chwa*	head
	ku-fiṭa	*ku-ficha*	to hide
	nḍoo	*njoo*	come!
	nḍia	*njia*	path
	ḍamu	*damu*	blood
	panḍa	*panda*	fork, slingshot

There is a striking difference affecting the tense/aspect system: with verb stems beginning with consonants Mombasa Swahili has *-n-* for the perfect-aspect marker (which, less the *a*, corresponds to the *-na-* of KiVumba).

(121)	KiVumba (Central)	KiMvita (Southern)	Standard (Southern)	
	ka-na-fika	*a-n-fika*	*a-me-fika*	he has arrived
	ka-na-soma	*a-n-soma*	*a-me-soma*	he has read
	ka-na-kaa	*a-n-kaa*	*a-me-kaa*	he is seated

but if the verb stem begins with a vowel *-me-* is used: KiMvita *a-me-ona* = standard *a-me-ona* "he has seen."

2.2.3 *Standardization* In the face of this kind of diversity, what dialect could the planners choose for their standard language? This would be the one they would develop as an educational tool, for purposes of administration, and for publishing. A partial solution had already been predetermined. By the end of the nineteenth century, the two major urban and trading centers were Zanzibar Town and Mombasa, and these, along with Dar es Salaam, had become early European administrative centers. Early missionaries who first located themselves in Zanzibar Town naturally learned KiUnguja; those who began their work in Mombasa or environs settled on KiMvita. The German missionaries, government administrators, and educators on the Tanganyika mainland learned versions of Swahili which were virtually identical to KiUnguja, the model for the Swahili of the inland trading centers. The first grammars to be produced, and the first books to appear—often the scriptures—were based on the dialects the Europeans had learned.

After the First World War and after all of East Africa came under the political control of the British, there were pressures to form uniform policies for all the East African territories. But the concern for the choice of a standard language had been present for some time. As early as 1882, the missionary Krapf commented on one aspect of the problem in his dictionary of the Swahili language: "What confusion must arise, if the University Mission at Zanzibar, the Church Missionary Society's agent at Frere Town [north of Mombasa] and in Uganda, the Free Methodists at Ribe [inland from Mombasa], the Scotch Mission near Lake Nyassa and the London Society near Lake Tanganyika, would have their separate orthography!"[9] Swahili poetry and religious works had been written in Arabic orthography. Europeans considered this ill-adapted for their purpose, however, and the Roman alphabet was rapidly introduced. Then the controversy developed on how to use the Roman alphabet. The graph *c* was suggested in place of *ch* for the palatal affricate /č/, and *ŋ* was proposed instead of *ng'* for the velar nasal (as in *ng'ombe* "cow, cattle"). But these proposals were rejected by the various education departments: *ch* and *ng'* were already too well established. Word division was a problem for a while as well. There were some who wanted to write the noun class prefixes and concords separated from their stems; under such a system *mtu/watu* "person/people" would have been written as *m tu* and *wa tu*. Others suggested that the possessive morpheme should be written attached to the possessed noun: *majani yamti* "the tree's leaves" (literally, the leaves of the tree") instead of the accepted practice then and today of writing these elements separately: *majani ya mti*.

Educators (who in many cases were missionaries) provided the first organized impetus to deal with the problem of standardization. The governor of Tanganyika's Education Conference in 1925 established a committee to keep track of Swahili school books to avoid duplication. But it was not until 1928, at the interterritorial conference, that a decision was confirmed to adopt KiUnguja, the dialect of Zanzibar, as the model on which all standardization efforts would be made. The decision was not made without argument, and it caused considerable bad feelings and bitterness. The choice of KiUnguja was supported by the Universities Mission to Central Africa, while Mombasa Swahili was advocated by the Church Missionary Society. Differences between scholars from the two areas had been long-standing.

There were quite compelling reasons for choosing KiUnguja. First of all, the Mombasa dialect was held in ill repute by the speakers of all the dialects to the north and south. This attitude was, and still is, a holdover from the times when there were open hostilities between various towns in an attempt to control trade; Mombasa, it seems, was at

---

[9]L. Krapf, *A Dictionary of the Suahili Language*, London, 1882 (republished in 1964 by The Gregg Press Incorporated, Ridgewood, N.J.), p. x.

the center of most of this conflict; furthermore, the Swahili that was spoken already at that time along the Tanganyika coast and in vast inland areas, including Kenya, was more similar to KiUnguja than to KiMvita. In these respects the decision was a pragmatic one.

2.2.4 *Literary Tradition*   Mombasa had for centuries participated in a rich literary tradition that thrived in the northern cluster of dialects. Except for Mombasa, the south lacked any such traditions, and by choosing KiUnguja, it was argued, language planners were going to cut East Africa off from an important part of its heritage. It is not surprising this argument failed to move the planners: the literary art that reached the highest levels of sophistication in the north was poetry, Islamic in original inspiration; the long heroic epic, the *tenzi* (*u-tenzi/t*^h*enzi* "kind of poem") dealt mostly with Islamic religious themes, the life of the Prophet, and the deeds of his early followers. The language planners were Christian missionaries, or if not missionaries, Western in culture, and not sympathetic with Islamic traditions.

Interestingly enough, the decision in favor of KiUnguja turned out to do little to diminish literary activity. Wherever Swahili has spread, one finds the quatrain, an extension of the traditional verse form. The quatrain, with *shairi* meter, is the verse form used for secular themes, from love to politics. The Mombasa poet Muyaka was famous for his poetry attacking the city's enemies at the height of its conflict with Zanzibar in the early nineteenth century. This tradition is carried on in every Swahili newspaper and magazine printed today, and it would be unthinkable for an editor to omit poetry from any edition. Poetry pages are public forums: one magazine calls its poetry page *Bunge la Washairi* "The Poet's Parliament."

The language and style of the earliest written poems date them from the 1700s and before. From the beginning one sees local and current themes side by side with Islamic ones: The *Utenzi wa Liongo* concerns the legendary folk hero, Liongo Fumo, and his feud with a paternal cousin over the inheritance of the throne of Shagga; the *Utenzi wa Al-Inkishfi* is a moralistic homily on the downfall of Pate (in the Lamu archipelago) in the late eighteenth century through intrigue, sedition, and assassination; the *Utenzi wa Vita vya Maji Maji* deals with the Maji Maji rebellion in Tanganyika against the German colonials in 1905.

Swahili poetry is not simply the domain of those educated in the traditional *chuo* (Koranic school). Much of it is didactic, exhorting people to live devoutly and virtuously, but even these poems are written in *shairi* meter and intended to be sung: they belong to the common man. Over thirty poets have been counted in Mombasa alone: their poems circulate orally and there are special evenings for "poetry fests"; a wedding is another occasion when poetry is sung or recited. Here is an example in standard Swahili:

(122) *Ma-pe-nzi ya-me-ni-va-a / na-mi ni-ko u-ge-ni-ni*
    a-ki-li i-me-ni-paa / ha-ta nji-a si-i-o-ni
    ma-pe-nzi ya-na ha-da-a / ya-kwe-li na-kwa-mbi-e-ni

Love has enveloped me / while I have been abroad
my mind has flown away from me, / I do not even see the road,
love is full of deceit, / let me tell you words of truth.[10]

This is one of four stanzas of a poem about the grief the poet feels over the lost love of his *mpenzi* ("lover/beloved"). It is typical of the quatrain form with shairi meter: a stanza contains three lines of sixteen syllables each; each line is divided into two *vipande* of equal length, and the final syllable of alternate *vipande* rhyme.

With the choice of the Zanzibar dialect for a standard, some of the best tradition of Islamic poetry was lost. But this situation is being redressed somewhat: for example, students at the University of Dar es Salaam today are attempting to use the *tenzi* epics as models for developing drama in standard Swahili. Standardization has had its costs, but one can see the literary tradition adapting and renewing itself in its new circumstances.

2.2.5 *Education and Publication*   The standardization of Swahili first of all has entailed the choice of KiUnguja over KiMvita. In the second place it has included standards of spelling and word division to be followed by educational and governmental organizations; and finally, it has led to the production of grammars and dictionaries, and standards of usage and style to be followed in all publications. The Interterritorial Swahili committee was established in 1930, and any book that did not meet the criteria did not receive its imprimatur and was usually then not published. The responsibilities of the committee were also to establish standards for orthography, to promote uniformity of grammar and syntax and uniformity in the use of existing vocabulary and of new words. It had little effect on the Swahili of those who already spoke it; its impact was chiefly felt in school textbooks and in the Swahili taught in mission and government schools.

Before large-scale publications and the spread of mass media, it was common practice to correct the Swahili appearing in books to conform to a norm supposedly based on KiUnguja. This was not easy because KiUnguja is a spoken and not a literary dialect. The language of school textbooks came to be influenced stylistically by European models; even syntactically the norm became idealized and unnatural, based on the

---

[10]J. Knappert, *An Anthology of Swahili Love Poetry*, University of California Press, Berkeley and Los Angeles, Calif., 1972.

abstract description in the grammars of Steere and Ashton.[11] Thus the language published under the auspices of the Swahili Committee was not always based on living tradition. As early as 1934, complaints were voiced:

> We have standardized Swahili and in the process Swahili seems to have become a new language. While, doubtless, all are ready to admit that Swahili, like any other language is bound to develop and grow, in form, idiom and vocabulary, as a result of the impact of the civilisations of the immigrant communities, yet surely the development must come from the Swahili mind, and must not be superimposed on them from without. But that is just what we have tried, and are still trying to do, with the result that we are in the somewhat ludicrous position of teaching Swahilis their own language through the medium of books, many of which are not Swahili in form or content, and whose language has but little resemblance to the spoken tongue. We are perhaps too apt to overlook the fact that the people themselves are not only capable of adapting their language to modern needs, but are doing so with amazing rapidity.[12]

Books written in the standard often seemed artificial and stilted; consequently it began to be known as *Kizungu* (European Swahili) or *Kiserikali* (Government Swahili). Even today one still hears standard referred to as *Kiswahili cha kitabu* (*kitabu* "book") "book Swahili," and sometimes *Kiswahili cha wastani* (wastani "average") "average Swahili," the latter referring to the view that in some sense no one actually speaks standard Swahili, that it is an idealized common denominator of all varieties and dialects of Swahili spoken today.

The excesses of the Swahili Committee did not last; their efforts eventually turned to the collection and preservation of the classical literature and to the study of Swahili dialects. Even the practice of granting an imprimatur to approved books was dropped. This resulted in a great deal more variety and experimentation in the style of writing that is appearing in print today.

Despite the artificial style, the uniformity of the textbook Swahili went far in spreading a Swahili which is similar, if not identical, to KiUnguja; however, for KiUnguja speakers the differences can sometimes be more important than the similarities; in their minds, the dialect that they encounter in radio, newspapers, schools, television (in Nairobi), and in ever-increasing quantity, in advertising, is not their language. At the extreme, the official standard is considered to be the invention of missionaries and other Europeans. It also sets off the

---

[11]E. O. Ashton, *Swahili Grammer*, Longmans, Green, London, 1944.

[12]Memorandum (no author), "Modern Swahili," *Bulletin of the Inter-territorial Language Committee* (now known as *Swahili*), vol. 7, 1934, pp. 3–10.

somewhat conservative and traditional coast from the westernized up-country areas, which were the most direct beneficiaries of European educational efforts, and which today, are the political and economic bases of power. The speech in these up-country areas tend to sound more like the standard than the KiUnguja dialect upon which it is based.

The success of the Swahili Committee's efforts for standardization has varied country by country. In Tanzania, where Swahili is the medium of instruction in the primary grades, and for some subjects in secondary schools, there is awareness and agreement among speakers of Swahili about the norms of the standard language. The situation in Kenya is different. Most second-language speakers of Swahili in Kenya have not learned Swahili in school; there the medium of instruction is usually either the local indigenous tribal language or English. They have learned their Swahili in the marketplace. For instance, the imperative for the verb "to come" among many educated Kenyans is the same as the infinitive, *kuja*; this is a recent innovation. Tanzanian speakers say *kuja* for the infinitive, but retain the irregular imperative *njoo*. For the Kenyans to impose the regular pattern on the verb "to come" and say *kuja* for the imperative is comparable to English speakers saying *goed* instead of *went*. This kind of detail makes up the negatively stereotyped image Tanzanians have of Kenyan speakers of Swahili.

In Uganda, little effort has ever been made to promote Swahili in schools, and it has always been vociferously rejected by the Baganda, a culturally prominent, and once politically powerful, tribe in Uganda. Nevertheless, the language is widely known and used, even by the Baganda. In Uganda, as in Kenya, Swahili has been learned for very practical reasons.

2.3 Cultural Change and Grammatical Processes

During the period of geographical expansion, Swahili underwent modification, not so much in its Bantu syntax or morphology, but noticeably in vocabulary and, to some extent, in pronunciation. The biggest outside influences were Islam, Arabic and Persian culture, and the Arabic language. More generally, rural society was transforming itself as increasing numbers of people involved themselves in long-distance trade, these people adapted their language to the changing circumstances.

When people alter their style of life they usually change their language. A change in jobs, hobbies, or living arrangements can bring with it new bonds between people as well as new things to talk about; words and ways of talking emerge in everyday use which only a short time before were regarded as novel. They enter into the standards for language behavior and become as much a part of one's self-image as conventions surviving from earlier times.

More often than not, it was the newcomers to the East African coast who underwent the greatest change. Their separate identities merged into the Swahili-speaking culture and their languages were usually lost: Arabic, for example, was superceded by Swahili except in narrowly defined settings such as the reading of the Koran and other functions associated with the mosque. The result of the assimilation process was not a simple mixture of two languages and societies, as has so often been said. It was more of an acceptance and integration of new elements into a language which has remained firmly defined in its grammatical base. A good deal of its vocabulary is borrowed, but the borrowings were always modified to fit the requirements of Bantu morphology and syntax (the analogous thing is true for English with its many borrowings from French, words which were nevertheless assimilated completely into its Germanic morphology and syntax). The borrowings had little but superficial influence on the structure of Swahili. It is in its character as a social tool that the change has been most dramatic, and here we must look to the interplay between structure and use, and examine the way in which Swahili pronunciation and vocabulary have accommodated themselves to social change.

2.3.1 *Pronunciation*   Because of the influx of large numbers of Arabic loans, and the prestige that Arabic held among the Moslem Swahili, the phonemes /ð/, /θ/, and /ɣ/ (orthographically *dh*, *th*, and *gh*) were added to the inventory of Swahili sounds. Examples of these occur in loan words: *dhamana* "surety, bail, bond," *themanini* "eighty," and *ghali* "expensive, scarce." Another addition from Arabic is the pronunciation of words which are spelled with *h*, pronounced as [x] or [h] depending on the education and status of the speaker. The sound [x] is difficult for English speakers; it is the sound of a *k* turned into a fricative; [ɣ] is similar but is voiced, a *g* sound turned into a fricative; [ð] and [θ] are interdental fricatives and are heard in English as the first sounds of *then* and *thin*. In most Bantu languages [l] and [r] are not separate sounds, but they are in Swahili. This is a consequence of the influx of words from Arabic, where these two sounds distinguish meaning, such as *mahari* "dowry" versus *mahali* "place." The prestige of Islam is reflected in a style of pronunciation that is heard in mosques and in the recitation of poetry: here there are a considerable number of Arabized pronunciations of loan words. Educated second-language speakers of Swahili away from the coast tend to imitate this style, but many consider this an affectation. Otherwise, away from the coast, and especially in the pronunciation of pidgin speakers, the fricatives /ð/, /θ/, and /ɣ/ tend to be modified, with [z] or [d] for /ð/, [s] or [t] for /θ/, and [g] for /ɣ/. For example, the word for a 50¢ piece, *thumuni*, is frequently heard as *sumuni.* The distinction between /l/ and /r/ is also merged, thus *mahali* "place" and *mahari* "dowry" are not distinguished.

Most Bantu languages are 'tonal'—that is, words can be distinguished by differences in relative levels of pitch. Notice the difference created by pitch in these examples from Kamba, a Bantu language of Kenya:

(123)   èìá   weed   èíá   milk   èìà   lake, pond
(`= low tone, ´ = high tone)

Swahili, however, has lost all tonal distinctions and has replaced tone with 'penultimate' stress—that is, stress on the next to last syllable, as in the English words *apartment, relation, catastrophic.* Although most Arabic loans have been changed to fit this pattern, some variation can be observed; for example, some speakers like to pronounce the words for "obligation" and "likewise" with their original Arabic accent placement: *lazima,* and *kadhalika* instead of *lazima* and *kadhalika.* Up-country, away from the influence of the Moslem coast, speakers are for the most part using penultimate stress, thus completely regularizing the pattern and nativizing loan words. This shift from a language employing tone to one with a fixed-stress pattern is undoubtedly due to its extensive use by nonnative speakers who failed to learn the complexities of a tone system. Other Bantu languages, like Lingala, along the Congo River in Zaire, have undergone the same evolution as they have become lingua francas.

These are a few of the things which have changed Swahili, but it is not a one-way process. Swahili changes what it borrows. Clusters of consonants other than Bantu /mb/, /nd/, /nj/, and /ng/ are generally not tolerated; a large number of loans coming into Swahili have had other sequences of consonants, and there has been a tendency for vowels to be inserted to separate them. English "brush," "blue," "blanket," "club," "mudguards" have become, respectively, *burushi, buluu, bulangeti, kilabu, madigadi.* This preserves the consonant–vowel–consonant–vowel pattern of Bantu lexical structure. This pattern is also the motivation for another change: nouns and verbs of Bantu origin always end in vowels. When loan words end in consonants, they are modified to fit this pattern by adding a final vowel in principled ways: /i/ usually is inserted following alveolar, palatal, and velar consonants (*t, d, s, z, l, r,* and *n* are alveolars, *ch* and *j* are palatals, and *k* and *g* are velars); /u/ is added following labials (like *p, b,* and *m*);

(124)   English   *bank*   becomes Swahili   *benki*
fine   *faini*
club   *kilabu*
team   *timu*

Swahili is currently borrowing a large number of English words along with their consonant clusters (like *skrubu* "screw," *eropleni* "airplane"). Time will tell whether these loans will bring a permanent change in the phonological pattern of Swahili. The situation is in flux: one hears both *daktari* with the English consonant cluster *kt* and *dakitari* with the vowel inserted. The great prestige of English puts pressure on Swahili to reshape its phonology, but Swahili, and not English, is the lingua franca of the masses: this makes it likely that the Swahili pattern will reemerge unchallenged. If this happens, people will have only pronunciations such as *dakitari*, *sikirubu*, and *eropuleni*.

2.3.2 Vocabulary

2.3.2.1 *Borrowing* The modifications in the phonological system of Swahili brought about by contact with other languages are rather minor compared to those in the lexicon. It has been calculated that 20 percent of the vocabulary is borrowed from Arabic and other Asiatic languages in spoken Swahili, 30 percent in the written language, and 50 percent in classical poetry. English provides some surprises along these same lines: in speech and writing the counts are at least as high with words from French, and there are substantial numbers of words from Latin and Scandinavian as well.

The loans from Arabic, Hindi, and Gujerati characterize Swahili culture as Moslem, maritime, urban, and mercantile. These are words brought by traders and entrepreneurs, some of whom settled on the coast. Even the Portuguese contributed something: they lived in garrisoned enclaves in the major coastal towns from 1500 to 1700 in an attempt to control and tax Indian Ocean trade, never integrating themselves in the local culture; yet there is evidence of their presence in the language.

In religion, most of the borrowing is from Arabic and includes both nouns and verbs:

(125) | | | | |
|---|---|---|---|
| *mtakatifu* | holy, person | *-abudu* | worship |
| *nabii* | prophet | *-amini* | believe, trust |
| *malaika* | angel | *-harimu* | forbid |
| *roho* | breath, spirit | *-sali* | pray |
| *tohara* | purification | *-bariki* | bless |

Military terms entered the language at different times; some are recent borrowings from the colonial period, such as *meja* "major" and *sajini* "sergeant"; others are earlier borrowings from Arabic, or Turkish, or Persian, but probably all introduced by the Arabs: *askari* "soldier, policeman," *jemadari* "general," *bunduki* "gun, rifle."

Unlike the Arabs and others, the Portuguese never became settlers;

they controlled a few major commercial centers and formed settlements only in Mozambique, where Swahili was largely unknown. One of their contributions was *gereza* "fort, prison" from the Portuguese *igreja* "church." Portuguese life was centered in their garrisons, where their chapels were located as well. Thus *gereza* became synonymous with the main structure and the place where offenders were held and punished. Today, however, *jela* from English "jail" seems to be replacing *gereza*. A good percentage of the loans from Portuguese is terminology for card-playing. We have *piku/ma-* "trick" from Portuguese *pecau* in Class 5/6. All of the following are in Class 9/10:

(126)			
	karata	cards	(karta)
	pao	clubs	(pao)
	shupaza	spades	(espada)
	kopa	hearts	(copa)
	uru	diamonds	(ouru)
	ree or *rei*	ace	(rei)
	seti	sevens	(sete)
	turufu	trump	(trunfo)
	ulitima	last round	(ultima)

Other words reflect the concern that surrounds sedentary, garrisoned life, as surely as card-playing does (all are in Class 9/10 except where otherwise indicated): *tabakelo* "snuff box," *foronya* "pillowcase," *bendera* "flag," *bweta* "small box," *leso* "handkerchief," *buli/ma-* Class 5/6 "teapot," *mvinyo* Class 3 "wine," *bomba/ma-* Class 5/6 "pump," *pipa/ma-* Class 5/6 "barrel," *mpira/mi-* Class 3/4 "ball." Some of these are seldom heard today. *Kandarinya* "kettle" has been replaced by Arabic *birika/ma-* Class 5/6, and *reale* (or *riali*) "dollar" has been replaced by terms from Arabic or English for various types of currency: *shilingi* "shilling," *fedha* "silver, money, coin, cash," and *dola* "dollar."

As urban life developed and commerce spread, Swahili borrowed from Arabic to the same extent that English borrowed from the French after 1066 with *baron, noble, gentility, monarch, court, liege, homage, tenure, manor,* and a mass of other loans. There were words to handle concepts that were foreign to rural people:

(127)	**Class 7/8**	*kitabu/vi-*	book/s
	Class 5/6	*zulia/ma-*	carpet
		duka/ma-	shop, store/s
		soko/ma-	market/s
		dirisha/ma-	window/s

Class 9/10	*fariji*	comfort/s
	barabara	highway/s
	kalamu	pen/s
	karatasi	paper
	kandili	lantern/s
	bilauri	glass/es
Verb	*-andika*	write

This is only a small sample, as is the following one for mercantile and political terminology:

(128)	**Class 11 or 14**	*u-shuru*	tax
	Class 9/10	*forodha*	custom house/s
		bahari	sea/s
		orodha	list/s, inventory/ies
		hawala	draft/s
		hesabu	account/s, math
		tarehe	date/s
		mali	wealth
		rasilmali	capital, assets
		akiba	reserve, savings
		ratili	pound/s
		biashara	trade, commerce
	Verbs	*-tawala*	rule
		-milki	possess, be owner
		-rithi	inherit
		-rubuni	cheat

But Swahili didn't simply borrow what it needed; it also integrated each lexical item into its noun classification system. The great majority went into Class 9/10, with just a few going into Class 5/6 (*duka/ma-* "shop") and other classes. The few that did enter other classes did so because of their original phonological shape: Arabic *kitab* was analogically treated as a noun of the *ki-* class and given a *vi-* plural (*ki-tabu/vi-tabu*); the initial *u-* of *ushuru* (Arabic) "tax" was interpreted as the *u-* Class 11 or 14 prefix. A similar example is provided by the word for "line" (*m-stari/mi-stari*) from Arabic *mistar*; here the initial syllable of the borrowed word—the *mi*—was interpreted as the Class 4 plural *mi-* and by the process of 'back-formation,' the singular was formed: all *mi-* words have *m-* singulars. Some other words, such as *nanasi* (Persian) (Pl *ma-nanasi*) "pineapple," *embe* (Hindi) (Pl *ma-embe*) "mango" were entered into their present classes because they fit semantically: Class 5/6 includes the names of most fruits. Such a semantic explanation is not always available, as it is not for the loanwords that entered Class 5/6 listed in (127).

As for why most borrowed nouns have ended up in Class 9/10, we do have some idea. Words like *motokaa* (English) "car" and *baisikeli* (English) "bicycle" are objects which are used by humans and conceivably could have been entered as Class 7/8 nouns (KI-/VI- Class). But they don't have *ki-* prefixes or any other phonological form (as in the case of *kitabu, ushuru,* or *mistari*) to help speakers assign class membership. Thus, most borrowed words fit quite nicely into a class with no clear-cut noun prefix and that already contains nouns of a wide range of meanings whose singular and plural forms are identical.

With the inception of European colonialism in the second half of the nineteenth century, a new period of borrowing began which has brought in names for a wide range of concepts and objects: the greatest number concern western technology and institutions: most have ended up in Class 9/10:

(129)	*baisikeli*	bicycle	*tai*	tie
	motokaa	car	*fulana*	undershirt (flannel)
	roketi	rocket	*jela*	jail
	eropleni	airplane	*gavana*	governor
	mashini	machine	*repoti*	report
	spaki	electricity (spark)	*kampuni*	company
	stimu	electricity (steam)	*maneja*	manager
	basi	bus	*injinia*	engineer
	skrubu	screw	*dereva*	driver
	petroli	gasoline (petrol)	*penesilini*	penicillin
	soksi	socks	*demokrasi*	democracy

The list goes on and on. We see here a demonstration of the flexibility of language to accommodate cultural change.

2.3.2.2 *Derivation and Semantic Extension*   Borrowing is not the only mechanism for acquiring vocabulary. Often speakers use the morphology of their language to derive new terms from old ones, or they extend the meaning of old terms to fit the new circumstances. Consider the political arena. *Ujumaa* is a Class 14 noun derived by affixing *u-* to the word borrowed from Arabic *jamaa* "family" to give the meaning "relationship, brotherhood, kin." But since the mid-sixties it has taken on a different connotation in political and philosophical writings. It now means "African socialism," a kind of political philosophy based on traditional concepts of family and society, as opposed to the borrowed word *usoshalisti* which means "socialism" in a more general sense. *Harambee* is a further example: originally it was used by stevedores, who had to move or pull heavy objects; the leader of a crew would shout *harambee* "all together now!" and on that signal everyone would pull or push. In Kenya today it is used as a slogan "Let's all work together to build a nation!" Semantic extension is not usually as obvious as borrowing, but it is actually more common: vocabulary is constantly shifting in meaning as circumstances and contexts of communication shift. Some further examples will help illustrate this:

		Nonextended Meaning	Extended Meaning
(130)	*ku-ji-tegemea*	to lean on oneself (from *-tegemea* "lean on")	to exercise self-reliance
	ku-ji-tolea	to offer oneself for (from *-tolea* "offer to/for")	to volunteer
	m-shawishi/wa-	tempter (from *-shawishi* "tempt, entice")	agitator/s

The noun *beberu* (Class 9/10) means "he-goat," an earlier extension was the meaning "bully," and now a new meaning is conveyed in the derivations *u-beberu* (Class 14) "imperialism" and *m-beberu/wa-* (Class 1/2) "imperialists." The nonextended meanings continue to be used side by side with the extended ones. Some examples from areas other than politics:

(131)	*kifaru/vi-*	rhino	(Class 7/8)	>	tank (military)
	porojo/ma-	idle talk	(Class 5/6)	>	propaganda
	shahada	covenant	(Class 9/10)	>	diploma
	msimu/mi-	northeast monsoon, season	(Class 3/4)	>	sports season (soccer)

Derivational morphology is a mechanism for developing vocabulary as old as the ancestral Bantu language. A great many new words can be added to the lexicon by utilizing a series of affixes to derive nouns from verbs. One of these is the suffix *-i*, which added to a verb form produces a noun stem. These noun stems then take on various noun class prefixes, and with each a distinctive meaning: with Class 1/2 (M-/WA-) and sometimes Class 7/8 (KI-/VI-) prefixes, the derived noun expresses a performer of the action of the verb; with the *ma-* Class 6 prefix the derived noun expresses the total sum of actions which bring about a goal expressed by the verb stem; with the *u-* Class 14 prefix, an abstraction is conveyed. The verb stem sometimes undergoes modification, but the connection can still be perceived:

(132)

Verb Stem	*-lea*	rear, raise
Derived Nouns	*m-lez-i/wa-*	tutor/s
	ma-lez-i	training, up-bringing
	u-lez-i	education
Verb Stem	*-tumika*	be employed
Derived Nouns	*m-tumish-i/wa-*	servant/s
	ma-tumish-i	servant's work, service
	u-tumish-i	service
Verb Stem	*-ongoza*	lead
Derived Nouns	*ki-ongoz-i/vi-*	leader/s
	ma-ongoz-i	direction, management
	u-ongoz-i	leadership

There are three other suffixes that are also employed in deriving nouns from verbs: the stative *-u* is used to derive adjectives; the instrumental *-o* derives nouns which denote objects used to perform actions (usually with *ki-/vi-* prefixes); this same *-o* suffix marks nouns which denote the result of an action (with *m-/mi-* or Ø/*ma-* prefixes); and finally *-e* marks nouns naming things which have undergone particular actions:

(133) *-u* **Stative**

m-tuliv-u/wa-	gentle, calm person/s	(from *-tulia* "be calm")
m-tukuf-u/wa-	glorious person/s	(from *-tukuka* "be exaulted")

-o **Instrumental**

ki-zib-o/vi-	stopper/s, cork/s	(from *-ziba* "stop-up")
u-fungu-o/ fungu-o	key/s	(from *-fungua* "open")
siki-o/ma-	ear	(from *-sikia* "hear")

-o Resultative

mw-end-o/mi-	trip	(from *-enda* "go")
m-chez-o/mi-	dance, game	(from *-cheza* "dance, play")

-e Patient

m-tum-e/mi-	messenger, apostle	(from *-tuma* "employ, send")
ki-umb-e/vi-	creature	(from *-umba* "create")
pʰet-e/pʰet-e	ring	(from *-peta* "bend round")

Most of the words in this list are old formations; nevertheless the process is available to form neologisms as the need arises. For example, two recent innovations are *u-baguz-i* Class 14 (derived from *-baguza* "cause to be separate"), which is used for "discrimination" and *u-chafuz-i* Class 14 (from *-chafua* "make dirty, soil, spoil"), which is used for "pollution."[13]

2.3.2.3 *Compounding* Since the Second World War, in which many East Africans saw service fighting along with the British in North Africa and Burma, and since the advent of *uhuru* (independence) for Kenya, Tanzania, and Uganda, East African cultures have felt strong influences for change both from within and from without. Most languages of the area have been affected by some of these pressures while they have remained insulated from others, fulfilling as they do just the function of communication in their home communities. Swahili, however, the lingua franca, has been part of innovation going on everywhere; it has responded with the addition of many new expressions to its lexicon. It has done this through borrowing (*usoshalisti*), and through derivation (*ujamaa, ubaguzi, uchafuzi*). Besides borrowing and derivation, there is one other major process languages have available for creating new vocabulary, and that is compounding.

Compounding is very old in Swahili, but until recently it was a device that had been used very little. The apparent prototype for all compounding in many languages is a model which uses *mwana* "child, offspring" (plural *wana*) plus another noun: *mwanamke* (*mwana + mke* "wife") is "woman" (that is, "child of wife"; compare this with expressions in English such as "daughter of Eve" in C. S. Lewis's works), and *mwanamume* (*mwana + mume* "husband") is glossed as "man"

---

[13]Neither of these words are listed in 1939 in the dictionary of Frederick Johnson, *A Standard Swahili-English Dictionary*. Oxford University Press, Oxford.

(compare with "son of man," or with "son of Adam" in C. S. Lewis); from this pattern a large number of new nouns have developed which involve borrowed nouns, derived nouns, or words that have been part of the lexicon for a long time. In each of these expressions, one can understand the composite meaning as coming from the pattern "child of . . . ." Hence "aviator" is *mwanahewu,* from *mwana* "child" and *hewa* "sky" ("child of the sky"), "scientist" is *mwanasayansi,* where one can see *sayansi* "science" ("child of science"). Other examples:

(134)

mwanafunzi	student
(*mwana + funzi,* from *-fund-* "learn")	
mwanamapinduzi	revolutionary
(*mwana + mapinduzi* "revolution")	
mwanachama	member
(*mwana + chama* "party, society, organization")	
mwananchi	citizen, fellow
(*mwana + nchi* "country, land")	countryman

Another pattern of compounding involves the juxtaposition of a noun, almost always a 'deverbative'—one derived from a verb root, followed by an object noun. This pattern is very productive, as in:

(135)	*mfanyi kazi*	worker
	(*-fany-* "do" + *kazi* "work")	
	mwuza samaki	fish seller
	(*-uz-* "sell" + *samaki* "fish")	
	kifunga bei	deposit
	(*-fung-* "tie" + *bei* "price")	
	chamshakinywa	breakfast
	(*-amsh-* "wake up" + *kinywa* "mouth")	

Two other nouns, *mfanyi biashara* "trader, businessman" (from *biashara* "business") and *mfanyi saa* "watch repairman" (from *saa* "watch") follow the pattern of the first example. All these expressions have an "agentive" pattern with an understood verb + object relationship: "workdoer," "fishseller," "pricetier," "mouthwakerupper," etc. Compare the English expressions *lawnmower, penholder, stockholder,* and *songwriter.* The order of the elements in English is exactly the reverse of what it is in Swahili (seller + fish in Swahili *mwuza samaki,* fish + seller in English), but the verb + object relationship is exactly the same.

The spelling of compounds in Swahili has not been completely regularized: the compounds based on *mwana* "child of" are nearly always spelled with the two elements written together; the other types are written separately or as single words, depending on the personal preference of the writer; we see the same tendencies in English with compounds like *gearshift* as opposed to ones like *steering wheel*. The important thing is that these expressions are pronounced as a single word with the characteristic stress on the penultimate syllable, *mwanafúnzi* and *mwuza samáki*, the stress on the first element either lost altogether or reduced. Note that the defining characteristic of noun compounds in English is stress, so that two-word phrases like *dark room* can be distinguished from single word compounds like *darkroom* by the way they sound.

Whereas derivation is a means of creating new words by adding affixes to stems, compounding combines stems with stems. English *boyhood* is a product of derivation because while *boy* is a stem (it can occur on its own or as the central meaning-bearing element of a larger word like *boys*), *-hood* is an affix, occurring only with stems, never on its own. *Boyfriend*, on the other hand, is a compound, since both *boy* and *friend* are stems. As is typical, the meaning of the compound includes the meaning of its parts, but it has more besides: a *boyfriend* is a friend who is a boy all right, but a special kind of friend. Different parts of speech can be involved, and different semantic patterns prevail: a *boyfriend* is a special kind of friend who is a boy, but an *eggnog* is not a special kind of nog that is an egg (rather nog that has eggs in it), nor is a *fireman* a special kind of man that is a fire (rather a man that does something about fires); a *playboy* may be a boy that plays, but a *callgirl* is not a girl that calls. The reader may find it interesting to discover and compare additional examples.

Now it should be easy to tell what is not a compound: *boycott* is not a compound, for example, since neither *boy-* in this sense nor *-cott* mean anything. The sense of *eggplant* as a compound may not be clear to those who do not make the connection to the ovoid shape of the fruit of this plant. *Cobweb* is a product of compounding in earlier times but is not alive as a compound any more: the meaning of *web* is clear enough today, but *cob* comes from an earlier word meaning "spider" we no longer recognize.

Dead compounds are a common phenomenon: languages will have productive processes of compounding that create needed expressions at one stage in their development and then while the larger expressions live on, the meanings of their parts fade away. We can see this in Swahili in some expressions formed from an adjective meaning "big, major, chief, distinguished," today pronounced *-kuu*. The compounds have become ossified and present-day speakers do not perceive this adjective within them anymore. This situation is reflected in the form of the compounds: We either get an old form ancestor to the modern words, *-kuru,* no longer used as an independent word, or a reduced *ku* (with a short vowel):

(136) *mkurugenzi*   leader, pioneer   (from *m-kuru-genzi*,
                                          where *-genz-* is a
                                          form of *-end-* "go")

       mkufunzi   skilled apprentice (from *m-kuu-funzi*;
                                          where *-funz-* is a
                                          form of *-fund-* "learn")

       mkulima   farmer   (from *m-kuu-lima*;
                                          -lima- "farm (verb)")

Swahili and English compounds frequently have similar semantic patterns but with opposite orders of elements (as with the expressions like "fishseller"). Consider the pattern of noun + noun compounds where the second noun functions as the qualifier of the first: *askari kanzu* (pronounced as a single word with stress on the penultimate syllable *ka*) means "plainclothes policeman," with the order *askari* "police" + *kanzu* (a type of civilian garment); compare English *plainclothes man*. Compare also:

(137) *mbwa mwitu*   jackal   (*mbwa* "dog" + *mwitu* "forest";
                                       compare the English com-
                                       pounds *mountain lion* "cougar"
                                       and *river horse* "hippopotamus")

       maji moto   hot water   (*maji* "water" + *moto* "fire";
                                       compare the English compound
                                       meaning "ardent spirits,"
                                       firewater)

It appears that this pattern has not been used extensively until recently. The expression for "detective" *askari kanzu* is a modern formation, as is *ukoloni mambo leo* "neocolonialism" which is formed from the juxtaposition of three nouns: *ukoloni* "colonialism" (from English) + *mambo* "affairs, matters" + *leo* "today." Compounds of this type appear to come from an earlier stage when they had the form of genitive (associative) constructions, and this would explain the order of elements in present day compounds. The idea would be that *mbwa mwitu*, for example, "dog-forest" came from a genitive expression, in effect "dog of the forest"; remove the marking for the possessive construction and we have, in effect, "dog-forest." In fact, in some cases both forms exist: *maji moto*, in effect, "water-fire," and *maji ya moto* "water of fire." We see this construction commonly in straightforward examples of the sort:

(138)   *mtoto wa Juma*   Juma's child / child of Juma
        kisu cha mama   mother's knife / knife of mother
        kikapu cha matunda   basket (*kikapu*) of fruit (*matunda*)

This same construction is used for expressions of a sort where English would use a noun modifier: for example, to say "cold water," there is the expression *maji ya baridi*, literally "water of cold," and to say "wooden cupboard" there is *kabati la mti* (*kabati* from English), literally "cupboard of wood." This pattern is being used to coin names for new objects brought in by modern technology, and here we can see that property characteristic of compounds that makes them like idioms, where the meaning of the expression as a whole cannot be inferred just from the meaning of its parts:

(139)   *gari la moshi*   locomotive train
                                 (lit. "vehicle of smoke")
        mtambo wa barafu   refrigerator
                                 (lit. "device of ice")

An interesting example of linguistic adaption in new cultural situations is found in a series of children's books which are part of a set used to teach schoolchildren the names of animals, birds, insects, plants, fish, musical instruments, machines, vehicles, and other objects. Of particular interest are two in the series entitled *Jifunze Majina ya Mashini* and *Jifunze Majina ya Magari* ("Learn the Names of Machines" and "Learn the Names of Vehicles").[14] Both of these picture and name objects which are for the most part not particularly germane to traditional African culture, but there is every reason to believe that they were prepared by native speakers of Swahili. Some of the things pictured in the books about machines include tools which would be found throughout East Africa in any local garage, or in any tradesman's kit: screwdriver, drill, wood chisel, wrench, and so forth. The names for these are commonly used and accepted terms of Bantu origin, like *nyundo* "hammer" (the Bantu were familiar with iron and had their own blacksmiths, and thus their languages have words meaning "to forge," "to hammer," bellows," "hammer"); others are early borrowings from Arabic and other languages and have been fully integrated into the language; however, in the realm of household articles the situation is different. There are kitchen appliances, for example, that one could find in many American homes, but not in the usual home of the Tanzanian *mwananchi* ("citizen, countryman"), and for these objects neologisms

---

[14]No author, *Jifunze Majina ya Mashini* and *Jifunze Majina ya Magari*, McGraw-Hill Far Eastern Publishers, Singapore, 1974.

are used. For example, new expressions have been invented for blender, toaster, electric range, percolator, and electric mixer. The situation is much the same for the picture book of vehicles. Familiar vehicles are given their commonly used names, but vehicles which are familiar only to filmgoers or to readers of history or historical fiction, vehicles such as the stagecoach or the horse-drawn buggy, are given new names.

A lot of the things are named by wholesale borrowing into Class 9/10 but not without modifying the phonological pattern to fit Swahili word structure. Consider these borrowings from English:

(140) *furiji*   fridge
       jeki   jack
       taipuraita   typewriter
       telepurinta   teleprinter
       redio   radio
       thamostati   thermostat
       helikoputa   helicopter
       hosikati   horse cart
       steitikochi   stagecoach
       pedikapu   pedicab
       rikisho   rickshaw
       stesheniwageni   station wagon
       limosini   limosine
       monoreli   monorail

Other objects are named by using the associative construction (with some of the constituents borrowed words) and derivation:

(141)

Associative Construction

treni ya mbizi	subway, underground	(*treni* "train," *mbizi* "dive, plunge")
basi ya gorofa	double-decker bus	(*gorofa* "story, level")
kamera ya televisheni	television camera	
gari la vita	chariot	(*gari* "vehicle," *vita* "war")

Derivation (-*i*, -*o* suffixes)

chukizi/ma-	transporter (kind of truck)	(-*chukua* "carry")
kinyunyizi/vi-	road sprinkler	(-*nyunyiza* "sprinkle")
kikorogeo/vi-	mixer	(-*koroga* "mix, stir")
pakizi/ma-	loader	(-*pakiza* "stow freight")
kifulio/vi-	washer	(-*fulia* "wash with/by")
kichujio/vi-	coffee percolator	(-*chuja* "strain, sieve")

Each of these patterns is productive, so it is not surprising that speakers utilize them to express new concepts, but what is of particular interest is the increasing use being made of compounding; there are a number of examples utilizing the 'verb + object' pattern (in this case all in Class 7/8, useful artifacts):

(142)	*kikaushanywele*	hair dryer	(*-kausha* "dry" + *nywele* "hair")
	kisaganyama	meat grinder	(*-saga* "grind" + *nyama* "meat")
	kifunguakopo	can opener	(*-fungua* "open" + *kopo* "can")
	kichongakalamu	pencil sharpener	(*-chonga* "sharpen" + *kalamu* "pencil")
	kivunanafaka	harvester	(*-vuna* "harvest" + *nafaka* "grain")
	kisombamali	delivery van	(*-somba* "carry" + *mali* "property")
	kizimamoto	fire truck	(*-zima* "extinguish" + *moto* "fire")

Furthermore, the 'noun + noun' pattern is represented where the second noun is modifier to the first. It is this pattern of compounding which has not been particularly productive until recently, but in these two books the items formed by following this pattern outnumber any of the others with the exception of the 'verb + object' compounds; a few examples suffice:

(143)	*baisikelimbio*	racing bike	(*baisikeli* "bicycle" + *mbio* "speedy run")
	lorijeshi/ma-	army truck	(*lori* "truck" + *jeshi* "army")
	terenikasi	express train	(*tereni* "train" + *kasi* "speed")
	pepeodari/ma-	ceiling fan	(*pepeo* "fan" + *dari* "ceiling")
	mtungimoto/mi-	water heater	(*mtungi* "water container" + *moto* "fire")
	saasitima	electric clock	(*saa* "watch" + *sitima* "electricity," from English "steam")
	pasisitima	electric iron	(*pasi* "iron" + *sitima*)
	kekeemkono	hand drill	(*kekee* "drill" + *mkono* "hand, arm")

daftaripesa/ma-	cash register	(*daftari* "ledger, register" + *pesa* "money, cash")
gurudumumaji/ma-	waterwheel	(*gurudumu* "wheel" + *maji* "water")
msumenogari/mi-	chain saw	(*msumeno* "saw" + *gari* "vehicle")

This compounding pattern has been·a part of Swahili for some time; on the other hand, one could argue that the prevalence of the pattern in English is the reason that it is seeing greater usage in Swahili; the expressions in (143) are simply literal translations of the English, with the order of the constituents reversed to reflect each language's own constraints. Apropos to this is the following piece which appeared in a Nairobi English-language newspaper a few years ago (*mbwa* means "dog" and *moto* means "fire, heat" or "hot"):

> Sometimes it is difficult to render a well-known English phrase accurately into Swahili but one refreshment-seller at Jamhuri Park during the celebrations decided the literal translation was best. As he moved among the crowd his cry of "hot-dogs" was changed at intervals to "mbwa moto, mbwa moto." Who thought up the name "hot dogs" anyway?

2.3.3 *Language Planning and the Grass Roots*   One of the long-standing concerns of language planners—linguists, educators, and government-officials—has been the development of a modern vocabulary for Swahili. This is seen throughout the pages of the journal *Swahili*.[15] For example, in Volume 24 (June 1954) is a list of terms which had been approved by the Swahili Committee to be used by financial institutions and businesses; for example, *account, gross profit, net profit, depreciation, assets, liabilities, rent, credit, debt, dividend.* In Volume 26 (June 1956) is a proposed supplement to the Standard English-Swahili Dictionary[16] of approximately thirty pages of vocabulary; Volume 28.2 (July 1958) has articles on Swahili slang, a supplementary list of words gleaned from poetry, aphorisms, and folk tales, and yet another of commercial terms. In Volume 35.1 (March 1965) are several lists: one for terms for stars and constellations, one for religious vocabulary, and

---

[15]Earlier the official publication of the Swahili Committee, published today by the Institute of Swahili Research of the University of Dar es Salaam, which has superceded the earlier committee.

[16]Frederick Johnson, *A Standard English–Swahili Dictionary.* Oxford University Press, Oxford, 1939.

another for mathematical terms. Volume 35.2 (Sept. 1965) has an article discussing the problems of translating English legal vocabulary, as well as a second list of mathematical vocabulary. The issue for March 1966 (Volume 36.1) has lists of terms that educators expect children to know before entering school and through the various grades in school, in addition to lists of mathematical terms for teaching math, and terms for other subjects: geography, history, the arts, and science.

A serious question that has to be asked, however, is whether external planning, planning from the top, has any effect on actual usage. For example, in the list of astromonical terms, *mchota maji* (literally, "water bearer" from -*chota* "dip up" and *maji* "water") is suggested for "Aquarius," but a very popular astrologer in East Africa today uses *ndoo* (literally, "bucket, pail") for that sign; for "Saggitarius" he uses *mshale* (literally, "arrow"), while the suggested list gives *mpiga shabaha* "shooter of the target"; in some cases, however, the astrologer's terms agree with the planners' list, whether by coincidence or design is not clear: *mapacha* "twins" for "Gemini," *simba* "lion" for "Leo," *mizani* "scales" for "Libra," *nge* "scorpion" for "Scorpio," and *samaki* "fish" for "Pisces."

Similarly for commercial terms, there are discrepancies as well as agreements between the 1954 list and a financial report of a company published in 1975, some twenty years later. For "dividend" both agree in using *mgao wa faida* "division of profit" (*mgao* derives from the verb -*gawa* "divide"), and the word for "profit" is also the same: *faida*, but "net profit" in the suggested list is *faida safi* (literally, "clean profit"), whereas the financial report uses both *jumla ya faida* "sum, or total of profit" and *faida kamili* "perfect profit." The word for income is the same for both: *mapato* (derived from the verb -*pata* "get"); they use the same word for debtor: *mdeni*, but different words for creditor: *mdai* (from -*dai* "claim, demand") in 1954 versus *mkopeshaji* (from -*kopesha* "loan") in 1975. Usage sometimes deviates from plans.

In Tanzania today, vocabulary devolpment has been decentralized. Individual institutions of government such as the national library are proposing lists of words that are needed in carrying on daily business. New vocabulary catches on and is used by the general population when it meets a communicative need sometimes coming from above and sometimes from the grass roots. The schools probably have had the biggest impact, with new vocabulary being used daily, and insofar as education is suited to the needs of students' home communities, such neologisms will spread there. The impact of mass media cannot be overlooked either, and especially radio. Some fifteen countries, including Tanzania, Kenya, South Africa, England, West Germany, the United States and China, broadcast programs in standard Swahili, and recently, Uganda has added Swahili to its list of languages used in broadcasting.

2.4 Conclusion: Swahili and the Social Fabric

Because of the attitudes of European colonialists and European missionaries, and partly because of the attitudes of some African ethnic groups, the reputation of Swahili has at times suffered. Swahili has always been the choice of the pragmatists in government, education, and religion. But very few, other than the native-speaking Swahili on the coast, ever appreciated its intrinsic merits as a cultural and linguistic entity. Opinions about Swahili have ranged from the sublime to the ridiculous: on the one hand the elegant praise of the Tanzanian poet Shaaban Robert, and on the other hand, remarks such as those of the English traveler Henry Salt, who in 1814 wrote "their language appears scarcely to deserve the name of a distinct dialect, but is a kind of mixed jargon . . . ."[17] European settlers in Kenya and some Asian merchants in Kenya, Tanzania, and Uganda, have learned what they have considered to be Swahili, but because they never thought too highly of the language or the people with whom they were trying to communicate, many of them have only bothered to learn highly fractured pidgins. The Baganda of Uganda have always resisted any effort to introduce Swahili in their schools or to adopt Swahili as a national language, because of ethnic pride and self-interest, and because they were mainly Christian, and Swahili for them was symbolic of the Moslem coast. Next to the forces operating against Swahili there has been the advantageous position of English, the language of the governing elite, both during colonial times and today. But the situation is changing.

In Kenya today, especially in the urban areas, Swahili functions to closely unite the working class who choose to use it rather than English or their own tribal languages in work-situations. English is viewed as an indicator of a higher status and is still identified as one of the primary qualifications for a good high-paying job or career. But, at least, among the working people, one can perceive resentment towards the prestige accorded to English. There is a popular Swahili song of a few years ago which somewhat cynically highlights the hypocrisy inherent in a sociolinguistic situation in which the same people use two languages, each for a distinct self-image. The songwriter, who comes from a rural area, comments that the people of Nairobi are a funny lot; it is only on payday that the pace picks up in the local bars (after-hour gathering places for Nairobi workers): everyone is happy, talk is loud and the beer flowing, boasting is unbridled, everyone touting the importance of his job, but, the song points out, all the talk and the boasting is in English. But, the songwriter continues, go into the same bar two or three days

---

[17]Henry Salt, *A Voyage to Abyssinia and Travels*, London, 1814 (quoted in Wilfred Whiteley, *Swahili, The Rise of a National Language*, Methuen, London, 1969, p. 1).

later, after payday, and every *bwana mkubwa* "bigshot" (literally, "important person, sir") is out of money, out of beer, and low on words, and curiously enough, everyone has reverted to speaking Swahili.

In Tanzania, one does not encounter this ambiguity, nor has Swahili been felt, especially since *uhuru* (independence), to be inferior. Outside the areas where Swahili was extended through the impetus of early trade, Swahili has spread through schools, radio, and newspapers. In the minds of recent generations, Swahili is associated with education, the prime means providing integration into the life of a developing nation. As during the German colonial period, knowledge of Swahili is a prerequisite for any African wanting to join the ranks of the civil service, although most top-level jobs are held by people bilingual in Swahili and English. The grass-roots development of the political party that led Tanzania to independence, uniting the country's many ethnic groups, would not have been possible without Swahili. The masses had Swahili and they were organized through it, while English functioned at the top in the actual negotiations with the British prior to independence. English, it is recognized, will remain the language of international relations and, for a considerable time to come, the language of higher education. In Tanzania there is a firm commitment to Swahili at all levels of society. In Kenya, there is still a great deal of ambivalence, as there is in Uganda.

A clear indicator of the different attitudes in Tanzania and Kenya was seen in the reaction against President Jomo Kenyatta's announcement in 1974 that Swahili would be used to conduct business in Kenya's Parliament. There were such strong objections voiced by members of Parliament that Kenyatta closed the Parliament the following day. He announced shortly after: "Whether some people will like my decision or not KiSwahili will be spoken in our *Bunge* [Parliament], because it is the language of the *wananchi* [citizens, countrymen, people]. English is not our language and the time will come when we will do everything in Swahili. I know many people will be annoyed but let them."[18] On the other hand, in Tanzania, Swahili has been used in conducting parliamentary business since the mid-sixties.

In Kenya there has always existed a public debate; this grew out of the ambiguity of the colonial policy: was it to be English, Swahili, or the vernaculars? In retrospect one can say that Tanzania is benefiting from the pre-World War I policy of the Germans. The Germans instituted Swahili as the universal language of education and administration, and the force of this policy continued after the British took over. But Kenya never was a German colony, only a British one; the British never

---

[18]Quoted in an East African Publishing House Supplement; "Swahili—Filling a Vacuum in the Language of the People" (no date or author available).

established a clear-cut language policy to unify that country. Recently, the attorney general of Kenya claimed that every Kenyan knows Swahili well, and that teaching it in schools "was a waste of time," and further, that teachers should concentrate on teaching a correct (British?) pronunciation of English.[19] His comments generated a lively response in the press; one reader commented: "Swahili has served as a means of uniting the 42 tribes in Kenya, big and small, all in pursuit of making our country a better and more comfortable place to live in. Indeed, it is the *lugha ya kazi* [the language of work]. Since Swahili is not a mother tongue, except for a minority, this necessitates us to teach it by all means at hand."[20] Most of the letters that appeared were in support of the teaching of Swahili.

In Uganda it is certain that Swahili is spoken widely, and by people who would not admit that they have any competence in the language.[21] It functions in ways similar to the role Swahili plays in urban Kenya. It is a marker of ethnic neutrality which allows people of an urban multiethnic society to communicate by a means which avoids the pitfalls and baggage of English at one end of the scale, and those of a local tribal language at the other. It occupies the middle ground and is essential in many areas of urban life including local politics and church affairs; without Swahili one might guess that football would not survive, since if a game were conducted in any one of the many local languages the passions of already volatile fans would only be inflamed further. It occupies the middle ground in the everyday work-a-day world: at the factories and in the union halls. At another level it is a vehicle for expressing and conveying pop culture: East African night life in the bars and clubs of Nairobi; the poetry that appears almost daily in newspapers; and in popular songs:

(144)   *Sheri, rudi, rudi, mpenzi wa roho.*
        Sheri, rudi, naomba kwa upendo.

Cher, return, come back, (my) sweet heart.
Cher, come back, I beg (you) with love.

The word *sheri* derives from the French *cher*, and is an import from Zaire, whose pop singers (who use French, Swahili, and Lingala) are often more popular in Kenya and Tanzania than are local musicians.

The newspapers and Swahili magazines cater to popular demand

---

[19]As reported in the *Daily Nation*, October 25, 1975.

[20]*Daily Nation*, November 3, 1975.

[21]See Carol Myers Scotton, *Choosing a Lingua Franca in an African Capital*, Linguistic Research, Edmonton, 1972, and also C. M. Scotton, "Strategies of Neutrality: Language Choice in Uncertain Situations," *Language* vol. 52, 1976, pp. 919–941.

with serializations of detective stories, and pulplike romantic fiction. People in the urban areas of East Africa find Swahili a bulwark against the loneliness of city life as well as a ready tool to exploit the glitter and attractions which the city offers.

While Swahili is a vitally functioning communicative tool there are still considerable problems that concern language planners. There have always been reading materials in Swahili for children to read, but a dearth of anything good for adults. There are indications, however, that soon even this gap will be filled. East African publishers are constantly providing the growing reading public with original Swahili novels, a lot of them dealing with romantic themes, and others with the general theme of the conflict of traditional values with westernization; detective stories and novels are gaining in popularity; and translations of titles originally written in English by African authors are appearing, Chinue Achebe's *Things Fall Apart*, for one example. Even some of Shakespeare's works have been translated by none other than Julius Nyerere, the president of Tanzania.

Concern has also been expressed from time to time about the effect English stylistics has on Swahili. For years Swahili newspapers have depended on English language news services for international news. Given the demands and exigencies of newspaper publishing, rapid translation of stories from English wire services is necessary, and out of this has evolved *Kigazeti* "newspaper Swahili," whose style is heavily influenced by English.

Code-switching (mixing two languages in the same discourse), among bilinguals, is often a target of criticism in letters which appear in newspapers. Code-switching is more apparent in certain situations and among certain people than in others.[22] It seems to be especially prevalent among those who have received a secondary or university education. The same group of people are also often accused of using an excessive number of loanwords in their speech when perfectly good and well-established Swahili words exist. And there is the continuing problem, many feel, of devising technical and specialized terminologies.

In many areas of East Africa, Swahili is competing for the loyalties of many who have other mother tongues. It is unlikely that Swahili will command the kind of respect these people have for their own languages any time soon, but it is as certain that with a thousand years of history behind it, Swahili is in East Africa to stay.

---

[22]For interesting examples of the social role of code-switching see studies in Wilfred Whiteley, ed., *Language in Kenya*, Oxford University Press, Nairobi, 1974.

SUGGESTIONS FOR FURTHER READING

For those who would like to do further reading on Swahili there are several readily available books. Edgar C. Polomé's *Swahili Language Handbook* (Center for Applied Linguistics, Washington, D.C., 1967) includes an extensive structural sketch of the phonology, morphology, and syntax of Swahili with a chapter on the writing system and a contrastive analysis of English and Swahili. Wilfred Whiteley's *Swahili, the Rise of a National Language* (Methuen, London, 1969) deals with several topics that were discussed in the second part of this chapter: the history and development of Swahili as a lingua franca, and problems of a national language; it also includes a select bibliography. For the reader who would like to begin learning Swahili, there is the author's text (with Sarah M. Mirza and Adelheid U. Stein, illustrator): *Kiswahili, Msingi wa Kusema, Kusoma, na Kuandika* ("Swahili, a Foundation for Speaking, Reading, and Writing," University Press of America, Washington, D.C. 1978). D. V. Perrott's *Teach Yourself Swahili* of the well-known "Teach Yourself" series (The English Universities Press, London, 1951) is a good beginning book. Also recommended is the manual by E. W. Stevick et al., *Swahili Basic Course* (Foreign Service Institute, Washington, D.C., 1963). This is a course that utilizes dialogues, pattern drills, and grammar notes. Used with the tapes that accompany the course, it can be successful in a home-study situation.

VI

Chinese
Dialect Variations and Language Reform

Charles N. Li

Sandra A. Thompson

1 THE FIVE MAJOR DIALECT GROUPS OF CHINESE

It is estimated that 900 million people, more than one-fourth the population on earth, are speakers of Chinese, whereas English, the second most widely spoken language in the world, can claim only 400 million speakers. Thus, on the basis of the immense number of speakers alone, Chinese commands our attention to its great practical and cultural importance. What, then, is Chinese? Genetically, it is an independent branch of the Sino-Tibetan family of languages which includes several major subfamilies parallel to Chinese: Tibetan, the languages of Tibet; Lolo-Burmese, the languages of Burma and scattered areas in southern China, southeast Asia, and the Tibetan borderland; and Karen, the

Charles Li was born and raised in China, and has been living in the United States since 1961. He teaches linguistics at the University of California, Santa Barbara. Sandra Thompson is an American who has been studying Chinese since 1961. She now teaches linguistics at UCLA. They have been collaborating since 1971 in an attempt to understand the facts of Mandarin grammar in the context of language universals and to try to explain how Mandarin expresses the same concepts as other languages do given its isolating nature. They are presently writing a grammar of the Mandarin language which will incorporate their findings.

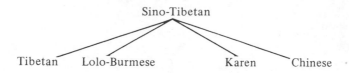

FIGURE 6.1   Sino-Tibetan Languages

languages of lower Burma. Schematically, the Sino-Tibetan family may be represented by Figure 6.1.

Tibetan and Lolo-Burmese are often lumped together into one group called the Tibeto-Burmese. But recent studies indicate that Karen and Lolo-Burmese also are closely tied together. On the other hand, Chinese is related to the other subfamilies very distantly although the genetic tie is reasonably well established. Each of the branches of the Sino-Tibetan contains a large number of languages. Within the Chinese branch, there are scores of dialects, some of them mutually unintelligible, spreading over the entire country. These dialects may be classified into five groups on the basis of their structural affinities.

1. **Mandarin,** the major dialect group in China. It varies the least from place to place within its region. It serves as the native tongue of more than half of the people of China, and it has the widest geographical extension embracing all the northern provinces and the west of the coastal provinces of central and south China. The term 'Mandarin' is an English translation of the old Beijing (Peking) expression, *Guānhuà*, "officials' language," which has been for many centuries the dialect of Beijing. In modern China, the Beijing dialect still serves as the standard of pronunciation for the national language, now officially called *Pǔtōnghuà* in the Peoples' Republic of China and *guóyu* "National Language" in Taiwan.

2. **Wu**, the dialects of the Yangzi estuary, typically those of the urban centers such as Shanghai, Suzhou, Wenzhou and other conclaves around the Yangzi river and its lower tributaries in the provinces of Jiangsu, Zhejiang, and Anhui.

3. **Min**, the dialects of Taiwan, Fujien, and Hainan, the second largest island of China situated in the Gulf of Tonkin. The northern subgroup of Min is typified by the dialect Fuzhou. Amoy represents the southern subgroup. The Min dialects of Hainan differ more from Fuzhou and Amoy than the other Min dialects differ from each other. In Taiwan, the Taiwanese people are mostly descendants of the Min speakers who immigrated from the coastal region of the Fujien province. They are still Min-speakers.

4. **Yue**, the dialects of Guangdong province. The Yue dialect of Guangzhou (Canton City), the provincial capital Guangdong, known

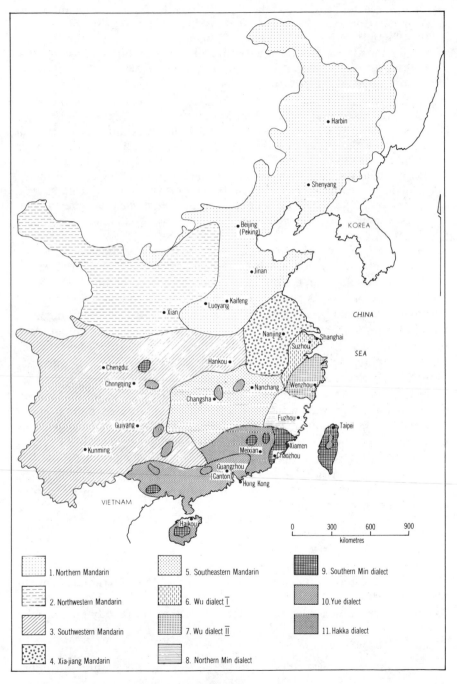

FIGURE 6.2 Map of Chinese Dialects

1. Northern Mandarin
2. Northwestern Mandarin
3. Southwestern Mandarin
4. Xia-jiang Mandarin
5. Southeastern Mandarin
6. Wu dialect $\overline{\text{I}}$
7. Wu dialect $\overline{\text{II}}$
8. Northern Min dialect
9. Southern Min dialect
10. Yue dialect
11. Hakka dialect

as Cantonese, is the standard language of Hong Kong and many
overseas Chinese settlements such as the Chinatowns in the cities of
the United States and Europe. Because of this fact, the English
words borrowed from Chinese usually have their origins in Cantonese, as do "kumquat" from Cantonese [kamkwat], "chop suey"
from Cantonese [tsap sui].

5. **Hakka**, the Hakka people are scattered throughout southeastern
China forming small, tightly knit agricultural communities in Guangxi
province and the Yue and Min dialect areas. One notable feature of
the Hakka dialects is that they are fairly uniform in comparison with
members of other groups. The Hakka spoken in Taiwan, for instance,
differs from the Hakka spoken in Guangdong minimally. Historically,
the Hakka people were northerners who moved south during several
waves of migration. The name, Hakka, which means "guests," indicates their nonnative status in their southern homeland.

We have chosen the term 'dialect' instead of 'language' for the
different forms of speech in China. There are two reasons. First, these
tongues are not separated from each other by national boundaries as are
the Romance languages such as French, Italian, Romanian, Spanish and
Portugese. Secondly, China has always had a uniform written language.
Although the vocabulary and the sentence structure of the modern
written language corresponds to that of Beijing Mandarin only, it does
have a unifying effect upon the culture of the people who speak mutually
unintelligible dialects. On the other hand, it should be pointed out that
there is no universally accepted basis for separating the terms 'dialect'
and 'language.' In the case of Chinese, one may cite mutual unintelligibility as a reason for regarding the various forms as languages. Our
decision to use the term 'dialect' merely reflects our conformity to a
long-established tradition in the study of Chinese. In later sections, we
shall discuss the written language and dialectal variations. At this point,
let us examine the characteristics of Chinese, that is, the properties
common to all the Chinese dialects.

2   THE STRUCTURE OF CHINESE

Although the Chinese dialects are numerous and the geographical spread
of these tongues covers an area larger than Europe, they share a number
of phonological and syntactic characteristics that are readily perceptible.

2.1   Tone

One of the most celebrated properties in the sound structure
(phonology) of Chinese is tone. Chinese dialects are tonal languages
because each syllable of a Chinese dialect under normal stress has a
significant, contrastive but relative pitch. The pitch may be level or

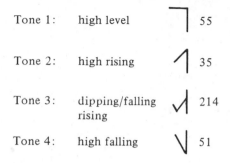

FIGURE 6.3   *Beijing Mandarin Tones*

contour, but it is an integral part of the pronunciation of the syllable or syllables of a word under normal stress, and it serves to distinguish one word from another. If a syllable has a weak stress instead of a normal stress, it loses its contrastive, relative pitch, and therefore, does not have a regular tone. In such a case, the syllable is said to have a 'neutral tone' meaning that the tonal contrast is neutralized. Hence, we can state that tone only goes on syllables under normal stress. Unstressed or weakly stressed syllables will not have a tone. In order to illustrate the tone system, let us consider the Mandarin dialect of Beijing as an example. It has four basic tones, as shown in Figure 6.3. The symbols in the column second from right are known as tone letters. They provide a simplified time-pitch graph of the voice. The vertical line on the right serves as a reference of pitch height. The time-pitch graph is drawn from left to right. The number represents the pitch register or pitch contour according to a scale of five levels, 1 being the lowest and 5 being the highest. If we take a syllable [ma] in Beijing Mandarin and put the four tones on it, the result is the paradigm of four different words shown in Figure 6.4.[1] (From here on when we are using phonetic transcription, we

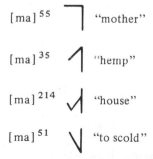

FIGURE 6.4   *Four Words [ma] in Beijing Mandarin*

---

[1]See the Appendix for an explanation of symbols used here to transcribe the sounds of Chinese.

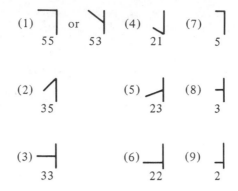

FIGURE 6.5   The Tones of Cantonese

will indicate the tones of Chinese by means of the numbers representing the pitch contours.)

Tonal variation is the most common difference among the dialects of China. Each dialect has its own tonal system, and the system may change from village to village within a short distance of each other. The Mandarin dialect has the least complex tonal system among all the dialects. It has the smallest number of tones, and the rules governing the behavior of the tones are relatively simple. Consider the tones in another dialect, Cantonese, for example. (See Figure 6.5.) It has seven tones of regular length and three short tones. The first two tones are related to each other through the phenomenon of 'tone sandhi' (which will be explained later). A syllable with the 55 tone ⌐ will change to the 53 ⅂ if it is followed by another syllable with the 55 tone ⌐ or the 5 tone ⌐ . As far as pitch level and pitch contour are concerned, the short tones do not create any new addition to the inventory of tones in Cantonese. The short tone, (7), has the same pitch level, 5, as tone (1), the short tone (8) has the same pitch level as tone (3) and the short tone (9) has the same pitch level as tone (6). The short tones (7), (8), and (9) are found only in syllables with short vowels and the final stops p, t, or k.

The complexity of the tonal systems of the dialect groups other than Mandarin is manifested not only in a larger number of tones but also in the phenomenon of tone sandhi. 'Tone sandhi' can be described as the change of tones when words are in juxtaposition. To put it differently, words tend to be of one syllable, and that syllable has a certain tone while standing alone, but will take on a different tone when it is followed by another word. We have already seen an example of tone sandhi in Cantonese. The most complex tone sandhi phenomenon is found in some of the Wu dialects and most of the Min dialects. Consider, for example, Chaozhou, a southern Min dialect. Considering

Isolation tones	5	2	33	11	35	53	213	55
Combination tones	3	5	33	11	31	35	53	13

FIGURE 6.6 *Chaozhou Tones*

syllables in isolation, there are eight tones, including two short tones belonging to syllables with final stops. We will call the tones on syllables in isolation the 'isolation tones.' When a syllable is followed by another syllable, tone sandhi occurs: each isolation tone changes to a different tone called a 'combination tone.' Figure 6.6 provides the Chaozhou isolation tones and their corresponding combination tones. Each column represents an isolation tone and its corresponding combination tone.

What this means is that speakers of the Chaozhou dialect have to learn for each word in their language its isolation tone, the tone it has standing by itself, and its combination tone, the tone it has when it is followed by another word. Just as speakers of English learn to pronounce the end of words like *beasts*, speakers of Chaozhou Chinese feel that using these tone variations is very easy; in fact, they aren't even aware that they're doing it.

Let us look at an example of how tone sandhi works in Chaozhou with the help of Figure 6.6. For example, the high short tone, 5, becomes the mid short tone, 3, in combination form. Thus, if we take the word for "one" in isolation, it looks like this in phonetic symbols:

[tsek] ⏉ one
    5

But if we put it in front of the words meaning "meal," it changes to

[tsek] ⏌
    3

like this:

[tsek] ⏌ [tɯŋ] ⏋ [puŋ] ⏉
    3   53   11   one meal

The isolation tone of the second syllable [tɯŋ], which is a grammatical particle called 'classifier' (to be discussed later), in "one meal" is ⏉ , as you can predict from Figure 6.6.
                213

Similarly, the Chaozhou word for "difficult" in isolation would be

[oˀ] ⌐
   2   difficult

Put in a phrase with another word after it, however, as you can guess, it changes to its combination form, like this:

[oˀ] ⌐   [poiˀ] ⌐   difficult to pull
   5   5

Although tone stands out as an important characteristic of Chinese, it is by no means confined to the Chinese dialects. In Asia, aside from the Sino-Tibetan family whose members are mostly tonal, there are other tone languages such as Thai, Vietnamese, and a number of the Highland languages in New Guinea. In Africa, most languages of the Niger-Congo family are tonal, while in Mexico, the languages indigenous to Oaxaca such as Mixteco, Chocho, Zapoteco, members of the Zapotekan family, are also tonal languages. (See pages 82–86 in the companion volume for a discussion of tone in the Niger-Congo language Maninka).

2.2 The Syllable in Chinese

Chinese is often said to be monosyllabic, with every word composed of one single syllable. This attribute is definitely applicable to the language in its ancient or archaic stages, thousands of years ago. But the trend of change in Chinese has been toward polysyllabicity. Mandarin nowadays can hardly be considered monosyllabic. The disyllabic compound has become the most prevalent word form in Mandarin. Some examples of disyllabic compounds in modern Beijing Mandarin:

língdǎo	to lead	*jiéguǒ*	result
zhīdào	to know	*xuéxiào*	school
láohǔ	tiger	*chàngpiān*	phonograph record

(When we are just talking about Beijing Mandarin, we will use the official spelling system of the Peoples' Republic of China, called Pīnyīn. In Pīnyīn, tones are indicated by diacritic marks above each syllable. (See Section 5 and the Appendix for more discussion.)

Let us examine the composition of a couple of these sample compounds. The first example, *língdǎo* "to lead," is historically derived from two monosyllabic words, *lǐng* "to lead" and *dǎo* "to guide." As you can see, these two monosyllabic words are almost identical in meaning. The combination of the two monosyllabic words with similar or identical meaning to create a disyllabic compound has been a productive process of compound formation in Chinese. Such a process is still active in present-day Chinese. The second example, *jiéguǒ* "result," is

derived from a different process. The first syllable, *jié*, is a verb meaning
"to bear." The second syllable, *guǒ*, is a noun object meaning "fruit." Thus,
the literal meaning of the two syllables should be "bear fruit," which is not
far from its meaning, "result." But when the two syllables combine to form
a compound, the compound becomes a new word with its own meaning.
The semantic aspect of this process is not different from the formation of
the English idiom "to kick the bucket" which means "to die." The other
four dialect groups are less advanced than Mandarin in the development
toward polysyllabic words. For instance, in Chaozhou, the Min dialect
we mentioned earlier, the word "to know" is [tsai]³³ as opposed to
zhīdào in Beijing Mandarin, and in Cantonese, a Yue dialect, the word is
[tɕi]⁵³ or [hiu]³⁵.

Phonologically, the syllable in Chinese is distinguished by the lack
of consonantal clusters; that is, combinations of several consonants such
as *st* in "stick," *fl* in "flow," *ft* in "soft" are not permissible in the
Chinese syllable structure.² Most syllables in Chinese begin with a
consonant, which is traditionally called the 'initial,' but some don't. For
example:

"short, low"

Mandarin (Beijing)	Mu (Wenzhou)	Min (Chaozhou)	Yue (Cantonese)	Hakka (Meixian)
[ai]²¹⁴	[a]⁴⁵	[oi]⁵³	[ai]³⁵	[ai]³⁵

On the other hand, the great majority of syllables in Chinese don't end in
a consonant. Beijing Mandarin, for instance, has only two nasal
consonants that may appear at the end of a syllable, the alveolar nasal
[-n], and the velar nasal [-ŋ]. The syllable-final consonants [-m], [-p], [-t],
[-k] that were present in Ancient Chinese have been lost in Mandarin
and most of the Wu dialects. The Yue, Min and Hakka dialects have
mostly preserved these consonants in the syllable final position. The
following example will illustrate this point:

"deer"

Mandarin (Beijing)	Wu (Wenzhou)	Min (Chaozhou)	Yue (Cantonese)	Hakka (Meixian)
[lu]⁵¹	[ləu]¹²	[lek]⁵	[lɒk]²	[luk]⁴

---

²Note that 'affricates' are not counted as consonant clusters here. While the conventions
of IPA lead us to transcribe them with double symbols [ts], [tsʰ], [tʂ], [tʂʰ], [tɕ], and [tɕʰ],
they *pattern* in the sound system as single sounds. A similar situation pertains in English
with the first and last sounds of "church." The IPA representation is with a double symbol
[tʃ], but other traditions use a single symbol [č], and there is evidence that the English *ch*
in fact patterns as a single sound.

In this example, the Beijing and Wenzhou monosyllabic words meaning "deer" end in a vowel, whereas their Hakka, Yue, and Min counterparts end in the consonant [-k]. In some dialects, the Ancient Chinese syllable-final consonants [-p], [-t], [-k] are replaced by the glottal stop [-ʔ]. For example, the word for "deer" in Suzhou, a Wu dialect, is [loʔ]^{23}, where the glottal stop [-ʔ] corresponds to the syllable-final [-k] of Chaozhou, Cantonese, and Hakka dialects already mentioned.

2.3   Chinese as an Isolating Language

We have seen that the major dialects of Chinese, although clearly related, are different enough from each other phonologically so that they are mutually unintelligible. When it comes to sentence structure, or 'syntax,' however, the dialects are quite similar. This is often the case with closely related languages; it is a result of the fact that, in general, sounds tend to change much faster than sentence patterns.

One of the first things a speaker of English or other European languages notices in Chinese is the lack of grammatical inflections in all Chinese dialects. Each word in Chinese has one immutable form. It does not change according to number, gender, or case. A language with such a characteristic is called an 'isolating' language. Let us illustrate Chinese as an isolating language by contrasting it with English, which is not an isolating language. In English, for example, the plural form of a noun is usually different from the singular: *man : men, book : books*. In Chinese, such a distinction does not exist. Thus, the same Chinese word stands for both "man" and "men," and the same Chinese word stands for both "book" and "books":

"man, men"
"book, books"

Mandarin (Beijing)	Wu (Suzhou)	Min (Chaochou)	Yue (Cantonese)	Hakka (Meixian)
[ren]^{35}	[ȵin]^{24}	[naŋ]^{55}	[jan]^{21}	[ȵin]^{12}
[ʂu]^{55}	[sɿ]^{44}	[tsɿ]^{33}	[sy]^{53}	[su]^{44}

Gender is another notion that is not grammatically manifested in Chinese. 'He' and 'she' is represented by the same word in Chinese:

"he, she"

Mandarin (Beijing)	Wu (Suzhou)	Min (Chaozhou)	Yue (Cantonese)	Hakka (Meixian)
[tʰa]^{55}	[li]^{44}	[i]^{33}	[kʰøy]^{23}	[ki]^{12}

We should observe that the words for "he" or "she" from the various dialects are not necessarily the descendants of the same Ancient Chinese word. In other words, different dialects do not always use the same vocabulary with different pronunciations. Often, they have different vocabulary for a certain term. We will discuss this aspect of dialectal variations in a later section.

Finally, there is no inflection or change of the form of a word due to grammatical functions. In English, for example, "I" is used as a subject or in a nominative case, but a different word, "me" is used as an object or in an accusative case. Thus, we say,

I like Susan.   NOT   ***Me** like Susan.
Susan likes **me**.   NOT   *Susan likes **I**.

Chinese, on the other hand, uses the same word for "I" and "me." In Beijing Mandarin, for example, the word is [wo]²¹⁴ (spelled in Pīnyīn as *wǒ*):

Wǒ xǐhuan Susan.   I like Susan.
Susan xǐhuan wǒ.   Susan likes me.

Since a Chinese word does not change according to gender or grammatical function, we can easily deduce that any Chinese dialect has only one word for "he," "she," "her," "him." For the same reason, we can also expect that Chinese verbs do not change their forms on the basis of number or person agreement with the subject noun, i.e., there is no verb conjugation. For example, the verb "to be" has only one form in Chinese. In Beijing Mandarin, it is [ʂɿ]⁵¹ (spelled in Pīnyīn as *shì*):

Wǒ shì Susan.   I **am** Susan.
Nǐ shì Susan.   You **are** Susan.
Tā shì Susan.   She **is** Susan.

Wǒmen shì Zhōngguó rén.   We **are** Chinese.
Nǐmen shì Zhōngguó rén.   You (Pl) **are** Chinese.
Tāmen shì Zhōngguó rén.   They **are** Chinese.

Let us compare the simple Chinese verb forms with the verbs of an Indo-European language. In Latin-American Spanish, for instance,

yo hablo   I speak
tú hablas   you (Sg) speak
él habla   he speaks

nosotros hablamos   we speak
ustedes hablan   you (Pl) speak
ellos hablan   they speak

Another illustration of the fact that each word in Chinese has one immutable form is in the area of tenses. In Spanish, for example, the verb, *hablar* "to speak" can take on five different forms according to the tense:

Present Indicative	*hablo*	I speak
Imperfect Indicative	*hablaba*	I used to speak
Preterit Indicative	*hablé*	I spoke
Future Indicative	*hablaré*	I will speak
Conditional	*hablaría*	I would speak

In Chinese, on the other hand, the verb remains unchanged whether it is used in a context indicating past, present, future, or conditional. Hence, the verb "speak" in Beijing Mandarin is simply *shuō* in all contexts. On the basis of these facts, one may get the impression that "Chinese has no grammar." But a 'grammar' is a set of rules that speakers of a language use to construct and understand original sentences. In this sense, it is absurd to regard any language as being without a grammar. The grammar of Chinese is different from the grammar of English or Spanish with respect to the manifestation of plurality, agreement, grammatical function, and so fourth. Although Chinese does not inflect a noun to denote plurality as English does, this does not mean that Chinese cannot express the concept of plurality. For example, if it is necessary to convey the information that there are books, not just one book, Chinese will employ a quantifier such as "many" or "some" to modify the noun "book." Similarly, Chinese can express any of the meanings of the various forms of the Spanish verb meaning "speak." For example, person and number of subjects can be expressed in the subject instead of the verb; time reference can be denoted by adverbs such as "yesterday," "tomorrow," and "now" just as easily as by verb tenses. (Cape York Creole, Chapter IV, shows similarities to Chinese in its word formation; the remaining four languages described in this volume are quite different. Compare how many meaningful elements are packed into verbs in Mohawk, Hua, and Swahili, Chapters I, II, and V. See also the discussion of flectional and agglutinative processes in word formation, with reference to Russian and Turkish, pages 99–108.)

It might be interesting to consider another implication of the isolating nature of Chinese. Notice, for example, that one of the ways in which English can combine two verbs is to use "to" the infinitive marker, before the second verb. Look at these examples:

(1) a. I **want to leave.**
    b. She **began to sing.**
    c. We **went out to see a movie.**

d. They **liked to eat the beans.**
e. I **bought some oranges to eat.**
f. That poem is **very hard to understand.**

Now, just as Chinese has no special marker to indicate past or future tenses on verbs, it also has no infinitive marker. So how would you suppose that combinations of verbs like this are expressed in, say, Beijing Mandarin?

If you guessed that the verbs are just combined with no marker at all, you are exactly right. Here is the Beijing Mandarin translation of each of the above sentences:

(2) a. *Wǒ   yào   zǒu.*
    I   want   leave
    I want to leave.

b. *Tā   kāishi   chàng-gē.*
    he/she   begin   sing-song
    She began to sing.

c. *Wǒmen   chū-qu   kàn   diànyǐng.*
    We   out-go   see   movie
    We went out to see a movie.
    We went out and saw a movie.

d. *Tāmen   xǐhuan   chī   dòuzi.*
    they   like   eat   bean
    They liked to eat beans.

e. *Wǒ   mǎi   júzi   chī.*
    I   buy   orange   eat
    I bought some oranges to eat.

f. *Nèi   shǒu   shī   hěn   nán   dǒng.*
    that   (Classifier)   poem   very   hard   understand
    That poem is very hard to understand.

In other words, verbal ideas in Chinese can often be combined with no special marker to indicate their meaning relationship.

By now you are probably wondering how speakers of Chinese ever do figure out these meaning relationships. The answer is, of course, the same as the one we gave when we were talking about tenses and plurals: a language can serve as a perfectly good tool of communication without signaling the same meaning relationships as English does. If you look at the combinations of words in each of the sentences in (1) or (2), you will see that the sentence meanings are entirely natural interpretations of these groups of words. For example, you don't need a "to" to tell you how to understand the sentence with the words meaning "I," "want," and "leave."

Looking at (2) c., however, you might object, saying that it has *two* meanings. That is,

Wǒmen   chū-qu   kàn   diànyǐng.
We   out-go   see   movie

can mean either:

We went out to see a movie.

or:

We went out and saw a movie.

How would the speaker of Chinese know which of these meanings is intended? But notice that these "two meanings" are not very different from each other. In fact, the best way to describe the situation is as follows: A Chinese sentence like (2) c. is unspecified as to whether it is telling us "**to see** a movie" or "**and saw** a movie," just as the noun *shū* is unspecified as to whether it means "book" or "books." In both cases, the people who speak Chinese either know that it doesn't matter which of the two possible meanings is intended, or they can figure it out from the context in which the sentence is used. And in both cases, if it becomes important to make the distinction, it can be made by adding more words.

2.4   The Classifier

Like noun, verb, and adjective, the classifier is a class of words or, in traditional terminology, a part of speech. It is used with nouns and is found in all the Sino-Tibetan languages, as well as a number of languages elsewhere in the world. In order to demonstrate how classifiers function in a language, let us first consider the following situation in English. The grammar of English requires its speakers to add the word, *do*, in questions like:

What do you think?

The question could be conveyed just as well without the word *do*,

*what you think?

But this last sentence is not acceptable in English. Yet if one were to ask what *do* means in the first question, one would have a hard time answering. The point being illustrated by the English example here is that the meaning of a word in a sentence can be very elusive sometimes although the grammar of the language requires the presence of such a word. The Chinese classifier is the kind of word whose meaning is difficult to pin down. But when a noun in Chinese is joined with a numeral, such as "one" or "two," or a demonstrative, such as "this" or "which," a classifier must be present. Thus, instead of saying the word-for-word equivalent of:

> this book
> which table
> three children
> seven snakes

the Chinese speakers must say the equivalent of:

> THIS CLASSIFIER₁ BOOK
> WHICH CLASSIFIER₂ TABLE
> THREE CLASSIFIER₃ CHILD
> SEVEN CLASSIFIER₄ SNAKE

The subscript number indicates that each of these nouns has a different classifier. In Beijing Mandarin, these four classifiers are:

běn	for	"book":	*zhè*	*běn*	*shū*	this book
			this		book	
zhāng	for	"table":	*něi*	*zhāng*	*zhuōzi*	which table
			which		table	
ge	for	"child":	*sān*	*ge*	*háizi*	three children
			three		child	
tiáo	for	"snake":	*qī*	*tiáo*	*shé*	seven snakes
			seven		snake	

Each classifier is used with one class of nouns. If the nouns belonging to the class share certain semantic characteristics, then the classifier will have a semantic base. For example, there is a classifier which is used with nouns denoting tiny, grainlike objects, such as sand, pearls, or rice. In Beijing Mandarin, it is *lì*.

yí lì shā	one grain of sand
yí lì zhēnzhu	one pearl
yí lì mǐ	one grain of rice
yí lì dànzi	one marble

It is this function of classifiers, which serves to divide nouns into different classes roughly according to certain semantic characteristics, that gives rise to the term 'classifier.' However, it is rare that the class of nouns with which a classifier co-occurs forms a semantically consistent class. For example, the classifier *tiáo* in Beijing Mandarin normally used with nouns denoting long and thin objects such as snake, rope, street, river, stick, and bamboo pole, can also occur with such nouns as cattle, rhinoceros, law, and decree. There are also classifiers which co-occur with a set of nouns that do not seem to share any semantic characteristics. For instance, the Beijing Mandarin classifier *bǎ* goes with such a motley group of nouns as chair, fan, knife, and rifle.

It is obvious from the foregoing discussion that the system of classifiers in Chinese must be learned item by item by the speaker of Chinese. In this sense, the Chinese classifier is not unlike the irregular plural nouns in English, that is, like *oxen, sheep, feet.* Each of these plural forms must be learned individually with respect to its corresponding singular form. In Chinese, the speaker must learn each classifier with respect to each noun or class of nouns. (See discussion of noun classes in Swahili, Chapter V, Section 1.2, and of noun classifiers in Jacaltec, pages 39–51 of the companion volume.)

2.5   A-not-A Questions

Simple yes/no questions—questions that require "yes" or "no" as part of an answer—are universal. But different languages may use different constructions for yes/no questions. In English, the yes/no construction is marked with a rising intonation and the placing of the auxiliary verb in front of the subject:

Can you leave?

Chinese has several forms of the yes/no question. All of them have the same intonation pattern as the simple declarative sentence. One particular form signals the interrogative meaning by combining the affirmative and the negative of the first verb or auxiliary. Thus, the Chinese counterpart of the English question, "Can you leave?" is:

YOU CAN NOT CAN LEAVE?

Let us look at some examples from Beijing Mandarin:

Nǐ   néng   bù   néng   zǒu?
you   can   not   can   leave
   Can you leave?

Tā shì bù shì Zhāng-sān?
he be not be Zhang-san
  Is he Zhang-san?

Tā qù bù qù Měiguó?
he go not go America
  Is he going to America?

Because this type of question involves the affirmative and the negative of the verb, it is called an 'A-not-A' question.

Now that you understand the principle for forming A-not-A questions, see if you can figure out what the A-not-A questions are which would correspond to the following statements. (Note that *huì* "likely" is in fact a verb in Beijing Mandarin.)[3]

a. *Tā huì qù.*
  he likely go
    He is likely to go.

b. *Tā kàn wǒde shū.*
  he read my book
    He's reading my book.

c. *Tā yào qù Zhōngguó.*
  he want go China
    He wants to go to China.

d. *Tā míngtiān kěyǐ gēn nǐ qù.*
  he tomorrow can with you go
    He can go with you tomorrow.

---

[3]The answer: the correct A-not-A questions corresponding to the statements in the text—

a. *Tā huì bù huì qù?*
  he likely not likely go
    Is he likely to go?

b. *Tā kàn bù kàn wǒde shū?*
  He read not read my book
    Is he reading my book?

c. *Tā yào bù yào qù Zhōngguó?*
  he want not want go China
    Does he want to go to China?

d. *Tā míngtiān kěyǐ bù kěyǐ gēn nǐ qù?*
  he tomorrow can not can with you go
    Can he go with you tomorrow?

Another way of signaling yes/no questions in Chinese is to add an interrogative particle at the end of a regular declarative sentence. The interrogative particle is unstressed and consequently carries no tone. For instance, the interrogative particle in Beijing Mandarin is *ma*:

Nǐ   néng   zǒu   ma?
You   can   leave   (Interrogative particle)
   Can you leave?

Tā   shì   Zhāng-sān   ma?
he   be   Zhang-san   (Interrogative particle)
   Is he Zhang-san?

2.6 Word Order and Definiteness

Definite noun phrases in English are normally signified by the definite article, *the*, whereas indefinite noun phrases are signified by the indefinite article, *a*. For example, *the boy* represents a definite noun phrase. When *the boy* is uttered, the speaker assumes that the hearer knows which boy he is talking about. On the other hand, *a boy* is an indefinite noun phrase. When *a boy* is uttered, the speaker does not assume the hearer knows the identity of the person to whom the noun phrase *a boy* refers. Thus, the notion of definiteness/indefiniteness plays an important role in discourse strategy. It is well known that Chinese does not have a definite article or an indefinite article. The function of signifying definiteness/indefiniteness is taken over by word order—the linear arrangement of words in a sentence. For example, consider the following two sentences in Beijing Mandarin:

Kè   lái   le.
guest   come
   The guest *has come.*

Lái   kè   le.
come   guest
   A guest *has come.*

In the first sentence, the noun, *kè* "guest," occurs before the verb, *lái* "come." Notice that it has a definite meaning "**the** guest." In the second sentence, the same noun, *kè* "guest," occurs after the verb, and it acquires an indefinite meaning, "**a** guest." These two sentences provide a typical illustration of the relationship between definiteness/indefiniteness on the one hand and the position of the noun relative to the verb on the other. The following generalization about word order and definiteness/indefiniteness can be stated for Chinese:

Nouns preceding the verb are usually definite, while those following the verb are usually indefinite.

Consider another pair of examples from Peking Mandarin:

> **Píngguǒ** wǒ chī le.
> apple   I   eat
>   I ate **the apple**.

> Wǒ chī le **píngguǒ** le.
> I   eat   apple
>   I ate **an apple**.

In the first sentence, the noun, *píngguǒ* "apple," occurs at the front of the sentence (hence, before the verb), and again, it has a definite meaning. In the second sentence, the same noun occurs after the verb and it normally has an indefinite meaning, although it may also be given a definite reading.

(You may have noticed that all of these sentences have one or two *le*'s in them; these *le*'s are special words which signal roughly that an action has been completed.)

As one might expect, the six general characteristics we have described are far from being an exhaustive account of the grammar of Chinese. We have selected these because they are some of the most striking characteristics of Chinese, and because they contrast well with English and other western languages. On the other hand, we would like to stress the fact that these characteristics are by no means unique to Chinese. Tone languages are widespread elsewhere in the world. Monosyllabism, prevalent in Ancient Chinese and to some extent in Modern Chinese dialects, is also found in Thai and Vietnamese, which are unrelated to Chinese. The lack of consonantal clusters is observed in many languages other than Chinese, including Japanese, Italian, and Tagalog. As for Chinese being an isolating language, we can cite Cambodian, a member of the Mon-Khmer family, as another example. Noun classifiers are also not unique to Chinese. For example, all of the Mon-Khmer languages have classifiers and so do languages in such diverse locations as America and Australia. The fact that these characteristics are not unique to Chinese does not diminish their value in contributing to a composite sketch of Chinese. There is no language that is composed of a set of properties which cannot be found in any other language in the world. To many linguists, it is the similarities rather than the differences among languages of the world that is most striking.

3   DIALECTAL VARIATIONS

In section 1, we introduced five major groups of dialects. Geographically, the greatest variety of dialects is in the southeastern coastal provinces including Guangdong, Fujien, Taiwan, most of Hunan, Jiangxi, and Zhejiang, and parts of Guangxi, Anhui, and Jiangsu. It is this area where four of the five dialect groups are located: Wu, Min, Yue, and Hakka. The rest of China proper belongs to the Mandarin-speaking region. At this point, we should also mention that not all languages indigenous to China are Chinese. There are over fifty non-Chinese ethnic minorities in China, ranging from Tibetans, Mongolians, and Uighurs in the west, to the Rukais and Tsous of the Malayo-Polynesian stock in Taiwan, the easternmost part of China, from the Lahus and Lisus of the Lolo-Burmese family in the south, to the Koreans and Hoches of the north. They all have their own languages. Some, such as Lahu and Tibetan, belong to the Sino-Tibetan family; others, such as Uighur, Rukai, and Hoche, belong to various other linguistic families. In modern China, efforts are made to promote the language and culture of the ethnic minorities. Autonomous regions have been established for many ethnic groups. Within these regions, newspapers, radio stations, and other forms of the mass media primarily use the native languages, although Chinese is taught in schools.

Since the Chinese dialects are closely related to each other, one way of viewing the differences among them is through the history of Chinese. Following the tradition in Sinology, we have labeled the earlier stages of Chinese as Ancient Chinese and Archaic Chinese. To be accurate, we should note that not all modern dialects are the descendants of one line of ancestors. At the time of Ancient Chinese (500 A.D.–600 A.D.) or even Archaic Chinese (1100 B.C.–100 B.C.), dialects were undoubtedly already in existence. Thus, the modern dialects may be the offshoots of several early dialects. The Ancient Chinese and the Archaic Chinese reconstructed by the linguists, notably the Swedish Sinologist, Bernard Karlgren, are eclectic systems embodying various old dialects. The differences between those early dialects were comparatively small, however, so we can make statements about the historical variations of the modern dialects with reference to one line of ancestors without any gross distortions.

Let us, then, discuss the differences among contemporary Chinese dialects from the point of view of their evolution from a single idealized earlier dialect. We can look at these dialect differences in four areas of the grammar: 1) phonology (pronunciation), 2) vocabulary, 3) morphology (word structure), and 4) syntax (sentence structure). Let us examine the differences in phonology first, since they are the most striking. We will see that the dialects can differ in numbers and types of tones, consonants, vowels, and syllables.

In section 2.2, where the syllable structure of Chinese was discussed, the consonants [-p], [-t], [-k] at the end of a syllable in Ancient Chinese were mentioned. The presence of any one of these consonants in syllable-final position normally causes the tone of the syllable to be reduced to a shorter duration. Among the modern dialects, these syllable-final consonants are preserved in Yue, Min, and Hakka only. In certain Wu dialects, they have been replaced by a glottal stop [-ʔ]. In Mandarin and other Wu dialects, they have been completely lost. Accompanying the loss of [-p], [-t], [-k] at the syllable-final position is the loss of all short tones in the Mandarin and some Wu dialects. In those Wu dialects which replaced the syllable-final [-p], [-t], [-k] with the glottal stop, the short tones are preserved.

Another historical phenomenon concomitant with the loss of syllable-final [-p], [-t], [-k] is the loss of the nasal [-m] in syllable-final position or the replacement of the syllable-final nasal [-m] by [-n] or [-ŋ], which were present in Ancient Chinese. Those dialects that underwent the loss of [-p], [-t], [-k] also underwent either the loss of [-m] or its replacement by another nasal segment.

A third difference among the dialects that can be viewed historically involves the loss of voiced consonants in syllable-initial position. Ancient Chinese had a series of voiced consonants such as [b], [d], [g], [z] in syllable-initial position. They are preserved only in Wu dialects and part of Hunan province called the Xiang dialect area, a branch of the Southeastern Mandarin dialect group. Elsewhere, they have become voiceless. In Hakka, they have developed into voiceless aspirated consonants.

To summarize, we have been differentiating modern Chinese dialects according to three factors with reference to Ancient Chinese:

1. Loss of syllable-final [-p], [-t], [-k]
2. Loss of syllable-final [-m] or replacement of [-m] at the end of a syllable by another nasal segment
3. Loss of syllable-initial voiced consonants

It is clear from the evidence presented that among all the dialects, the Mandarin group has changed the most in the evolution from Ancient Chinese. All three losses took place in Mandarin. In order to illustrate the differences described, we will present the different pronunciations of six words from representatives of the five dialect groups in Table 6.1. (The pronunciations are written in the International Phonetic Alphabet, IPA, for which there is an explanation in the Appendix.)

Table 6.1 shows, for example, that the word for "pen" in Mandarin is not pronounced with a final consonant, but its corresponding counterparts in Min, Yue, and Hakka are pronounced with final stop [-t]. Among the two Wu dialects chosen for Table 6.1, we notice that one of them has a glottal stop [-ʔ] instead of [-t] for the word "pen," and one of them does not have a final consonant for the word "pen." Table 6.1 also shows that the Wu dialects are the only ones with voiced initial consonants as in the words "skin" and "firewood." Finally, the various pronunciations among the dialects for "needle" in Table 6.1 shown that the Ancient Chinese syllable-final [-m] is preserved only in Min, Yue, and

TABLE 6.1 The Result of Sound Loss from Ancient Chinese

	Mandarin (Beijing)	Wu (Suzhou)	Wu (Wenzhou)	Min (Chaozhou)	Yue (Cantonese)	Hakka (Meixian)
pen	pi^{214}	$pi^{ʔ4}$	pi^{23}	pit^{2}	$pɛt^{5}$	pit^{2}
pigeon	$kə^{55}$	$kɤ^{ʔ4}$	ky^{23}	kap^{2} (Xiamen pronunciation)	kap^{3}	kap^{2}
bamboo	$tʂu^{35}$	tso^{4}	$tɕiu^{23}$	tek^{2}	$tsɔk^{5}$	$tsuk^{2}$
needle	$tʂən^{55}$	$tsen^{44}$	$tsay^{44}$	$tsam^{33}$	$tsɐm^{53}$	$tsəm^{44}$
skin	$pʰi^{35}$	be^{24}	bei^{31}	$pʰue^{55}$	$pʰei^{21}$	$pʰi^{12}$
firewood	$tʂʰai^{35}$	$zɒ^{24}$	za^{31}	$tsʰa^{55}$	$tsʰai^{21}$	$tsʰai^{12}$

Hakka; it is lost in one of the two Wu dialects and it is replaced by [-n] in Beijing Mandarin and the other Wu dialect.

Table 6.2 provides a survey of the number of tones, syllable-initial consonants, and syllable finals—the syllable minus the initial consonant—in a sample from the five dialect groups: it shows that Mandarin has the least number of tones and syllable finals. Another fact from Table 6.2 to be noted is that the number of initial consonants among the various dialect groups does not vary a great deal, whereas the number of syllable finals fluctuates considerably.

Table 6.3 illustrates more of the differences in the pronunciations of a few sample words among the representative dialects. The data in this table show that for each sample word, aside from the dialectal differences illustrated by examples in Table 6.1, there are many other differences among the pronunciations of the dialects. In regular speech, in fact, the differences are sufficient to hinder communication between speakers of different dialects.

The data in Table 6.4 contain the pronunciations of three Chinese dialects for ten words. Based on what you have learned about the differences among the Chinese dialects from the point of evolution, you should be able to reconstruct the initial and final consonants for each of these ten words in Ancient Chinese (we are ignoring the tones here because you have not learned how to reconstruct tones). If the vowel for a word is unchanged for all three dialects, you may assume that Ancient

TABLE 6.2   The Sound Components of Words

	Tones	Initial Consonants	Syllable Finals
Mandarin (Beijing)	4	21	38
Wu (Suzhou)	7 (2 short tones)	26	49
Min (Chaozhou)	8 (2 short tones)	17	82
Yue (Cantonese)	9 (3 short tones)	19	53
Hakka (Meixian)	6 (2 short tones)	18	75

TABLE 6.3   Divergence in Pronunciation

	Mandarin (Beijing)	Wu (Wenzhou)	Min (Chaozhou)	Yue (Cantonese)	Hakka (Meixian)
mist	u^{51}	$m\o^{11}$	bu^{11}	mou^{22}	vu^{42}
pond	$ts^h\iota^{35}$ $t^haŋ^{35}$	$dzei^{31}$ $duɔ^{31}$	ti^{55}	$tɕ^hi^{21}$ $t^hɔŋ^{21}$	ts^hi^{12} $t^hɔŋ^{12}$
gold	$tɕin^{55}$	$tɕiaŋ^{44}$	kim^{33}	$kɐm^{53}$	kim^{44}
shrimp	$ɕia^{55}$	ho^{44}	he^{55}	ha^{53}	ha^{12}
cooked rice	fan^{51}	va^{11}	$puŋ^{11}$	fan^{22}	fan^{42}
to peel	pau^{55}	po^{23}	pak^{2}	$mɔk^{3}$	$pɔk^{2}$

TABLE 6.4   Reconstruct Initial and Final Consonants for Ancient Chinese

	Cantonese (Yue dialect)	Shanghainese (Wu dialect)	Beijing (Mandarin dialect)	Ancient Chinese
1. chat	t^ham	$dɛ$	t^han	
2. doctrine	tou	$dɐ$	tau	
3. door	mun	$mən$	$mən$	
4. necessary	pit	pi	pi	
5. end	muk	muo	muo	
6. fix	tiŋ	diŋ	tiŋ	
7. bottle	$p^hiŋ$	bin*	$p^hiŋ$	
8. field	t^hin	die	$t^hɛn$	
9. shop	tim	di	tiɛn	
10. pile up	tip	di	tiɛ	

*The word for 'bottle' in Shanghainese is slightly irregular; reconstruct it as if it ended in -ŋ.

Chinese has the same vowel for that word. Otherwise, ignore the vowels.[4]

The second area of dialectal differences is manifested in the vocabulary—the choice of words for common use. This area also constitutes a significant difference and contributes to unintelligibility between the dialects. Examples are provided in Table 6.5. You will note that some dialects use single words that correspond to compound expressions in other dialects.

There is an important difference between the data in Table 6.3 and the data in Table 6.5. In Table 6.3, each row gives the different pronunciations of the same word in the different dialects. In other words, these different pronunciations may be viewed as the various descendants of the same word in Ancient Chinese. The data in Table 6.5 are not in the same situation. Although the different dialect forms in each row have the same meaning, they often represent different words; that is, they are not the different descendants of the same word in Ancient Chinese. Hence, the variation between those dialect forms cannot be considered a matter of pronunciation difference. It is primarily due to the different choice of words. For example, only Cantonese and Meixian Hakka use the same word for "he" or "she." Otherwise, the word for "he" or "she" differs among the dialect representatives in Table 6.5.

A third area of difference among the dialects is that of morphology or word structure. Earlier we pointed out that Mandarin should not be considered a monosyllabic language anymore, because of the large

TABLE 6.5 *Divergence in Vocabulary*

	Mandarin (Beijing)	Wu (Suzhou)	Min (Chaozhou)	Yue (Cantonese)	Hakka (Meixian)
he, she	t^ha^{55}	li^{44}	i^{33}	$k^h\o y^{23}$	ki^{12}
to push	t^huei^{55}	$t^h\varepsilon^{44}$	u^{55}	$\mathrm{\Omega}\mathrm{\eta}^{35}$	$su\eta^{31}$
rubber	$\text{ç}ia\eta^{51}t\text{ç}iau^{55}$	$zia\eta^{22}bi^{33}$	$ts^hu^{12}ni^{35}$	$t\text{ç}\oe\eta^{22}kau^{53}$	$su^{42}jin^{17}$
thief	$\text{ç}iao^{214}t^hou^{55}$	$z\gamma^2ku\gamma^4du^{21}$	$ts^hu^{24}ts^hak^{21}$	$\text{ç}iu^{35}t^hou^{35}$	$ts^h\varepsilon t^4ku^{31}$
to drink	$x\ni^{55}$	$t\text{ç}^hi^{?4}$	lim^{33}	$j\text{e}m^{35}$	$s\ni t^4$
don't want	$pu^{35}iau^{51}$	$fi\ae^{513}$	mai^{213}	$\mathrm{m}^{21}\mathrm{ɔi}^{33}$	$\mathrm{m}^{12}\mathrm{ɔi}^{42}$

[4]The answer: reconstruction of Ancient Chinese pronunciations (V stands for vowel that is not reconstructed). 1) dVm 2) dV 3) mVn 4) pit 5) mVk 6) diŋ 7) bVŋ 8) dVn 9) dVn 10) dVp.

TABLE 6.6   *Disyllabic versus Monosyllabic Expressions*

	Mandarin (Beijing)	Yue (Cantonese)
clothing	i^{55}ʂaŋ	sam^{53}
pliers	tɕʰiɛn^{35}tsɿ	kʰim^{21}
crab	pʰaŋ^{35}ɕiɛ	hai^{35}
quilt	pei^{51}uo	pʰei^{21}

number of compounds it has. However, certain other dialects, such as the Yue, have many fewer compounds; that is, they are closer to the monosyllabic form of Ancient Chinese. Let us look at a few examples where the Beijing Mandarin disyllabic compounds correspond to the monosyllabic words in Cantonese (Yue), as shown in Table 6.6.

The explanation for this difference between dialects is a very interesting one. Mandarin has changed more than any of the other dialects from the Ancient Chinese source. In particular, it has lost all the earlier syllable-final stops and replaced the final [-m] with another nasal, and it now has the smallest number of tones of any of the dialects. As a result, many words which used to sound different have come to sound the same; that is, they have become homophones. It is reasonable for a language to tolerate a certain percentage of homophones. But excessive homophony may impair communication. To compensate for the development of large numbers of homophones which resulted from the loss of a number of earlier phonological distinctions, Beijing Mandarin resorted to a change from monosyllabic words to disyllabic words in a great portion of its vocabulary, thus decreasing the amount of homophony again. Earlier, we discussed two processes by which disyllabic compounds can be formed—the combination of two monosyllabic words identical or similar in meaning, and the fusing of a Verb–Object construction. Another common process of forming a disyllabic compound is to combine a monosyllabic word with a syllable that is devoid of any meaning. The syllable *zi* in the Beijing Mandarin compound *qiánzi* "pliers" is such an example. Formerly in Ancient Chinese, the syllable *zi* was a word with diminutive meaning. But in present-day Beijing Mandarin, as it occurs in a compound such as *qiánzi*, it has no meaning by itself and it does not affect the meaning of the compound. But it does serve the purpose of making a compound to reduce homophony.

The fourth respect in which the dialects in China can differ is syntax. This is the least significant respect because there is a great deal of uniformity in the syntactic systems of the dialects. For example, the *A*-not-*A* question exists in all dialects; the correlation between word order and definiteness/indefiniteness holds true for all dialects; the lack of inflection and concordance or agreement in person, number, gender, is uniform in all dialects. We can go on and on listing the basic syntactic characteristics common to all dialects in China. Significant variations are rare. In the following discussion, we will present two types of variation between Mandarin, the major dialect group, and the other four dialect groups.

The first type of variation concerns a particular syntactic construction widespread in Mandarin but not in other dialects. This syntactic construction employs the use of a grammatical particle *bǎ* and therefore is called the *bǎ-construction* by the Chinese grammarians. Normally, in a simple Chinese sentence with a transitive verb, the word order is identical to that of English, namely, the verb occurs between the two nouns:

JOHN CRITICIZED PETER.

In linguistic terminology, the noun, "Peter," that follows the verb is the 'accusative' noun. When the *bǎ* particle is used, the word order of a sentence with a transitive verb becomes different. The accusative noun now precedes the verb instead of following the verb, and the particle *bǎ* is placed in front of the accusative noun:

JOHN *ba* PETER CRITICIZED.

For example,

John bǎ Peter pīping le.
John *ba* Peter criticize
   John criticized Peter.

This is the so-called *bǎ*-construction. It is widespread in Mandarin, having come into existence during the ninth century. It is responsible for a gradual shift in the basic word order of Mandarin sentences: from verb-medial type, in which the transitive verb occurs between the nouns, to verb-final type, in which the transitive verb occurs in the final position of a sentence. However, the *bǎ*-construction is extremely rare in the dialects other than Mandarin. It represents another step taken by Mandarin, which is already the most radical dialect group in its deviation from Ancient Chinese, in moving away from the structure of Ancient Chinese.

The other syntactic variation among the dialects concerns the type of sentences involving such verbs as those meaning "give," "present," "award," "donate." In Mandarin, such sentences are constructed with the following word order:

JOHN GAVE **ME A PENCIL**.

where "me" is known as the dative noun and "a pencil," the accusative noun. The word order in Mandarin has the dative noun preceding the accusative noun. In other dialects, however, the prevalent word for the postverbal nouns in this type of sentence is exactly the opposite, so that the accusative normally precedes the dative:

JOHN GAVE **A PENCIL ME**.

This concludes our discussion of the differences among the dialects. We observe that there is no logical limit to the subtle distinctions that may exist among dialects, particularly in the area of pronunciation. Even within one urban center, it is often possible to discriminate local differences in pronunciation. For example, in the western section of Guangzhou (Canton City) known as Saikwan, the local pronunciation is noted for the buzzing quality of the vowels in the syllables, *tsi*, *ts*^{h}*i*, and *si*, which do not occur in the speech of the other sections of the city. Hence, it is impossible to describe all the various dialect forms. Our presentation here is confined to only a few fundamental and important variations among the dialects of Chinese.

4   THE WRITING SYSTEM

In a description of most languages, the writing system consititues the most insignificant part. In the case of Chinese, however, the writing system occupies a position of unusual importance. One reason is that the Chinese writing system is unique. Another reason is that it serves as the vehicle for some of the finest literatures ever produced. The third reason is that it provides a medium through which the investigation of Ancient and Archaic Chinese can be conducted. To the westerner who is accustomed to an alphabetical script, the writing system of Chinese is probably the most fascinating and bewildering aspect of the language.

Writing in China began over 4,000 years ago with the drawings of natural objects. Each picture in its first form represented a natural object. The pictures were then simplified so that only the essential outlines are preserved. This is the origin of the pictorial characters in written Chinese, called the pictographs. Although characters with such an origin have undergone drastic changes, we can still perceive their

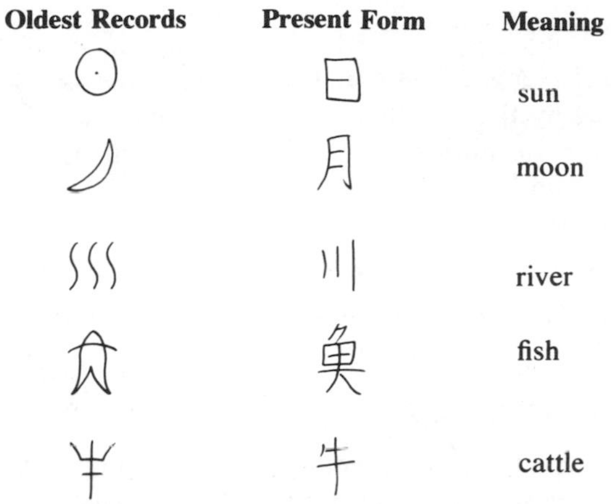

Oldest Records	Present Form	Meaning
⊙	日	sun
☽	月	moon
〻	川	river
𩵋	魚	fish
⅄	牛	cattle

FIGURE 6.7 *The Pictoral Origin of Chinese Characters*

pictorial nature on the basis of their modern appearance. (For examples see Figure 6.7.) The pictographs constitute only a small fraction of Chinese characters. It is obvious that the drawing of natural objects alone cannot serve as an adequate written representation of a spoken language. For example, locomotions, abstract concepts, experiences, and grammatical particles are difficult to render in pictures. Even natural objects can present insurmountable obstacles for pictographs. How do we devise different pictographs for different kinds of trees without relying on some system other than drawing? Hence, as the Chinese writing system began to emerge, several methods other than the drawing of natural objects were employed to form new characters.

4.1 Diagrammatic Representation of Ideas

The use of diagrams to symbolize certain abstract notions represents one method of creating characters. Formerly, the diagrams ──᛫ and ᛫── were created for the notions "beyond" and "below." The horizontal line symbolizes a boundary. The dot above the boundary represented "beyond"; the dot underneath the boundary represented "below." Today, the Chinese characters signifying "beyond" and "below" have become 上 and 下 . Similarly, the symbols created for the numbers, "one," "two," "three," were ─ , ニ , 三 , where "one" is represented by one horizontal stroke, "two" is represented by two horizontal strokes, and "three" by three horizontal strokes. They remain as the characters for "one," "two," and "three" in present-day Chinese. The characters so created are known as ideographs.

4.2 Compound Ideographs

A compound ideograph is a new character whose meaning is in some way represented by the combination of the meanings of its parts. Thus, the character for the notion "bright" was created by compounding the characters for "sun" and "moon." The semantic motivation for such a compound is obvious. Since the sun and the moon are the two natural sources of light, the notion "bright" can be symbolized as the sum total of the sun and the moon. The character for "bright" is 明. The left component, 日, means "the sun"; the right component, 月, means "the moon." The former character for the notion "to surround" has the form. The middle component, 口, represents "city"; each of the peripheral components represents "foot." The composite character indicates a city being surrounded by people. Hence, it has the meaning, "to surround." Compound ideographs are also formed by the duplication of the same character. For example, the word 木 "tree" is duplicated to form the word 林 "forest," since a forest is a dense growth of trees; the ancient character 从 "crowd," is formed by duplicating three times the character 人 "human," since a crowd is a gathering of people; finally, the character for "loquacious" is, formed by repeating three times the character "speak," since "loquacious" means "talkative."

4.3 Loan Characters

Loan characters resulted from the practice of borrowing a character for a word which has the same sound as the original word denoted by the character. For example, the character for "depart, separate," 離 originally was the name of a bird. It was borrowed to signify "depart, separate" because it had the same pronunciation as the bird in Archaic Chinese. In modern Chinese, its meaning as a species of bird is no longer retained. Similarly, the character 易 originally was a pictograph for "scorpion," it was then borrowed to denote the word "easy," which had the same pronunciation as the word for "scorpion." In modern Chinese a new character stands for the word "scorpion," and the character 易 means "easy." Thus, loan characters do not involve the creation of new characters. They represent an extension of the existing characters. The use of loan characters was practiced in the earliest written records in China. One side effect of this practice is that the present-day deciphering of the archaic documents is quite difficult and complex.

324

4.4 Phonetic Compounds

The phonetic compounds account for more than 90 percent of all the Chinese characters today. Basically, a phonetic compound is the combination of two characters, one representing a semantic feature of the word, called the 'signific,' the other representing the pronunciation of the word, called the 'phonetic.' The process of forming phonetic compounds has been the standard method for creating new characters for more than 2,000 years. For example, when the new chemical element radium was discovered, it was decided that the Chinese word should approximate the sound of the first syllable, [re-], in the English word. Thus, the character for "thunder," 雷 , with the pronunciation [lei][35] was used as the phonetic, and the character for "metal," 金, was used as the signific, since radium is a metallic element, and a new character, which is a phonetic compound, was born for the word "radium": 镭.

Since the vast majority of the Chinese characters are phonetic compounds, they can be arranged occording to their component parts for the purpose of reference. The system of arrangement most widely used by the scholars of Chinese is the one that employs the use of 'radicals.' During the seventeenth century, a Chinese scholar and lexicographer compiled a list of 214 radicals for his dictionary. In most cases, a radical is the signific of the character. For example, the radical of the character 吐 "to vomit" is 口 "mouth"; the radical of the character 江 "river" is 氵 "water." In those cases where the character is not a phonetic compound, the decision as to which part of the character is a radical becomes a matter of arbitrary convention. One simply has to memorize the analysis of such a character. The radicals provide a basis of reference for Chinese dictionaries. All Chinese dictionaries are divided into sections according to radicals. Thus, in order to look up an unrecognized character in a dictionary, one must know the radical of the character. The radical confines one's search to a particular section of the dictionary. Within that section, the characters, all of which share the same radical, are arranged according to the number of strokes they have. The one with the least strokes comes first and the one with the most strokes comes last. The character is then located according to the number of its strokes.

Although the method of constructing phonetic compounds offers a reasonably systematic process for analyzing the Chinese writing system, the very nature of the characters means that attempting to learn Chinese can be a formidable task. One of the largest Chinese dictionaries contains over 40,000 different characters, which seems overwhelming. However, in actual practice, things are not as bad as we might imagine. It is estimated that a knowledge of 2,000 to 3,000 characters will suffice for one to function as a literate person in Chinese society. Such a person will be able to read newspapers, magazines, and modern textbooks. The fact that most of these characters are phonetic compounds also facilitates the learning process, since a phonetic compound is merely the combination of the radical with another character serving as the phonetic part.

Since the initial appearance of the Chinese written system more than 4,000 years ago, the Chinese people have had only one written language. Thus, no matter how different the dialects are, literate Chinese people from different parts of the country have always been able to communicate with each other through writing, and they all have access to the same body of literature. In this respect, the written language provides an invaluable service to the country as an instrument of cultural unification. It also played a role in the cultural dominance of China over many of its neighboring countries in the past. Japan, Korea, Vietnam, during their early historical periods, all adopted the writing system of China. The written language of Japan to this day still remains a mixture of Chinese characters and the Japanese syllabic system.

5   LANGUAGE REFORM IN MODERN CHINA

Because of the high percentage of illiteracy (over 85 percent in 1949) and the communication problem complicated by the scores of mutually unintelligible dialects in China, the government of the People's Republic of China after it came to power in 1949 set fourth a policy to establish a uniform spoken language and to simplify the written language. In October, 1955, at the National Language Standardization Conference, a common language for the People's Republic of China was proclaimed. It embodies the pronunciation of the Beijing dialect, the grammar of northern Mandarin, and the vocabulary of modern vernacular Chinese literature. This newly proclaimed national language has since been known as *Pŭtōnghuà*, which literally means the "common language." The style and vocabulary of this national language, according to the decision adopted by the Conference, must remain close to the language of workers and farmers and not become a standard language remote from the language of everyday life. Since the enactment of the policy to establish Pŭtōnghuà as the national language, tremendous effort has been made to teach it to the populace. It is reported that the effort has been successful, and that the absolute majority of the Chinese people nowadays are fluent in Pŭtōnghuà. At the same time, the government has not attempted to discourage the use of local dialects. As a result, the various dialects remain active in China and there has been a marked increase of bilingualism among the people of the Min, Yue, Wu, and Hakka dialect groups. For example, the Linguistics Delegation which visited China in 1974 reports:

The county of Datian in Fujian province was cited as an example of the progress achieved. It has three major and over ten minor dialects— "people separated by a blade of grass could not understand each other." A cadre from the North needed three to seven interpreters to make a speech. Party leaders took an active role in promoting Pŭtōnghuà, concentrating on schools, evening schools, and public gathering places; and recently in the movement to criticize Lin Piao and Confucius there was further advance in the popularization of Pŭtōnghuà. In a recent radio report a county official addressed 120,000 people without need of an interpreter.[5]

Similarly, Lin Shou-ying reports of a trip that he made in 1975:

Invariably, in every city or district, one could hear the local people speak their own dialect. But when these people were spoken to in Pŭtōnghuà, they answered in the same. Some of these people spoke Pŭtōnghuà with their local accent, but the accent was generally slight enough to be intelligible to a person who could only understand Pŭtōnghuà.[6]

A result of the coexistence of a national language and local dialects is the interaction between them. Hence, the Pŭtōnghuà of different locales inevitably takes on local accents due to the influence of the indigenous dialect, and conversely the dialects are affected by Pŭtōnghuà in their vocabulary and pronunciation. However, there is no stigma attached to regional accents in Pŭtōnghuà or to local accents in other dialects. There is a significant absence of social distinction on the basis of accent of speech. For example, several of the national leaders, like the late Zhou En-lai, the late Mao Ze-dong, and Deng Xiao-ping, have noticeable regional accents in their Pŭtōnghuà.

Since the establishment of the new national language, Pŭtōnghuà, and the successful elimination of illiteracy among the great majority of the populace, the Chinese language in the form of both the new national language and the various dialects has acquired a number of new features. In the area of vocabulary, under the impact of new social conditions in the People's Republic of China, many old vocabulary items which are considered either elitist or derogatory have been abandoned, and new words have been created as replacements. For example, the old usages *taitai* "wife" and *xīansheng* "husband," have been replaced by the new term *airen*, which literally means "lover." Today, *airen* is the universal term for both "husband" and "wife" in Pŭtōnghuà. The old expressions *taitai* and *xīansheng*, which also stood for "Mr." and "Mrs.," referring to people of higher social status than workers have

---

[5]Winfred P. Lehmann, ed., *Language and Linguistics in the People's Republic of China*, University of Texas Press, Austin, 1975. See discussion of this volume in the "Suggestions for Further Reading" section at the end of the chapter.

[6]Lin Shou-ying, "Changes and Reform in the Language of the New China," *Journal of the Chinese Language Teachers Association*, vol. 12, no. 3, Oct. 1977, pp. 210–214.

been abandoned. Another old usage, *kǔlì* "coolie," which gave rise to the English word *coolie* is now replaced by *gōngrén* "worker." The old expression *kǔlì*, which literally means "bitter labor," has a derogatory overtone from the days of western colonialism. The following is a selected list of old expressions which have yielded to new vocabulary:

Old Expression			**New Expression**	
xiǎojiě	miss	⎫		
fū-rén	madam	⎬ ⟶ *tóngzhì*		comrade
xīansheng	Mr., teacher	⎭		
nóngfū	peasant	⟶ *shè yuán*		commune member
chēfū	driver	⟶ *jiashǐ yuán*		operator
hǔofū	cook (military)	⟶ *chuī shì yuán*		cook

The word *fū* in the last three items has the connotation of a lowly, inferior person. Hence, all the expressions using that word are replaced.

Some old expressions have been abandoned because they are divorced from the ordinary speech of the workers and peasants. For example, the formal and archaic usages, *lìnzhūn* "your honorable father" and *lìntáng* "your honorable mother" are no longer used. One simply says:

Nǐ	*de*	*bàba*		*Nǐ*	*de*	*māma*
You	(Genitive	father		You	(Genitive	mother
	Particle)				Particle)	
	your father				your mother	

Other old usages have been abandoned because what they stood for have been eliminated under the new social order. For example, the term *lǎo māzi*, formerly denoting "amah, servant," is no longer used because such a dependent social role no longer exists.

On the other hand, the new social conditions in China have created new expressions for the language. Such new expressions are particularly abundant in the area of political usages and propaganda. For example:

hóng wèi bīng	red guard (member of the cultural group)
chì jiǎo yīshēng	barefoot doctor (a doctor, often a paramedic, who travels on foot to treat patients in a rural area)
sān tuō lí	three divorces (divorced from reality, proletarian politics, and production)
yòu hóng yòu zhuān	red and specialized (politically active and technically well prepared)

The abolition of the old, inappropriate expressions and the use of new vocabulary is achieved in the national language, Pǔtōnghuà, without any apparent difficulties. There has been no need for official action or governmental decrees in this respect. The people of China regularly participate in political discussions, debates, mutual criticism and group study of political documents. In the course of such activities, the same critical attitude has been focused on language as on other aspects of culture, new vocabulary has evolved, and old terms, judged inappropriate, have been rejected. There is a widespread desire for the style and vocabulary of the national language to be as close as possible to the everyday language of workers and peasants. Since every citizen in China at least until recently had to spend some time each year laboring with peasants and workers, and therefore, every citizen could be considered to that extent a peasant or a worker, there has been a basis for an evolution of language in just this direction. The change taking place is dramatic, and all the more so when we realize we are comparing the present-day national language, Pǔtōnghuà, with the prerevolution Beijing Mandarin, which was far from being a language of the common people.

The other aspect of the language reform movement deals with the written language. The reform of the written language has two goals: 1) the simplification of characters and 2) the creation and popularization of a national phonetic alphabet. The simplification of characters began immediately after the founding of the People's Republic of China. The major motivation behind this reform is to facilitate the eradication of illiteracy. In 1956, 515 commonly used characters were simplified. In 1964, over 2,000 characters had become simplified. The 214 radicals which we mentioned in section 4 have been reduced to 189. Figure 6.8 provides a sample of simplified characters in contrast to their original form.

The national phonetic alphabet, known as *Pīnyīn*, serves as a tool to aid in the popularization of Pǔtōnghuà and in teaching the pronunciation of characters. The Chinese examples in this section other than the characters are written in Pīnyīn. In earlier sections, we also provided sentences written in Pīnyīn. An explanation of the Pīnyīn symbols is given in the Appendix.

Aside from serving as a tool for facilitating the learning of the Chinese characters and the popularization of Pǔtōnghuà, the Pīnyīn system has also been used as a base for creating alphabetical writing systems for minority languages. It is possible that the government of the People's Republic of China may decide to replace the written characters completely with the Pīnyīn writing system in the future. At this point, the ultimate replacement of characters remains a mere possibility. One thing is certain: if the Chinese writing system is changed to Pīnyīn, the nation will undergo a drastic cultural upheaval that may last for a generation, and the change will undoubtedly have far-reaching effects on the literary tradition of the nation.

Original Form	Simplified Form	Gloss
餐	歺	meal
勞 動	劳 动	labor
工 廠	工 厂	factory
國	囗	country
賽	宎	to compete
門	门	door
風	风	wind
知 識	知 识	knowledge
獨 立	独 立	independent
生 產	生 产	produce
讓	让	let
邊	边	side

FIGURE 6.8 Characters in Their Original and Simplified Forms

FIGURE 6.9   *Pīnyīn in Practice—A 1959 Photograph of Commune Members in Hopei Province*

SUGGESTIONS FOR FURTHER READING

Chao, Y. R. *A Grammar of Modern Spoken Chinese.* Berkeley and Los Angeles: University of California Press, 1968.

This 850-page tome is a gold mine of information for those who are intrigued about the linguistic structure of Chinese. It is best suited for those who know some Chinese and who can be tolerant of its very idiosyncratic organization.

Karlgren, B. *Easy Lessons in Chinese Writing.* Stockholm: Naturmetodens Språkinstitut, 1958.

The eminent Swedish Sinologist has sequenced Chinese characters in lessons on the basis of phonetic and semantic relations among the characters. For the student who is seriously attempting to become literate in Chinese.

Karlgren, B. *Sound and Symbol in Chinese.* London: Oxford University Press, 1923.

This little history book tells how Chinese scribes ingeniously used their limited stock of pictographs as building materials for a full-blown writing system. Very rewarding reading for both students of Chinese and those who do not intend to learn the language.

Kratochvíl, Paul *The Chinese Language Today—Features of an Emerging Standard.* London: Hutchinson University Library, 1968.

The strengths of this book are its excellent treatments of the sounds, tones, and word-formation patterns in Chinese, and its discussions of the writing system and the standardization of Mandarin in China.

Lehmann, Winfred P., ed. *Language and Linguistics in the People's Republic of China.* Austin: University of Texas Press, 1975.

This book is a report of a four-week visit to the People's Republic of China of a delegation of linguists made in the fall of 1974. Very readable and highly informative, it includes chapters on the situation as seen by the delegates with respect to Pǔtōnghuà, language reform, language teaching, national minority languages, dictionary writing, and language-related research.

Newnham, Richard *About Chinese.* Baltimore, Md.: Penguin, 1971.

Discussing the sounds and sentence patterns of Chinese, the writing system, and writing reforms, this small paperback is perhaps the best introduction to the Chinese language for the layman. It also contains a list of forty-eight further references.

Wieger, Léon *Chinese Characters.* Hsien-hsien: Catholic Mission Press, 1927. (Reprinted by Dover, 1965).

While Karlgren's *Sound and Symbol* expounds the general principles of Chinese character development, Wieger traces their building blocks, one at a time, back to the primitive engravings in which the characters had their origin.

APPENDIX: THE TRANSCRIPTION OF CHINESE SOUNDS

Symbols from the International Phonetic Association's alphabet (IPA) are used throughout whenever dialects other than Mandarin are discussed. In discussing Mandarin we use both IPA transcription and Pīnyīn, the national phonetic alphabet of China. IPA transcriptions in the text are in square brackets [ ], tables comparing dialects are in IPA.

A. Consonant Sounds Found in Mandarin

	Pīnyīn Transcription	IPA Transcription	Description of Sound
Stops	b	p	voiceless unaspirated bilabial
	p	p^h	voiceless aspirated bilabial
	d	t	voiceless unaspirated alveolar
	t	t^h	voiceless aspirated alveolar
	g	k	voiceless unaspirated velar
	k	k^h	voiceless aspirated velar
Affricates	z	ts	voiceless unaspirated alveolar
	c	ts^h	voiceless aspirated alveolar
	zh	tʂ	voiceless unaspirated retroflex
	ch	tʂ^h	voiceless aspirated retroflex
	j	tɕ	voiceless unaspirated pre-palatal
	q	tɕ^h	voiceless aspirated pre-palatal
Fricatives	f	f	voiceless labio-dental
	s	s	voiceless alveolar
	sh	ʂ	voiceless retroflex
	r	ʐ	voiced retroflex
	x	ɕ	voiceless pre-palatal
	h	x	voiceless velar
Nasals	m	m	bilabial
	n	n	alveolar
	ng	ŋ	velar
Laterals	l	l	alveolar

B.   Tones Found in Mandarin

Pīnyīn Transcription	Tone letters	Description of Tone
−	⌐ 55	high level
´	⌐ 35	rising
ˇ	⌐ 214	falling-rising
`	\ 51	high falling

C.   Additional Consonant Sounds Found in Other Dialects

IPA Transcription	Description of Sound
ʔ	glottal stop
m̥	syllabic bilabial nasal
ɳ	retroflex nasal
v	voiced labio-dental fricative
z	voiced alveolar fricative
h	voiceless approximant
r	rolled alveolar (trill)
j	palatal semi-vowel

D.   Vowel Sounds of Mandarin and Other Dialects

	Front	Central	Back
Close	i y	ʉ	ɯ u
Close-lowered	ɪ ʟ		ʊ
Half close	e ø		ɤ o
		ə	
Half open	ɛ ɜ œ		ɔ
	æ	ɐ	
Open	a		ɒ

(Lips are rounded for the vowels y, ø, œ, ʉ, u, ʊ, o, ɔ, and ɒ. The lip position for the other vowels is spread or neutral. The symbol ι stands for the retroflex apical vowel of Mandarin.)

Explanation of how these sounds are produced can be found in:

Principles of the International Phonetic Association, Department of Phonetics, University College, London WC1E 6BT.

Peter Ladefoged, *A Course in Phonetics*, Harcourt Brace Jovanovich, New York, 1975.